LITERATURE AND TOURISM

Related titles

Christopher M. Law: *Urban Tourism*
John Lennon and Malcolm Foley: *Dark Tourism*

Literature and Tourism

Edited by
Mike Robinson and Hans Christian Andersen

CENGAGE
Learning·

Australia • Brazil • Japan • Korea • Mexico • Singapore • Spain • United Kingdom • United States

CENGAGE
Learning·

Literature and Tourism, 1st Edition

Authors: Mike Robinson and Hans Christian Andersen

For product information and technology assistance, contact **emea.info@cengage.com**.

For permission to use material from this text or product, and for permission queries, email **emea.permissions@cengage.com**.

British Library Cataloguing-in-Publication Data
A catalogue record for this book is available from the British Library.

ISBN: 9781844800742

Cengage Learning EMEA
Cheriton House, North Way, Andover, Hampshire, SP10 5BE United Kingdom

Cengage Learning products are represented in Canada by Nelson Education Ltd.

For your lifelong learning solutions, visit **www.cengage.co.uk**

Purchase your next print book, e-book or e-chapter at **www.cengagebrain.com**

Printed in the UK by Lightning Source
1 2 3 4 5 6 7 8 9 10 – 13 12 11

Contents

List of Plates

List of Figures and Tables

Figure

Tables

Acknowledgements

I would like to thank Phil Long of the Centre for Tourism and Cultural Change for his readings of, and comments on, Chapters 1 and 2. Thanks also go to Janet for just being there at the right time! Particular thanks must go to Hans Christian for all his work from the outset: his support, friendship and enthusiasm for putting this work together. I have gladly put up with the poorly disguised looks of disbelief and astonishment upon people's faces, and consequent detours of explanation when telling them that my co-editor is Hans Christian Andersen! It has been a great pleasure to work with a Dane of such standing. I would also like to acknowledge the support of Sheffield Hallam University and the Centre for Tourism and Cultural Change for my continuing research in this fascinating area.

Mike Robinson

I would like to thank Mike Robinson for illustrating that only the imagination sets the limits for tourism research. And to Dr Elizabeth Andersen for professional and personal support and continued encouragement in this work. Thanks also to Andrew Skinner of the University of Innsbruck, Marianne Asmussen of the Karen Blixen Museum (Denmark) and Miriam Harte of Bede's World (South Shields) for help and inspiration. The support from the University of Northumbria, in particular the Centre for Travel and Tourism in Newcastle Business School, is gratefully acknowledged.

Hans Christian Andersen

Both editors would like to offer generous thanks to all the contributors to this volume; for their ideas and thoughtful contributions and for their patience while all was being brought together.

Notes on the Contributors

Hans Christian Andersen was born in Denmark and is a Senior Lecturer in Tourism Management at the University of Northumbria. He has worked for the *Guardian*, lectured at the Universities of Hull and Newcastle and specializes in attractions management, arts and heritage tourism and arts marketing. His earlier research and publications involve museums management, attractions management, British and Danish theatre, and travel as a motif in the works of Hans Christian Andersen (1805–75).

Michael Barke is Reader in Human Geography at the University of Northumbria. His love affair with Spain started with his first visit as a student in 1968 and has continued undiminished ever since. He has travelled widely throughout the Iberian peninsula and has conducted research into several aspects of social and economic change, including tourism, in Andalucia in particular. He has published over 20 articles on Spain and co-edited *Tourism in Spain* (1996).

Robert Barnard was born in Essex, and after attending Colchester Royal Grammar School, went up to Balliol College, Oxford, in 1956. His first job was with the Fabian Society, and later he taught briefly in Accrington, before going to Australia in 1961 as a lecturer in English at the University of New England. He married in Australia, and he and his wife came back to Europe in 1966 to the University of Bergen, Norway, where he later took his doctorate. In 1976 he went to the University of Tromsø, the world's most northerly university, as Professor of English. His first crime novel, *Death of an Old Goat*, had been published in 1974, and since then he has produced over thirty crime novels, either under his own name or as Bernard Bastable, the pseudonym he uses for historical crime mysteries. He and his wife came back to live in Britain at Leeds, in 1983. In addition to fiction he has written books on Dickens, Agatha Christie (*A Talent to Deceive*) and a *History of English Lit-*

erature. He is an active member of the Crime Writers' Association, the Detection Club, and the Brontë Society of which he was chairman from 1996–99.

Lawrence I. Berkove is Professor of English at the University of Michigan-Dearborn and the Director of its American Studies Program. His area of specialization is American literature of the nineteenth and early twentieth centuries. He has published widely in this area, but most extensively on authors of the American West. In addition to Mark Twain, he is also an authority on Ambrose Bierce, Jack London, and the literature of Nevada's Sagebrush School.

Bill Bramwell is Reader in Tourism at Sheffield Hallam University, UK. He has edited books on rural tourism, sustainable tourism in Europe, and tourism collaboration and partnerships, and he has published numerous papers in tourism-related journals. He is currently editing a book on sustainable tourism in the Mediterranean. In 1992 he co-founded the *Journal of Sustainable Tourism*, which he continues to co-edit. Among his current research interests are influences on policies for managing tourism growth, community responses to tourism's impacts, and Mediterranean tourism.

Patricia Cormack is Associate Professor in the Department of Sociology and Anthropology, St Francis Xavier University. She specializes in sociological theory, analysis of political and autobiographical texts, and cultural studies.

Graham M. S. Dann is a founder member of the International Academy for the Study of Tourism and of the research committee on international tourism of the International Sociological Association. With interests in tourist motivation and the semiotics of promotion, he has over seven books and ninety articles/chapters to his name. Currently he is Professor of Tourism at the International Tourism Research Institute, University of Luton, and serves on the editorial boards of four leading tourism journals.

Clare Fawcett is Associate Professor in the Department of Sociology and Anthropology, St Francis Xavier University. She has conducted research on Japanese cultural resource management, nationalism and archaeology, and Japanese tourism on Prince Edward Island.

John Woodrow Presley is Provost at the State University of New York at Oswego and Professor of English. He has been writing on the works of Robert Graves since 1974, and on the subject of tourism for almost as long. While his list of publications includes poems, textbooks, a book on Graves, and many articles on language and modern literature, his greatest interest is on the intersection between 'high art' and mass culture. He is currently general editor of *Gravesiana*, the journal of the Robert Graves Society and vice-president of the Robert Graves Society.

Mike Robinson is Professor of Tourism and Director of the Centre for Tourism and Cultural Change at Sheffield Hallam University, UK. Mike's general research interests lie in the dynamic relationships between tourism and forms of cultural expression. The representation of tourism in fictive texts is one of Mike's particular interests. He is editor of eleven books on tourism's inter-relationships with the cultural domain and has organized numerous international conferences on such themes. Mike serves on the editorial boards of two journals and is editor of the book series on *Tourism and Cultural Change*.

Sarah Tetley gained her BSc and PhD qualifications in Tourism in the Centre for Tourism at Sheffield Hallam University, UK. Her thesis examines visitor attitudes to authenticity at a literary tourist destination, with the PhD being awarded in 1999. She subsequently developed her interest in place imagery through employment as a researcher in Liverpool's city marketing organization, The Merseyside Partnership.

Dr John Towner, BA (Dunelm), MA (York Ontario), PhD (Birmingham) was formerly Senior Lecturer in Geography at the University of Northumbria. His research interests are in the history of leisure and tourism and he has published extensively in this field, including *An Historical Geography of Recreation and Tourism in the Western World, 1540–1940* (1996). Until recently, he was Associate Editor (History) for the Annals of Tourism Research. He is now a Senior Research Associate in the Department of Child Health, University of Newcastle, undertaking research on the history of injury.

Donald Ulin's most recent publication in *Victorians Institute Journal* is on William Howitt's middle-class politics of domestic tourism. He is working on a book *Seeing the Country: Tourism and Literature in Nineteenth-Century England* and has published articles in *Victorian Studies, Victorian Poetry*, and *Cultural Critique*. He is currently Assistant Professor of English at the University of Pittsburgh at Bradford.

Amber Vogel (University of North Carolina at Chapel Hill) has served as editor of *The Journal of African Travel-Writing* since 1996. Previously she edited *The Black Warrior Review* (1987–88) and *The Carolina Quarterly* (1992–96). She is currently at work on *Getting Across the Intervening Space: Selected Letters of Laura (Riding) Jackson*. With Joseph M. Flora she is co-editing the updated *Southern Writers: A Biographical Dictionary*. Her essays have recently appeared in *The Companion to Southern Literature, The Seventies: The Age of Glitter in Popular Culture, Safundi: The Journal of South African and American Comparative Studies*, and *Chelsea*. In 1997 she served as consultant for the BBC documentary *Being There: East Africa*.

David T. H. Weir is Professor of Management at CERAM, Emeritus Professor of the University of Northumbria, Visiting Professor in Management Development at Lancaster University and Chairman of Fourth Paradigm Consulting and has also held a series of leading positions in the academic and commercial world. He is the author of numerous articles, and several books including the best-selling *Modern Britain* series. He also published two volumes on risk management in 2000. He is currently completing a book entitled *Nevil Shute: The Untypical Englishman*, and a manuscript on management in the Arab world entitled *The Fourth Paradigm: Arab Managers in a Global World*.

Introduction

Over the last two decades of the twentieth century, various researchers have investigated the multi-dimensional, multi-layered relationships that exist between literature (fiction and travel writing) and place, particularly, though not exclusively, from a cultural geography perspective. However, while it is clear that such relationships do exist, overall these have, to a large extent, resisted structured interrogation within the context of tourism studies *per se*. This collection of essays is an attempt to raise awareness of literature as being an important element in the structures and development of tourism and the behaviour of tourists, and to establish the tourism–literature relationship more firmly in the realm of tourism studies.

The book deals with both literature as a created cultural form and with its creators, the writer, and the interconnectivity between the two. As creative people, some writers become great sources of inspiration to their readership, who are not content merely to read and collect their works. They may also want to visit the writers' homes, in order to connect with the space where 'great' books came into being, to walk where the writers walked, to see what the writers saw. They may go on journeys to follow in the footsteps of the admired writers, perhaps to go where the latter went for inspiration. They may even follow the writers on their lives' journeys to the very end and 'worship' at their graves.

Such personality-based tourism goes back many centuries and accounts for the preservation and/or design of a wide range of sites and attractions, including literary museums and commemorative plaques on buildings inhabited or visited by the famous, whether they are creative artists or have made their mark on history in other ways. It is a kind of cultural tourism in the anthropological sense, in that it involves tourists and visitors identifying with, discovering, and creating signifiers of cultural values with those people who have become part of the cultural mythologies of places. In this respect, a visit to Napoleon's grave in Paris or to Bertold Brecht's house in Augsburg are of the same nature: both can express a need to find evidence that the great personality 'really existed', that there is a human being behind the myth. In the case of literary tourism we are, as tourists, looking for evidence of the writer's real life, perhaps to use symbolically for inspiration or as an addendum to our reading. It can clearly be argued that writers are among the great personalities who attract tourists.

But literary tourism is obviously also cultural tourism in the aesthetic sense: it is tourism based on creative art. Again we are dealing with a type of tourism with a tradition going back centuries, certainly to the time of the Roman Empire, and which played an important part in that distinctive European tradition of the 'Grand Tour' of cultural sites.

As aesthetic cultural tourism, literary tourism is distinctive. Literature (prose fiction, poetry and drama) is not like other art forms. Unlike the visual arts and music, literature can potentially be engaged with at a personal level by anybody who can read and who understands the conventions used by the author in telling a story or arranging words to create aesthetic and semantic patterns. The author and the reader are closer to sharing the art, you might say, than the sculptor or ceramic artist and their audience. As human beings, we may all have the capacity for drawing and painting at some level, we may all be able to develop that capacity at least to some level of competence, and we may – and this is of course hypothetical – all be able to respond to sculpture at some kind of instinctive level, enjoying it without necessarily being able to formulate a view on it. But literature, being word-based and (in a normative sense) story-based, has an advantage: if we can speak, if we can talk to other people about ourselves and other people, then we are already in the world of the author, we already share some understanding of the author's linguistic raw material, simply through our use of it for everyday purposes.

Our argument would be that literary tourism is special for that reason: as readers, as members of the audience for word-art, we have much more immediate access to the work of art, because we can grasp how it can be used formally and stylistically and because we share the author's interest in telling stories about human beings and in using words to express emotions.

This would, then, account for a range of literary tourist experiences beyond the 'worshipping' at sites made attractive through allusion with the author as person-ality. The literary tourist also engages in tourism related to the art itself. One very direct way of doing so would be to engage in special-interest tourism and attend creative writing summer courses, where the tourists might attempt to become practitioners. Visits to literary museums – often in the shape of national libraries but also in some cases to actual museums devoted to literature and the production of books – would also be examples of niche tourism of a highly specialized kind.

The aspect of literary tourism that makes it stand out is tourism based on the content of the works, something which painting may approach, if we consider, for example, visits to locations portrayed in paintings, or which music may emulate on an abstract level in the case of programme music. But only with literature are we able to say that the art work itself can lead us on actual journeys to real places, as we engage in aesthetic cultural tourism based on the wonderful, hazy, imprecise world of fact and fiction we inhabit.

Such travel is based on the stories told or the world expressed through poetry and involves visits to locations which an author has incorporated in a literary work. An argument may arise over the 'reality' of real locations mentioned in works of fiction: does it 'make sense' to visit a real location, just because is has formed part of a narrative plot? Prince Amled – the Danish model for Shakespeare's Hamlet, Prince of Denmark – may have existed. The castle at Elsinore certainly does exist. But if Amled really did exist, he would have died centuries before the construction of the castle. The point usually made by critics is that a location in a narrative is always, by definition, part of the narrative, part of the fiction. It is *not* the same as the real location. Hamlet's castle only exists in the narrative, on stage, in the imagination, but not in reality.

And yet, it seems fair to assume that for the cultural or literary tourist visiting the town of Elsinore, Hamlet's castle on the shores of the Øre Sound, opposite the coast of Sweden, is not only real but is real in a particular way. It exists on two levels at the same time: both as a castle originally constructed to perform a particular strategic function and as the location associated with one of the great stories in world literature and world theatre. The literary critic might not agree but the cultural geographer and the tourism studies specialist would, and they may be two of the guides which literary tourists also need on their quest for literary tourism experiences.

We are therefore dealing with tourism and travel at several levels, inspired both by literary authors and by literary works. It is our contention that since our understanding (as readers) of literature is arguably so personal and immediate, the study of literary tourism requires a simultaneous study of literature *and* tourism. The editors have sought to establish the foundations for such a study in Chapter 1 'Reading between the lines: literature and the creation of touristic spaces', where we discuss how the imaginative spaces of literature and literary biography lend themselves to the creativity of tourism, the supply of tourist attractions and events, and the curiosity of tourists past and present. We examine the commodification and promotion of literature and the literary within a tourism context, involving various processes of transformation from perceptual to physical space, and from fictive reality to touristic fact. In drawing out the ways in which the creativity of writers and their works continues to spark the creative process within the tourism sector, we highlight how literary tourism is intimately joined with social and cultural constructions of spaces and time.

Understanding the motivations for tourist visits to particular destinations, the reasons for specific tourist activities and the behaviour of tourists, are omnipresent themes in tourism studies. As Mike Robinson explores in Chapter 2 'Between and beyond the pages: literature–tourism relationships', literature is a powerful, if often tacit source of knowledge for the tourist at all stages of a journey. While tourist promotional brochures are clearly central to the functioning of contemporary national and international tourism, the ideas, images, identities and imaginings derived from our normative encounters with fiction provide an essential context for our motivations and behaviour as tourists. Robinson locates the inspirational, motivational and transformative qualities of literature as emanating from both the text itself, internally as the 'written word' and externally from various manifestations and interpretations of the text and its author.

Literature can have a complex and direct influence on the 'real world', as Michael Barke explains in Chapter 3 '"Inside" and "outside" writings on Spain'. Literature, whether produced by domestic or foreign writers, can accumulate a lasting image of a country as a tourist destination. In Barke's words 'Although the superstructure of modern mass tourism in Spain was built around sun, sea, sand, ease of modern travel, the convenience of the "package" and relative cheapness, the substructure relied heavily on a set of images which stretched back into Spanish literary history and external writings about Spain.' The creation of an image for tourist Spain becomes a matter of implicit negotiation between native and tourist writers of different kinds: (i) writers/works associated with places; (ii) writers describing particular places in their works, and (iii) travel writers writing about particular places.

In Chapter 4 'Frizzling in the sun: Robert Graves and the development of mass tourism in the Balearic Islands', John Presley illustrates how complex the relationship between tourism and a particular creative writer can be. Graves, who spent much of his life on Mallorca, was both a student of tourism (writing about earlier visitors to the island), a tourist attraction in his own right (as others came to see the place where he, the 'personality', lived), personally involved in advising on and investing in elements of the local tourist industry and a critic of the rapidly developing mass tourism on the Balearics and in Spain generally. Thus, the man already well understood as a writer and poet also becomes describable in terms of tourism.

David Weir, writing in Chapter 5 about 'Nevil Shute and the landscape of England: an opportunity for literary tourism', illustrates that the personal relation between writer and tourism is paralleled by the relationship between tourist-reader and tourism. Just as Shute constructs his plots and the landscapes where they take place, with a straightforward engineer's approach, so the tourist-reader deconstructs the texts, seeking out and visiting the locations that appear in the author's works.

Appropriating and controlling the image of the literary destination and the nature of the literary tourist experience becomes a matter of cultural politics, as Robert Barnard explains in Chapter 6 'Tourism comes to Haworth'. What starts off, during the lifetime of the author, as tourism based on curiosity and opportunism soon becomes a matter of controlling the image of the authors (Charlotte Brontë specifically) through biography and the collection and exhibition of realia, as a tourist industry of accommodation, catering and retailing develops around the actual attractions. Barnard's essay exemplifies the personal/human aspect of literary tourism: the main Brontë attraction, the preserved/reconstructed home of the family, is now controlled by a literary society whose membership and leadership represent a readership rather than, say, a cultural élite or the tourist industry.

How the visitor responds to the image projected by the destination generally is the subject of Bill Bramwell and Sarah Tetley's Chapter 7 'Tourists and the cultural construction of Haworth's literary landscape'. They investigate how myths of place, and the physical features of the town and the surrounding landscape help visitors understand the literary and cultural landscape of a major international literary destination. It is clear from this example that visitors do understand the signals transmitted to them by those who maintain/design such a destination, but also that they understand it in the open-minded manner of the tourist: they create their own, personal understanding of the destination and expect to find those (retail and catering) features which might be anathema to the literary purist. Literary tourists may be students of literature but perhaps they are so in general, individual, lay terms rather than, typically, as professionals.

L. M. Montgomery has left an equally important cultural legacy behind on Prince Edward Island, as Patricia Cormack and Clare Fawcett explain in Chapter 8 'Cultural gatekeepers in the L. M. Montgomery tourist industry'. They reveal how the image of Montgomery on which that industry is based is a matter of contention on the island, where tourist authorities, academics and the current owners of the rights to the L. M. Montgomery intellectual property are seeking to satisfy a variety of cultural needs, while also ensuring the preservation of a quality image for the destination. Far from being unproblematic, this in fact leads to an image based on very different ideas about both 'what' L. M. Montgomery tourism should be and who is in the target audience for that tourism.

How widespread is literary tourism? It has been one of the intentions of this volume to look beyond a purely British context, and the tourist experience of Spain, Canada, Africa and the United States is included in this volume, albeit supplied by writers from Anglo-Saxon countries.

There is, perhaps, an emphasis on the British experience and this is, we would argue, neither unexpected nor irrelevant in a volume that hopes to reach at least some level of generality. For one thing, the British have long celebrated their authors as national heroes. The existence of the so-called 'Poets' Corner' in London's Westminster Abbey is evidence in itself. Westminster Abbey is where the monarch is crowned and it is also where the nation's greatest writers are either buried or commemorated with monuments. The nation cannot express its respect for literature more clearly. Furthermore, the study of English-language literature has had a special status in the British academic world, where it has filled the intellectual space which other nations would fill with, say, philosophy or political science. Literature is where generations of British schoolchildren and students have learned to play with abstract ideas and concepts, in a country which reputedly values pragmatism above abstraction. To study literary tourism in that context, given the precedence set in the Grand Tour for cultural tourism, is not illogical.

The Grand Tour is, however, the real clue to the perspective taken in this volume. The Grand Tour, albeit an essentially British phenomenon in its origins, was widely copied throughout Europe, leaving an inheritance behind in the shape of a continued interest in a particular cultural tradition and a particular set of continental European tourist destinations and attractions. The Grand Tour is essentially a European phenomenon, drawing on a European cultural tradition, and the fact that it appears and reappears in this volume emphasizes the fact that the phenomenon considered here is European to its fullest extent and more.

In a sense, Mark Twain represents a particular and long-lived version of the Grand Tour. In Chapter 9 'The two Mark Twains as tourists,' Berkove highlights how the two aspects of Twain the writer are reflected in his travel books, the 'two Twains' being the humorous narrator of the books whose *naïveté* makes us laugh, and the other less conspicuous and much more critical narrator who appears below the surface of the stories. Lawrence Berkove's approach is one of literary criticism rather than touristic analysis, and its conclusion makes a strong case for the study of literary tourism: 'As Twain demonstrates in all his books, the true traveller must prepare himself or herself spiritually as well as mentally to be honestly open to new insights as well as sights. Otherwise, one merely travels with a list of sights to be seen and checked off, sees only surfaces, and experiences quantity rather than quality' (p. 205).

Literature can have a very fundamental relationship with tourism, not merely providing tourist attractions or destination image. In Chapter 10 'Matthew Arnold's guerilla in the glade: the politics and poetics of tourism', Donald Ulin explores a development in the 'ideology' of tourism. Matthew Arnold, Ulin suggests, exemplifies the development of modern tourism in the UK as that country finds itself, for the first time ever, a nation with a predominantly urban population and an increasingly influential middle class. As a result, the traditional ideology of the (countrified) aristocracy is challenged and a new work ethic begins to dominate. Matthew Arnold, as an Inspector of Schools, tours this developing nation as a 'meta-tourist', incorporating both professional and leisure aspects of travel, and in his poetry he expresses how, as a guerilla soldier observing the romantic glade from the cover of the shrubs, he sees a new view of the landscape evolving, one where we may choose to tour the actual geographical landscape but may also prefer, instead, to visit it by proxy, by witnessing how artists have portrayed it.

The aestheticization of the landscape is also a theme in John Towner's Chapter 11 'Literature, tourism and the Grand Tour'. This archetypal form of tourism, cultural tourism for (primarily but not exclusively) the young aristocracy, has given rise to a large body of travel literature, whose writers have often preferred to provide their readers with an idealized view of the Grand Tour, with many borrowings from earlier writers. Travel literature has not coincided with the facts (or even the truth) of travel. However, although fiction rather than fact has dominated Grand Tour publication, the true outcome, in print, of centuries of ambitious touring is not a literary legacy of consequence but rather the guidebook.

On the other hand, in Chapter 12 'La Serenissima: dreams, love and death in Venice', Graham Dann looks at how creative and travel writers have accumulated central motifs over centuries, motifs that form the core experience of a particular destination. In this case, we can not only see how the image of a destination owes much to the work of creative writers as they appear in promotional literature, but also how, eventually, the same motifs can be seen to reflect, in much wider terms, how we experience tourism generally.

The close connection between travel and literature is clear from Amber Vogel's Chapter 13 'African sublime: the dark continent joins the Grand Tour'. Vogel shows how the (British) perception of Africa was formed in literature in the eighteenth century, as the new kind of (less aristocratic) Grand Tour that was developing in Africa merged with existing literary concepts such as the Sublime and the Picturesque. Eventually, writers such as Oliver Goldsmith, who never travelled in Africa himself, is able to reflect a view of travel in Africa that includes Gothic elements of death, ruination, and lonely and highly dangerous exploration, some of which we can still see reflected in contemporary tourism.

The relationship between literature and tourism exists at many levels. It may be tourism inspired by the lives of authors or by their works. It is tourism that can act as an aspect of the study of literature, but it is more likely to be informal than formal study, performed (we would suggest) by readers rather than critics, and it is articulated through a series of tourist attractions and events that forms not only a specific type of 'cultural' tourism but also forms an integral part of tourism in a more generic sense.

Literature and authors can influence the development of tourist attractions in a very direct and personal way, both providing the core experience (through the literary attraction and literary heritage) which others negotiate and maintain, and the image for the destination generally through the way they themselves create and negotiate that image. Literature may also, much more fundamentally, reveal the development of tourism as a human activity in the context of cultural and historical development. It is our hope – and also our expectation – that the exploration of this field is now established, but also that it will provide further avenues for academic exploration.

Mike Robinson and Hans Christian Andersen

Chapter 1

Reading Between the Lines: Literature and the Creation of Touristic Spaces

Mike Robinson and Hans Christian Andersen

INTRODUCTION

Some 450 years on, the half-timbered house of Shakespeare's birthplace in Stratford-upon-Avon has undergone a significant makeover. Not only does it now boast original period items, painstakingly recreated artefacts and recrafted decorative fabrics, it also features a reconstruction of Shakespeare's father's glove-making workshop, improved access for disabled visitors and a new visitor exhibition. This is all part of a continuing programme to attract and manage the some 520,000 visitors (1998 figures) it receives annually. The exhibition informs us that the house has been a literary shrine for over 250 years and particularly since the building was purchased by public subscription in 1847 by the body of trustees that still manages the property. Varlow (1996) notes the monograms of Sir Walter Scott and Thomas Carlyle on the window of Shakespeare's 'birthroom' as evidence of notable literary visitors. The four other properties associated with Shakespeare and his family (New Place, Anne Hathaway's Cottage, Hall's Croft, and Mary Arden's House) in close proximity, and indeed Stratford-upon-Avon *in toto*, are a well-established tourist product, the focus of what Holderness (1988) refers to as 'bardolatry': a devotional worship of the man, his works and the places and times he inhabited. In addition to the role of Stratford, Holderness (1988) also notes the longstanding power of Shakespearean theatre performances in London to attract 'tourists'. And now, the recreated Globe Theatre at London's Bankside (opened in 1997) with its programme of performances and exhibitions continues the process of linking the literary with tourism.

At one level there is nothing surprising or complicated about such linkages between literature and tourism. However, set against the dynamics of globalization, the rapidity of international tourism development, what Urry (2000) terms the 'sociology of mobilities', emerging discourses of hyper-reality and instantaneous media, the diversity of cultural expressions, and searches for meaning and understanding in tourism, there is much to examine and explore. If we extend the

Shakespeare example further, we find that ideas of pilgrimage, and supply and demand economics, important though they be, are inadequate in helping us to understand fully the relationships between literature and tourism. How do we explain the full-sized replica of Anne Hathaway's Cottage with its 'authentic' furnishings located in Victoria, British Columbia? Anne Hathaway's Cottage bed-and-breakfast establishment south of Perth in Western Australia, complete with its Romeo and Juliet Suite? That to tourists, Kronborg Castle in Denmark is better known as Hamlet's Castle? That the Alabama Shakespeare Festival attracts more than 300,000 visitors each year from over 60 countries and is only one of approximately 35 Shakespeare festivals across the USA?

Such examples represent the consumption, production, re-production, commodification, transformation, communication, and distribution of literature for tourism purposes. On the surface, what is commonly referred to as 'literary tourism' can be seen as an obvious development: a dimension of cultural tourism, representative of yet another set of experiences that we find 'exciting, edifying, pleasurable, estranging, broadening' (Clifford 1997). But, as with so many aspects of seemingly straight-forward encounters, the processes by which literature is utilized by and for tourists are riddled with issues of contestation, social and political tension, powerplay and of meaning. The focus of this chapter relates to the exploration of such processes in considering how tourism constructs, reconstructs and utilizes – 'commodifies' – historic and contemporary manifestations of literary arts. However, before examining the various commodified forms of literature, the chapter examines the boundaries between and across literary forms, with the intention of uncovering how literature and tourism overlap and interact.

As an initial assumption, we regard the relationship between literature and tourism as two-sided: the study of either can illuminate the other in the right circumstances. It is, for instance, quite likely that tourism involving locations with literary associations can ignite an appreciation and understanding of literature as means of reflection and self-reflection and as a portal to innumerable realities: we read, and by sharing the author's insight and understanding of the real world, our insight and understanding is also broadened. But, it would be argued, the corollary is also true: literature – in the sense of 'fiction' or 'creative writing' – is an important, but under-used instrument through which we can explore the nature, development and meaning of tourism. Tourism as history, politics, as a cultural dynamic and as emotion can be understood through an engagement in literature. As Lowenthal (1985: 224) states 'more people apprehend the past through historical novels, from Walter Scott to Jean Plaid, than through any formal history'. It has to be acknowledged that the boundaries between fiction and non-fiction are becoming increasingly blurred anyway, and that fiction has increasingly had to yield to literary theory and the essay as the point where critical thinking takes place. But this does not leave literature without powers as an instrument for evolving views about the nature of the relationship between human beings and their environment from a blatantly subjective but also publicly revelatory angle. It is not the aim of this chapter to seek to disclose the significance of tourism through direct literary analysis, but, the recognition of the value of creative writing in doing so is very much part of the undercurrent that sweeps the chapter along.

In examining questions that surround the tourism/tourist–literature relationship, this chapter builds on previous discourse that has positioned literature as a reservoir of cultural understanding. The focal point for this study has been the tri-partite relationship between authors, their writings, and the concepts of place/landscape. Works of literature are recognized as expressive of economic, cultural and political change, replete with intimate and revealing perspectives on the relationships between people and place at various space scales (Crang 1998; Drabble 1979). Raymond Williams' (1973) text *The Country and the City* used literary works from the eighteenth and nineteenth centuries to explain what he saw as the divide between the urban and the rural, each with its attendant mythologies and language. Pocock (1979, 1981*a*), perhaps chiefly with his edited volume *Humanistic Geography and Literature* (1981*b*), mapped out the ways in which literary expressions of places, sites and landscapes can gain us greater insight into the social, economic and political order of the world, together with an understanding of identities, the constructions of culture and the dynamics of landscape change. It is the ability of writer and writings alike to filter, explore and intellectually meander that makes literature such a valuable instrument of geographical and social inquiry. As Pocock (1981*b*: 10) states: 'It is the deliberately cultivated subjectivity of the writer which makes literature into literature and not, say, reporting.' He goes on, 'such a process is not to deny factual reproduction, for literature is often referred to as a mirror, reflection or microcosm of reality'.

The relationships between literature and physical space have provided a focus in cultural geography, in the sense that literature can reflect real space and its use, even if it does not invariably do so. Moretti (1998) focuses on 'space in literature', whereby writers define and redefine spaces through their works. Space is fictionalized by virtue of its literary expression. Through the use of maps, Moretti's *Atlas of the European Novel* sets out a fascinating spread of interwoven literary geographies, enabling us to track the plots and storylines of novels and genres as well as the wider social themes they display. A similar approach is taken in Bradbury's (1996) *The Atlas of Literature*, in which detailed maps and street plans are used to highlight the spaces that writers and writings inhabited, created and transformed. Such volumes provide a useful entry point into considering touristic uses of neo-fictional space.

Previous works that have explicitly explored the multifarious relations between literature and the various facets of tourism include Herbert (1996), Hilty (1996), Newby (1981), Pocock (1992), Rojek (1993), Squire (1992, 1994, 1996), and Urry (1995). Perhaps unsurprisingly, history has been a particularly strong feature in earlier studies. Scholars have sought to explain the evolution of sites, regions and nations as tourist destinations by focusing upon their past portrayal in works of literature and the ways in which such portrayal has shaped present perceptions and images. The connections between location as a source of literary inspiration and as a place to visit are generally transparent. The physical landscapes and sociopolitical history of Scotland were, for example, influential in shaping the style and content of two of the country's most celebrated literary figures, Robert Burns and Sir Walter Scott. In turn, their lives, works and the myths woven around both became durable cultural commodities, successfully relocating Scotland from the cultural periphery to the centre of romanticism, and in so doing they generated substantive tourism legacies (Andrews 1989; Butler 1985; Gold and Gold 1995; Prickett 1981; Seaton 1998).

But despite some academic excursions into tourism and literature relationships, there seems to have been surprisingly little analysis of the relationship between the two, particularly in the light of two fundamental realities, namely, firstly, that much tourism is based on the written word, and, secondly, that tourists read and are inspired by literature. In his examination of the political economy of cyberspace, Luke (1999: 47) points out that '[w]hat exists for human beings is mostly disclosed by words'. Tourism is certainly no exception. Words are the building blocks of image creation and projection, as well as being the means by which we convey our expectations and experiences. In tourism terms, 'literature' can initially be seen broadly as a fundamental reservoir of words that can inform, envision, stimulate, motivate and inspire.

But literature means more to us than such a reductionist definition reveals. The literature which forms the focus for this chapter – creative writing/fiction – does not seek deliberately to say anything about the processes of tourism or about tourist destinations and attractions. Rather, they inhabit the world of what Gunn (1972) calls 'organic information sources', and it is through these we learn of tourism – of destinations and landscapes, of culture and peoples, about how to interpret them and understand what they mean. Literature is a potent and pervasive force, running deep within and across societies, shaping the way we see the world and each other. As Anderson (1983: 40) puts it: 'Fiction seeps quietly and continuously into reality, creating that remarkable confidence of community in anonymity which is the hallmark of modern nations'. Certainly, but not exclusively, within the western developed world, literature is a powerful and dynamic field of cultural expression. Of course, not all literature is pregnant with landscape imagery to tempt the tourist to destinations, or possesses strong themes and characters to form the basis for the creation of literary theme parks. Nor does every author offer that richness of personality and lifestyle that might encourage tourists to explore their preserved literary homes. But considered generally, literature as accumulated 'cultural capital' does provide wellsprings of information, points of imaginative departure and inspiration for tourists. Within the wide gamut of creative writing, sometimes deeply buried, sometimes just below the surface, lie the seams for writers of tourist brochures to mine.

LITERATURE AND THE LITERARY: BOUNDARIES AND ISSUES

How is the term 'literature' used in this chapter? Since we are in the world of tourism rather than of literature exclusively, the starting point must be an acceptance that the manifestations of literary tourism – the literary homes, the trails, museums, landmarks, landscapes, theme parks, etc. – come into existence because there is a 'consumer demand' for them. The demand is for physical evidence that can support what we know about and have learned from literary works and the careers of their authors. The field of interest – the literary attractions, if you like – evolves gradually, as literary sites become available, as they come into the limelight with the developing popularity of works and authors, as theme parks are designed in response to anticipated demand. Visitors are motivated in many different ways: perhaps by a professional, academic or journalistic interest in literature, perhaps by a more personal interest in exploring the world of loved works and authors in greater depth.

The understanding of what literature is must be equally pragmatic and eclectic in this chapter. The definition cannot simply follow the concepts of a particular critical school. Rather, literature must be seen in terms of what you find on the shelves in libraries and bookshops marked 'Fiction', (i.e. the novel and the short prose narrative), 'Poetry' and 'Drama': the traditional genres of creative writing, whose main shared feature is the use of the written word to create 'aesthetic objects' or 'literary works of art'. Any definition will invite debate and protest and this definition will no doubt do so. Indeed, this chapter invites controversy from the very beginning by making Shakespeare the first example: the dramatist's stage works are only partly describable as 'literature'. Arguably, as drama they are something quite different, namely 'blueprints for performance'. In the context of this chapter, primacy is given to Shakespeare, the 'word-artist', and the implication should be clear: what matters here is not to cross the boundaries of how 'literature' is understood but how the relationship between literature and tourism is constituted. Underlying this is a strong suspicion that literary tourism is not in itself a manifestation of radical and innovative exploration of tourism as an art form.

As has been suggested above, both the authors and their works attract visitors. To account for this aspect of the power of literature, it is necessary to define literature further, not only in terms of genre but also with reference to at least two different kinds of critical framework. Firstly, biographical criticism forms a cornerstone of what literature is, in touristic terms. Literature is an example of inter-human communication and the person of the author, the creative artist, is crucial in allowing us to appreciate the work, since the work is the artist's deliberate communication with the reader. This may seem like a step backwards in the development of literary criticism but helps explain the fact that it is intrinsically interesting to know something about the author: for a literary tourist to visit the author's home and look into the author's study is a worthwhile activity which enhances both the holiday and one's appreciation of the literary work. Secondly, it is also assumed that the work itself (seen in abstraction from the author) will attract the attention of the tourist/visitor. It is therefore also proposed that the work in its own right, *qua* literary work, has sufficient stature to attract the tourist. In that respect, this chapter leans towards Formalism with its emphasis on 'literariness', or even towards the by now outdated and somewhat discredited Neo-critical stress on the work proper, in abstraction from tangentially interesting details such as the author's career. As you will perceive, this chapter also acknowledges the validity of a critical school that sees literature as reflecting social reality and perhaps political ideology.

Far from wanting to display a lack of critical focus, the purpose is to acknowledge the many roles which literature can play in the lives of individuals and communities, paralleled by the many ways in which literature can manifest itself as part of the contemporary tourist product. The apparent critical indiscipline is, rather, an insistence that a broad-based pillaging of the coffers of literary criticism will assist the understanding of literary tourism and lead to a better understanding of how such an apparently unstructured complex of tourist attractions and tourist experiences as described on the first page of this chapter can be seen to contribute rationally to the world of literature.

Functional perspectives

A description of the kind of object under consideration here is important. Literature is made up of instances of the written text, usually in published form, created for aesthetic purposes. Primacy is given to the 'book'. However, the implications of using the term 'text' are acknowledged. The term 'text' is now very widely applied to examples of inter-human communication, based on linguistic systems of many kinds. The phrase 'written work' might serve better, acknowledging that the author's 'work' can appear in different guises. Not only is *Romeo and Juliet* a Shakespearean tragedy, it is also opera, ballet, film, television and, of course, the printed text will be manifested in many ways as actual stage productions. Each of these manifestations give us a 'text' to work with, a system of signification which we can decode and whose meaning we can try to explain.

Our understanding of what can legitimately be analysed in these terms has been considerably extended in recent decades, so that critical interest is now not only focused on 'literary works of fine art' but also on a range of other kinds of word-based 'text': diaries, letters, labels, advertisements, etc., which can legitimately be analysed to see how they reflect and shape the economic, political and sociocultural realities of the world. For the observer of literary tourism, this extends the range of verbal texts that can be included in the touristic presentation of the author.

However, the widened definition of what a 'text' is – a 'system of signification' – also allows us to look at the literary tourist attraction itself as a text which we can analyse and seek to make sense of. Given that tourist attractions are commonly the result of interpretation and deliberate design from the point of view of their owners and managers, we are entitled to attempt to observe, analyse and interpret them ourselves from the visitor/academic point of view. Consequently, what we are interested in here is the verbal work of art, but we acknowledge that our critical faculties need also to be directed at other kinds of linguistic (perhaps non-verbal) communication which we encounter in the literary tourism sphere.

Literariness

In using the term 'literature' we are referring to something more than mere 'collections of words'. Any verbal message is more than merely a 'collection of words': a verbal message is a 'linguistic event', words arranged for a purpose, whether to form the instructions for the use of machinery or to form a short lyrical poem. A work of literature is here a 'linguistic event', displaying special patterns and orders of language. Literature possesses what we could identify as 'literariness', an accepted, defining characteristic of literature as distinct from other kinds of linguistic event.

Broadly speaking, as readers and critics we recognize the phenomenon 'literature' through the way language is used. Deliberate patterning – in the shape of e.g. rhyme, rhythm, metre, rhetorical structure – are typical linguistic features that mark out the work as literary, attracting the attention of the reader to it as such and making the work identifiable as literary. The same is true about the deliberate use of style in the work, understood as the vocabulary selected and the ways in which meanings and sounds are combined, patterned and integrated. These features are part of what constitutes 'creative writing'.

Experience suggests that these features are not exclusive to 'literature': other types of text use literary conventions and linguistic features that we would expect to read in a novel or poem. Thus, as Dann (1996) has illustrated, tourism promotion brochures exhibit a range of linguistic features, techniques and literary devices with roots in literary art, such as alliteration, repetition, rhyme, metaphor, simile, onomatopoeia. What is more, over the years tourism promotional texts have evolved from simple description to more elaborate narratives, even to the poetic, and in so doing they have created their own colourful discourse complete with cliché and ambiguity. Consequently, it is recognized that the functions which language performs in creating literature cannot be sole defining characteristic of literature. As texts, tourist brochures may have features of 'literariness', yet they are not accepted literary works of art in the same way as the works of say, Charles Dickens.

Fictional worlds

A common reference point in defining literature is the concept of fiction. We read a newspaper, a journal article, or indeed a text such as the present one, and we accept that these represent and present primarily a world of facts, not necessarily as markers of truth, but as phenomena that have existence in the real world. In such texts, ideas are generally conveyed in factual terms and via language that is normally precise, direct, and free from ornamentation and poetics. But in general use, the term 'literature' implies more than 'a vehicle for communicating facts'. The presentation of fact would not normally be the creative writer's first goal: (s)he would be more concerned with 'truth' than with 'fact', where the truthfulness of a literary text is not merely established with reference to (scientific) fact but also with reference to emotional 'fact': that which we feel to be true, that which our experience, social conscience, personal morality tell us to be true or truthful. In major forms of literature – the drama and the novel – such emotional truth is explored in fictional worlds, where imaginary characters move in imaginary worlds and engage in imaginary events and activities.

As readers – and as writers – we engage in a different kind of activity from exchanging knowledge about fact when we involve ourselves in these fictitious, imagined worlds: we play a game of make-believe, exploring a parallel, created universe in order to escape into it and, perhaps, learn about the 'real' universe. The forms and structures of language used to create this parallel universe is used and read differently from the language of 'fact'. Lodge (1992: x) sees fiction as a rhetorical 'art', where 'the novelist or short-story writer *persuades* us to share a certain view of the world for the duration of the reading experience'. We accept the rhetoric for what it is and for what it gives us.

As will be discussed later, there are complications in identifying, with any sort of precision, the boundaries between real and imaginary worlds in literature. The author may locate fictional events in more or less thinly disguised, actual locations or base the events on actual, historical events. However, in the context of literature, only the fictional universe has primacy, as a distinguishing aspect of literariness. It can lead to a kind of 'literary tourism of the mind', as evidenced by books showing pictures of imaginary buildings made famous by appearing in famous books, such as Ashe's *Literary Houses* (1982) and *More Literary Houses* (1983).

Literature also deals with imaginary characters, who inhabit fictional worlds and engage in imaginary events. At one level characters such as Mary Shelley's monster in *Frankenstein*, Abraham Stoker's Dracula, or Lewis Carroll's Queen of Hearts are wholly creatures of the imagination, yet even they behave as if they were real with their behaviour patterns rooted in our own humanity. At another level, characters can be autobiographical and seem to be exceedingly close to a known reality. It is for the reader to interpret where the boundaries lie exactly, and this is the explicit nature of fiction: to leave us with questions regarding the existence of characters and the worlds they 'live' in.

Pollard-Gott (1998) presents an interesting, though obviously subjective overview of the 100 most influential (read 'popular') fictional characters in world literature. Hamlet is placed at the top of the chart, whilst Conan Doyle's Sherlock Holmes is at number nine, Jane Austen's Emma resides at number seventy, and Rice Burrough's Tarzan is at number ninety. The very fact that such a list should have been created, based on the assumption that characters of fiction are 'influential', testifies both to the power of fiction and fictional character and, by implication, to our willingness to take fictional character seriously. Hamlet may, indeed, be influential in con- temporary society, like other mythical personalities such as Che Guevara, John Lennon or Ernest Hemingway. Similarly, we may find it hard to divorce such characters of fiction from the 'real' landscapes which they inhabit: we visit Hamlet's Castle in Elsinore, although the 'historical' Hamlet lived elsewhere and the castle was built centuries after the time when Hamlet is thought to have lived. Shakespeare has given Hamlet – and in some ways also Elsinore itself – a reality that is entirely meshed with the fiction. Other examples here are Lucy Maud Montgomery's *Anne of Green Gables* and Charlotte Brontë's *Jane Eyre*.

Narrative structure

In the drama and prose narrative, the plot often forms the organizing principle that makes sense of the narrative. The author's fiction may be based on fact, but the narrative – the plot, the ordering of events – gives meaning to the fiction. The narrative gives significance to individual events by giving them the right place relative to other events.

The same organizing principle is at work both in many visitor attractions and in tourist trails: the visitor attraction is interpreted for the visitor in such a way that it makes sense to the visitor. The author's home is laid out and explained so that it, in itself, becomes a narrative about the author. In a similar manner, the tourist trail gives order (often an artificial order) to a sequence of locations, which are selected for inclusion in the trail because together they will make sense, form a whole. Here, too, we may speak of the tourist trail as a narrative.

Such a narrative is not fixed. It is changed, in detail or completely, in response to fashion trends in interpretation and in visitor attraction choice, as is the case with Shakespeare's birthplace referred to above. In literary tourism, as in literature itself, we find the same principle at work: the desire to tell stories, to give significance to an apparently random reality by selecting and ordering elements of reality in a way that makes sense in a specific cultural context.

Biography

In recent years, book signings and public readings by authors have become a common phenomenon in the world of contemporary literature. It is not sufficient for us to know authors from their works: we now expect them to appear in person, to present and explain their work, to allow us to hear the voice of and see the person behind the work. The poet becomes not just a writer but also a performer.

At one level, this is just part of the contemporary demystification of the public personality. We expect those who live from the public (e.g. by publishing and selling their works) to place themselves before the public for scrutiny, in press interviews, arts programmes in the electronic media, public appearances. Publicity becomes second nature to the contemporary artist.

Biographical criticism has not always been popular in academic circles. Indeed, in the twentieth century it has been far more important (and in many ways much more rewarding, from a critical point of view) to look at the work than at the author and, even more, the way in which the audience relates to the work. There is of course, a logic to this: as readers (and critics) we experience the *work* at first hand rather than the author, and it is the work rather than the author that becomes part of our collective consciousness, because we can share and debate our views of the literary text.

On the other hand, criticism that focuses on the work at the expense of the author misses out on an important dimension: literature is also communication between individuals. The poet or novelist communicates impersonally with a large audience, perhaps across centuries and national borders. We need not know Molière to appreciate Molière's plays; the *Mahabharata* speaks to us from an age we cannot fully imagine. And yet the human dimension of creative writing is always there: creative writing, literature, appeals to us because it deals with human experience. By reading *The Golden Ass* we engage in a dialogue with fellow members of the human race across millennia.

Literary tourism allows us to indulge in the human aspect of literature: we can freely indulge in the biography of the author, visit locations where the author went, tell ourselves that by being in the presence of the great writer's quill we are also, somehow, closer to the hand that held it and the great talent that created the work.

Literary tourism bypasses the scepticism which many critics feel towards biography, allowing us openly to ask whether a particular kind of person would create a particular kind of literature. Fame comes into the equation: where lowbrow writers might not find a place in literary histories, literary tourism includes those writers who can attract mass audiences. Reader demand overrides critical acclaim. The reason is the same regardless of the apparent 'quality' of the author's work: we are fascinated by creative artists, who can create the literary works that most of us can only appreciate and admire.

Creative writing or 'travel literature'?

The focus within this chapter is on the role of the fictional text and its creators. Thus, we bypass a strongly emerging field of interest in tourism studies, that of travel writings and guide books, and the relationships they share with tourists and the evolution of tourism cultures. The guide book, as Fussell (1980: 203) points out, is 'not sustained by a narrative exploiting the devices of fiction'. Its primary function is that of information transfer for the deliberate end result of better defining the touristic experience. The travel book, on the other hand, is a far more complex creation, drawing freely upon literary motifs and the subjectivity one would expect from autobiographical accounts of travel. Holland and Huggan (1998: 12) argue that it may be 'best to see travel writing as pseudoethnographic', displaying a type of objective reporting but invariably coloured by the personal. Increasingly, travel writings move beyond spatial geography confines to deeper explorations of meaning, self and cultural change exemplified in the works of Pico Iyer and Umberto Eco. Furthermore, frequent wanderings into storytelling approaches, the use of fiction techniques, literary embellishments, and a flair for elongating the truth has meant that travel books edge into the terrain of literature.

Again, there has been a particular focus on travel writings as providing valuable historical accounts on the evolution of travel and tourism patterns and the cultural contexts within which these are drawn. Studies, many of them focusing on the eighteenth and nineteenth century, have explored the various discourses and scriptings of travel as 'gateways of understanding' to geographies of cultural difference, colonialism/imperialism, feminism, romanticism and aesthetics (Bohls 1995; Buzard 1993; Chard 1999; Duncan and Gregory 1999; Fussell 1980; Gilroy 2000; Jarvis 1997; Mills 1991; Morris 1993; Pratt 1992). Holland and Huggan's (1998) *Tourists with Typewriters* concentrates on contemporary travel writers and their writings, and the insights which these imperfect works provide on such issues. In doing so, they endorse, though not uncritically, the literary status of travel writings and their role as cultural reflectors.

We can identify cases where fiction and travel writing appear to overlap. Thus, Hans Christian Andersen's 1835 novel *A Poet's Bazaar* is really an autobiography camouflaged with the impressions which Andersen gained from travelling through Italy. Also, Jules Verne's *Around the World in Eighty Days*, set in 1872, shows the invented character Phileas Fogg following accurate schedules (Withey 1997). However, these apparent borderline cases are, in fact, clear examples of fiction and we would include them as such, in order to consider the popularity of Verne's novel and the effect it had in stimulating interest in world travel and tourism (Rothman 1998; Withey 1997).

On the other hand, this chapter excludes non-fiction, including the travel writings and 'factual' accounts of travelling by creative writers. Novelists and poets exhibit a general tendency to travel and explore, often to the very limits of their known world, bounded by the culture and technology of the time. Chaucer made business trips to Genoa and Florence in the latter quarter of the fourteenth century and his own trips from London to Canterbury would seem to have influenced his own works in both subject matter and style. Robert Louis Stevenson's travels throughout his life, through Europe, to California, and his 'island hopping' in the South Pacific until making Samoa his home are all the more remarkable, given the practical problems of long-haul travel of the time.

Fussell (1980) examines the phenomenon of British authors travelling between 1918 and 1939, positioning them as élite 'anti-tourists'. However, Fussell's study is drawn from a nostalgic lament on the death of 'real' travel and the British (English) proclivity for the uncomfortable exploration of all things 'foreign'. His accounts are internalist in the sense that they deal with a well-delimited and atypical selection of British writers (as opposed to modern tourists), who travelled or, more aptly in some cases, emigrated. Now, well within the realities of democratized, postcolonial travel and tourism, we are primarily interested in the external legacies of creative writers who have travelled. We concentrate not primarily on what they had to say (write) about their journeys but on the 'trace' they left, their bequest of extensive international routes of associations and sites, which have become markers on the routes which modern literary 'pilgrims' can follow, in part or completely.[1]

The relationship between experiences in real time and space, and created spaces and places is complex and at times contradictory. The relatively extensive geography of Shakespeare's works are largely derived from secondary sources and not his own very limited travel experience. Byron's *Childe Harold* is widely interpreted as a personal travelogue based upon the poet's 'grand tour' between 1809 and 1811. Stevenson wrote *Treasure Island* years before sailing the South Seas. Rupert Brooke wrote of Grantchester and ultra-Englishness from Berlin. Graham Greene's extensive travelling links directly to his fictional works so that Sierra Leone where he worked during the Second World War provided the setting for his novel The *Heart of the Matter*, and his journeys through Mexico in 1938 provided the inspiration for *The Power and the Glory*.

In addressing the question of what it is it within a novel or poem that initiates, defines and confirms the follow-up actions of visiting a destination represented, or of making the imaginary real via a literary attraction or trail, the nature of fiction, or more precisely the nebulous boundary between fiction and reality is central. Arguably – and somewhat paradoxically – the lack of distinction between the real and the imagined within the literary form is one of its distinguishing features. Readers are allowed to cruise the real world within their imagination and to fuel their imagination through glimpses, representations and deliberate distortions of realities. McHale (1987: 33) positions fictional text in this hazy and wonderfully imprecise zone 'as being in-between, amphibious – neither true nor false, suspended between belief and disbelief'. Readers are able to travel without moving and indulge in the shadows of creative play and metamorphic situations.

CULTURAL PERSPECTIVES

Moving away from linguistic and ontological features, literature occupies a dualistic role in cultural terms as being both an object of culture and a process of creative development that results in such an object. We take literature to be a defining element of culture: a characteristic indicator, activity and interest of a people (Eliot 1948). It is reflective of our way of life, but also a marker of collective achievement and social identity. Literature is generally recognized as a social and cultural practice, whereby in daily life we share frameworks for its recognition, if not its precise definition. Thus, Olsen (1981: 533) claims 'A literary work must ... be seen as being offered to an audience by an author with the intention that it should be understood with reference to a shared background of concepts and conventions which must be employed to determine its aesthetic features.' We may not agree with what these features are exactly, but we recognize that literature emerges from, and is understood within, cultural settings and social institutions that allows us to speak of literariness.

Literature has been absorbed into that set of cultural resources that form the basis of what Wynne (1992) terms the 'cultural industries': that broad sweep of the creative and decorative arts now recognized as having significant economic value as well as social worth. Literary works as created objects for sale, or what MacCannell (1976) terms 'cultural productions', are part of the cultural industries. The production of novels and poetry in the UK is buoyant, as is their consumption. In 1999, 106,390 books were published in the UK, including 'computer books' (Leisure Forecasts 2000). This figure includes the substantial categories of non-fiction and children's/educational books. However, a high proportion of published books can be classified as creative writing or fictional texts. Creative writing in the UK finds profile and legitimization with a stream of literary review programmes on the television and radio, regular newspaper reviews, and with calendared events such as the Booker Prize and Whitbread Prizes for contemporary fiction, and the highly successful National Poetry Day, established in 1994.

The tradition of literary tourism

The spaces and places of literature have long been noted as sites to visit and engage with, in the context of homage, pilgrimage and education. A persistent, and in the main, accurate view is that spatial expressions of the lives and works of creative writers have largely held appeal to the traveller rather than the tourist. Following Fussell (1980), they are positioned more in bourgeois nostalgia rather then the proletarian realities of the 'moment'. Whether defined by their size, grandeur, location, architecture, etc., literary sites could claim to attract the literati, by virtue of their expression through their own text and the trappings of literary fame. The topographical settings of Homer's *Iliad* and the journeys from Troy to Ithaca that underpin his second epic, *The Odyssey* were readily absorbed by the grand tourists, travelling scholars and writers of the eighteenth and nineteenth century. Calaresu (1999) notes how eighteenth-century guidebooks would urge élite European travellers to make the pilgrimage to Virgil's tomb in Naples. Calaresu makes the point that the Grand Tour becomes more of a confirmation of ancient history rather than an encounter with new worlds. This is echoed by Chard (1999), who points out this apparent discovery of ancient sites was more a product of literary mediation, whereby the traveller was already familiar with the landscape through the readings of the classics. In this way the Greece of Lord Byron was arguably as much a product of his time at Harrow and Trinity College Cambridge, as it was of his first visit to Greece in 1809.

Not surprisingly, the pattern of literary tourism development in the nineteenth century reflected wider sociocultural trends and access/transport developments. Interests in landscape, the pastoral, science, antiquities and the lives of 'great' social and political figures were central to the romantic movement and were filtered down to the educated middle classes through the artists, novelists and poets of the day. Urry (1995) for example, has examined the contemporary tourist popularity of the English Lake District through the generation of place-images and place-myths (Shields 1991), fuelled by the 'Lake poets' (notably Wordsworth, Coleridge and Southey), through their works and lives. Urry notes that the combination of the poets' celebrity status, and the fact that the generic metaphysical, romantic themes were exemplified in the area where they lived, provided strong motivations for others to visit the Lake District. Thus, as Urry (201: citing Ousby, 1990), notes, 'as early as 1802 Coleridge's residence in Keswick was being noted as an additional attraction of the area; while by the 1840s it is thought that Wordsworth was receiving 500 visitors a year at Rydal Mount'.

The notion of celebrity in literature assisted in shaping early tourism 'trails'. Fuelled by his early death at 37, and his passionate and direct celebration of Scottishness through his life, his poems and songs, Robert Burns was a true literary celebrity. As Gold and Gold (1995) note, the birthplace of Robert Burns in Alloway, Scotland was attracting American travellers in 1817, only twenty-one years after the poet's death. Sites associated with the poet's life, more than the landscapes he wrote of, were toured and formed an itinerary for the educated curious. As Gold and Gold (1995: 63) note: 'Even his widow and children were objects of interest.' Similarly Butler (1985), Glendening (1997), Gold and Gold (1995) and Seaton (1998) have discussed the importance of Sir Walter Scott in developing Scottish tourism. In part this was a function of Scott's overt intention to display *his* Scotland and to attract tourists through his works (Seaton 1998). But in part tourism grew around the cult of Scott's personality as a prolific, professional writer, a precursor of Victorian taste, and as a self-professed patron of 'Scottishness'.

Though we can cite instances of embryonic touristic developments associated with creative writing and authors throughout the nineteenth and into the twentieth century, these largely remained at the small scale and focused upon middle-class enthusiasts and emergent literary societies.

Commodifying literature for tourism

In recognition, and often in anticipation, of the interests of tourists in the lives and works of creative writers, the tourism industry has long claimed literary sites and associations as part of its increasingly diverse resource base. Following Henri Lefebvre's (1991) notion of the 'production of space' in the pursuit of capital accumulation we have moved from passive, informal, almost incidental, encounters with literary locale to deliberate creations of literary spaces for tourists. Sites, and sights, of literary association are no longer projected to, and experienced by, the travelling minority, but are consumed directly and indirectly by the touring majorities.

The processes of commodification and consumption are central in tourism (see for instance Cohen 1987; MacCannell 1976; Robinson 1999; Watson and Kopachevsky 1994). Literature lends itself well to both processes. As a production process, creative writing is an economically 'quiet' activity, which at the individual level carries little in the way of exchange value. Books exist to be consumed, if we can accept that reading is indeed a consumptive act. The writer aspires to exposure of his or her works, to diffusion of their meanings and, rather more pragmatically, to high volume sales.

Books as objects attract visitors. The 250-year old British Library with its stock of 16 million books and periodicals and numerous collections of manuscripts and maps of international importance attracts approximately 410,000 reader visits per annum (http://www.bl.uk/). Indeed, the British Library, like other national libraries, is the nation's literary museum, paralleled in some countries by actual literary museums, like those of Estonia, the Czech Republic, Scotland and Ireland, where the national literary tradition, as well as sometimes even the book itself as artefact, can be celebrated. The book, as museum exhibit, forms the foundation of this quite traditional type of attraction, as will be the case in the intended British National Centre for Children's Books. Similarly, antiquarian and second-hand book fairs and auctions attract significant numbers of visitors, indicating the status of books as collectors' items with a life well beyond the one they enjoy when they are new in the market. Seaton (1996) has examined the role that 'book towns' can play in rural tourism, drawing upon the case of Hay on Wye in the Welsh Borders which, as a noted centre for bookshops, is estimated to generate over a million tourists a year. Such examples illustrate the power of the physical form of literary works. The permanent and temporary ownership of literature is now a well-established practice across western democracies, forming the basis of literary culture. New developments in internet technologies and increasing access to literature on the world-wide web is unlikely to challenge this. Access to the 'virtual' book and the works of Shakespeare on screen can be seen as new additions (albeit in a different form) to cultural capital (Bourdieu 1984) and are more likely to deepen our literary culture and increase the sales of books. Evidence of this may well be found in the continuing popularity of the 'hardcopy' book, whose readership continues to thrive, certainly in the UK, where it is firmly supported through the education system.

The inherently selective and managerial process of commodifying cultural expressions for tourists can lead to erosion of meaning and authenticity (Greenwood 1989). Assertions that meaning is somehow 'lost' as the literary is packaged for tourists appear weak and, at times, irrelevant, given the openness of interpretation which creative writing invites. It would be equally appropriate to argue that interpretation and presentation for tourists can expand the insight of the visitor into the art and craft of writing and that the world of literary art gains rather than loses through the process. Of course, it can be argued that interpretation and presentation, in the shape of tableaux and rides at theme parks, are a 'distraction' from the actual written work, in the same way that a film adaptation of a novel or play can be said to impose a particular interpretation on the onlooker. Not all writers think that the public's study of themselves as human beings necessarily adds to our understanding of them as creative artists. A case in point is Hans Christian Andersen's contempt for the notion of a museum to the artist, containing everyday items from the artist's home (Andersen 1999). However, this is surely an unavoidable risk, which we are bound to encounter whenever we attempt to share an interpretation as a community/audience, rather than insisting that the experience of the fiction can only take place in private, and the argument would certainly not hold where the drama is concerned: the interpretation amounts to a 'staging' or 'production' of an aspect of the literary universe and must stand and fall by its reception by visitors and critics.

Commodification of literature takes place in various guises in the contemporary touristic realm, ranging from well-visited theme parks and packaged trails of fictionally derived experiences, to the preserved and revered places associated directly with the writer's creativity, and subtle or less subtle denotations of literary association. What we are talking about here is the commodification of the imagined and the imaginers. In the ascendancy of cultural tourism, literature has been claimed by tourists and the tourism industry as an increasingly important resource and below is considered the various ways by which literature is presented to the tourist. What is evident from the following review is that literary tourism well illustrates the cultural merging that continues to take place. Literary attractions and sites draw upon the built and artefactual heritage, landscape, the performing arts; and they tap into diverse tourist preferences and motivations, including personal and collective nostalgia, reminiscences of nationalism, and cultural enlightenment, or at least cultural engagement.

The writer's home

The home of the writer is arguably the most powerful tourism resource with appeal across a range of markets. Contained within this notion of 'home' are houses, apartments and rooms that have borne witness to various stages of a writer's life from birth to death. Writer's homes as focal destinations provide tangible connections between the created and the creator, allowing tourists to engage in a variety of emotional experiences and activities. For literary pilgrims, however we may choose to define them, here lies the potential for intimacy, authenticity: a 'real' sense of Goffman's (1959) 'behind the scenes'. The notion that the visitor is where the author's pen physically touched paper or his/her fingers the keys on the typewriter, may be remote from the actual human insights, revelations and experiences that feed the creative process for the writer. The writing process is generally a solitary, staccato process, requiring a setting of tranquillity, familiarity, presence of information and a measure of inspiration. As such, to the outsider the work and the spaces of that work are imbued with mystique: here, in the writer's home, we are in the surroundings where that private process took place.

Interestingly, the idiosyncrasies of writers and their works are often evident in only subtle ways within their homes. Fully admitting exceptions, a cursory review of writer's homes reveals a marked degree of commonality. Internally, writers' spaces display some hybrid order between home and office, often located within libraries reflecting their craft, and reminding them of their bookish heritage. Desks and chairs are surrounded by accumulations of collected materials from travelling as sources of on-hand knowledge. Restful, bucolic views without and natural light within prevails. As one would expect, locations are quiet, somewhat hidden within a tract of natural or manufactured countryside. These unifying features reflect an occupation of social distance and privilege, though we must qualify the point that what is presented to the tourist as the writer's home is often their last home, and as such reflects an accumulation of fame and fortune, and not the less salubrious steps on the way.

The home of the writer provides a focus for pilgrimage, because it is assumed to have been a central influence in the generation of the writer's creative works, almost as a reflection or extension of their character. This assumption is greatly facilitated by collective hindsight and exposure to the works of the author. Thus, one can accept that the gothic grandeur of Abbotsford fits the atmosphere of Sir Walter Scott's romantic novels: both home and works are very much part of the same project, to recover Scots history and create a new notion of what unites Scotland as a nation. Similarly, we can imagine the three terraced houses, and one semi-detached house, in the former mining town of Eastwood in Nottingham that were at various times homes to D. H. Lawrence: they reflect, and are indeed woven into his early novels (Cook 1981; Crang 1998; Shields 1991). In visiting such places, the literary tourist can hope for some similar inspiration (and aspiration), or a least a shared moment of connection between creativity and these particular 'homely' spaces.

The D. H. Lawrence example is interesting in the sense that it highlights the fact that the writer's 'home' which the tourist visits could be many places at differing parts of an author's life, or, not really 'home' at all. Indeed, nostalgic notions of 'home' are frequently constructed at some physical distance. During the First World War Lawrence and his German bride Frieda spent an uncomfortable period renting a cottage near the village of Zennor on the north coast of Cornwall. While effectively seeking to escape from conscription into the army, Lawrence worked on *Women in Love* here. However, the couple were subject to the scrutiny of a suspicious population who believed the Lawrences to be spies, signalling to German submarines, and they were eventually served with a military exclusion order that forced them to leave Cornwall for London (Worthern 1991).

How the writers' home is presented to, and interpreted for tourists varies considerably. For some properties a simple 'blue plaque' (or similar) on the exterior of the house explaining who lived there and when, denotes a place in literary heritage. But this suggests that the site has a rather passive role in literary tourism, as a site to note and perhaps add to the many visited on a trail rather than one to explore fully. Much more aligned with the notion of an experience for the tourist are writer's houses that are effectively attractions complete with admission charges, designated routes through furnished rooms and an adjoining gift shop and catering facility.

Over the years, the focus of presentation in writer's homes has moved away from the traditional museum approach with its formal displays of objects, to the currently prevailing style of realistic, 'lived-in' settings which the author would have inhabited beyond the writing process. Thus the birthplace of George Bernard Shaw, a Victorian terraced house in Dublin, is presented to visitors as having 'the appearance that the family have just gone out for the afternoon'. Notwithstanding the search for period authenticity, the emphasis upon the generation of 'atmosphere' and what Brostrøm (1997: 36) refers to as 'the sense of the magic presence of the inmates', appeal to the visitors' sense of the romantic and of history. The following reaction of an Argentinean visitor to her visit to the Brontë Parsonage at Haworth, West Yorkshire is a typical illustration:

> When I returned to the town, I visited the Parsonage. I could not believe how well kept it was! Emily could have appeared at any moment to continue writing on the table I was looking at. Everything was just perfect. I could easily picture Mr. Brontë coming back from work, greeting his daughters, going to his studio, having dinner in the little kitchen. (The Brontë Society 1999)

The writer's home thus becomes a series of settings for the tourist's emotional engagement with the writer and his or her works. Ordinary rooms are transformed into staged backdrops for recollection and imagination (Asmussen 2000). Central to the connectivity experienced by visitors on a tour of the writer's home are objects, artefacts of daily reality. In the homes of the 'great' writers (as with other 'great' historic figures), common objects are conferred with hyper-significance and reverence. Brostrøm (1997), for example, notes that writer's beds appear to be a favourite attraction, symbolic of an intimacy with the author. Other notable literary objects are, not surprisingly, pens, typewriters and desks. This labelling process, where objects are given significance is partly undertaken in the mind of the tourist, but increasingly it is initiated, stimulated, planned and maintained by the owners and managers of the home, constituting 'public discourse' that signifies wider socio cultural values (Neumann 1988).

Orchard House, the former home of Louisa May Alcott and her family, is typical of the way the ordinary (or what was considered ordinary by the Alcotts at the time) is reconstructed as the extra-ordinary through textual references, meanings, subsequent public acclaim and the Louisa May Alcott Memorial Association, who operate and mediate the tourist gaze. The kitchen, often among the least significant of rooms, is first legitimated in the promotional literature by a quotation from one of Louisa's Journals:

> All of the philosophy in our house is not in the study, a good deal is in the kitchen, where a fine old lady thinks high thoughts and does good deeds while she cooks and scrubs. (*LMA Journal*, December, 1860, cited on www.louisamayalcott.org)

Then, with reverent authority, the visitor is told that 'Mrs. Alcott, Louisa, Anna and May prepared and preserved food, and washed and ironed laundry in this room' (www.louisamayalcott.org). The objects of the room gather their significance and symbolism from their own history of ownership and use:

> Original features include the soapstone sink given to Mrs. Alcott by Louisa, a hot water reservoir, and a drying rack designed by Mr. Alcott for laundry. Mrs. Alcott's bread board, mortar and pestle, tin spice chest and wooden bowls are displayed on the Hutch table and countertops.

The realistic and personalized room settings appear to bless the personal effects, or indeed any effects, taking the tourist experience beyond that of a museum. These are no longer personal settings. An apotheosis has taken place: the writer's home has become the tourist's house.

Somewhat removed from the idea of 'home' for the writer are those places of transitory association: the places where a literary figure dined, was entertained, slept or made some remembered stop in his or her passage through life. Here once more spaces and places have symbolic significance conferred upon them, borne out of moments of passage. The general propensity of writers to travel means that many places across the world have had such significance bestowed upon them. Backwaters and the mundane are transformed by momentary association and off-beat locations are elevated to meaningful points on trails of pilgrimage and discovery. Associations can be markedly ethereal and encapsulated within numerous literary tourist guides as places bearing the 'spirit' of a writer or character. Paris, and particularly the Left Bank, capitalizes on its 'bohemian' heritage, and the visitor is invited to imagine the narrow streets of Montparnasse as somehow populated by the spirits of literary figures, artists and intellectuals.

Other associations are more tangible. The Inn of the Turquoise Bear in Santa Fé, for instance (www.turquoisebear.com), plays upon a host of literary associations from when the place was the home of city noteworthy Witter Bynner. Bynner's entertaining of literary celebrities such as W. H. Auden, Robert Frost, Christopher Isherwood and D. H. Lawrence allows the Inn to promote itself on the strength of these associations.

A more offbeat literary association relates to the National Lottery-funded renovation and preservation of the Victorian public lavatory in Hampstead, North London where gay playwright Joe Orton used to visit for sex and general observation of 'cottage culture' (Chittenden 1999). Whilst the rationale for renovation relates to the lavatory's architectural importance, the association with Orton is recognized to be part of the reason for obtaining funding. It remains to be seen whether this association will be developed on any tourist trail.

Better a dead author ...

What greatly facilitates the symbolism and attraction of the writer's house is the fact that the writer is usually no longer in residence. He or she has often died and the home is preserved as a memorial. As is the case with music composition, the process of creating the work itself – writing – is not easily turned into a public performance. The process of writing is not intrinsically interesting (as that of glassblowing or sculpting might be) and watching a writer or composer set pen to paper is not likely to tell us much about the creative process. What the preserved home – or other location – can do is to provide a glimpse of the intimate sphere inhabited by the writer during the process and that will satisfy the curiosity of the literary culture vulture. The preserved home of the deceased author offers the promise that the writer might at any point re-enter the home. The certainty that he never will ensures that the visitor can, perpetually, collude with the staff of the literary attraction in imagining what the home would be like if the writer was actually on the other side of the next door we come across or behind a hedge in the garden: our creative imagination helps form the illusion that the creative writer is real and with us, as are her books.

Having said this, living authors do of course also attract visitors. Appearances at book signings and readings at literary festivals allow the public access to people who normally appear as names on covers. High-profile authors possess considerable 'pulling power', particularly if they also have parallel exposure as a media personality. Public, live performance has become a typical aspect of the career of the modern author and its importance cannot be underestimated in an age where promotion – and self-promotion – is the rule rather than the exception. Living authors are perhaps more unwittingly subject to the tourist gaze, as their houses, favourite restaurants and holiday locations are pointed to as part of the more established tours and trails of personalities. In a world of competitive celebrity, living writers and their homes cannot match the 'spectacle' of the tours that take in the homes and haunts of film and television stars. A tour around the condominiums of Malibu will point out the luxurious driveway (such tours do require a healthy imagination) of the home of Jackie Collins, but mainly because she is part of the 'rich and famous' set which includes her actress sister Joan Collins.

Dead authors are so much more flexible in touristic terms. Their demise locates them as part of our collective heritage and the accompanying processes of selectivity, contestation and the vagaries of the market. Whilst death is not a pre-condition for 'distinction', it helps tremendously. As already pointed out, by being dead, authors (or at least some of them), are more easily made accessible to the tourist gaze. Once the lives of authors have passed, they acquire that sense of completeness and distance that allows them to be institutionalized, subjected to formal celebration through anniversaries of births and deaths and festivals, stimulating the tourism industry to greater creativity in presentation and interpretation. Unlike the Hollywood coach tours of living film-stars' homes, most literary tours do not take in the homes of dead writers. However, on their death authors can become heroes, icons, focal points for generations and symbols for an age. This lends itself well to an industry that trades on symbols, icons and anniversaries, where writers do not really die, they just become more powerful brands.

For the tourism industry dead authors provide several advantages. Dead authors (usually) provide us with graves and memorials to visit. These are tangible signatures of a writer's presence and commonly accessible to the public. Graves and monuments vary from flamboyant celebrations of posthumous literary greatness, such as the grouping of marble tombstones in 'Poets' Corner' in Westminster Abbey, or the soaring Walter Scott Memorial on Prince's Street Edinburgh, to the simple granite headstone of Franz Kafka in the Jewish Cemetery at Olsany, Prague. Using the wonderfully engaging website www.findagrave.com one can discover where authors are buried. Thus we can find out that Charles Lutwidge Dodgson (a.k.a. Lewis Carroll) is buried in Mount Cemetery, Guildford, Surrey, England, and that Raymond Chandler died on 26 March 1959 and is buried in Mount Hope Cemetery, San Diego, California. Over 1,000 writer's graves are listed, many with photographs of the actual tombstone, memorial or site where the author's ashes were scattered. One can identify clusters of dead authors in certain cemeteries. A trip to Le Père Lachaise Cemetery in Paris for instance, will net you the graves of Honoré de Balzac, Marcel Proust, Gertrude Stein and Oscar Wilde.

Though the vast majority of writers' graves are not significant attractions themselves, they are important elements in literary trails. They are more the focal point for literary pilgrimage, the tombstone allowing people to come as close to a 'famous' author as they would ever get. There are those who visit writers' graves inspired primarily by the works of the author. Cousinuea (1999) recalls a pilgrimage made by film maker John Antonelli to Jack Kerouac's home town of Lowell, Massachusetts and in particular Antonelli's actual confrontation with Kerouac's grave. Somewhat uncomfortably and uncertainly Antonelli speaks to the tombstone, thanking Kerouac. The thanks were given for *The Dharma Bums*, *On the Road*, *Desolation Angels*, *The Subterraneans* and *The Town and the City*: Kerouac's works that at various points had inspired this film maker's own life and works. The fact that he knew little about Jack Kerouac's life and the town of Lowell was secondary to the inspiration his books had provided: a characteristic reason for a literary pilgrimage.

Others visit the graveside inspired by the biography. The grave of Sylvia Plath, American poet, and one-time wife of future Poet Laureate Ted Hughes lies in the new cemetery beside the Church of St Thomas à Becket in Heptonstall, a small village above the town of Hebden Bridge in West Yorkshire in the UK. Plath's tragic suicide in 1963 at the age of thirty projected her as a feminist icon of betrayed womanhood, and her grave remains a site of pilgrimage for many of her followers, a few of whom, on more than one occasion have chiselled away her married name 'Hughes' from the headstone.

In the footsteps of . . .

Tourists do not recognize administrative boundaries. They pass, often unknowingly, from district to district, county to county and state to state. Over recent years new such territories have been marked out, not based on administrative or political convenience but in accordance with to reference points drawn from writers and their works. The word 'country' that is thus created on the basis of literary fact and fiction reflects the self-contained nature of fictional settings, but it also refers to the spatial and temporal geographies of the writer. So in England we encounter 'countries' that span centuries and a variety of literary genres, reflected in examples such as 'Shakespeare's Country', 'Hardy's Wessex', 'Brontë Country', 'Tarka Country' (after the novels of Henry Williamson), and 'Heriott Country'. As Duffy (1997) points out, Ireland's 'Yeats Country', 'Goldsmith Country' and 'Kavanagh Country' are amongst the literary motifs which the tourism authorities are successfully using in their promotion to redefine and re-invent the Irish 'place'. Ireland is prominent among nations using their literary heritage as a central element in their cultural tourism promotion, and elsewhere we find entire nation states that have been pre-fixed by writers closely associated with them. Thus, we can holiday in, and explore, Byron's Greece and Hemingway's Spain.

The tourism industry, in pursuit of image creation/re-creation and ultimately economic gain, is largely responsible for the designation of notional bounded areas associated with writers and their works. But this has been no recent 'top-down' imposition. Literary association is a far more organic performance, acted out with various stakeholders proud and astute enough to be associated with their factual and fictional progenies as part of identity building. Claims are made for geographical associations by local communities, local and regional authorities, literary societies and figures of academic authority.

Included in the latter are 'travellers who can write' and who have set out to report and claim new geographies as mapped out by (usually 'great') writers and poets. Edward Thomas's volume, *A Literary Pilgrim in England*, originally published in 1917, sets out a now well-established framework for exploring and encountering literary places. Thomas's starting points are the lives of authors and the regions of England they are associated with and from which they drew their inspiration. Through the use of highly selective sampling, the works of the authors are raided for allusions to their local/regional landscapes. The emphasis is clearly upon 'landscape' as that which links the personal creative sources of inspiration with the ultimate public expression of the works. In the process literary territories are created and confirmed. So, for instance, Sussex is 'claimed' for Hillaire Belloc and Northampton is 'claimed' for John Clare. It is as though these spaces, once they have been given these artificial labels, can then only be defined by reference to literature.

A wide range of publications are now available, exploring landscapes and city-scapes with reference to literary associations (Blythe 1984; Borish 1984; Daiches and Flower 1979; Drabble 1979; Dudgeon 1989; Eagle and Carnell 1977, 1981; Hardwick and Hardwick 1968; Hardyment 2000; Kent 1945; Kitchen 1980; Marsh 1993; Mitchell 1967/86; Morley 1980; Myers 1997; National Trust 1985; Price 1983; Somerville 1985; Stead 1989; Thompson 1985; Troughton 1989; Webb 1990). These vary from works devoted to the worshipping of particular writers (see for example Walter Dexter's *The England Of Dickens*, 1925), literary critical guides that link geography with the history of literature (e.g. Daiches and Flower 1979), the straightforward table-top volume (Premoli-Droulers 1885), selective regional and historical geographies of literature (see for example David Carroll's *A Literary Tour of Gloucestershire and Bristol*, 1994) and national populist gazetteers that vary in the extent of their coverage (see for instance Richard Shurey's *Walking Through Literary Landscapes*, 1984). The structure of these publications also varies from personal accounts of literary locations, strong on autobiographical narrative, to elongated forms of promotional text, with a strong message that readers should follow in the footsteps of particular writers and their characters. Michael Pearson's (1992) *Imagined Places* is representative of the former. Pearson links his own boyhood experiences of reading and encounters with 'real' characters with his visits to

Steinbeck's California, Twain's Missouri, Hemingway's Key West, the Vermont of Frost, Faulkner's Mississippi, and Flannery O'Connor's Georgia.

Representative of the latter is Varlow's (1996) *A Reader's Guide to a Writer's Britain*, endorsed by the Tourist Boards of England, Scotland and Wales. Subtitled *An Enchanting Tour of Literary Landscapes and Shrines*, the volume is a detailed gazetteer of literary places the tourist can visit, with an unsurprising focus upon the 'great'. Books such as these not only help crystallize the geographies of the literary, they also assist in developing and deepening public reverence for 'great' literature and tourist expectations that it will be somehow neatly packaged and cogently presented.

The concept of themed tourist trails is well established and works within (and across) regional, national and international boundaries. Linking individual attractions and sites of interest together creates a more potent and penetrative tourist product, not just in promotional terms but in a wider intellectual sense too. Concomitant with the mix of 'on the ground' signs and schematic maps setting out a trail, is a narrative that seeks to knit together the otherwise disparate, rationalizing *why* we should look at the world in this 'joined-up' way.

Hughes (1998), drawing upon the work of Silbergh *et al.* (1994), discusses the role of tourist trails as important spatial manifestations of tourism, arguably illustrative of 'the most direct relationship between the organising principle of tourism and its transformation of physical and cultural reality' (Hughes 1998: 29). Tourist trails that are inspired by literary sites and authors provide prime examples. Here, the boundaries between history and heritage are characteristically blurred as 'facts' surrounding authors' lives and works. Their locations of work and play, their inspirations and affections are captured by promotional authorities and tour operators eager for new saleable structures. Rojek (1993) cites the examples of 'The Dickens Trail' and 'The Catherine Cookson Trail', comparing the various physical markers of these trails to the landmarks that occur in the texts. For Rojek, literary landscapes are 'escape areas' and he positions such creations as indicative of new post-modern 'realities' and the blurred boundaries of the real and the imaginary. Two reflections emerge. Firstly, in what sense do these literary trails 'lead' us/the tourist anywhere? Following Rojek's idea of escape they lead us to the places in space and time where we would wish to be, at least momentarily. Furthermore they do this with minimal risk. And secondly, trails encapsulate the packaging ideology that is at the heart of contemporary tourism and that we, as tourists, now innately recognize and come to expect.

The tourism industry is now well versed in structuring the sites and symbols of literature into organized routes. These are wide ranging in their level of organization and formality. Study tour organizations offer classes, education breaks, opportunities to write, read and discuss literature, and can be focused upon both the process of writing and the products of a particular author. Often the motivation for such experience is one of emulation draped with a feeling of homage to a particular writer or genre. Literary societies of varying constituencies organize opportunities to travel and retrace the lives and works of their 'heroes' and 'heroines'.

Complete packaged experiences where a tour company provides a guided literary tour (usually by coach) are offered by a relatively small number of specialist and non-specialist operators with varying degrees of literary knowledge. Often labelled as a subset of heritage (Price 1996), such tours are offered chiefly because of their capacity to generate income and provide a niche and an edge in a highly competitive environment. Operators are keen to capitalize both on popular literary interests with strong markets and on opportunities such as the anniversary of a writer's birth or death. Not surprisingly, commercial tourist routes in the UK tend to be focused upon the popular, high-profile literary markers relating to Shakespeare, the Brontës, and Jane Austen.

IMAGININGS MADE REAL

The interface between tourism and literature represents an alliance of imaginations. The tourism industry continues to respond to consumer preferences for activity, interaction, adventure, high visibility, education and sensory experience all within increasingly compressed time-scales. In this sense, perhaps the ultimate way of packaging literature is represented by purpose-built attractions; theme parks and heritage parks that have sought to condense elements of imaginative writing – characters, story, and setting – within a created, controlled and largely artificial environment. Trying to locate firm conceptual boundaries between theme parks and museums, the 'staged' and the 'authentic', the real and the virtual appears increasingly problematic (MacDonald and Alsford 1995; Swarbrooke 2000). That is not to say that it is impossible to make the distinction. Visiting the author's home, being in the presence of actual physical evidence of the author's life and creative activity, is intrinsically a different experience from visiting a staged representation of the author's 'creative universe', complete (say) with characters from the works. Most visitors would appreciate this.

However, since the theme park is in itself a staging, far removed from an exhibition of real artefacts, the interpretation behind that staging becomes a matter of controversy and even public argument. You need only look at the story of the Danish Hans Christian Andersen theme park, which has been running since the 1970s, when the first such project was not only rejected but ridiculed in Denmark by a population who saw it as a threat to the preservation of the writer's proper reputation (see Kvam 1983). The resistance to what is seen as potential misrepresentation of the author has remained until recently – clearly the Danish population as such, not just the intelligentsia, sees itself as the guardians proper of their native writer's reputation – and only now, since the late 1990s, has the debate led to actual plans, this time for two competing theme parks (*Børsen*, 1999; *Aktuelt*, 2000), one in Andersen's native town of Odense, the other close to Copenhagen with its rather larger catchment area. It is obviously significant that such controversy can arise.

This chapter is deliberately pragmatic in its approach to literary theory, picking and choosing theories that will help explain, broadly, what motivates the tourist to visit a literary tourist attraction. But such pragmatism is only meant to reflect what is seen as the tourists' motivation. The Hans Christian Andersen Theme Park controversy is, to an equal extent, a reflection of public views and suggests that tourists and other visitors are not uncritical, just because they happen to be contemplating a theme park, nor are they only capable of being critical of catering and levels of fun and excitement: content also plays a part, where the theme park reflects already existing themes and texts.

Inspiration for attractions and theme parks continues to emerge from every branch of popular culture, from film, television, music and literature. Indeed, theme parks themselves have essentially become texts activated by their relations to the cultures they emerge from and the people that visit and consume them. On reflection it is a little puzzling that more theme parks and attractions have not been developed on the back of imagined worlds and invented characters, given the wealth of literature to draw from. Even so, we can, for example in the UK, encounter large rabbits at the 'World of Beatrix Potter', Bowness, Cumbria, at the 'Alice in Wonderland Centre', Llandudno, North Wales and large moles and badgers at the 'Wind in the Willows Attraction', Rowsley, Derbyshire. As Phillips (2000: 98) points out: 'If Rider Haggard and Conan Doyle, Hans Christian Andersen, the Brothers Grimm, Bram Stoker, Malory and Tennyson are not directly acknowledged, variations of their stories are to be found in Disneyland, and in almost all other theme parks.'

Jonathan Swift's pointed satire on the religious politics of the Irish Parliament and the Irish Court, *Gulliver's Travels* (*Travels Into Several Remote Nations of World. In Four Parts*), published in 1726, is of course concealed within a narrative of vivid imagination and the earliest traditions of fantasy travel writing. The central character, ship's surgeon (and later Captain) Lemuel Gulliver, experiences numerous adventures including that of being shipwrecked on the virtuous island of Lilliput (somewhere to the south of Sumatra), where the inhabitants are less than six inches high. Over the years the fantasy element of Lilliput in this barbed and decidedly adult book has been extracted, adopted and adapted for children and now has a physical presence, of sorts, in three theme parks in the UK and one in Japan. The family business of Weavers Close Ltd successfully runs the UK theme parks – Gulliver's Kingdom, Gulliver's Land and Gulliver's World – which are aimed at families with children aged between two and thirteen (see Table 1.1). In Japan, Gulliver's Kingdom, billing itself as an 'ecological amusement park', features (in a gloriously illogical admixture of a reproduced Scandinavian town, 'Bobsleigh Land' and the 'Fureai open zoo farm') Gulliver's Island with its forty-five metre long fibreglass model of Gulliver surrounded by shops and a French Puppet theatre to tell the story of Gulliver's Travels. It is in the transformation of literature into touristic space, as 'packages of meanings and meaningful forms' (Hannerz 1996), that we can identify the conjunction between so many dynamics and tensions: the global power of the fictive text, the dominance of first-world literature and language, articulations of post-modern capitalism, hybridity, 'the compression of the world into a single place' (Robertson 1992), interconnectedness, and national discontinuity.

Children's fiction provides a rich vein for purpose-built attractions and theme parks in the entertainment industry and for several reasons. Firstly, by definition, their appeal is largely to children (and parents: the family market), a large and highly influential segment of the tourist market. Secondly, children's literature is sometimes bold and highly explicit in its settings and characters. The lack of subtlety entails a fairly smooth translation to three-dimensional settings. Thirdly, the designers may

Table 1.1   UK theme parks based on *Gulliver's Travels*

Theme park	Key attractions	Further features
Gulliver's Kingdom, near Matlock, Derbyshire	30 rides and attractions in themed areas of Little Switzerland; Fantasy Terrace; Western World; Lilliput Land; Palais Royale Play Area; and Bourbon Street.	Lilliput Ices available and Gulliver's Travels Restaurant; children under 90 cms enter free of charge.
Gulliver's Land, Milton Keynes	45 themed rides and attractions across Fairy Tale Land; Lilliput Land; Main Street; Discovery Bay; and the jungle-themed Adventure Land.	Typical catering outlets includes Gulliver's Travel Restaurant; The Kings Fish & Chip Bar; The Queen's Ice Cream Parlour; and the Lilliputian Lunch Box; children under 90 cms enter free of charge.
Gulliver's World, Warrington	Attractions are dispersed within Alice's Wonderland; Count's Castle; Adventure World; Circus World; Dinosaur World; Water World; Smugglers Wharf and Western World.	There is a main restaurant serving hot meals, a fast-food outlet serving burgers and chips, and a fish and chip restaurant. Branded merchandise offered to visitors includes T-shirts, caps, pens, pencils and rubbers.

stress what they see as relatively 'simple' story lines that can transcend national boundaries and so maintain a wide cultural appeal. Fourthly, the extremes of imagination that are used in children's fiction frequently allow for 'larger-than-life' characterization and animation, and allow for broad interpretation to an audience that is generally seeking excitement and entertainment rather than authenticity. Importantly too for tourism theme-park developers, these features allow extant merchandizing based around the writings featured. Moreover, in the consumption of Peter Rabbit pencil cases, Little Mermaid T-shirts and Lilliput burgers, meanings relating to tourism and literature are generated and circulated intertextually.

It is worth noting that children's literature does not inevitably lead to caricature treatment in the theme-park world. Not only is creative quality and intellectual subtlety possible in the theme-park, for instance by allowing creative artists to interpret narratives three-dimensionally. The Swedish Museum for Children's Literature exemplifies a theme-park treatment that turn narrative into three-dimensional tableau yet leads the visitor to the logical conclusion, where literary theme park meets literary merchandise: the children's bookshop. It is the mission of the theme park that informs the physical manifestation of the theme park. Not all literary theme parks aim to lead the visitor to the book: many simply use literary image as the basis for theme-park entertainment. It is, as they say, 'horses for courses'.

Perspectives on the packaging of literature

There are other packaged manifestations of literature that the tourist can access. Literary festivals and events though frequently fashioned for local communities and contemporary writers can draw tourists with programmes of live readings and performances. Creative-writing holidays, focusing on a specific genre or in a particular location, are also increasingly popular niche offerings. Of course, the development of literary tourism attractions has been, and continues to be, *ad hoc*, opportunistic and idiosyncratic, reflecting a myriad of sociocultural variables, market trends and the caprice and passions of the literati. However, we can discern some broad themes or features of the tourism–literature relationship that frame the commodification process, and three of these are discussed below.

The literary as heritage

Locating literature as possessing some sort of public legacy, expressed in emotional as well as spatial terms, enables us to talk of a literary heritage. Though literary fashions may come and go, we can turn to a collective and cumulative past as defined by published works, their performance and interpretation. These are our cultural reference points that sit with conceptions of social and cultural identity, ideas and ideals of nationality and nationhood, and popular discourses of historical development. Thus, we understand terms such as Shakespeare's England, Wordsworth's Lake District, and Hardy's Wessex, not only in geographical terms but also as passages of time.

But as numerous scholars have noted (see for example Graham, Ashworth and Tunbridge 2000; Lowenthal 1985; Tunbridge and Ashworth 1996) have noted, heritage is open to contestation and conflict, partly as an internal function of its propensity to commodify, commercialize and select, and partly due to conflicting, or dissonant, external interpretations relating to its utilization, ownership and meanings. Here we are not focusing upon works of literature themselves as being open to contradictory and critical appraisal, which they clearly are, but upon them as cultural capital: the mix of physical manifestations identifiable from literary works and associated with their creators. The packaging of literary heritage as cultural capital for tourists generates dissonance at various levels: amongst tourism promoters/developers, between tourism promoters/developers and literary *aficionados*, and amongst tourists seeking the authentic. Rojek (1993) points to examples where the literary heritages of D. H. Lawrence, Thomas Hardy and the Brontës, together with their associated tourism potential, have been mobilized and politicized in planning and resource disputes. Nostalgia is important here and it seems that literary tourism increasingly plays to an audience that wishes to travel in time as well as space. The pre-war Surrey of John Betjeman's poetry, Rupert Brooke's Grantchester, the childhood playgrounds in Arthur Ransome's *Swallows and Amazons* series, the carefree jolly japes of Enid Blyton's Famous Five, and the working-class values enshrined in Sid Chaplin's works: all, in their different ways, appeal to the tourist in search of 'pastness' (Fowler 1992) and worlds of meaning.

Who 'owns' literary heritage is a central question and begs the further question of the ownership of literature itself. As McClarence (2000) reports, rivalries are increasingly common in the realm of literary tourism. 'Somerset is challenging the Lake District's exclusive claim to Wordsworth and Coleridge. Coventry and Hull are fighting it out over Phillip Larkin. The Brontës have prompted a friendly skirmish between northern villages.' McClarence's main focus is that of the claims being made for associations with Lewis Carroll by the North Wales seaside resort of Llandudno, and Whitby on the Yorkshire coast. Based upon the fact that Alice Liddell, the child who was the inspiration for Carroll's Alice books, spent a family holiday in Llandudno in Easter 1861, the town is home for an 'Alice in Wonderland Centre' at The Rabbit Hole which attracts over 20,000 visitors a year. Carroll visited Whitby several times and his first published work, a poem called *The Lady of the Ladle* was set in Whitby. Based upon this, a 'White Rabbit Trail' has been developed that allows tourists to explore nineteenth-century Whitby. But the location of, and the competition for, Lewis Carroll's literary heritage does not stop with Llandudno and Whitby. Claims of various authenticity are also made for Carroll and his work by Darlington, Sunderland and South Tyneside in the North East of England, Daresbury, the village of his birth in Cheshire, and Christ Church College, Oxford, his place of education and where he taught mathematics for 47 years.

At one level such claims and counterclaims are nothing more than promotional posturing with the net effect that more tourists are exposed to literary works. At another level this contestation reflects deeper cultural sensitivities revolving around regional and national identities, community pride and prejudices, and how we relate to the images presented in literature. At an even further level, it indicates the economic importance of literary connections and is symptomatic of the creativity (economic desperation) of tourism development agencies eager to exploit literary sites and associations. For Stratford-upon-Avon, tourism brings in £135 million and supports 7,500 jobs (Calder 2000). Without the Shakespearean inheritance it is hard to imagine Stratford as being in any position to generate such economic benefits.

Greatness thrust upon 'Them'

Within the realms of literary tourism we find an emphasis upon the 'great' works and 'great' authors. The label of 'great' or 'classic' is significant in the context of literary tourism and one we must deal with up front. From a superficial point of view it might be thought that the establishment of a literary canon would help the tourism system in establishing appropriate literary tourist attractions. The literary canon – like the lists of 'must-have' classical music CD's for music collectors – is a straightforward list of literary works that have acquired special status by having been read by readers over decades and even centuries. Arnold Bennett's 1909 *Literary Taste* is exactly such a list, with prices, of 'great' English literature, aiming to help the book buyer identify works of quality. Such lists continue to be published to this day. In 1993 the British National Curriculum Council presented such a list, recommending standard works for British schoolchildren to study.

Such lists have to be made, so that a national school curriculum can be standardized. However, they also continue to create controversy, because it is so difficult to identify objective criteria for inclusion on the list. Arnold Bennett refused to identify specific criteria: great literature is something which you recognize when you see it. Similarly, in *How to Read* (1931), the American poet and critic Ezra Pound stated that: 'Great literature is simply language charged with meaning to the utmost degree.' But whereas we can debate levels of meaning, just as we can debate the potency of language and its capacity to engage the reader through various linguistic combinations, ranging from simplicity to the most elaborate, we are unlikely to attain much common ground where the works on the list of 'great' literature is concerned. Nevertheless, hierarchies do exist in literature: they are socially and culturally determined rather then being based on objective criteria. Few would argue that the works of Shakespeare are not 'great' and most could point to various indicators to justify this view, ranging from the broadly quantitative (longevity, number of performances of the works, number of translations into other languages) to the qualitative (beauty and creativity of language, and the universality of human emotions revealed). However, whether the works of Shakespeare are any *greater* than those of Oscar Wilde, Noel Coward or Jeffrey Archer, is another issue fraught with arguments over of subjectivity and cultural context.

In literary tourism, the term 'great' generally equates with 'popular' and we therefore have to move beyond concern solely for the written word, to bring in issues of cultural dissemination and social taste: literary tourism comprises a readership with a will of its own, it does not restrict itself to those works and authors who have somehow won a place on the literary Parnassus. Literary tourism is both supply-led (what is available, which literary homes are available for preservation) and demand-led (what actually interests the literary tourist). This partly helps us explain why Catherine Cookson tours in South Tyneside in the North East of England can be so successful, although there are few tangible and authentic traces of her life and works in the area, save the site of her birthplace 'marked by an information panel in the shadow of a railway embankment at the side of a traffic roundabout'. (Fowler 1992: 49). The lack of physical markers in a post-industrial, regenerated South Tyneside is compensated for in this instance by Cookson's popularity: the need for authentic evidence of the author's presence in the area is superseded by the evidence provided by the intangible legacy she has left behind in the region, as the author of over one hundred books between 1950 and 1990, selling more than a hundred million copies. Literary celebrity drives literary tourism, and this explains why the most recent edition of the British Tourist Association's own 'literary canon' includes Catherine Cookson.[2]

As the Cookson example also displays, in literary tourism the 'great', or the 'popular' need not inevitably be located in the past. With great speed contemporary fiction can generate a touristic legacy. Robert James Waller's first novel in 1992, *The Bridges of Madison County*, which in 1995 became the best-selling fiction book of all time (according to the *New York Times*), propelled Madison County, Iowa, into prominence as a tourist destination (Hilty 1996). This position would be con-solidated with the 1996 release of the film adaptation of the name. Similarly, the small Texan frontier village of Seguin experienced a dramatic increase in tourist activity after the 1994 publication of Janice Woods Windle's *True Women*. As Hilty (1996: 191) reports, 'visitors can relive history as they visit the gravesites of heroines, the author's childhood home, the Guadeloupe River, other homes, hotels museums, churches and parks. A tour of these sites has been mapped out for visitors.'

By denoting literature as 'great', we fuel the tourist fire and generate further popularity. Following Bourdieu and Passeron (1977), we may well be reproducing a social hierarchy and defining socially accepted taste, thereby arguably maintaining an élite, or a least a middle-class élitism, in terms for determining what is acceptable 'good' reading. In this vein, tourist encounters with literary attractions are mediated by inherent social preferences in respect of what works – or what physical mani-festations and associations with those works – are worthy of the tourist gaze and which ones are not. However, simultaneously with this value grading, another principle is at work, namely the democratizing processes of consumption, modernity and subsequent postmodernity of tourism and literature, resulting in such (apparent) paradoxes as 'great' works being put for sale at the highly accessible price of £1 per volume, or Wordsworthian solitude being made available on the shores of Lake Ullswater, to a succession of coach parties.

THE AESTHETICS OF LITERATURE AND LANDSCAPE

From a tourist perspective, many sites associated with writers and their works are only elements of a wider perceptual experience, of which the aesthetic is an impor-tant component. In British literary tourism, landscapes of scenic beauty and pic-turesque spaces have become prominent features: rolling parklands, dramatic 'wilderness', rustic cottages and Gothic mansions. Thus, when we speak of the tourist experience of 'the literary' we are speaking of a much deeper entanglement with conceptions of beauty and nostalgia within real and imagined landscapes. The reasons are historical. Literature – and painting – was, and remains, influential in inventing and re-inventing landscapes. From our earliest encounters with literature, not only do we learn of landscapes in a geographical sense, we also learn to consider them in a moral context. We learn of beauty as encapsulated and interpreted by and through the writer, who holds a pivotal role because his/her work has taken inspiration from a particular landscape and has dispersed the idea of landscape itself (Eagleton 1983). But literature not only provides us with representations of land-scape, complete with embellishments and elaborations. Concepts of beauty are dif-fused throughout society to the point where they become a form of cultural 'truth'. As Inglis (1990: 199) says, positioning landscape as popular culture, 'the facts *are* the values as you walk or drive through the English landscape'.

In Western European(ized) cultures, the role of romantic literature in creating a tourism of the 'picturesque' is well-documented (Adler 1989; Andrews 1994; Drabble 1979; Moir 1964; Urry 1995; Watson 1970). The ethic of romanticism has created a powerful legacy for contemporary tourism (Adler 1989; Shoard 1999). The reaction against the cold scientific objectivity of the European Enlightenment in the late eighteenth century was channelled through the passionate, subjective, spiritual literature of the time, which came to be known as romanticism. In the process, it widened the range of acceptable 'recreational' landscape types from the cultivated and accessible (which the formal Baroque garden exemplified so well) to include remote, peripheral and wilder areas. This included the coastline, where the seaside emerged as 'part of romantic taste for sublime effects' (Towner 1996). Areas such as the Scottish Borders, the English Lake District, Switzerland and the Italian Lakes, which were at the time very much on the remote margins of the urbanizing and industrializing Europe (Olwig 1981), were transformed into settings for poets, novelists and travel writers.

Much literary tourism is difficult to disaggregate from the broader experiences of landscape. In this sense, literature is an important intensifier of the tourist experience as well as being an experience in its own right. When we consider tourism à la Jane Austen, or Hardy, or Scott, or Brontë, or Goethe, or Clare we are intimately bound to a *picturesque* legacy.

However, if romantic notions of landscape are at the root of European literary tourism, it is no longer bound to landscapes of love, truth and beauty. The tourist reader extracts more than landscape from a novel or poem and, consequently, demand-led literary tourism must offer more. Modernist British fiction, with its focus on social realities, economic change and heavy detail, is just as much part of literary tourism as is Wordsworth. From the vantage point of the early twenty-first century, this is arguably a more 'sincere' literature–tourism relationship because it stands without the buttressing of the picturesque. Writing shortly before the boosterist regional tourism agendas of the 1980s, Drabble (1979: 195) notes that: 'We admire Lowry, we read Lawrence and Sillitoe. But we do not go for our holidays to Wigan, or Smethwick or Merthyr Tydfil.' Endeavours to generate tourism in previously industrialized centres, using the 'literary hook', have met with varying degrees of success. True, such place types as Drabble mentions are not thriving holiday resorts, but they are now recognized as visitor destinations, in part due to their literary associations. Bradford boasts Priestley, Stoke-on-Trent points to Arnold Bennett, South Tyneside majors on Catherine Cookson, and Wigan, in an ironic twist, brushes off George Orwell's 1936 failure to find 'Wigan Pier' as an allegory of industrial decline, creating its own heritage tourist attraction of the same name.

From meaningful words to meaningful spaces?

Within the context of an expanding tourism culture, literature's role has been underestimated and largely under-researched. This chapter has only touched upon some aspects of the relationships that exist between literature and tourism, in the knowledge that further work needs to be carried out. As an interim conclusion we offer the following brief observations and thoughts.

Firstly we have sought to establish a field of literary theory, based on a pragmatic and eclectic choice of existing theory, to help demonstrate that a single strand of theory will not help us understand what makes literary tourism attractive and interesting for tourists to explore.

We have argued that literature – in the sense of creative writing/narrative prose/ drama/poetry – possesses qualities that feed into a particular kind of tourist experience. Not only is literature aesthetically pleasing, it also presents the reader with fictional worlds that invite to exploration in their own right, directly in theme parks and less indirectly in writers' homes and in landscapes and townscapes related to those fictions. This kind of tourism, based on the fictional world, is well established.

It has also become clear that creative writers, who have long enjoyed the admiration of their fellow human beings for their special talents, are becoming increasingly active as public personalities, even as celebrities. Our admiration for those who have the talent to create leads to a curiosity in the reader/tourist which in turn leads to an interest in visiting both places associated with the world of the writing and with locations which are directly related to the writers' lives and careers. The notion of visiting the home (or grave, etc.) of the great writer, to pay homage to that person, is an ancient phenomenon and continues to play a part in contemporary tourism.

The world of literary tourism – the attractions available for visiting – is built up serependitiously, from a range of places that have entered the field because they were available and/or because there was a demand for them. Literary tourism is based on a dynamically evolving complex of sites, responding to and interacting with market demand, in line with fashion and with the 'accepted' canon. In the main one would expect literary tourism to fall in line with that canon, providing an additional means of accumulating Bourdiesque literary cultural capital, but there is clear evidence that the market mechanisms can carve a space for literary heritage lying outside the (bourgeois) canon.

The way in which literary tourism is articulated – the 'packaging' – has also become clear. The writer's home, perhaps, attracts particular attention since that is where the tourist is brought into contact with the artist, the exceptional, creative human being whose talents fascinate and attract. However, the literary heritage trail is also a powerful concept, whether based on single authors (or their works) or several. Finally – and this may well be a recent innovation – the theme park provides a physical designed experience, based on fiction, in line with the kind of leisure park that now forms such a central part in tourism at many levels. These theme parks are, as yet, mainly based on children's works and it is likely that the computer game will be able to fulfil any similar need in the grown-up adult market for theme parks based on literature for the more mature reader.

Certainly, but not exclusively, within the western developed world literature is a powerful and dynamic field of cultural expression. Despite the rising curves of hyper-realities and the virtual, we nevertheless continue to inhabit a culture of books and literature. As Bradbury notes:

> The inescapable fact remains: literature is an aspect of society. It coheres, structures and illuminates many of its most profound meanings. It is, in a particular sense, an institution of society, an inheritance of artistic practices and values, a point of formal interaction

where writers and audiences meet, a means of social communication and involvement, and a manifest expression of our curiosity and our imagination. (Cited in Short 1991)

What is interesting is how easily this analysis can be applied to contemporary tourism. We encounter the world and meaning through tourism as a first-world institution and as a form of communication that is in itself an 'expression of our curiosity and our imagination'.

Clearly not all literature is pregnant with landscape imagery to tempt the tourist, or strong themes and characters to create literary theme parks. Nor are all authors rich of character and lifestyle that would encourage tourists to explore their homes. But the continuing transformations and packaging of the literary for tourists would appear to endorse the social and cultural value of both literature and tourism alike. The process of commodification is however, invariably selective and, following Walter Benjamin, in the course of reproduction literature, as 'art', loses its authenticity. But the authenticity of literature is in itself a challenging and nebulous concept, and one that relates more to the idea of the literary pilgrim than to the post-modern tourist as an absorber of de-differentiated experiences.

At one level the commodification of the literary marks a process of democratization allowing touring societies to gaze upon yet another dimension of cultural capital. This increasingly entails a form of tourism literacy whereby tourists read the adapted and translated texts of physical markers, each in their own way and to varying degrees, acting as mediators for the creative writings and writers they represent. At another level the touristic spaces that are being created from literature convey a plethora of meanings that exist beyond the text but which are fundamental to our cultural understanding of tourism. Our reading of literature as tourists (or more precisely our reading of literary tourism as tourists) invites us to consider questions relating to our individual and collective identity, the images, messages, meanings and boundaries we project in an inter-connected world.

NOTES

1. But, unlike the travel writer, it is clearly not a necessary condition for a creative writer to have travelled in order to produce a literary work: perhaps best exemplified through science-fiction writing.
2. See Liddall (ed.) (1993) *Literary Britain* and Liddall (ed.) (1997) *Literary Britain*. These two promotional leaflets not only illustrate a change in the selection of authors for inclusion but also a broader and more varied view of both the audience for literary tourism and of literary tourism as a tourism product.

REFERENCES

Adler, J. (1989) 'Origins of Sightseeing', *Annals of Tourism Research*, **16**, 7–29.

Aktuelt (2000) 'Eventyret kommer til Høje-Taastrup', *Aktuelt*, 13 April 2000.

Andersen, Dr H. C. (1999) 'The author at the museum', in J. de Mylius, A. Jørgensen and V. H. Pedersen (eds), *Hans Christian Andersen: A Poet in Time*. Odense: Odense University Press.

Anderson, B. (1983) *Imagined Communities*. London: Verso.

Andrews, Malcolm (1989) *The Search for the Picturesque: Landscape, Aesthetics and Tourism in Britain, 1760–1800*. Aldershot: Scolar Press.

Andrews, M. (ed.) (1994) *The Picturesque: Literary Sources and Documents*. Mountfield: Helm Information Ltd.

Ashe, R. (1982) *Literary Houses: Ten Famous Houses in Fiction*. Limpsfield: Dragon's World.

Ashe, R. (1983) *More Literary Houses*. New York: Facts on File.

Ashe, R. (1984) *Children's Literary Houses. Famous Dwellings in Children's Fiction*. Bicester/New York: Facts on File.

Asmussen, M. W. (2000) 'Two museums devoted to one writer', in Mike Robinson (ed.), *Expressions of Culture Identity and Meaning in Tourism*. Sunderland: Business Education Publishers, 17–22.

Bennett, A. (1909) *Literary Taste*. Ed. Frank Swinnerton (1938). Harmondsworth: Penguin Books.

Blythe, R. (1984) *Characters and Their Landscapes* (orig. UK title: *From the Headlands*). Orlando: Harcourt Brace Jovanovich.

Boddy, K. (1999) 'The European journey in post-war American fiction and film', in Jas Elsner, and Joan-Pau Rubies (eds), *Voyages and Visions: Towards a Cultural History of Travel*. London: Reaktion Books, 232–51.

Bohls, Elizabeth A. (1995) *Women Travel Writers and the Language of Aesthetics, 1716–1818*. Cambridge: Cambridge University Press.

Borish, E. (1984) *Literary Lodgings*. London: Constable.

Børsen (1999) 'Engelsk developer bygger H. C. Andersen-park i Odense', *Børsen*, 12 December 1999.

Bourdieu, P. (1984) *Distinction: A Social Critique of the Judgement of Taste*, Routledge: London.

Bourdieu, Pierre and Passeron, J.-C. (1977) *Reproduction in Education, Society and Culture*. London: Sage.

Bradbury, M. (1996) 'Dreams of empire', in M. Bradbury (ed.), *The Atlas of Literature*. London: De Agostini Editions, 148–51.

British National Curriculum Council, the (1993) 'From Sendak to Shakespeare: recommended reading for pupils aged five to 16', in *The Guardian*, 16 April 1993.

Brontë Society, the (1999) 'A visit to Haworth by Maria Lujan Tubio', *Brontë Student*, Haworth: The Brontë Society, Issue No. 3.

Brostrøm, T. (1997) 'Homes of writers and remembrance', in *10 Digterhjem/Writers' Houses*. Rungsted Kyst: Karen Blixen Museet, 34–6.

Butler, Richard W. (1985) 'Evolutions of tourism in the Scottish Highlands', *Annals of Tourism Research*, **12**: 371–91.

Buzard, James (1993). *The Beaten Track: European Tourism, Literature and the Ways to 'Culture', 1800–1918*. Oxford: OUP.

Calaresu, M. (1999) 'Looking for Virgil's tomb: the end of the Grand Tour and the cosmopolitan ideal in Europe', in J. Elsner, and J.-P. Rubies, (eds), *Voyages and Visions: Towards a Cultural History of Travel*. London: Reaktion Books, 138–61.

Calder, S. (2000) 'From Cornwall to Braemar, Du Maurier to Wesley, literary Britain is on the map', *The Independent*, 19 September, p. 3.

Carroll, D. (1994) *A Literary Tour of Gloucestershire and Bristol*. Stroud: Alan Sutton.

Chard, C. (1999) *Pleasure and Guilt on the Grand Tour*. Manchester: Manchester University Press.

Chittenden, M. (1999) 'Orton's loo is preserved for the nation with Lottery loot', *The Sunday Times*, 3 January, p. 3.

Clifford, James (1997) *Routes: Travel and Translation in the Late Twentieth Century*. Cambridge, Mass.: Harvard University Press.

Cohen, E. (1987) 'Authenticity and commoditization in tourism', *Annals of Tourism Research*, **15**, 371–86.

Collins, R. (1990) *Culture, Communication and National Identity: The Case of Canadian Television*. Toronto: University of Toronto Press.

Cook, I. G. (1981) 'Consciousness and the novel: fact or fiction in the works of D. H. Lawrence', in D. C. D. Pocock, (ed.), *Humanistic Geography and Literature*. London: Croom Helm, 66–84.

Cousinuea, P. (1999) *The Art of Pilgrimage*. Shaftesbury, Dorset: Element Press.

Crang, M. (1998) *Cultural Geography*. London: Routledge.

Crawford, R. (1997) 'Redefining Scotland', in S. Bassnett *Studying British Cultures*. London: Routledge, 83–96.

Daiches, D. and Flower, J. (f. p. 1979) *Literary Landscapes of the British Isles: A Narrative Atlas*. Harmondsworth, 1981: Penguin.

Dann, G. (1996) *The Language of Tourism: A Sociolinguistic Perspective*. Wallingford: CAB International.

Dexter, W. (1925) *The England of Dickens*, London: Cecil Palmer.

Drabble, M. (1979) *A Writer's Britain: Landscapes in Literature*. London: Thames & Hudson.

Dudgeon, P. (1989) *Daphne du Maurier: Enchanted Cornwall. Her Pictorial Memoir*. London: Michael Joseph.

Duffy, P. J. (1997) 'Writing Ireland: literature and art in the representation of Irish place', in Brian Graham, (ed.), *In Search of Ireland: A Cultural Geography*. London: Routledge, 64–83.

Duncan, James and Gregory, Derek (eds) (1999) *Writes of Passage: Reading Travel Writing*. London: Routledge.

Eagle, D. and Carnell, H. (eds) (1977; 2nd rev. edn 1981). *The Oxford Literary Guide to the British Isles*. Oxford: Oxford University Press.

Eagleton, T. (1983) *Literary Theory: An Introduction*. Oxford: Blackwell.

Eliot, T.S. (1948) *Notes Towards the Definition of Culture*. London: Faber & Faber.

Fowler, P. (1992) *The Past in Contemporary Society: Then, Now*. London: Routledge.

Fussell, P. (1980) *Abroad: British Literary Travelling Between the Wars.* Oxford: Oxford University Press.

Gilroy, Amanda (ed.) (2000) *Romantic Geographies: Discourses of Travel 1775–1844.* Manchester: Manchester University Press.

Glendening, John (1997) *The High Road: Romantic Tourism, Scotland, and Literature, 1720–1820.* New York: St Martin's Press.

Goffman, E. (1959) *Presentation of Self in Everyday Life.* Harmondsworth: Penguin.

Gold, J. R., and Gold, M. M. (1995) *Imagining Scotland: Tradition, Representation and Promotion in Scottish Tourism since 1750.* Aldershot: Scolar Press.

Graham, B., Ashworth, G. J. and Tunbridge, J. E. (2000) *A Geography of Heritage: Power, Culture and Economy.* London: Arnold.

Greenwood, D. (1989) 'Culture by the pound: an anthropological perspective on tourism as cultural commoditization', in V. Smith (ed.), *Hosts and Guests*, 2nd edn. University of Pennsylvania Press: Philadelphia, 171–85.

Gunn, C. (1972) *Vacationscape: Designing Tourist Regions.* Austin, Bureau of Business Research: University of Texas.

Hannerz, Ulf (1996) *Transnational Connections.* London: Routledge.

Hardwick, M. and Hardwick, M. (1968) *Writers' Houses: A Literary Journey in England.* London: J. M. Dent.

Hardyment, Christina (2000) *Literary Trails: Writers in Their Landscapes.* London: National Trust Enterprises.

Herbert, D. H. (1996) 'Artistic and literary places in France as tourist attractions', in *Tourism Management.* **17**(2), 77–85.

Hilty, A. (1996) 'Tourism and literary connections: how to manage the image created', in M. Robinson, N. Evans and P. Callaghan, (eds), *Culture as the Tourist Product.* Sunderland: Business Education Publishers, 185–98.

Holderness, G. (ed.) (1988) *The Shakespeare Myth.* Manchester: Manchester University Press.

Holland, Patrick and Huggan, Graham (1998) *Tourists with Typewriters: Critical Reflections on Contemporary Travel Writing.* Ann Arbor: University of Michigan Press.

Hughes, G. (1998) 'Tourism and semiological realization of space', in Greg Ringer, (ed.), *Destinations: Cultural Landscapes of Tourism.* London: Routledge, 17–32.

Inglis, F. (1990) 'Landscape as popular culture', in Simon Pugh, (ed.), *Reading Landscape: Country–City–Capital*, Manchester: Manchester University Press, 197–213.

Jarvis, Robin (1997) *Romantic Writing and Pedestrian Travel.* London: Palgrave Macmillan.

Kent, W. (1945) *London for the Literary Pilgrim.* London: Rockliff.

Kitchen, P. (1980) *Poets' London.* London: Longman.

Kvam, K. (1983) 'Fra værkstedsteater til gruppe- og egnsteater', in S. K. Jensen, K. Kvam and U. Strømberg: *Dansk Teater i 60erne og 70erne. En artikelsamling.* Teatervidenskabelige Studier VIII. Copenhagen: Borgen.

Lefebvre, H. (1991) *The Production of Space.* Oxford: Blackwell.

Leisure Industries Research Centre (2000) *Leisure Forecasts 2000–2004.* Sheffield: Leisure Industries Research Centre.

Liddall, J. (ed.) (1993) *Literary Britain*. London: British Tourist Authority.
Liddall, J. (ed.) (1997) *Literary Britain*. London: British Tourist Authority.
Lodge, D. (1992) *The Art of Fiction*. London: Penguin.
Lowenthal, D. (1985) *The Past is a Foreign Country*. Cambridge: Cambridge University Press.
Luke, T. W. (1999) 'Simulated sovereignty, telematic territoriality: the political economy of cyberspace', in Mike Featherstone, and Scott Lash (eds), *Spaces of Culture*. London: Sage, 27–48.
MacCannell, D. (1976) *The Tourist: A New Theory of the Leisure Class*. New York: Schocken Books.
McClarence, S. (2000) 'War breaks out in Wonderland', *The Times*, 1 April, 34.
MacDonald, G. F., and Alsford, Stephen (1995) 'Museums and theme parks: worlds in collision?', *Museum Management and Curatorship*. **14**(2), 129–47.
McHale, Brian (1987) *Postmodernist Fiction*. London: Methuen.
Marsh, K. (ed.) (1993) *Writers and Their Houses: A Guide to the Writers' Houses of England, Scotland, Wales and Ireland. Essays by Modern Writers*. London: Hamish Hamilton.
Mills, Sarah (1991) *Discourses of Difference: An Analysis of Women's Travel Writing and Colonialism*. London: Routledge.
Mitchell, W. R. (1967/86) *Haworth and the Brontës*. Clapham via Lancaster: Dalesman Publishing.
Moir, E. (1964) *The Discovery of Britain: The English Tourists 1540 to 1840*. London: Routledge & Kegan Paul.
Moretti, Franco (1998) *Atlas of the European Novel 1800–1900*. London: Verso.
Morley, F. (1980) *Literary Britain: A Reader's Guide to Writers and Landmarks*. London: Hutchinson.
Morris, J. (1993) *The World of Venice* (rev. ed.). London: Penguin.
Myers (1997) *Myers' Literary Guide: The North East* (2nd edn) Myers.
National Trust (1985) *Writers at Home* (National Trust Studies). London: Trefoil Books in association with National Trust.
Neumann, M. (1988) 'Wandering through the museum: experience and identity in a spectator culture', in *Border/Lines*, Summer, 19–27.
New, C. (1999) *Philosophy of Literature*. Routledge: London.
Newby, P. T. (1981) 'Literature and the fashioning of tourist taste', in Douglas C. D. Pocock, (ed.), *Humanistic Geography and Literature*. London: Croom Helm, 130–41.
Olsen, Stein Haugom (1981) 'Literary aesthetics and literary practice', *Mind*, **90**: 521–41.
Ousby, I. (1990) *The Englishman's England*. Cambridge: Cambridge University Press.
Parry, B. (1993) 'The contents and discontents of Kipling's imperialism', in Erica Carter, James Donald and Judith Squires (eds), *Space and Place: Theories of Identity and Location*. London: Lawrence & Wishart, 221–40.
Pearson, M. (1992) *Imagined Places: Journeys into Literary America*. Jackson: University Press of Mississippi.
Philips, D. (2000) 'Narrativised spaces: the function of story in the theme park', in David Crouch (ed.), *Leisure/Tourism Geographies*. London: Routledge, 91–108.

Pocock, D. C. D. (1979) 'The novelist's image of the North', in *Transactions of the Institute of British Geographers*, NS 4, 62–76.

Pocock, D. C. D. (1992) 'Catherine Cookson country: tourist expectation and experience', in *Geography*, 77, 236–44.

Pocock, D. C. D. (1981*a*) 'Place and the novelist', in *Transactions of the Institute of British Geographers*. NS 6, 337–47.

Pocock, D. C. D. (ed.), (1981*b*) *Humanistic Geography and Literature*. London: Croom Helm.

Pollard-Gott, Lucy (1998) *The Fictional 100: A Ranking of the Most Influential Characters in World Literature and Legend*. Sacramento: Citadel Press.

Pound, E. (1931) *How To Read*. London: Harmsworth.

Pratt, Mary Louise (1992) *Imperial Eyes: Travel Writing and Transculturation*. London: Routledge.

Premoli-Droulers, F. (1995) *Writers' Houses*. London. Cassell.

Price, B. (1983) *Creative Landscapes of the British Isles. Writes, Painters and Composers and Their Inspiration*. London: Oregon Press.

Price, S. (1996) 'Tourism and literary connections', in M. Robinson, N. Evans and P. Callaghan, (eds), *Culture as the Tourist Product*. Business Education Publishers: Sunderland, 375–82.

Prickett, Stephen (ed.) (1981) *The Romantics*. London: Methuen.

Robertson, R. (1992) *Globalization*. London: Sage.

Robinson, M. (1999) 'Cultural conflicts in tourism: inevitability and inequality', in M. Robinson and P. Boniface (eds), *Tourism and Cultural Conflicts*. Wallingford: CAB International, 1–32.

Robinson, M. (2001) 'Tourism encounters: inter- and intra- cultural conflicts and the world's largest industry', in Nezar AlSayyad (ed.), *Consuming Tradition, Manufacturing Heritage*. London: Routledge, 34–68.

Rojek, C. (1993) *Ways of Escape: Modern Transformations in Leisure and Travel*. Basingstoke: Macmillan.

Rothman, H. K. (1998) *Devil's Bargains: Tourism in the Twentieth-Century American West*. Lawrence: University Press of Kansas.

Said, E. (1993) *Culture and Imperialism*. New York: Random House.

Seaton, A. V. (1996) 'Hay on Wye, the mouse that roared: book towns and rural tourism', *Tourism Management*, 17(5), 379–85.

Seaton, A. V. (1998) 'The history of tourism in Scotland: approaches, sources and issues', in R. MacLellan and R. Smith (eds), *Tourism in Scotland*. London: International Thomson Business Press, 1–41.

Shields, R. (1991) *Places on the Margin*. London: Routledge.

Shoard, Marion (1999) *A Right to Roam*. Oxford: Oxford Paperbacks.

Short, J. R. (1991) *Imagined Country: Environment, Culture and Society*. London: Routledge.

Shurey, R. (1984) *Walking Through Literary Landscapes*. Newton Abbot: David & Charles.

Silbergh, D., Fladmark, M., Henry, G. and Young, M. (1994) 'A strategy for theme trails', in Magnus J. Fladmark (ed.), *Cultural Tourism*. London: Donhead, 123–46.

Somerville, C. (1985) *Twelve Literary Walks With Ordnance Maps*. London: W. H. Allen.

Squire, S. (1992) 'Wordsworth and Lake District tourism', *Canadian Geographer*, **32**, 237–47.

Squire, S. (1994) 'The cultural values of literary tourism', *Annals of Tourism Research*, **21**, 103–20.

Squire, S. (1996) 'Literary tourism and sustainable tourism: promoting *Anne of Green Gables* in Prince Edward Island', *Journal of Sustainable Tourism*, **4**(3), 119–34.

Stead, M. J. (1989). *Literary Landscapes*. Oxford: Lennard Books.

Swarbrooke, J. (2000) 'Museums: theme parks of the third millennium?', in Mike Robinson (ed.), *Tourism and Heritage Relationships: Global, National and Local Perspectives*. Sunderland: Business Education Publishers, 417–32.

Tambling, J. (1995) *E. M. Forster: Contemporary Critical Essays*. Basingstoke: Macmillan Press.

Thomas, E. (1917) *A Literary Pilgrim: An Illustrated Guide to Britain's Literary Heritage*. This 1985 edition ed. by Justin Davis. Exeter: Webb and Bower.

Thomas, E. (1917) (1980 edition). *A Literary Pilgrim in England*, Oxford: Oxford University Press.

Thompson, J. (1985) *Orwell's London*. New York: Shocken Books.

Towner, John (1996) *An Historical Geography of Recreation and Tourism in the Western World, 1540–1940*. Chichester: John Wiley.

Troughton, M. (1989) *Pens, Profiles and Places: A Literary Tour Round Yorkshire*. Otley: Smith Settle.

Tunbridge, J. E. and Ashworth, G. J. (1996) *Dissonant Heritage: The Management of the Past as Resource in Conflict*. Chichester: John Wiley.

Urry, J. (1995) *Consuming Places*. London: Routledge.

Urry, J. (2000) *Sociology Beyond Societies*. London: Routledge.

Varlow, S. (1996) *A Reader's Guide to Writer's Britain*. London: Prion.

Watson, G. L. and Kopachevsky, J. P. (1994) 'Interpretations of tourism as commodity', *Annals of Tourism Research*, **21**, 643–60.

Watson, J. R. (1970) *Picturesque Landscape and English Romantic Poetry*. London: Hutchinson.

Webb, E. (1990) *Literary London: An Illustrated Guide*. Tunbridge Wells: Spellmount.

Williams, R. (1973) *The Country and the City*. London: Paladin.

Withey, Lynne (1997) *Grand Tours and Cook's Tours: a History of Leisure Travel, 1750–1915*. London: Aurum Press.

Worthen, J. (1991) *D. H. Lawrence: The Early Years 1885–1912*. Cambridge: Cambridge University Press.

Wynne, D. (1992) *The Culture Industry*. Aldershot: Avebury.

www.bl.uk

www.findagrave.com

www.louisamayalcott.org

Chapter 2

Between and Beyond the Pages: Literature–Tourism Relationships

Mike Robinson

> But words are things, and a small drop of ink,
> Falling like dew, upon a thought, produces
> That which makes thousands, perhaps millions, think;
>
> (Byron, *Don Juan*, Canto 3, LXXXVIII)

INTRODUCTION

Tourism is routinely and summarily regarded as an important mobilizing force between and within cultures. The continuing metamorphosis of tourism from modern capitalism to postmodern capitalism (Rothman 1998), is marked by transnational rapidity and fluidity (Urry 2000). It is also distinguished by a multiplicity of relationships with cultural forms and networks. It no longer makes much sense to speak of tourism as some coherent, formulaic entity of experience. Experiences are multiple, fragmented, dispersed and intimately intertwined with the full diversity of cultural products and practices. It is in the light of new connections being made with various cultural forms and practices that this chapter considers the unfolding relationships between literature, tourism and tourists.

The relationships we share with literature are wide, varied and riven with complexity. What readers gain from literature in terms of emotional and intellectual engagement, inspiration, new perspectives and, deeper understanding of the human condition, has long been the subject of literary academic inquiry. But more recently as literary theory has morphed ever more into cultural studies, the focus has also been upon the ways in which literature constructs histories, shapes political discourse and influences the processes of social and cultural change. Literary texts exercise a duality of roles in providing critical source material for understanding cultural resonances, and in possessing a capacity to affect and effect cultural being profoundly. Inglis (2000*b*) in his *Delicious History of the Holiday* provides a prime example of the way literary accounts can infuse our understanding of ourselves as tourists by drawing upon a wide variety of texts ranging from Joseph Conrad's *The Shadow Line*, and the poems of Philip Larkin, to Kenneth Grahame's *The Wind in the Willows*. It is precisely because such works deal with human emotions and imaginings that they are of use in capturing the essence of tourism, but the insights gleaned for the academic also reflect the relationship that tourists share with literature in a more general sense.

The purpose of this chapter is to explore and examine the nature of the relationships that exist between tourism/tourists and literature. Broadly, a distinction can be made between two sets of relationships, and this distinction lightly structures the discourse. The first is centred upon what the tourist is able to extract from the text itself. What is there contained between the covers of a book that can induce, inspire, motivate and transform readers into tourists? In this sense, literature is accorded a quasi-promotional role. Though this is largely an unintentional function, falling outside of capacities to track and measure, literature can nevertheless present the reader with implicit and explicit representations of places as potential destinations, at various stages of the tourist experience, and thus influence, directly and indirectly, where tourists go and what they do. Charters (1991: xxvii) for example, quotes William Burroughs on the influence of Jack Kerouac's seminal novel of 'beat' culture, *On the Road*: 'After 1957, *On the Road* sold a trillion Levis and millions of espresso coffee machines, and also sent countless kids on the road.' We increasingly come across tourists exploring the world as depicted in literature, discovering real locations used in fiction and seeking to correlate fictional locations with some markers of reality. However, the problem with this phenomenon is one of attribution, as there is seldom any straightforward cause-and-effect relationship between the reading of literature and the tourist act. The process of conversion from the reading of literature to being a 'literary tourist' is dislocated and complex, but this is no reason to avoid exploration and examination.

In addition to its promotional role, literature also plays a significant part in shaping the culture of tourism and the 'being' of tourists. Fictional representations of the world exist as reservoirs of particular knowledges from which readers can extract images, identities and imaginings of places and peoples. In addition, literature as language, ideas and imagination is very much part of the world 'cultural flow' (Hannerz 1989) in the immediate physical realm, as mobile objects (Urry 2000) to be consumed, and as a more ethereal vector of globalization (Hannerz 1992), modernization (Giddens 1990), post-modernization (Robertson 1992), nationalism (Anderson 1983), transnationalism (Martín-Barbero 1993), and colonialism/post-colonialism (Huggan 2001; Said 1993; Sardar 1999). Tourists-as-readers and readers-as-tourists are exposed to literature in a dynamic sense, as it carves out ways in which we see and structure the world. Thus, this chapter also addresses the question: what is there within the pages of a literary text that can influence the behaviour of tourists and shape tourist attitudes, expectations and behaviour?

The second set of relationships between tourists/tourism and literature that concern us here exist beyond the text; past the pages, outside the book covers. In practice it is difficult, if not impossible, for creative writings merely to exist as words on the page. In the act of reading, in the conversion of the written texts and the multi-dimensional spaces they occupy (Barthes 1977) to the spoken, in the lending of a book to a friend, in post-reading discussion, interpretation and analysis, actions are generated, ideas are circulated, spaces are created and various realities emerge. All literature (one could say all texts) is subject to the cultural processes of trans-mutation and transvaluation, to the extent that it is now highly problematic to speak of literature solely in terms of 'the written word'. *Winnie the Pooh* is the charming children's book by A. A. Milne, but it also exists as, and represents, a range of other joined-up cultural forms and objects. Therefore, Winnie the Pooh *is* Ashdown Forest in Sussex ('Pooh's forest'), *is* Pooh Sticks Bridge, *is* the game of 'Pooh Sticks', *is* a spiritual treatise (Hoff's 1998 *The Tao of Pooh and Te of Piglet*) and, most notably through 'disneyfication', *is* a 'classic' cartoon, *Tigger the Movie*, a comic book, a cuddly toy, a Piglet pencil case, an Eyore balloon, a brand of honey, and cardboard packaging for a Big Mac meal.

Readers and non-readers, tourists and non-tourists thus encounter literature in a variety of spaces and times. This chapter is also concerned with these exogenous literary existences and how they convert to, and shape, tourist visits and the con-struction of tourism spaces.

RELATIONSHIPS WITH THE TEXT: THE ACT OF READING

Tourists read literature. On the surface, this fact may not appear a particularly surprising revelation. It is nevertheless a critical feature worthy of exploration. As Loselle (1997), following MacCannell (1976) indicates, tourists do 'read' sights and signs. Here, primarily we are concerned with the actual and potential effects of reading creative writings and how the practice of reading can determine people's propensity to engage in some aspect of the touristic process and influence patterns of supply and demand. But in this sense we cannot differentiate tourists from the wider reading public. In theory we can conceive of the latter population as potential tourists, though praxis informs us that only a proportion will participate in tourist activity. Our initial emphasis, then, must be upon the relationships generally shared between readers and texts. Understanding the impacts of literary engagement as they relate to the social and economic phenomena that constitute tourism comes a pos-teriori.

Airports, railway stations and bus terminals are significant arenas of literary engagement. Along with the consumption of newspapers and magazines, casual observation shows us that travellers and tourists read books and novels in particular. Indeed, it is frequently the case that holidays afford us the time in which we can 'relax with a good novel'. The act of tourism, however exotic or energetic, is nonetheless constructed around periods of 'doing nothing'. Waiting in the departure lounge for the next flight, travelling on the train, lounging on the beach or resting in a hotel room all provide opportunities for reading the books we have had little time to read within the confines of our working routines.

One is tempted to argue that engaging with tourism and travel not only allows us to read literature: it positively encourages it. When else do we get the time to indulge in a leisure pursuit that is defined by an openness of space and slowness of time? This notion of reading in the spaces that tourism creates for us exemplifies a multi-layered feature of post-modern tourism, that of leisure within leisure within leisure. The tourist visiting the landscape represented in a novel will increasingly and simultaneously reside in multiple leisure worlds. He or she will probably have read about the landscape, read about the author who portrayed the landscape, have seen a screen adaptation of the novel that was filmed in the landscape, will be in the landscape, and as (s)he relaxes in the landscape, be reading another book by a different author featuring a different landscape altogether.

Rojek (2000) distinguishes between 'fast' and 'slow' leisure. *Fast leisure* encompasses superficial, ephemeral and multi-dimensional leisure pursuits, characterized by computer games, which in Rojek's words (23) 'encourage the development of fragmentary consciousness since they permit the individual to concentrate on one part of the game instead of the unfolding whole'. He contrasts these new forms with *slow leisure* activities such as reading a novel, which although it may in itself be restrictive and finite as an activity, nevertheless allows the reader's imagination to flourish and develop. The idea of defining leisure by virtue of pace, rhythm and flow is useful in allowing us to emphasize the position of the act of reading literature as an imaginative and liberating encounter. The physical parameters of the novel – the first and last chapters, opening and closing pages – are usually matched by a beginning and ending, a culturally informed understanding of self-containment. Even within serial novels we recognize the boundaries and come to expect that all will be resolved, justice will prevail, happiness will triumph, the sun will set, love will conquer all, and the journeys through the characters will end. And yet, despite recognizing novels as finite parcels, between the pages, within those parameters, we are encouraged, enticed and empowered to wander and explore seemingly infinite connections of meaning. In the most obvious sense the text is 'open', inviting different perspectives.

In reading creative writings, we escape to other places with other people. As New (1999: 53) comments: 'Nothing could be clearer than that works of fiction arouse emotions, or, more generally, psychological reactions, in us, and that it is fictional characters and events that are the objects or the source of those reactions.' However, there is a level of analysis that challenges the apparent reality of this. The places, characters, events and happenings that we read about, and which provoke reactions in us, are not, of course, real in any way and thus how can we 'experience' fear, loathing, sympathy, sadness and the complete palimpsest of emotional responses that we clearly do experience and which are part of the reading experience? The answer is, predictably, complex and inconclusive, but two features are worth alluding to. First, it does seem that we *suspend our disbelief* when we read, but we do so knowingly. When we say we are 'immersed' in a novel and its plots, this is not entirely true. As New (1999: 55) points out, 'we participate in the fictional world, but, inevitably, in that world everything including our psychological reactions, is make believe'. This does not deny the reality or the rationality of our emotional experiences (we really cry, really laugh, really feel sadness), but it does qualify them. We *know* the difference between crying over the death of a relative and crying over the death of favourite character, but we engage in the act of pretending (Currie 1990).

Iser (1979) suggests that as readers we primarily react to the surface structure of the text but this can set off a process that unmasks a deeper structure to which the reader can relate in a more universal way. Thus, we can move beyond the disbelief that we are suspending. Tuan (1995) points to the meaning of reading literature as moving beyond the fictional so as to extract deeper levels of knowledge and meaning. He comments:

> Reading them [the great nineteenth century novels] broadens our knowledge, enlarges our human sympathies, and forces us to attend to realities beyond the self, which may be radically different from our own, and yet have the power to penetrate and nest in the core of our being. (223)

When we read the text of a tourist brochure, or a tourist guide, although the language may borrow from literature, we know the text to be somehow real and not imaginary. Furthermore, in reading promotional literature, we do not usually allow ourselves to suspend our disbelief, or move into deeper levels of meaning. That is not to say that tourist brochures do not invoke *any* psychological reactions in us: they clearly do. Rather, it is a question of extent. The intricacies of plot, story line and characterizations need time/space/order to develop, elements that are not available in tourist brochures. Also crucially missing is the intention to say anything significant about the human condition. Instead, 'book a holiday with us' is the much more important message.

Second, in the act of reading we employ the elusive concept of *imagination*. The fiction we read is, of course, a product of the author's imagination. It is not (to follow Coleridge's (1817) early exploration) simply a flight of fancy or a mechanistic association of ideas, but rather it is something more sustained, creative and organic. The imagination that forms the text has to be inventive and persuasive enough to draw us into imaginary dimensions. Literature confronts our imagination so that we can 'make-believe'.

Tourism literature makes some attempt to be imaginative within bounds of accuracy and true representation. But imagination resides within the reader too. Tourism promotional brochures work, in part, through the act of the reader imagining him or herself, in an anticipatory and partial way, say, on the beach, or in the swimming pool, in place of people featured in the brochure and within the setting portrayed in the text (Cohen 1979).

It is the facilitator for 'losing oneself' in the text, as Barthes (1975) puts it; part of the 'eroticism' of the text. For Barthes, the reader is born from the necessary 'death' of the author. Important in this consideration of relationships between tourism and literature is Barthes' distinction between what he terms 'readerly' and 'writerly' texts (Barthes 1975). In the former, the expectations of the reader are confirmed or verified on reading. In the latter, the text unseats and challenges the reader's expectations. Tourist experiences contain elements of both confirmation and challenge and this can be related to the core sources of information/inspiration, whether derived from a tour-operator's brochure or from a work of fiction.

Whereas the physical/psychological act of reading – as an act of personal, cognitive communication, a meeting of eye and text – can be considered ubiquitous, the cultural practice and context of reading is highly variable. Somewhat paradoxically, the reading of literature is both an intimate, singularly personal act *and* a subset of a wider and longer cultural ecology (Miall and Kuiken 1998). In this sense, reading, and the meaning of the read, is a cultural practice in the same way as tourism. It is defined by settings and meanings that are socially coded and understood within spatial and temporal boundaries. The act of touring/being a tourist is at one and the same time a personal, subjective experience and a component of a vast cultural phenomenon, complete with defining generic characteristics.

INTERNAL LITERARY ELEMENTS

Between the covers of a novel, or between the first and last line of a poem, there are various features that can have a bearing on any subsequent relations with tourism. When we read literature something happens to us. We arrive at a novel or poem with nothing and after we have read, we come away with something. Reading is the act in which transference and transformation takes place. Within the reader lies a host of ways to read, and between readers lies a seemingly infinite number of interpretations. As he pronunces 'the death of the author', Barthes (1977) locates meaning within the reader. Thus, whatever the intention of the author may have been, texts (an extremely broad term for Barthes and one that is applied beyond the definition of literature as employed here) are subject to ever-changing interpretations and they are thus left as endlessly 'open' in their meanings. Following Barthes, Iser (1974) argues that the author creates the text in artistic mode but that the reader realizes the text in an aesthetic way. Meaning, for Iser, lies somewhere between the two, but is certainly a function of reading.

There are 'internal' features of creative writings that not only help to define literature in the sense of 'being literary', but which also lay the foundations for our reading and interpretations of literature, and for how we pursue the text in other ways. It is difficult to ascribe the precise influence, if any, of some of these features in any touristic sense. Elements such as *presentation* (who narrates, from what position and with what authority: major or minor characters, observers; conscious or self-conscious telling of the story? Who are the narratees and what assumptions are made about them? How is narrative timed: before or after events? What languages are adopted in the narrative?); *focalization* (point-of-view: with whose 'eyes' is the story seen; when and how: with hindsight, as a 'fly-on-the-wall'?); and *characterization* (invented personalities, traits and histories that readers identify with, like, dislike etc.) are well-debated dimensions of literary theory, but they have not been examined in relation to their 'tourist' readings.

Far from being mere intellectual frippery, the argument here is that in a general sense such elements have a role. Novels in which the narrator within the fiction seems to 'befriend' the reader may well inspire more to pursue the contents of the novel through tourism. Some tourists do seem particularly prone to identify with some types of characters, particularly heroes and heroines. Thus we find young Japanese girl tourists dying their hair red in homage to *Anne of Green Gables* during their visits to Lucy Maud Montgomery's home on Prince Edward Island. Similarly, there are well-trodden paths to Top Withens Farm near Haworth in West Yorkshire, reputedly the site of Heathcliff's moorland farmstead in Emily Brontë's *Wuthering*

Heights, where tourists commune with the spirits of the Gothic tragic characters of Heathcliff and Catherine Earnshaw.

A key internal feature of creative writing is that of story or plot. Aristotle maintained that stories, through their simulation of life's experiences and through their rhythmic ordering, provide us with pleasure, and that pleasure is a desirable state. We largely work on the assumptions that literature is rooted in, and reflective of, human experience and this is how we relate to it. The conventional Aristotelian plot, with its beginning, middle and an end, has constantly been challenged, certainly throughout the history of the novel, but as a way of structuring the events of the narrative it maintains its power. Telling and listening to stories is something we learn from an early age and something that cuts across cultural boundaries. Stories are capable of translation across languages and different media. Essentially a story/plot involves transformation of some kind to take it away from a simplistic sequence of events to a more complicated evolutionary/revolutionary narrative of people, places and relationships. Technically, plot is deduced by the reader from the text and thus relies on his or her learnt literary competence. Plot is the shaping of events by the layering of turns and various twists of complexity that leads to an endpoint, which then usually relates back to the beginning, revealing why events emerged in the particular way they did.

Overly-descriptive accounts of places and events, as we might come across them in a travel guide, make little appeal to our emotions, nor do they elicit those 'inspirational' feelings of spontaneity, release and escape. However, even the most undesirable of places and events can be enlivened when embroidered by incident, accident, drama, surprise, mystery, puzzle-solving, suspense, humour and action. Dann (1996) recounts how literary devices, and various linguistic techniques are increasingly imported from literature to sell tourism products and have become embedded in the 'language of tourism'. Dann does not really explore the device of plot/story in tourism promotion, focusing more on the functions of language in accordance with Jakobson's (1960) linguistic framework. This omission is not surprising since Dann's focus is largely on tourism promotional literature, texts largely constructed as short and piquant bursts of text with limited capacity for plot development. Nonetheless, story telling is a potent promotional tool in tourism, a point picked up on by tourism marketers over the years.

It would seem that we can 'read' tourism as a form of story telling, so that a holiday is conceived of as something more than just a sequence of events: it becomes a 'story' whose development will lead to a logical conclusion. We know there is an ending to the holiday in temporal terms: it will come to a conclusion; but we are not always sure of what the story will be. The events that take place during a holiday are structured and sequenced so as to make sense to us. Events move between ourselves as both the 'meta-narrators' and participants in the action (on the one hand) and the different characters and environments we come into contact with (on the other), creating and exploring themes, revelations and coincidences. Interactions are overlaid with emotions, remembrances and passions of the characters and can exhibit, in various measures, elements of mystery, adventure and the unexpected. And in our personal recollections of holiday experiences after the holiday has ended, we reject simple 'reporting', preferring to relay our recollections as stories and joined-up anecdotes, embellished and polished in order to make them more entertaining. There is much more to explore in terms of conceptualizing tourism as 'story' and 'story telling' but this is outside of this chapter.

There is also more research to be done into how the internal structure of literature, over and above language, influences tourist readings. Furthermore, there is room for more detailed investigation into the relationships between tourism and different literary genres, and the differences and similarities they display in terms of features and techniques. Literature has long been divided up into certain classes and types – 'genres'. Obvious categorization draws a distinction between prose, drama and poetry, or between tragedy and comedy. However, in part as a reflection of social diversity and cultural merging, we are used to dealing with many mixed genres and sub-genres of literature. The taxonomies of literature are clearly not objective, nor are they fixed. Apart from being convenient (they allow us to discuss literature in certain terms and at certain levels), they are abstract, fluid and capable of displaying multiple traits (Fowler 1982). Thus, we can have 'romantic classics' and 'historical thrillers'. Table 2.1 displays typical genres applied to literature together with an indication of their relative popularity.

Table 2.1   Percentage sales of fictional literature by genre

Children's books (includes non-fiction)	27
Crime/mystery/thriller	18
Classics, e.g. Dickens	11
Historical romance, e.g. Catherine Cookson	9
Romance, e.g. Barbara Taylor Bradford	8
Science fiction/fantasy	8
Horror, e.g. Stephen King	8
Modern literary fiction, e.g. Martin Amis	7
Poetry	6
Book of film/TV programme	5
Play/film script	3
Other fiction	10
Comedy/jokes	5
Cartoons	3

Source: Mintel 1999

Even the most superficial investigation of literary tourism points to certain genres dominating the tourism–literature relationship. Children's fiction, for instance, metamorphoses into theme parks, and the genre of crime mystery has given rise to a plethora of short-break holiday products, loosely based upon Agatha Christie, Conan Doyle, P. D. James-type thrillers. These allow tourists to 'solve' crimes in role-play situations, usually within the evocative and pleasant surroundings of a country house hotel.

At the heart of the tourism–literature relationship is the idea/ideal of *romantic fiction*. As a literary genre this is extremely broad in its interpretation and mani-festations. Romanticism, as a surrogate for the imaginative, fictitious, fabulous and the extravagant (Lamont 1987), was the motor for a powerful literary and cultural movement in the western world that has shaped tourism past and present (Squire 1988). However, while a historical perspective on romanticism would theoretically result in tourists connecting with the poetical works of Samuel Taylor Coleridge and William Wordsworth, the historical novels of Sir Walter Scott, and the neo-gothic novels of the Brontë sisters, and the respective landscapes and interpretations of 'nature' of these writers, that perspective misses an important dimension. More everyday notions of 'romance' and the 'romantic' are also located within such texts as those mentioned above. Thus, there is an emphasis on a love of nature, landscape and setting; and the clichéd response of 'I fell in love with the place' is perhaps indicative of this, with tourists being fed by fictional as well as factual accounts.

But romance, love, sex and passion, or at least a desire for these, are also very firmly in the minds of many readers. Tourism as an emotional encounter, as a search for 'love' and romance in all its various guises (Lee 1976), is still under-researched. Fussell (1980: 113) declares that 'Making love in novel environments, free from the censorship and inhibitions of the familiar, is one of the headiest experiences travel promises.' Stewart (2000: xvii) who quotes Fussell on this continues 'The promise of a foreign affair, that enticing combination of the erotic and the exotic, can prove unbearably alluring.' While the travel brochures and tour operator's advertisements may hint at opportunities for such encounters, it is imaginative fiction that feeds these promises, when we read before and during our holiday. What is involved here is imaginative fiction generally, not only in the sense of 'great' literary works but also the vast spread of titles with their distinctive 'clench covers' and 'placeless' exotic settings as issued by publishers such as Mills and Boon, Harlequin, Silhouette, Rapture Romance and Avon Books, and written using similarly exotic pseudonyms and aliases.

Romance novels have their roots in highly moral 'domestic fiction' consumed by the female middle classes in the nineteenth century and they invariably told of struggling heroines in search of a hero. Today, as then, these books are remarkably popular. According to the American Bookseller Association, there were 2,289 romances released in 2000 in the USA, this genre generating $1.37 *billion* in sales in 2000 and comprising 55.9% of all popular paperback fiction sold in North America (www.bookweb.org/research/stats). Despite a predilection for imagined locations replete with stereotypical portrayals of the exotic, rather than the real, it is the possibility and promise of romance, adventure and encounter in travel that not only sells vast quantities of books but also generates a desire for travel. There is a dearth of research into the role of such fiction and its influence on the tourist motivations of specific travelling groups, such as for instance, thirty- to forty-year-old female readers and the increasing numbers of single females taking holidays alone. Lack of research may be due to the general absence of specific geographical locations in this kind of fiction, and arguably because of a pejorative view that such novels occupy the realms of pulp fiction rather than 'high' literature.

Place representation

In the often long and elaborate search for information on destinations, activities and experiences, the potential tourist collects a range of written sources, some of which are subsequently read, whereas others are not. This accumulation of knowledge, facts and impressions is understood to be a fundamental and formative process in tourism. Indeed, the apparent reliance we place upon the printed words and images of tourist brochures and leaflets is a core convention in the culture of tourism. Tourist destination promoters are increasingly well versed in providing us with words and images as substitutes for the actual experience of being in a particular place. The language of tourism is a powerful language in terms of both its sophistication and simplicity, and by virtue of our willingness to read and believe. As with any language, we engage in the social and cultural conventions of use, accepting the boundaries of understanding and meaning. The holiday brochure and other formats of promotional literature have clear and significant roles to play in the formulation of destination image, in our perception of place, and in the creation of desire and recognition of need for such places.

The relationship between specific tourist literature and the tourist is built upon mutual understanding of an anticipated outcome. The tourist visit or experience can be tracked back to the reading of a particular brochure, advertisement, or maybe a piece of travel writing. This link, whilst not without problems of measurement, is nonetheless relatively straightforward. This cannot be said of the relationship between creative writings and the tourist. The tourist does not usually recognize literature as having much bearing on the decision-making processes. Put simply, if we are seeking a holiday in Spain we would not normally base that decision on reading Hemingway. However, our encounters with relevant creative writings may well be counted as influencing our decisions, in terms of adding information to the process, helping to generate positive and negative preconceptions and images of destinations and enriching our experiences of places subsequently. Moreover, they do this through words alone. Demonstrating this with scientific rigour could prove complicated: pictures are clearly important in the generation and communication of image (MacKay and Fesenmaier 1997), and the lack of visuals in the process we are concerned with here means that the acutely subjective information transfer process from the page to the mind of the potential tourist is complex to model.

The key position of the visual image in destination selection is well established (see for instance: Baloglu and McCleary 1999; Echtner and Ritchie 1993; Fakeye and Crompton 1991; Gartner 1986, 1989, 1993; Gunn 1972; Hunt 1975; Kotler, Haider and Rein 1993; Milman and Pizam 1995). Figure 2.1 serves to illustrate that the image-formation process is fed by both organic and induced sources. Fakeye and Crompton (1991) suggested that organic factors, which would include the reading of literature, were important in image formation before the individual had contact with any promotional literature. Induced factors would then dominate, once an active search for information had been initiated. Presumably organic sources would also continue to be used and absorbed during the process.

This model and others fail to indicate the relative importance of each information source, and as Baloglu and McCleary (1999) point out, little consideration is given to how images are developed. Baloglu and McCleary, in seeking to address this, indicate that 'books/movies/news' can influence the formulation of image, though there is no attempt to disaggregate this, nor to examine it in much detail. Dann (1996) in his thorough analysis of the uses (and abuses) of language in tourism, usefully synthesizes previous conceptualizations of information sources used by tourists in the generation of images and destination selection (Gunn 1972; Gartner 1993; Cohen 1993). Dann does criticize Gartner's model of image formation for omitting literary sources of information but they are not accorded great attention by Dann, who chronologically positions them at the pre-trip stage, where he sees them as having the greatest influence. As mentioned earlier, paying such scant attention to the influence of literature is understandable, given the inherent problems of measurement and of tracking the what, how, where and when of what people read. However, this should not sway us from acknowledging the role of creative writings in shaping images of place and destination, nor should it deter the researcher from fully exploring this role.

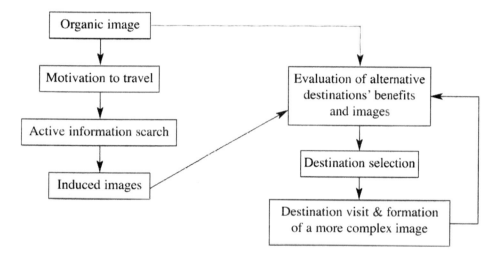

Figure 2.1 The image-formation process
Source: Fakeye and Crompton (1991)

It should be clear that the very point of creative literature is usually not to offer accurate representations of places. Guide books and gazetteers, with their inventories, fulfil this role. In these, the narrative flows from what the tourist wants and expects to see. The travel writer may depart from such expectations and in some cases may also be far removed from any notion of accuracy, but nonetheless is also generally grounded in attempts to provide accessible representations of real places. In fiction, however, the author uses place less as a material reality and more as imaginative space (Miller 1995) within which characters and events unfold and relationships develop. Places are transformed into backgrounds which action, story and plot are projected onto, and into, diachronically. Far from having to conform to standards of objectivity, places become deeply interwoven with the outpourings of imagination from author, characters and the reader.

This would seem to render literature an uncertain or even highly misleading source of information on places and potential destinations. But this wholly misinterprets the way we approach creative writings and any relationship they may share with tourism. Novels, short stories and poetry can impart useful information on places but they do so unknowingly, unintentionally, and outside of the usual structured timeframes of tourist decision making. Images created through reading fiction in childhood for instance can remain with us into our adult lives, shaping our preconceptions of places and communities and our expectations of experiences. These images are built around constructs of space, allowing us to recognize distant and distinct geographies. But they also rest on admixtures of temporal and emotional constructs, such as remembrance, recollection, nostalgia, permanence, innocence and a range of subtle Proustian sensory associations.

Books read in childhood can retain an important shaping influence upon our perception of places up to and beyond our visiting them. Thus, in Arthur Ransome's children's adventure novel *Swallows and Amazons* (and his subsequent 'Lake' novels), Lake Windermere in the English Lake District provides the setting for various adventures of the characters of Roger, John, Susan and Titty. Derived in part from his own childhood experiences in the South Lake District and inspired by his own reading of classic children's adventure tales, Ransome creates images in the text that are not only evocative of physical landscape but are also deeply nostalgic at both a personal and a social level. Importantly, though not extensively, these images are re-enforced rather than created by the use of illustrations in the books. Fantasy, discovery, adventure, play and enjoyment are the very essence of *Swallows and Amazons*, all within an environment that its 'lovely', 'nice', 'happy', 'safe' and 'moral'. The positive aspects of childhood, as fond remembrances or desired states, are hard to disentangle from the idyllic shores and islands of Lake Windermere. Arguably it is these fixed-in-time images that retain a prominence in contemporary tourist minds as they now visit the heavily crowded area.

What the reader can extract from creative writings is more a 'sense of place' than a mere objective description. It is also a 'sense of the past' (Lodge 1992). Not necessarily in terms of creating historical backdrops but in relation to the unlocking of our own personal place histories and associations. This is largely a process of extraction by the reader and not any imposition by the author, who has different uses for 'place' and is probably wholly ignorant of any potential tourist uses. The organic interpretative process of the reader (as reader foremost and possible tourist at some point) is one which is selective, resulting in multiple discolouration of realities, and taking place in a rather *ad hoc* manner, remote, yet connected to, tourist experiences and encounters with destinations. In the face of the messiness surrounding the ways in which literature sculpts our images of place and how this translates into destination choice and visit, it would be easy to dismiss it as having little impact. But this would be to deny an important flow of information.

To pursue how places are portrayed and read in creative writings and to tease out their implications for tourism, three categories of represented place are briefly discussed

Fantastic lands

Arguably one of the most powerful traits of fictive literature is its ability to generate wholly self-contained places which the reader is invited into. Fantastically imagined geographies range from discrete sites such as the enormous and highly elaborate Gormenghast Castle in Mervyn Peake's novels, to the extensive lands of Frank Baum's Oz and Tolkien's Kingdoms of the Middle Earth. Manguel and Guadalupi (2000) have produced a comprehensive and revealing *Dictionary of Imaginary Places* that captures the power of the writer's imagination and the extent to which it has penetrated our everyday discourse. In this, Manguel and Guadalupi present the reader with an opportunity to engage in touring the boundaries of both the imaginations of the writer and ourselves.

In relation to literary tourism there is not much that can be drawn from the above save two points that are worthy of note. A first point, as was noted in Chapter 1, relates to the ways in which fantastic places provide inspiration and themes for tourism developments, trails, activities and theme parks. The concept of extreme fantasy as a focal point for tourists is picked up in the fiction of Michael Crichton. Crichton translocates Conan Doyle's fantasy of living dinosaurs into the setting of the unopened island theme park of Jurassic Park island of Isla Nubla, off the coast of Costa Rica. Crichton's 1973 screenplay for the film *Westworld* similarly, and more poignantly, created Delos, an amusement park with pleasure zones, based on Roman, medieval and cowboy themes where realistic robots help tourists fulfil their fantasies with disastrous consequences.

Secondly, encounters with fantastic places and landscapes can stimulate a desire to trace the original sources for such creations. This, of course, is premised on the notion that the roots of the mythic are located in reality. This provides a route of exploration that can be followed by the more adventurous tourist. For instance, the physicality of Coleridge's Xanadu as depicted in the fragmentary poem of *Kubla Khan* is traced to Shangdu in the Republic of Inner Mongolia in the travels of William Dalrymple (1990) and Caroline Alexander (1994). Alexander comments (xii) that 'Kubla Khan's great strength, it seemed to me, was that it could transport one to a realm of the imagination by means of images that were altogether of this world.' The links between the fantasy and reality of place vary considerably, some examples being more straightforward than others. We are connected to the fantastic by common assumptions and culturally shared conventions enabling us to comprehend and partake in created geographies. Interestingly these connections frequently surface in touristic encounters as when we overhear someone refer to a castle as being 'just like Dracula's'.

In the fictive world of Daniel Defoe's *Robinson Crusoe*, Crusoe's Island, where the character spent nearly thirty years, was located off the tropical Venezuelan coast. Defoe's novel is drawn from the historical account of Alexander Selkirk, the Scottish seaman shipwrecked for four years upon the rugged volcanic island of Juan Fernandez located in the temperate waters 400 miles off the Chilean coast (Seidel 1991). The Chilean government renamed Juan Fernandez Island, Robinson Crusoe Island, in recognition of its tourism potential and it now positions itself as an ecotourism destination attracting relatively small numbers of tourists. Meanwhile, in the

Caribbean, the timeshare company of RCI, in partnership with the government of Trinidad and Tobago, have developed 'Crusoe's Island Resort' on Tobago. Here the fantastic and the mythic of literature persists in preference to the reality. Indeed, the extraordinariness of Robinson Crusoe's island, along with other tropical island environments featured in popular novels such as Stevenson's *Treasure Island*, Ballantyne's *Coral Island*, and the island featured in Johann David Wyss's *Swiss Family Robinson*, have had a marked influence on the construction of contemporary visions of exotic tourist paradises far removed from European home (Seidel 1991; Varney 1999).

Invented and disguised places

Wang (1999), in a carefully worked treatise, reveals the ambiguities and tensions of MacCannell's (1976) notion that authenticity in the tourist experience is a question of 'objectivity' measured scientifically, against evidence, as a historian would have to do. Instead, Wang favours the idea of 'existential objectivity', where tourists search for 'their own authentic selves and inter-subjective authenticity' (365). This perspective is far more meaningful in contemporary tourism studies and is straightforwardly applied in the context of literary tourism. Literary tourism, it might be argued, is based on the subjective act of reading, an initially intimate and private activity where the reader engages in 'self-making'. Such 'self-making' is echoed in the tourist's search for the sites, symbols, places and experiences encountered in literature. In this context there is little room for such a thing as an objective authenticity that derives from *imaginative* sources. In literature, we are dealing more with a simulated reality (at the least), and variants of the inauthentic (at the most), albeit with roots in the objective reality of the published text itself and the shared interpretation of that text that follows from the fact that readers share their humanity and may also share the culture to which the text refers and from which it grows.

The 'inauthentic' as somehow 'not *being* the real thing' has long been a feature of the tourism industry. Whatever we may argue with regard to what the tourist may want, what he or she actually gets is another matter entirely. It is not difficult to conceive of a situation in which Shakespeare's birthplace was found not to be Shakespeare's birthplace but was still promoted as such to tourists, many of whom would be none the wiser, and many others who would still be able to absorb an interesting presentation of social heritage without the hook of any famous association. Indeed, this is exactly what happened with Hans Christian Andersen's birthplace, which was preserved during his lifetime in honour of his achievement but was also denounced by him as not being the birthplace at all (Andersen 1996). Now referred to as 'the house traditionally associated with Hans Christian Andersen', it is still the core of the 'Hans Christian Andersen Museum' in Odense. Thus, authentic pilgrimage continues to centre on an inauthentic location.

Such is the denotative power of a tourism industry that trades more on hedonism and entertainment than history and education. This is not that far from the desire of some writers to entertain, captivate and exorcise, rather than provide an accurate description of the world; the real world frequently employed as a means to an imaginary end. To echo structuralism's canon of signs as being arbitrary, for some writers real places may as well be invented ones and the invented ones real. This, of course, does not invalidate the claim that some writers also see it as their task to reflect the reality of the human condition in a *truthful*, if not scientifically exact, manner. The contentious issue of authenticity in heritage, literature and tourism arises on the supply side, exactly because the aims of artists and historians can be informed by a moral ambition which the tourism industry may not find relevant, because it focuses on the supply side. That is in itself revealing: at what point does the focus on the expectations and ambitions of the tourist become a relevant or even an inevitable part of our investigation of literary tourism?

For that grouping of tourists we might loosely call 'explorers' (Cohen 1972), or what Smith (1989) terms 'off-beat' tourists' certain literary representations of place present attractive opportunities. The inherent imprecision and equivocation of creative writings can leave the reader with an agenda of mystery and delightful confusion regarding the exactness of place and setting. In part this is a reflection of the literary process and its essence of eternal open-endedness. But it also reflective of a culture of tourism that seeks to uncover and unmask, to satisfy curiosity and somehow discover the 'real thing'.

Literature abounds with disguised places, some 'concealed' more than others in the way they are described and referenced in fiction (Paterson and Paterson 1981; Ousby 1990). David Lodge's University of Rummidge, somewhere in the West Midlands of the UK, and the workplace of the character Philip Swallow in Lodge's comic novel *Changing Places*, is close to Birmingham University, where Lodge taught. The existentialist stories of Franz Kafka reveal implicitly the cityscape of Prague, then acting as a signifier for the urban and industrial alienation that had replaced the lively old districts such as Josefov, where Kafka had grown up (Akkerman 2000) and now exists as a cosmopolitan European centre, fit for the tourist's attention. In the USA, 'new' literary landscapes were created by William Faulkner in novels such as the *The Sound and the Fury* (1929), *As I Lay Dying* (1930) and *Absalom, Absalom!* (1936). Faulkner invented the County of Yoknapatawpha in Mississippi as the setting for his novels, basing the geography and history of the area on Lafayette County and combining some 'real' features such as the Tallahatchie River with 'disguised' places such as Oxford (Jefferson in reality).

In the UK, perhaps the most oft-quoted exponent of the 'disguised' place is Thomas Hardy, who, in his series of novels at the end of the nineteenth and early twentieth century, re-invented Wessex, the old Saxon Kingdom in the south-west of England (Birch 1981). In 'Hardy's Wessex', Dorchester became Casterbridge, Salisbury became Melchester, and Yeovil became Ivell, in the author's deliberate attempt to define the locale of his works by reference to a 'partly real, partly dream-country' (Colour Library Books 1989). Hardy even produced his own map, complete with its own history, which was carried through the series of Wessex novels, each time impressing the fictional area upon his readers. 'Hardy's Wessex' was arguably the first deliberate attempt to manufacture and market a region that fans and tourists could visit (Hardyment 2000).

The only authoritative source as to where invented or disguised places 'actually are' is likely to be the writer, but this information is not always available, nor is it ever really reliable: a place in fiction does by definition not exist and cannot be visited, any more than you can speak to a character in a novel. A case in point is George Eliot's mill 'on the Floss', which the author created as a composite of real locations which went into the novel's Dorlcote Mill, but which drew on her own experiences and research of a mill at Arbury (her birthplace in Warwickshire), her observation of the tidal surges of the River Trent and a mill near Weymouth in Dorset. Anthony Trollope's cathedral city of Barchester, the focal point for a series of six novels set in the imaginary county of Barset, was conceived while the author was visiting Salisbury, and at various times has been taken as being based on Salisbury, Wells, Exeter, Winchester, Hereford and Gloucester.

Writings and readings of 'real' places and spaces

One of the great strengths of literature is the way it can combine the structured realities of place with the immense possibilities of action and characterization in self-supporting narratives. A writer's own experience of place(s) is an obvious foundation for the development of the text and can be reflective and reflexive of the relationship that he or she has with that place. Writers regularly confirm that their works rely on their personal experience (Marsh 1993), including (one assumes) their experience of actual locations, and in some types of fiction – preeminently realism and naturalism – the accurate portrayal of the real, observable world is part of the artistic project, even if the current post-modernist approach tends to deny the validity of such an endeavour. Nevertheless, linking fictional place with real location is often, if not always, legitimate: creative fiction does not exist in isolation from the 'real world', it is part of it. Certainly, within literature there are a myriad examples of places apparently portrayed 'as they are': real settings for fictional events. Levels of detail may vary considerably, as may the intensity of description and the style of writing, but nonetheless images of real places are absorbed into the consciousness of reader and tourist alike.

The way real places are presented in fiction varies in terms of depth. In some works they may simply form a backdrop, creating mood or atmosphere to characterization and story. In others, they are very much in the foreground, shaping and feeding the characters and their behaviour or even assuming an importance as great as the characters. The idea of place as 'backdrop' having a symbolic function over and above the physical, is common in literary criticism. In Moretti's (1988) view, the novel's use of physical space is largely as a 'prop to narrative temporality'. Johnson (2000), focusing specifically upon cities, highlights the ways literature has tended to deal with places, as either imaginary spaces or representations of material reality, contrasting the way Dublin is laid out in great physical detail for the reader in Joyce's *Ulysses* with Virginia Woolf's more superficial usage of London in her novel *The Years*. The contrast relates to a greying extent rather than any sharp definition and is hardly likely to make significant incursions into tourist's perceptions of cities. Arguably, Woolf in her other novels such as *Mrs Dalloway* (Daiches and Flower 1979), creates a more precise image of London.

Lodge (1992) compares the way Henry Fielding writes of London as a backdrop for his novel *Tom Jones* with the way Dickens writes of London in *Oliver Twist*. While both are detailed in their descriptions and use actual spatial reference points, they vary in their impact. Lodge (57) argues that in Fielding's account 'there is no attempt to make the reader "see" the city or to describe its sensory impact ... ' Dickens, who drew heavily upon his own childhood experience of early nineteenth-century London, exemplifies the way in which real places are given depth in literature. The author mobilizes the sensory, to evoke and to layer geography with emotional resonance. Of course this 'sensorization' can be applied to wholly invented places as well, but in relation to real places it provides an added perspective to the actual location for the reader and it distinguishes literary description from the more superficial sources of tourist knowledge.

Arguably the prime example of how real places can be conveyed through literature is James Joyce's *Ulysses*, a lengthy and lofty paragon of the modernist novel published in 1922. Mimicking Ulysses in Homer's epic *Odyssey*, the central character Leopold Bloom makes an estimated 18-mile journey of Dublin on one day, 16 June 1904, sharing his thoughts with the reader through interior monologue. Joyce portrays the city in immense detail, thereby turning the urban environment into 'an element in which the characters live. Indeed, it pervades them, flows through them, all the time, for it is through them, as they walk its streets and are aware of its impinging upon the periphery of their consciousness, that we principally know it'. (Allen 1958: 354)

The accuracy with which Joyce conveys Dublin in *Ulysses* has led to comments that the novel could well be used as a guide book for the city (Allen 1958). Johnson (2000: 199) quotes Joyce as saying: 'I want to give a picture of Dublin so complete that if the city one day suddenly disappeared from the earth it could be reconstructed out of my book.' Although it is likely that Joyce was referring to the artistic intentions underlying his realistic description, he has also *de facto* created a useable guide for the modern-day Ulysses tourist. Indeed, it is not uncommon to see tourists following maps seeking out the 'real' places of Joyce's fiction (www.robotwisdom.com/jaj/jajdublin.html). Indeed, 'Bloomsday' is celebrated on 16 June, and in Dublin, *Ulysses* fans celebrate with readings and by retracing of the Bloom's steps. 'Bloomsday' is also celebrated in spirit in Toronto, New York, Melbourne, Tokyo and Buenos Aires. From the tourist's perspective close detail of place becomes an *aide-mémoire*, an opportunity for almost spiritual absorption. This may look like exaggerated or even misguided behaviour on the part of the celebrant-tourists, but it does underline the fact that pure detailed description of real location in literature without symbolic value lacks artistic significance. As Lodge (1992: 60) says: 'The danger of most set-piece descriptions of place (the novels of Sir Walter Scott provide plenty of examples) is that a succession of well-formed declarative sentences, combined with the suspension of narrative interest, will send the reader to sleep.'

The author's use of real places within creative writings is laden with a number of complications that manifest themselves in the tourist realm. Firstly, wholly value-neutral communication of information through literature is rare. Descriptions of real places in literature is inevitably loaded with sets of interpretations; some emanating from the author via first-or third-person narration, others from the reader, and what we may term *the 'being-ness' of reading*. The latter reflects Heidegger's (1962) position that we are essentially temporal beings, extracting meaning from where we are in particular times and, by implication, spaces (Bergson 1991). Thus, we read at various locales in time (particular emotional times and spaces: youth, adolescence, middle-age, etc., late at night, alone, amongst other readers, when ill, etc.), all of which adds to the contextualization of the experience of reading and the 'how' of 'seeing'. Places in fiction are generally anchored to the emotions generated at particular times by the characters of a novel, or more explicitly in the author providing the narrative. Thus, from a tourism point of view, the reader is presented with destination images laden with predispositions, shaped by feelings of the moment and the spectrum of life experiences. Whether or not there is such a thing as an objective reality, existing outside the human being, the act and process of reading is characterized by a tacit subjectivism, coming from both the author and the reader.

Secondly, this tacit subjectivism somehow implies that we cannot 'trust' a description of a place if we read it in literature. Partly this is framed by the division that has been drawn above between literary and induced/organic information sources. Over the years, an expectation has been nurtured that the latter will be reliable and the former not. But the division is not as clear-cut as we may think. We seldom rely on one information source only, preferring to draw on several, but the expectation nonetheless remains. However, this is not to say that we cannot extract valuable information about 'real' places from literature.

Thirdly, authors frequently jump between real and imagined or disguised places within the same text (Ousby 1990). The narrow southern England geography of Jane Austen's novels exemplify this with their key centres of reality such as London, Bath, Lyme Regis and Brighton. But these are interspersed with references to imaginary places as in *Pride and Prejudice* which features Meryton (a supposed village in Hertfordshire), Hunsford (in Kent) and Kympton (in Derbyshire).

Finally, whilst we can relate to the geography of real places in literature, they are destined to be frozen in time in the universe of the fiction. In some ways this holds great appeal for the tourist, eager for glimpses of literary pasts, the views of the writer, and the streets and buildings inhabited by their characters. In part, the success of the Catherine Cookson tours of South Tyneside in the North East of England or the Helen Forrester Walk around Liverpool, based on the saga fictions of Liverpool in the 1930s (Williamson 2001) draw heavily upon the nostalgic appeal of places just within memory and surrounded with fond reminiscence. In other ways it can weigh heavy on the residents of tourist destinations such as Bath, who find themselves as prisoners of Austenesque fictional representation, or which can hamper the efforts of destinations eager to rid themselves of outmoded factual and fictional images.

THE DISCOLOURATION OF THE TOURIST GAZE

Reflections on the myriad of informational texts available for tourists, including some travel writings, leads to a familiar question of where the 'truth' about destinations is to be found. The democratization of sources of opinion about tourist places and the development of new media vehicles to diffuse them has resulted in the production of contesting scripts. Foucauldian multi-truths prevail and singularly 'truthful' representations of tourist destinations are as elusive as Plato's shadows on the cave walls. Indeed, fiction presents us with varying truths and multiple authenticities of place, which can be readily turned to the purpose of tourism and the deliberate manufacture of place images (Graham 2001). However, what needs to be remembered is that literary truths are fundamentally different, existing as they do in time-specific constructs.

While there is a realization that literary representations of places may be misleading, and positioned at various points in personal and collective pasts, they nevertheless can exert considerable influence on the contemporary and ego-fuelled consumptive tourist gaze. Urry (1995) notes that the anticipation that accompanies the tourist gaze is constructed though non-tourist practices and we can include in this the reading of literature, and specifically the reading of place through literature. Urry also points out that 'the gaze is constructed through signs and tourism involves the collection of such signs', (p. 133). He continues by quoting Culler (1981): 'All over the world the unsung armies of semioticians, the tourists, are fanning out in search of the signs of Frenchness, typical Italian behaviour, exemplary Oriental scenes, typical English pubs.' In the consumption of literature we are indeed collecting signs, the signs of others, signs of otherness, signs constructed for us by the writer, signs seen through the eyes of another, signs that affirm and challenge, signs that can lead us to see places differently.

Creative writings provide us with multiple realities of places, distortions and fragments of geographies located in various time dimensions. Paradoxically, there is a honesty about how places are presented in fiction, an honesty that tourism promotion bodies sometimes struggle with. Upbeat factual, banal descriptions of towns, cities, countries, buildings are jettisoned in favour of emotional, intimate, romantic, disturbing, dissonant, hyper-real versions of places as backgrounds, settings and contexts. While such accounts can enrapture the reader and generate positive and curious feelings toward a place, they can also create a negative image that can remain with tourists for a considerable time and that the tourism industry has to manage.

Meethan (1996) highlights the importance of destination image in shaping touristic consumption of place and makes the point that such images are seldom homogeneous nor stable. Meethan takes the example of the UK seaside resort of Brighton, which has positive and romantic literary associations with Jane Austen, Arnold Bennett, William Thackeray and Charles Dickens. However, the publication of Graham Greene's 1938 novel *Brighton Rock* (subsequently filmed in Brighton in 1947) portrayed the resort as a new centre of 'gangster capitalism' (Punter 1997), revealing a previously hidden hard edge to the town. At the time this literary revelation was condemned as a threat to the tourist trade by the local council and press (Meethan 1996). Arguably the backlash to the place as portrayed in *Brighton Rock* was forceful for the very fact that it was in direct counterpoint to previously published positive or, at the very least, benevolent literary accounts.

A case could be made that there were indeed two, if not more, sides to Brighton then and now, as there are to most places. However, for some places literary representations have played an almost unrelenting part in the construction of negative images to both tourists and the wider public. Examples abound, but three are worthy of mention here as illustrative of their influence. A first example relates to the way that even the briefest extract of literature can shape public and by implication tourist perceptions of place. John Betjeman's poem *Slough*, published in 1937, vents his dislike of industrialism, suburban sprawl and the impacts of expansion upon this Berkshire town and prophetically invites an aerial bombardment of the place:

> Come friendly bombs and fall on Slough!
> It isn't fit for humans now,
> There isn't grass to graze a cow.
> Swarm over, Death!

And later:

> Mess up the mess they call a town –
> A house for ninety-seven down
> And once a week a half a crown
> For twenty years.
>   (Betjeman, 1989)

In these few stanzas of social commentary and tongue-in-cheek verse, learned by vast numbers of schoolchildren, Slough is burdened by a label that it still finds difficult to shake off. Though by no means a tourist destination, Slough's appropriation by Betjeman has been the bane of promotional bodies, estate agents and the local authority, who remain explicit in their desire to counter the poet's now dated rant (www.slough.gov.uk/CommunityLife/claims_fame.asp). This defence culminated in 1998 when local poets were invited to compose tributes to the town, along with Booker prize-winning author Ben Okri.

A second example relates to the way that 'the troubles' in Northern Ireland continue to provide reality settings for fictional events. Numerous novels have used the political, social and economic conflicts and conditions of Northern Ireland either as a backdrop or as a central part of the story (see for instance: Parker 1995; Pelaschiar 1998). While the Republic of Ireland basks in the touristic glow of its literary heritage, the North, or at least the key locations of Belfast, Derry and Armagh, continue to provide an evocative, rich, dynamic and disturbing framing for contemporary creative writings. In terms of expressing the communal strife and conflict scenarios which the people of Northern Ireland are dealing with, the literature that has emerged over the past thirty years from writers such as Joseph O'Connor, Roddy Doyle, Ciaron Carson, Mary Beckett and Danny Morrison, has played an important part. However, ironically, the utilization of 'the troubles' in literature assists in the discolouration of external and tourist perceptions of Northern Ireland and contributes to the negative imagery that keeps tourist numbers low, when economically it would help if they were high.

The third example relates to the way in which creative writings have endowed the North of England (a vague and shifting term but one that would generally extend north of Birmingham) with a persistent image of darkness, depression and dejection.

This is usually contrasted with literary images of the South of England presented as lively, cosmopolitan and affluent.

Shields (1991), following earlier work by Pocock (1978, 1979) on the legacy of novels about the North, identifies a stream of literary representations of grimness rooted in the nineteenth century when the social and environmental degradation of the industrial revolution were present in wholly unregulated excess. Frederich Engel's influential, factual, observations of working lives and organizations in Manchester's mills of 1844 were also buttressed by numerous fictionalized and arguably more penetrative accounts. Elizabeth Gaskell's *Mary Barton* (1848), and *North and South* (1855), Disraeli's novel *Sybil* (1845), Charles Dickens's representation of Preston in Lancashire as Coketown in *Hard Times* (1854), represented the North of England as grim and despoiled, which was largely an accurate portrayal of the region at the time. Describing the North as bleak and dirty continued well into the twentieth century with Arnold Bennett's novels set in the smoky pottery towns of Stoke-on-Trent, D. H. Lawrence's back/blackcloth of the Nottingham coalfields in *Lady Chatterley's Lover* (1929), Walter Greenwood's (1933) tale of *Love on the Dole* set in Manchester during the depression, George Orwell's *The Road to Wigan Pier*, Sid Chaplin's novels of the depressed Durham coalfields and other fiction set in the provincial North.

Even into the 1950s, 60s, 70s and 80s, the North of England was represented as the hardest hit by the waves of economic depression, the slowest place to recover, the place where prosperity passed by and as a place to escape from. Novels such as Stan Barstow's *A Kind of Loving* (1961) and Barry Hines's *A Kestrel for a Knave* (1968), the poetry of Yorkshire's Tony Harrison, and the drama of Alan Bleasdale and Jim Cartwright, all captured a 'sense of place', and continued the theme of the North as bleak. From a literary perspective these stark and often angry works of social realism, dark images and deep characters have made for excellent literature and powerful sociopolitical commentary. From the perspective of tourism promotion bodies seeking to attract visitors to parts of the previously heavily industrialized, but now regenerated, 're-invented' North of England, such literary representations have contributed to, and continue to act as an incalculable and intangible perceptual barrier to tourists and investors (Fowler, Robinson and Boniface 2001). The tourist gaze toward the North is still clouded by a fictional legacy of mill smoke and drizzle. No matter how 'real' literary representations of the North were in the nineteenth and twentieth centuries, and arguably, no matter whether they still accurately represent parts of the North in the twenty-first century, their legacy lives on presenting a perpetual challenge for image-makers in tourism.

What these examples point to is the power of literary texts to frame the tourist gaze, or indeed, to negate it. Places, communities, history are imagined through the communicative power of literature. Furthermore, this power is cumulative, incessant and difficult to counteract. The creative writer has the beauty and poetic charm of language, plot and character to convey and represent places, as well as a long 'shelf-life'. The tourism promoter is armed with a few ephemeral brochures. It would appear to be a one-sided contest.

THE PROCUREMENT OF TOURIST ATTITUDES TO OTHERNESS

The art of true surprise is swiftly disappearing from tourism. Tourists no longer encounter destinations and host communities with vacant anticipation but rather with an expectation that their preconceptions will normally be endorsed, part of what Dann (1999: 165) refers to as the 'passive tautology' of tourism. Tourist literature, travel guides and travel writings all have a role in shaping images of, and attitudes to, the places we visit and the communities we encounter. So, too, does creative writing.

The slow and cumulative process of absorbing certain literary works can shape our worldviews as readers and tourists. We reach destinations forearmed with images and ideologies cultivated from the pages of the novels and poems we have read over the course of our lives. While literature enriches our knowledge of the world and assists in shaping our perceptions generally, it is particularly relevant when it extends to knowledges of others and otherness, and to shaping national, regional and local identities from the armchair. Literature can imbue the tourist with attitudes forged outside of contemporary events and time-specific realities. It can reify nationalist boundaries and perpetuate hegemonies that are not only located in the developed west, but also seem to be fixed within a hyper-nostalgia for an uncritical past. Literature is a commanding feature of national identity and remains as a defining reflection of residual colonialist attitudes, partly through the dominance of the English language as the 'language of advantage' (Collins 1990) and partly through reproduction and continual re-invention. Creative writing has a central role to play in the historical and political analysis of international relations. The work of Said (1980: 1993) has been vital in illustrating the ways literature has played its part in constructing, projecting and maintaining the notion of the European self and by extension the subjugation of the 'rest' of the world. Said demonstrates the sheer and corrupting face of power of fiction. As Darby (1998: 25) puts it: 'Fiction's constructions and apprehensions cannot be seen as merely incidental to the processes of imperial expansion. On the contrary, they were fundamental to the existence of empire itself.'

In the nineteenth century and well into the twentieth century, distant and expansive empires provided a wealth of source material for writers, particularly the increasingly popular literary form of the novel. The British Empire provided novelists with new dimensions of fiction that exaggerated the facts of military and commercial expansionism, bringing heroic adventure and exotic cultural encounters back to an increasingly literate Britain. The works of Rider Haggard, Rudyard Kipling, John Buchan, Joseph Conrad and later E. M. Forster were laden with images of distant and different cultures. At the time, these stories of Empire were tremendously popular: Haggard's *King Solomon's Mines* was an instant best-seller, with Edgar Wallace's *Sanders of the River* close behind, and Kipling's books sold seven million copies in Britain and some eight million in the United States (Bradbury 1996). It is not only fiction about the Empire that generated the cultural attitudes that still pervade tourism. Sax Rohmer's *The Mystery of Dr Fu Manchu*, published in 1913, in which the Chinese were given fantastical and grotesque identities, gave rise to a persistent and racist attitude that saw China as a nation of inscrutable villains

(Donald 1993). Similarly, cold-war spy novels such as those by Len Deighton, John le Carré, and indeed Ian Fleming's Bond books, arguably contributed to a deep suspicion of Eastern Europe and Eastern Europeans as poor, threatening and 'grey', that continues to permeate tourist minds to this day.

Hidden beneath the labels of literary heritage and literary greatness is a deeper influence that shapes our contemporary tourist experiences and our expectations of 'otherness' in touristic encounters. Scotland's identity (particularly as distinct from that of England), reinforced over the years by the Scottish Tourist Board, owes much to the achievements of its great literary figures, whether it be the linguistic innovation of Burns, the locations featured by Scott, the Scottish novels of Stevenson, or the re-invented romanticism of Buchan (Crawford 1997). Literary 'greats', whose lives and works are well employed for commercial purposes in tourism, are also lingeringly used in defining, presenting, projecting and protecting national identities. The novels of E. M. Forster project an essentially English, rural and non-industrial notion of England (Buzard 1993; Tambling 1995), a view endorsed by later screen adaptations. In his imperialist writing, Kipling (whose poem *If* was recently voted as Britain's favourite poem) has shaped the perceptions and values of generations of tourists and, of course, non-tourists, with regard to the 'other' of India and the Far East (Parry 1993). Even Jane Austen's works can be viewed as upholding national hier-archies and nationalistic anachronisms. Said (1993) for instance points to Austen and her narrowness in positioning a small expanse of southern England as somehow universal and central, and in doing so fortifying the emergent British Empire. That position is carried on in the Hollywood remake of Austen's *Emma* as the film *Clueless*, which portrays Los Angeles, and in particular Beverley Hills, as the centre of the universe (Stern 1997).

The tourism industry, driven by populism and, by extension profit, is able to ride over dissonance and contestability, to select and promote literary commodities that have a wide appeal. However, as it does so, it invokes literary 'greatness' when addressing the market, rather than standing up to post-colonial scrutiny and a new cultural pluralism. As it homes in on 'great' writers and their works, it obviously excludes others. It remains to be seen how, and whether, the tourism industry will, and can, present emergent post-colonial literary figures such as Rushdie, Naipaul, Marquez and their works, and whether they can be so neatly packaged in an age that moves beyond the post-colonial into the global and multi-cultural.

RELATIONSHIPS BEYOND THE TEXT

The internal workings of a novel and the messages and imagery it conveys are not in themselves enough to explain the popularity of literary sites and the high profile they appear to command within formal and informal tourist itineraries. In tourism terms there is definitely 'life beyond the text'. Over the centuries, because of the dominance of print, we have come to think of narrative and literature as one and the same thing. Narrative, whether originally presented to the public as literature, now exists in a variety of cultural forms, and as a cultural commodity literature is appropriated, traded, transformed and carried along with the global flow of cultures. What are considered to be the most important of these exogenous manifestations of literature are discussed below.

Lives, loves and celebrity

Literature and the writers of literature are beset by a range of contradictions. The creative process may depend upon various interactions and observations of inter-actions but the writing process is solitary. The reading process is also solitary and yet one novel can be consumed by millions. The writing and reading processes are singular and plural. The work can be read independently of any consideration of the author, as a creation of itself, yet at other times in reading the work we are 'reading' the author too. The writer may seek fame and public exposure for him or herself, or for the created work, for both or neither. Celebrity status may be sought but not awarded, or maybe accorded and not wanted.

Baudrillardian-type claims that in a fluid, eclectic, postmodern world of discourse and mass media, the author no longer commands the importance he or she once had, do not sit comfortably with the realities of literary tourism. From a tourism per-spective, literature is rarely defined only in terms of the work alone. The commo-dification of texts for tourists also involves exploring the intimacies of their creators, and in some cases the lives and deaths of authors make for an equally, if not a more fascinating 'gaze'. Insights into writers' lives creates a tourism of the personal, of the real, and provides a touchstone for the understanding of what is an otherwise quasi-mystical process of creating a novel, poem or play. As discussed in Chapter 1, the writer's home is perhaps the most 'sacred' space in literary tourism. Here is the physical embodiment of those we cannot usually see, or speak to, and whose works we worship. This extends beyond the mere tourist gaze to a voyeurism. For it is not just the text that can be taken to be 'erotic', but the lives of the writers, as artists, as geniuses, as eccentrics, as heroes and heroines, as cultural icons, as famous people, but ultimately as 'other' people. Tourism reflects human curiosity and a society that increasingly seeks to distinguish between celebrity and 'the rest', and upholds this polarization through its rites of display. The 'otherness' of the writer and artist is exploited by the tourism industry and the tourist participates, not only in the quest for knowledge and understanding, but also eager for glimpses, revelation, exposé and scandal.

Reputations and the 'off-the-page' behaviour of some authors elevate them to a point where the tourist derives more pleasure from, and gives more attention to, their lives and times than from their works. Byron's comment following the publication of his epic poem *Childe Harold's Pilgrimage* in 1812 that 'I awoke to find myself famous', was to be prophetic of his later notoriety, a notoriety that perhaps had more to do with his life than his literary talents. The young Baron Byron whose works charmed the public was known for his reckless behaviour, numerous affairs (including one with Lady Caroline Lamb) and later for his commitment to the Greek cause against the Turks. But public outrage regarding his incestuous relationship with his half-sister, Augusta Leigh, forced Byron to leave Britain in 1816. Following his death in 1824, Byron was buried in the family vault but permission for him to be buried in Poets' Corner in Westminster Abbey was refused. Indeed, such was the stigma attached to Byron's name, given that he was a member of the House of Lords, that it was not until 1969 that a plaque of dedication to him appeared in the Abbey.

Indeed, there would seem to be a powerful and positive correlation between public/tourist interest and the more extreme forms of behaviour. The fascination we hold for Coleridge's and de Quincy's opiate addictions, the drug culture surrounding Kerouac, Keasey, Ginsberg and Burroughs; the way we readily pigeonhole D. H. Lawrence as a pornographer; our fascination for the highly public homosexuality of Oscar Wilde and the injustices done to the same man who gave us *Lady Windermere's Fan*; the scandal surrounding the savage murder of playwright Joe Orton by his lover Kenneth Halliwell; the way we portray Dylan Thomas as a hard-drinking 'jack-the-lad'; the way we continue to scrutinize the suicide of Sylvia Plath and the mysterious eleven-day disappearance of Agatha Christie in 1926; all point to our fixation with *discovering* the facts behind the fiction. The figures behind our literature are not immune from a wider cultural preoccupation for the salacious, the different, our search for hero and anti-hero, and the rise and fall cycle of celebrity. Arguably, that is why some writers shun their publics, as did J. D. Salinger, the author of *Catcher in the Rye*, who banished himself from the world, his public and his family (Salinger 2000). Others are perhaps more ambiguous about their relationship with the public gaze, such as the author Barbara Taylor Bradford. Rose (1998) recounts:

> One of my favourite moments was Barbara Taylor Bradford renewing her marriage vows in the total privacy of a completely deserted tropical island on which no tourists step; with only black luggage carriers in attendance, as well as the whole photographic and editorial team of *Hello!*

We continually observe, unearth and reveal the lives of literary talents, dead and alive, as we do so with all public figures. Although the tourism industry can often obscure some truths in its promotional literature, it can also play to them. In Dublin, visitors can indulge in a 'Literary Pub Crawl' (sponsored by Jameson Whiskey), which revels in the drinking exploits of the city's favourite authors including Brendan Behan, Flann O'Brien and Joyce. One comes away from this carefully orchestrated experience better armed with an interior view of these writers and their writings but feeling rather ambiguous about them as people. The experience arguably works because they are portrayed as 'characters' and 'caricatures', rather than the complex, and in some cases, much troubled writers of fiction.

As Rose (1998) points out, and as the example of Byron reminds us, the cult of celebrity is not a new phenomenon. Particularly after the publication of Mrs Gaskell's *Life of Charlotte Brontë* in 1857, Miller (2001) notes the rise in celebrity status of the author. The biography fuelled public interest in Charlotte, a point accentuated by the fact that Haworth and the parsonage, the place where she lived and worked, provided an identifiable shrine. Miller (p. 98) continues:

> The almost religious awe in which she was held soon came to be focused on the place where she had spent nearly all her life, and a fully-fledged cult developed complete with pilgrims and relics. Although literary cults were not confined to the Brontës in the latter half of the nineteenth century, Charlotte inspired a uniquely intense devotion.

What is new is the way that celebrity status is thrust powerfully and seemingly perpetually across transnational communication networks to the point where we cannot escape it. Ewen (1988), like Boorstin (1963) before him, relates the notion of celebrity to the 'mass reproduction' of works, with exposure and dissemination fuelling prestige. However, where reproduction is clearly a driver of celebrity status, Bourdieu's (1993) formulation of 'symbolic capital' is also relevant in the context of literature, where writers, and their work, accumulate symbolic markers such as public/critical recognition and prestige to a point where the text can be thought of as, in secular terms, 'consecrated' and the author as 'canonized'. Biography assists in this canonization process as it purports to make publicly accessible the 'real' pysche of the writer and helps in revealing the fact behind the fiction. Complimentary or otherwise, biographies of writers are not only markers of prestige but highly effective promotional devices with the power to elevate writers to celebrity status, such as Mrs Gaskell's *Life of Charlotte Brontë*, or to revive the popularity of writers, such as Anthony Trollope's biography and bibliography did in the 1920s (Hall 1993).

But on the whole, and when compared to film and television stars, writers do not experience the excesses of inter/transnational exposure, partly because of language barriers, partly because of the writing experience being solitary, disjointed and *ad hoc*, but mainly because of the dominance of ocularcentrism (Synott 1993): the visual media and the 'faces' that occupy our large and small screens rather than the inside of a dust jacket. Where some contemporary writers have attained celebrity status and are widely recognized through the media, such as Salman Rushdie and Jeffrey Archer, this is largely more a result of their non-literary activities.

The establishment of literary societies and 'fan' clubs are in part a recognition of celebrity, and the formalization of public attitudes toward literature, ranging from professional appreciation to personal adoration. In relation to the development of literary tourism, little research has actually been carried out. However, such organizations perform two key roles. The first is perhaps the most obvious and direct one and relates to the organization and hosting of visits to sites with literary connections, the organization of conferences and performances, the promotion and maintenance of literary sites and the lobbying for the care and restoration of literary heritage. The second, but more intangible role, is one of advocacy, in the sense that such clubs and societies assist in the process of fixing literary figures and works in public, national and international consciousness. The Dickens Fellowship, for instance, which was founded in 1902, not only has branches across the UK but also across the world including the USA, India, Argentina, France and Japan. Over ninety literary societies are members of the UK Alliance of Literary Societies and collectively they represent a potent and supportive role in the presentation of literature to wider society.

The literary souvenir

Closely allied to the idea of celebrity is the notion of the literary souvenir; some physical memento associated with a writer or a text that extends the idea of the writer or text into the world. As researchers have long noted the concept of the memento is an essential part of the contemporary tourism experience (MacCannell 1976; Graburn 1987; Litrell 1990), and literature is not immune to the generation and mobility of merchandise that is used to mark tourism. Again, the idea of literary souvenirs to pacify tourists is not in itself new. Miller (2001: 100) notes that 'In the aftermath of the *Life*, Charlotte's father had found himself cutting up her letters into small squares to cope with the demand for samples of her handwriting.' Memorabilia surrounding the likes of Burns, Scott and Wordsworth were also well-established features of early literary tourism.

However, the increased branding of tourist (and non-tourist) merchandise with literary associations and motifs is now a significant economic activity in its own right (Price 1996). Items such as Shakespeare's Cottage tea-cosies, Jane Austen embroidery kits, Peter Rabbit T-shirts and myriads of tea towels featuring images of authors, characters and locations are now mass produced and mass consumed. The connections with literature are often tenuous to say the least. Iyer (2000: 247) notes that 'in Keat's house, you can buy a teddy bear wearing a sash that says I AM A R♡MANTIC'. Miller (2001: 107) points out that 'Brontë' has become a nationally marketed brand for biscuits that bear little connection to the Brontës or Haworth but which is there instead to 'confer home-made status on a mass-produced product, reaching back through history to Victorian clichés of Charlotte the housewife'. We have quite got to the point where a Mrs Gaskell lawn-mower or an E. M. Forster multi-speed food blender is commonplace, but we are increasingly accustomed to the process of imaginative 'heritage' branding.

Aside from the obvious economic dimension of literary souvenirs as purchased by the tourist, and the culturally defining nature of the objects themselves as they are consumed, they also act as extensions of the texts/authors whose brand-name they carry. However dislocated they may be from the spirit of literary connection or however contrived they may seem, they nonetheless disseminate the idea of a literary culture, and exist as part of that diffuse, immeasurable cloud of subconscious reference points that feeds tourist curiosity.

The changing politics of print

In considering the tourism–literature relationship as existing beyond the interior of the text and as we attempt to explain the magnitude, transnationalism and cross-culturalism of literary tourism, we need to position literature as both product and process/media and message within a framework of social and political mobilities. Whilst it would be folly to argue that in the context of international tourism, literary tourism occupied anything more than a niche, it is nonetheless a significant and well-established niche.

Although we can track changes and trends in literary form and devices, the essence of literature as the making of poietic realities has not shifted significantly. What is clear is that interpretations of literature have developed apace to the point where literature can be viewed as being defined by criticism. But arguably, the history and development of literary tourism relates less to the nature of literature itself and to the emergence of literary criticism, and far more to the issues of production, diffusion and consumption of texts. Following Adorno and Horkheimer (1979), we can locate literature as part of the 'culture industry', subject to mass production methods, driven by profit motives and increasingly focused upon delivering literature to mass audiences. It is not the place of this chapter to delve deep into the development of 'print capitalism' and the sociology of literature *per se*. Varying historical perspectives on the development and diffusion of literature, and the growth of literacy are provided by the likes of Badaracco (1995); Boorstin (1963); Escarpit (1966, 1971); Hoggart (1957); Jordan and Patten (1995); Lowenthal (1984). However, several inter-related points are worth reflecting on in relation to literary tourism.

PRODUCTION AND CONSUMPTION ISSUES

For its markets, literary tourism is ultimately dependent upon the production/ replication and public consumption of books. In that they can be mechanically reproduced, printed books provide a fixity to their imagined contents, and their generally long shelf life (assured through increasingly well-defined 'second-hand' markets) maintains a powerful inter-generational dimension that feeds the concept of literary heritage. The creative process in terms of 'new' titles continues apace and societies accumulate ever-extending libraries of ideas and perspectives. In the UK in 1999, over 9,700 titles of adult fiction published were published (*The Bookseller* 2000). In addition to the generation of new titles, new editions and reprints of earlier titles are also published and continue to permeate public consciousness. The production of literature varies considerably from one country to another, as a function of literacy rates and the distribution policies and networks of publishers. Thus, in the United States between 1994 and 1996, 25 book titles were published per 100,000 people, compared to 252 in Finland, 183 in the UK, 17 in Chile and 2.2 in Algeria over the same period (UNESCO 1998).

What is more important from a literary tourism perspective, however, is the consumption of literature, though it is frequently difficult to decide whether it is the literary works or their authors (or both) that are being consumed. Table 2.2 shows fourteen titles that have sold over ten million hardback and paperback copies worldwide and are taken to be the world's best-selling fiction, though precise sales figures are hard to obtain. It is useful to bear in mind the distinction between best-selling titles and best-selling authors since the two do not necessarily coincide. According to Ash (1997), the best selling fictional book of all time is Jaqueline Susann's 1966 'pulp' novel *The Valley of the Dolls*, which spent a record number of weeks at the top of the New York best sellers list, selling over 28 million copies. However, the world's best selling writer of fiction is Agatha Christie, whose 78 crime novels are estimated to have sold 2 billion copies (Guinness 1999).

The bestsellers identified above have generated fairly limited tourist legacies, though we can identify sites and 'attractions' associated primarily with those authors on the list who have died. For instance, Margaret Mitchell's apartment, where she wrote *Gone with the Wind*, has been developed in the centre of Atlanta, Georgia, complete with a museum, galleries and a shop, and tourists can visit the Erskine Caldwell Birthplace Museum in Moreland Georgia. As with Susann's *Valley of the*

Table 2.2   The world's best-selling fiction

Author	Title
Bach, Richard	Jonathan Livingstone Seagull
Blatty, William	The Exorcist
Benchley, Peter	Jaws
Caldwell, Erskine	God's Little Acre
Heller, Joseph	Catch-22
Lee, Harper	To Kill a Mockingbird
McCullough, Colleen	The Thorn Birds
Metalious, Grace	Peyton Place
Mitchell, Margaret	Gone With the Wind
Orwell, George	1984, Animal Farm
Puzo, Mario	The Godfather
Robbins, Harold	The Carpetbaggers
Salinger, J. D.	Catcher in the Rye

Source: Ash, R. (1997) *The Top Ten of Everything*

Dolls, (and this is implicit generally in Table 2.2), the extensive consumption of fiction has for the past forty years or so related to its availability in cost-effective paperback form. Popular fiction is now highly visible alongside magazines in airports and railway stations and in a very real sense 'travels' widely.

Diffusion, translation, adaptation

Hannerz (1996) uses the term 'the global ecumene' as a way of referring to the interconnectedness across nations and cultures; a linking-up of ideas and diversity within the dynamic of collapsing time and space. This is a useful if imperfect way of conceptualizing the world. In the global ecumene, riven as it is with tensions between uniformity and fragmentation, global/local, centre and periphery relationships, national and supra-national identities, modernity and postmodernity, and tensions between culture and economy, the production, consumption and distribution of media are central processes. If we are to attempt any understanding of, for instance, the fascination of Japanese women tourists with Lucy Maud Montgomery's *Anne of Green Gables*, the 800 members of the Shakespeare Society of Japan, the global appeal of Hans Christian Andersen's Fairy Tale theme-park rides, or of Dracula and vampires, then we must position literature/creative writing as part of these processes.

In his *Atlas of the European Novel*, Moretti (1998) provides a historical account of the way that literature diffused its way across Europe in the nineteenth century from its core centres of Britain and France. Moretti's study is detailed down to genre and author and provides an insight into not only fictional geographies as created and captured by the novel, but also into the realities of the diffusion of literature to new audiences across nations and into different cultural territories. The mechanisms of diffusion are implicit rather than explicit in Moretti but nationally they relate to the availability and circulation of novels in public lending libraries, and transnationally they relate to the translation of the novel into various languages and to suit varying literary tastes. For example, the success of Sir Walter Scott's translated novels across a number of states accords to the European taste of the time for novels of the 'melodramatic imagination' (p. 177). Circulation is also dependent upon the distributive capacity and the 'reach' and power of publishers, and increasingly their promotional efforts prior and post-publication.

Bourdieu and Passeron's (1977) conception of literature as an inherent symbol within bourgeois society – a political tool wielded by the middle class – is a powerful but nonetheless historicized view. While we may certainly recognize an 'élite' in terms of publishing control and in terms of artistic evaluation, it would seem apparent that the trend towards the democratization of bookishness in terms of ownership and readership continues. The idea that literacy is defined by print technologies and distributive networks (Goody 1977, 1987; Ong 1982), is rapidly being challenged by new developments within each and by melting boundaries between literature and the electronic media including film, television and the internet. Arguably, literary tourism is still pervaded by an air of the affluent white 'middle-classness' found across the broad canvas that is presented as cultural tourism (Richards 1996, 2001). But this would be an over-simplification if one takes the full spread of literary attractions into account (including large theme parks featuring characters from children's literature). The truth is that there is little in the way of empirical data to work with.

Certain literary works seem to have permeated the globe more than others. Demand for particular literary genres is linked to particular fashions, trends, time-specific cultural tastes and, in the cases of romance and horror genres for instance, to deeper psychological and emotional needs (Tudor 1997). To an extent this helps in the explanation of certain cross-cultural proclivities with regard to literary tourism. However, more direct reasons relate to the idea of translation as a basic tenet of the spatial and cultural diffusion process. As Cronin (2000) points out tourism is woven with delicate and indelicate instances whereby the traveller/tourist has to continually negotiate between languages, words and meanings, and is confronted with the need to translate to some degree or other. In Cronin's words (p. 38): 'Translation can be the ultimate expression of linguistic hospitality welcoming new languages, cultures and ideas into the mother tongue, or it can be a fortress of hegemonic difference translating people into the language of dominant cultures and annihilating difference.' This, in effect, is another layer of complexity that informs the relations between tourism, tourist and literature, but here we deal with the more superficial and mechanistic aspects of translation. Translation here relates to two processes. The first is concerned with the conversion of texts written in one language into another language. The second relates to the translation of literary works into different media and communicative forms.

It is clear from the outset that when we are speaking of translating creative writings from one language to another we are doing so against a backdrop of decided unevenness. Creative writings are constantly translated into various languages largely reflecting market popularity of a particular work and writer. But while it is common to find copies of *Jane Eyre* or *Pride and Prejudice* translated into Japanese on the shelves of Tokyo Airport's book stands, it is uncommon to find nineteenth-century Japanese novels translated into English at Heathrow. The 'flow' of translation is decidedly from English into 'other' languages. According to the International Clearing House for Endangered Languages there are 6,760 different languages spoken in the world, however, some 96 per cent of these are spoken by only 4 per cent of the world's population (Kubo 1998). For the rest of the world the English language is increasingly dominant. Estimates vary but Crystal (1997) suggests that in addition to some 573 million people who speak English as their first or second language, there are also some 670 million who possess 'native-like' fluency in the langauge.

While there are clearly issues relating to cultural de-territorialization/re-territorialization and the privileging power of the English Langauage, its ubiquity is particularly relevant to international flows of visitors to literary sites. It would seem a necessary, though not sufficient condition for the generation of international interest that visitors are familiar with creative writings and to a lesser extent their creators. Table 2.3 shows the top ten most frequently translated authors in 1980 and 1996. Although this only deals with the number of translations and not which langauges these books are translated into, it is clear that in a post-Soviet world, writers of English-langauage fiction dominate. Indeed, in 1996 some 69 of the first 100 most frequently translated authors are either from the UK or the USA; all writing fiction. Clearly while such statistics suggests transnational readership of such authors, this does not point to any manifestation of literary tourism, though we can identify strong touristic forms associated with the likes of Agatha Christie, Jane Austen and Shakespeare. Even Stephen King's horror stories have generated their own literary tours and trails around the small towns and hamlets of Maine on the US East Coast marginally disguised and used by King as the settings for gruesome happenings (Beahm 1999), despite King's own attempts to put tourists off the scent with false directions and names (Ezard 2001).

It is an acknowledged shortcoming of this examination of the literature–tourism relationship that it has almost exclusively focused upon English Literature, or certainly literature created by writers that have English as their primary language. This is a function of not being able to 'step outside one's own langauge' and of the more practical issue of not being able to access to non-English research sources. There are clearly myriad texts laid down and translated in languages other than English, as there are non-English writers of distinction with huge readerships. There are also numerous examples of developments in literary tourism that are centred upon non-English texts and non-English writers. Moscow is developing its extensive literary connections (Benn and Bartlett 1997) capitalizing on the former homes of such names as Tolstoy, Chekhov, Bulgakov and Pasternak, and museums including those focusing on Pushkin and Gorky. Intourist, the former Russian State tour operator, provides tours of Moscow taking in the streets and buildings where literary scenes took place. The city of Weimar in Germany attracts 'pilgrims' to the houses of Goethe and Schiller (Coughlan 1998). Rouen is capitalizing upon its links with Gustave Flaubert through its Flaubert museum, his nearby home, and the city settings for *Madam Bovary* (Ruck 1997), and Cabourg in Normandy markets the connections it has with Marcel Proust (Herbert 2001).

However, the development of literary tourism coterminously reflects the culture of tourism generally and thus would seem to be dominated by a 'western', developed,

Table 2.3   Most frequently translated authors

Rank	Authors	Associated country	Number of translations	Number of countries translating
1980	1980	1980	1980	1980
1	Lennin V. I.	USSR	468	15
2	The Bible	Palestine	232	48
3	Christie A.	UK	189	20
4	Verne J.	France	172	21
5	Blyton E.	UK	147	12
6	Marx K.	Germany	136	20
7	Cartland B.	UK	135	13
8	Engels F.	Germany	132	17
9	Shakespeare W.	UK	112	22
10	Breznev L. I.	USSR	109	14
Rank	Authors	Associated country	Number of translations	Number of countries translating
1996	1996	1996	1996	1996
1	Christie A.	UK	192	25
2	Steel D.	US	141	22
3	King S.	US	137	21
4	Shakespeare W.	UK	125	25
5	Cartland B.	UK	115	11
6	Stine R. L.	US	107	8
7	Blyton E.	UK	94	9
8	Koontz D. R.	US	82	14
9	Vandenberg P.	Germany	78	2
10	Austen J.	UK	74	19

Source: UNESCO, World Culture Report, 1998

strongly Eurocentric marketplace. In the context of international travel, literary tourism remains strongly defined by English Literature; moreover, a relatively small bandwidth of English Literature, acutely hierarchical and still dominated by 'the classics'. Given the agency and authority of the English langauge as the medium for global communication (albeit with some creolization), coupled with the continued engraining of westernized variants of the culture of tourism, it would appear that the international supply–demand patterns of literary tourism will persistently reflect the translations of classic 'English' works alongside popular fiction into 'other' languages. The fact that the majority of people who speak 'English' as their first language have long lived outside the UK, indeed, outside of Europe, coupled with the idea of 'international writers' who, like Salman Rushdie, transcend single nation literary geneologies, may well be a pressure towards redefining literary studies. However, it would seem to matter little in the realms of a literary tourism still very much defined by, and linked to, national heritages and cultural nationalism.

The second form of translation we are concerned with here is that by which creative writings are reproduced into forms outside the conventional book. For aesthetic, ethical and political reasons, creative writings old and new continue to be reproduced in and accessed through cyberspace. New contested spaces of identity are being created and reimagined (Morely and Robins 1995), and following Anderson (1983) literatures are central to such processes. Though some creative writings are being specifically produced for electronic space, it is the reproduction and digitalized distribution of existing works of literature that dominates the infoscapes of the internet. Whole collections of complete literary works, condensed versions of the classics, novels by subscription, biographies and intimate details of writers lives, ready translations into an increasing number of languages and books to buy electronically, are all now fixed as part of a society of generalized communication and mass media (Vattimo 1992). In the context of literary tourism, what cyberspace provides is yet another layer of literacy, and the promotion of its essential ingredients to an interconnected world, complete with its politics of power, identities and silences.

Arguably the most potent driver for literary tourism over recent decades has derived from audio-visual adaptations of creative writings. It is not the purpose of this chapter to delve into the matters surrounding such transformations, save to say that they are numerous and include issues of technical praxis, ownership, legal rights and fidelity/faithfulness to the text (McFarlane 1996). Structured transformation and translation of written texts into audio-visual productions (film, television, radio) are the most tangible manifestations of life beyond the text. In Foucault's words: 'The book is not simply the object that one holds in one's hands' (1974: 23). Books are increasingly defined by reference to other texts and exist intertextually within a general milieu of fluctuating boundaries between and across genres and media. Thus we may encounter the works of Jane Austen through a television serial, a Hollywood film (*Emma* and *Clueless*) or even through an advertisement borrowing from Austen-type characters.

Behind each adaptation lies a network of interpretive decisions tempered by resource practicalities and the boundaries of time and space. Such decisions may or may not involve the writer but have more to do with remote variables such as global market penetration. Beyond each adaptation lies ongoing controversies and comparisons. However, first and foremost in the context of this chapter, screen (and to a lesser extent radio) adaptations of literature has the effect of generating tourist interest in both the fictive text dramatized and the writer who first created the text. Notably, the filmmaker/director does not become the object of tourist attention.

Effectively, screen adaptations in particular, act to greatly increase public exposure to literary works and sites. As previously observed there is a dearth of research into the role of creative writings generally upon the shaping of destination images and patterns of tourist motivation/behaviour. This information gap is compounded and complicated when we attempt to assess the impact of the various adaptations of literature in addition to the general circulation of literature in book form. Researchers to date have largely failed to factor-in the role of adaptations into studies of visits to literary sites.

Whatever the measure of criticisms to emerge relating to the fidelity of the adaptation, visually re-produced texts generate audience levels rapidly and far in excess of readership figures. Moreover, in acts of literary democratization, they are able to reach new, transnational, multi-cultural audiences, or more specifically, new, transnational, multi-cultural audiences are able to access (both physically and intellectually) creative writings. Arguably, more people are likely to have come into contact with the works of Dickens, Thackeray, Hardy, Austen, Brontë, George Eliot and others through large- and small-screen adaptations than through reading the novels themselves. Hall (1993) points to the British television serialization of the Palliser novels in the 1970s and the Barchester novels in the 1980s as a major factor in generating interest in the works and life of Anthony Trollope. We can posit that Dylan Thomas's *Under Milk Wood*, his play specially written for radio and broadcast shortly after his death in 1953, attained its high level of popularity because it was broadcast, or, conversely, that it would have taken far longer to reach the population and attain its appeal if it had solely relied on live performances and the sales of the written play. Unfortunately, limited research in this area makes it difficult to ascribe certainty to such assertations. Much of the work on screen adaptations of literature has focused upon textual transformative processes rather than their impacts upon the literacy and consumptive patterns of wider society. However, it would appear eminently reasonable to assume that there exists some element of causality between widely distributed adaptations and the popularity of the works and creators.

It would also appear reasonable to assume that adaptation provides another potential touristic opportunity. Visual representations of novels, particularly the 'classics', rich in their melodrama, lavishness and nostalgia, links the written with the visual. In early screen adaptations of literary works, the confines of the studio, whilst bringing a book 'to life', prohibited the audience from even considering exploration of setting and landscape. More recently however, utilization of reality locations for adaptations of literary works feeds the curiosity and desire of viewers and can generate a flow of tourists. The visualization of literature through screen adaptation fits neatly with the ocularcentrism of the tourist. Thus tourists, who may, or may not, have read the book, will seek out literary landscapes and sites as represented on the screen. For those undertaking the adaptation of books, problems clearly exist in finding 'authentic' settings than can be used as locations. What emerges from the adaptation process are re-created places, effectively, new 'revealed' dimensions of the text, rewritings, and new 'extensions' to authorship. As Ellis (1982: 4) observes, 'adaptation trades upon the memory of the novel, a memory that can derive from actual reading, *or*, is more likely with a classic of literature, a generally circulated cultural memory' (quoted in Sheen 2000: 14).

In terms of literary tourism, 'generally circulated cultural memory' is increasingly a significant motivating factor for tourist visits and experiences. Perceptions of place are constructed not only through close reading of literature, but from decades of screen adaptations in 'general circulation', on film, on television, on video, on the front cover of television guides and as part of those everyday 'did you see?' conversations. Arguably then, society absorbs the imprecise location of 'The Cobb' (harbour wall) of the Dorset town of Lyme Regis, not so much through a reading of Jane Austen's *Persuasion*, or even John Fowles's *The French Lieutenant's Woman*, novels in which it features, but via its use as an authentic and faithful setting in the BBC film version of *Persuasion* in 1995 and from the image of Meryl Streep as Sarah

Woodruff walking a dramatic rainswept Cobb in Harold Pinter's 1981 screen adaptation of *The French Lieutenant's Woman*. The Cobb itself is an informal attraction for visitors, but the use of 'heritage' attractions, historic houses and castles in adaptations of nineteenth-century classic novels emerge almost as a genre in their own right and feed the tourism industry.

Inglis (2000*a*: 192), in recognizing the touristic legacy of the television dramatization of Evelyn Waugh's *Brideshead Revisited* in the early 1980s, speaks of the serial as 'an architectural education and a celebration of cultivated tourism such as Waugh would have despised, yet which he in much of his writing inaugurated'. Using Castle Howard in North Yorkshire as Waugh's Brideshead (although Waugh visited Castle Howard it is uncertain whether this corresponds directly to his idea of Brideshead), boosted tourism to the site, so much so that the owners, the Howard family, were able to fund renovations of the estate (Adams 2000).

This additional layered impact of adaptation upon the tourism–literature relationship continues to be recognized and exploited by the tourist, the tourism industry and indeed by those involved with the production and distribution of adaptations. J. K. Rowling's Harry Potter novels employ a mixture of real and imaginary places as story settings. The film version of *Harry Potter and the Philosopher's Stone* takes this a stage further and uses a variety of existing locations not in the book (mostly existing popular heritage attractions) including the National Trust's Lacock Abbey, Durham and Gloucester Cathedrals, and Alnwick Castle (Heptinstall 2001). None of these are specifically literary sites in themselves, aside from broad allusion, but their inclusion in the screen adaptation of the novel gives them a literary dimension.

There is a further dimension to the translation concept that resonates with the tourist, and that is the commodification of literature itself. Be they read as 'great' or 'niche', literary sites, museums, trails and the like, provide the best evidence of an increasingly accessible cultural form. Indeed, literary tourism is now part of a 'new' literacy. As tourists, the public now access and encounter writers and their works through guided tours, literary museums, heritage centres, festivals, theme parks, hotels with literary allusions, and a vast range of related merchandise. In these popular arenas of literary encounters, new audiences for creative writings are being forged, arguably reflecting new ways of story telling and a shift, not to back to the oral traditions whose passing was mourned by Benjamin (1936) and Ong (1982), but forward to a genesis of multi-media, hyper-sensory 'traditions'.

REFERENCES

Adams, M. (2000) *Movie Locations: A Guide to Britain and Ireland*. London: Boxtree.

Adorno, T. W. and Horkheimer, M. (1979) *Dialectic of Enlightenment*. London: Verso.

Akkerman, A. (2000) 'Harmonies of urban design and discords of city-form: urban aesthetics in the rise of western civilization', *Journal of Urban Design*, **5**(3), 267–90.

Alexander, C. (1994) *The Way to Xanadu*. London: Phoenix.

Allen, W. (1958) *The English Novel: A Short Critical History*. London: Penguin.

Andersen, H. C. (1996) 'The author at the museum', in M. Robinson, N. Evans and P. Callaghan (eds) *Culture as the Tourist Product*. Sunderland: Business Education Publishers, 5–32.

Anderson, B. (1983) *Imagined Communities*. London: Verso.

Ash, R. (1997) *The Top Ten of Everything*. New York: Dorling Kindersley.

Badaracco, C. H. (1995) *Trading Words: Poetry, Typography, and Illustrated Books in the Modern Literary Economy*. Baltimore: Johns Hopkins University Press.

Baloglu, S. and McCleary, K. W. (1999) 'A model of destination image formation', *Annals of Tourism Research*, **26**(4), 868–97.

Barthes, R. (1975) *The Pleasure of the Text*. New York: Hill and Wang.

Barthes, R. (1977) *Image, Music, Text*. (trans. Stephen Heath) London: Fontana.

Beahm, G. (1999) *Stephen King Country*. Philadelphia: Running Press.

Benjamin, W. (1936) 'The storyteller: reflections on the work of Nikolai Leskov', in H. Arendt (ed.) (1968) *Illuminations*. New York: Schocken Books, 83–109.

Benn, A. and Bartlett, R. (1997) *Literary Russia*. London: Picador.

Bergson, H. (1991) *Matter and Memory*. New York: Zone Books.

Betjeman, J. (1989) *John Betjeman Collected Poems*, 4th edn. London: John Murray.

Birch, B. P. (1981) 'Wessex, Hardy and the nature novelists', *Transactions of the Institute of British Geographers*, NS 6, 348–58.

Boorstin, D. J. (1963) *The Image: Or What Happened to the American Dream*. London: Penguin.

Bourdieu, P. (1993) *The Field of Cultural Production*. New York: Columbia University Press.

Bourdieu, P. and Passeron, J. C. (1977) *Reproduction in Education, Society and Culture*. London: Sage.

Bradbury, M. (1996) 'Dreams of empire', in M. Bradbury (ed.) *The Atlas of Literature*. London: De Agostini Editions, 148–51.

Brontë Society, the (1999) 'A visit to Haworth by Maria Lujan Tubio', *Brontë Student*, The Brontë Society, Issue No. 3, p. 3.

Buzard, J. (1993) *The Beaten Track: European Tourism, Literature and the Ways to 'Culture', 1800–1918*. Oxford: Oxford University Press.

Charters A. (1991) 'Introduction', in J. Kerouac, *On the Road*. London: Penguin, 1991 edn, viii–xxix.

Cohen, E. (1972) 'Towards a sociology of international tourism', *Social Research*, **39**(1), 64–82.

Cohen, E. (1979) 'A phenomenology of tourist experiences', *Sociology*, **13**, 179–201.

Cohen, E. (1993) 'The study of touristic images of native people: mitigating the stereotype of the stereotype', in D. Pearce and R. Butler (eds), *Tourism Research: Critiques and Challenges*. London: Routledge, 36–69.

Coleridge, S. T. (1817) *Biographia Literaria: Or, Biographical Sketches of my Literary Life and Opinions*. Oxford: Oxford University Press, 1907 edn.

Collins, R. (1990) *Culture, Communication and National Identity: The Case of Canadian Television*. Toronto: University of Toronto Press.

Colour Library Books (1989) *Great British Writers*. Godalming: Colour Library Books.

Coughlan, S. (1998) 'Goethe, Schiller and a slice of sausage', *The Times*, 25 July.

Crawford, R. (1997) 'Redefining Scotland', in S. Basnett (ed.), *Studying British Cultures*. London: Routledge, 83–96.

Cronin, M. (2000) *Across the Lines: Travel, Language, Translation*. Cork: Cork University Press.

Crystal, D. (1997) *English as a Global Language*. Cambridge: Cambridge University Press.

Culler, J. (1981) 'Semiotics of tourism', *American Journal of Semiotics*, 1, 127–40.

Currie, G. (1990) *The Nature of Fiction*. Cambridge: Cambridge University Press.

Daiches, D. and Flower, J. (1979) *Literary Landscapes of the British Isles: A Narrative Atlas*. London: Paddington Press.

Dalrymple, W. (1990) *In Xanadu: A Quest*. London: Flamingo.

Dann, G. S. (1996) *Tourism: A Socio-linguistic Analysis*. Wallingford: CAB International.

Dann, G. S. (1999) 'Writing out the tourist in space and time', *Annals of Tourism Research*, 26(1), 159–87.

Darby, P. (1998) *The Fiction of Imperialism: Reading Between International Relations and Postcolonialism*. London: Cassell.

Donald, J. (1993) 'How English is it?, Popular literature and national culture', in E. Carter, J. Donald and J. Squires (eds), *Space and Place: Theories of Identity and Location*. London: Lawrence & Wishart, 165–86.

Echtner, C. M. and Ritchie, B. (1993) 'The measurement of destination image: an empirical assessment', *Journal of Travel Research*. 31(4), 3–13.

Ellis, J. (1982) 'The literary adaptation: an introduction', *Screen*, 23(1), 4.

Escarpit, R. (1966) *The Book Revolution*. Paris: Harrap, UNESCO.

Escarpit, R. (1971) *Sociology of Literature*. London: Frank Cass.

Ewen, S. (1988) *All Consuming Images: The Politics of Style in Contemporary Culture*. New York: Basic Books.

Ezard, J. (2001) 'King and Country', *The Guardian*, 24 February.

Fakcyc, P. C. and Crompton, J. L. (1991) 'Image differences between prospective, first-time, and repeat visitors to the lower Rio Grande', *Journal of Travel Research*, 30(2), 10–16.

Foucault, M. (1974) *The Archaeology of Knowledge*. London: Tavistock.

Fowler, A. (1982) *Kinds of Literature*. Oxford: Oxford University Press.

Fowler, P. J. (1992) *The Past in Contemporary Society: Then, Now*. London: Routledge.

Fowler, P. J., Robinson, M. and Boniface, P. (2001) 'Pride and prejudice: two cultures and the north east's transition', in J. Tomaney and N. Ward (eds), *A Region in Transition*. London: Ashgate.

Fussell, P. (1980) *Abroad: British Literary Travelling Between the Wars*. Oxford: Oxford University Press.

Gartner, W. C. (1986) 'Temporal influences on image change', *Annals of Tourism Research*, 13, 635–44.

Gartner, W. C. (1989) 'Tourism image: attribute measurement of state tourism products using multidimensional scaling techniques', *Journal of Travel Research*, 28(2), 16–20.

Gartner, W. C. (1993) 'Image formation process', in M. Uysal and D. R. Fesenmaier (eds) *Communication and Channel Systems in Tourism Marketing*. New York: Haworth Press, 191–215.

Giddens, A. (1990) *The Consequences of Modernity*. Cambridge: Polity Press.

Giddings, R. and Sheen, E. (eds), (2000) *The Classic Novel: From Page to Screen*. Manchester: Manchester University Press.

Goody, J. (1977) *Domestication of the Savage Mind*. Cambridge: Cambridge University Press.

Goody, J. (1987) *The Logic of Writing and the Organization of Society*. Cambridge: Cambridge University Press.

Graburn, N. H. H. (1987) 'The evolution of tourist arts', *Annals of Tourism Research*, **11**(3), 393–420.

Graham, C. (2001) 'Blame it on Maureen O'Hara: Ireland and the trope of authenticity', *Cultural Studies*, **15**(1), 58–75.

Guinness (1999) *Guinness World Records*. Guinness World Records Limited.

Gunn, C. (1972) *Vacationscape: Designing Tourist Regions*. Austin: Bureau of Business Research, University of Texas.

Hall, J. N. (1993) 'Trollope's entry into Poets Corner in Westminster Abbey', *The New York Times Book Review*, March, 4.

Hannerz, U. (1989) 'Notes on the global ecumene', *Public Culture*, **1**(2), 66–75.

Hannerz, U. (1992) *Cultural Complexity*. New York: Columbia University Press.

Hannerz, U. (1996) *Transnational Connections*. London: Routledge.

Hardyment, C. (2000) *Literary Trails: Writers in Their Landscapes*. London: The National Trust.

Heidegger, M. (1962) *Being and Time*. Oxford: Blackwell.

Heptinstall, S. (2001) 'Harry Potter and the locations for hire', *The Mail on Sunday*, 11 February, 98–9.

Herbert, D. H. (2001) 'Literary places, tourism and the heritage experience', *Annals of Tourism Research*, **28**(2), 312–33.

Hoff, B. (1998) *The Tao of Pooh and the Te of Piglet*. London: Methuen.

Hoggart, R. (1957) *The Uses of Literacy: Aspects of Working-class Life*. London: Chatto & Windus.

Huggan, G. (2001) *The Post-Colonial Exotic: Marketing the Margins*. London: Routledge.

Hunt, J. D. (1975) 'Image as a factor in tourism development', *Journal of Travel Research*, **13**(3), 1–7.

Inglis, F. (1990) 'Landscape as popular culture', in S. Pugh (ed.), *Reading Landscape: Country–City–Capital*. Manchester: Manchester University Press, 197–213.

Inglis, F. (2000*a*) '*Brideshead Revisited* revisited: Waugh to the knife', in R. Giddings and E. Sheen (eds), *The Classic Novel, From Page to Screen*. Manchester: Manchester University Press, 179–96.

Inglis, F. (2000*b*) *The Delicious History of the Holiday*. London: Routledge.

Iser, W. (1974) *The Implied Reader: Patterns of Communication in Prose Fiction from Bunyan to Beckett*. Baltimore: Johns Hopkins University Press.

Iser, W. (1979) *The Act of Reading: A Theory of Aesthetic Response*. London: Routledge & Kegan Paul.

Iyer, P. (2000) *The Global Soul*. London: Bloomsbury.

Jakobson, R. (1960) 'Linguistics and poetics', in T. Sebeok (ed.), *Style in Language*. Cambridge, Mass.: MIT Press, 350–77.

Johnson, J. (2000) 'Literary geography: Joyce, Woolf and the city', *City*, **4**(2), 199–214.

Jordan, J. O, and Patten, R. L. (eds), (1995) *Literature in the Marketplace*. Cambridge: Cambridge University Press.

Kotler, P., Haider, D. H. and Rein, I. (1993) *Marketing Places: Attracting Investment, Industry and Tourism to Cities, States and Nations*. New York: The Free Press.

Kubo, K. (1998) *www.tooyoo.l.u-tokyo.ac.jp*

Lamont, C. (1987) 'The Romantic period 1780–1830', in P. Rogers (ed.), *The Oxford Illustrated History of English Literature*. Oxford: Oxford University Press.

Lee, J. A. (1976) *Lovestyles*. London: Dent.

Litrell, M. A. (1990) 'Symbolic significance of textile crafts for tourists', *Annals of Tourism Research*, **20**, 228–45.

Lodge, D. (1992) *The Art of Fiction*. London: Penguin.

Loselle, A. (1997) 'History's double: cultural tourism in twentieth-century French writing'. New York: St Martin's Press.

Lowenthal, L. (1984) *Literature and Mass Culture*. New Brunswick: Transaction Books.

MacCannell, D. (1976) *The Tourist*. New York: Schocken Books.

MacKay, K. J. and Fesenmaier, D. R. (1997) 'Pictorial element of destination in image formation', *Annals of Tourism Research*, **24**(3), 537–65.

McFarlane, B. (1996) *Novel to Film: An Introduction to the Theory of Adaptation*. Oxford: Clarendon Press.

Manguel, A. and Guadalupi, G. (2000) *The Dictionary of Imaginary Places*. San Diego: Harcourt Inc.

Marsh, K. (ed.) (1993) *Writers and their Houses*. London: Hamish Hamilton.

Martin-Barbero, J. (1993) *Communication, Culture and Hegemony: From the Media to Meditations*. London: Sage.

Meethan, K. (1996) 'Place, image and power: Brighton as a resort', in T. Selwyn (ed.), *The Tourist Image: Myths and Myth Making in Tourism*. Chichester: John Wiley, 179–96.

Miall, D. S. and Kuiken, D. (1998) *The Form of Reading: Empirical Studies of Literariness Poetics*. **25**, 327–41.

Miller, J. H. (1995) *Topographies*. Stanford: Stanford University Press.

Miller, L. (2001), *The Brontë Myth*. London: Jonathan Cape.

Milman, A. and Pizam, A. (1995) 'The role of awareness and familiarity with a destination: the central Florida case', *Journal of Travel Research*, **33**(3), 21–7.

Mintel Report (1999) *Books*, 01/05/99, Mintel International Group Limited.

Morely, D. and Robins, K. (1995) *Spaces of Identity: Global Media, Electronic Landscapes and Cultural Boundaries*. London: Routledge.

Moretti, F. (1988) *Signs Taken for Wonders: Essays in the Sociology of Literary Forms*. London: Verso.

Moretti, F. (1998) *Atlas of the European Novel 1800–1900*. London: Verso.

New, C. (1999) *Philosophy of Literature*. London: Routledge.

Ong, W. (1982) *Orality and Literacy: The Technologizing of the Word*. London: Methuen.

Ousby, I. (1990) *The Englishman's England*. Cambridge: Cambridge University Press.

Parker, M. (ed.), (1995) *The Hurt World*. Belfast: Blackstaff Press.

Parry, B. (1993) 'The content and discontents of Kipling's imperialism', in E. Carter, J. Donald and J. Squires (eds), *Space and Place: Theories of Identity and Location*. London: Lawrence and Wishart, 221–40.

Paterson, J. H. and Paterson, E. (1981) 'Shropshire: reality and symbol in the work of Mary Webb', in D.C.D. Pocock (ed.), *Humanistic Geography and Literature*. London: Croom Helm, 209–20.

Pearson, M. (1992) *Imagined Places: Journeys into Literary America*. Jackson: University Press of Mississippi.

Pelaschiar, L. (1998) *Writing the North: The Contemporary Novel in Northern Ireland*. Trieste: Edizioni Parnaso.

Pocock, D.C.D. (1978) 'The novelist and the north', Department of Geography, *University of Durham Occasional Publications*, (New Series) 12.

Pocock, D.C.D. (1979) 'The novelist's image of the north', *Transactions of the Institute of British Geographers*, NS 4, 62–76.

Price, S. (1996) 'Tourism and literary connections', in M. Robinson, N. Evans and P. Callaghan (eds), *Culture as the Tourist Product*. Sunderland: Business Education Publishers, 375–82.

Punter, D. (1997) 'Fictional maps of Britain', in S. Basnett (ed.), *Studying British Cultures*. London: Routledge, 65–80.

Richards, G. (ed.), (1996) *Cultural Tourism in Europe*. Wallingford: CAB International.

Richards, G. (ed.), (2001) *Cultural Attractions and European Tourism*. Wallingford: CAB International.

Robertson, R. (1992) *Globalization: Social Theory and Global Culture*. London: Sage.

Rojek, C. (1993) *Ways of Escape: Modern Transformations in Leisure and Travel*. Basingstoke: Macmillan.

Rojek, C. (2000) *Leisure and Culture*. Basingstoke: Macmillan.

Rose, J. (1998) 'The cult of celebrity', *London Review of Books*, **20**(16), 20 August, www.lrb.co.uk/v20n16/rose2016.htm.

Rothman, H. K. (1998) *Devil's Bargains: Tourism in the Twentieth-Century American West*. Lawrence: University Press of Kansas.

Ruck, A. (1997) 'On the trail of the lonesome parrot', *The Sunday Telegraph*, 8 June.

Said, E. W. (1980) *Orientalism*. London: Routledge & Kegan Paul.

Said, E. W. (1993) *Culture and Imperialism*. New York: Random House.

Salinger, M. (2000) *Dream Catcher*. London: Scribner.

Sardar, Z. (1999) *Orientalism*. Buckingham: Open University Press.

Seidel, M. (1991) *Robinson Crusoe: Island Myths and the Novel*. London: Twayne Publishers.

Sheen, E. (2000) ' "Where the garment gapes": faithfulness and promiscuity in the

1995 BBC *Pride and Prejudice*', in R. Giddings and E. Sheen (eds), *The Classic Novel, From Page to Screen*. Manchester: Manchester University Press, 14–30.

Shields, R. (1991) *Places on the Margin*. London: Routledge.

Smith, V. (ed.) (1989) *Hosts and Guests: The Anthropology of Tourism* (2nd edn), Pennsylvania: University of Pennsylvania Press.

Squire, S. (1988) 'Wordsworth and Lake District tourism: romantic reshaping of landscape', *Canadian Geographer*, **32**, 237–47.

Stern, L. (1997) '*Emma* in Los Angeles: *Clueless* as a remake of the book and the city', *Australian Humanities Review*, (7), August, www.lib.latrobe.edu.au/AHR/archive/Issue-August-1997/stern.html.

Stewart, L. (2000) *Erogenous Zones: An Anthology of Sex Abroad*. New York: Modern Library.

Synott, A. (1993) *The Body Social: Symbolism, Self and Society*. London: Routledge.

Tambling, J. (1995) *E. M. Forster: Contemporary Critical Essays*. Basingstoke: Macmillan.

The Bookseller (2000) 'Trade stats give mixed results', 3 November.

Tuan, Y. (1995) *Passing Strange and Wonderful: Aesthetics, Nature, and Culture*. New York: Kodansha Globe.

Tudor, A. (1997) 'Why horror? The peculiar pleasures of a popular genre', *Cultural Studies*. **11**(3), 443–63.

Varney, A. (1999) *Eighteenth Century Writers in their World*. Basingstoke: Macmillan.

Vattimo, G. (1992) *The Transparent Society*. Baltimore: Johns Hopkins University Press.

UNESCO (1998) *World Culture Report*. Paris: UNESCO.

Urry, J. (1995) *Consuming Places*. London: Routledge.

Urry, J. (2000) *Sociology Beyond Societies*. London: Routledge.

Wang, N. (1999) 'Rethinking authenticity in tourism experience', *Annals of Tourism Research*, **26**(2), 349–70.

Williamson, V. (2001) 'Re-reading Liverpool: literary tourism 1974–2001', paper presented at the Tourism: Environments, Conflicts, Identities and Histories Conference. University of Central Lancashire, UK, June 2001.

www.bookweb.org/research/stats

Chapter 3

'Inside' and 'Outside' Writings on Spain: Their Relationship to Spanish Tourism

Michael Barke

... wounded Spain, dressed up for carnival ...
(Antonio Machado)

INTRODUCTION: IS SPAIN 'DIFFERENT'?

Although written long before the arrival of mass tourism in Spain, Machado's caustic observation is representative of the response of many Spanish intellectuals to the way that significant parts of their country appeared to be usurped and potentially misrepresented, for the apparently frivolous purpose of tourism promotion. Yet, even the best informed of commentators could be forgiven for thinking that there is no immediately obvious relationship between Spanish literature, literature on Spain and the modern tourism phenomenon in that country. Spain is one of the world's main tourist destinations with an estimated 51.7 million visitors in 1999. Ostensibly, it does seem rather difficult to find a connection between the two phenomena of 'tourism' and 'literature' in Spain, principally because of the nature of the former. Spanish tourism is dominated still by mass, coastal tourism to the Balearic Islands, the Canaries and the coasts of Catalonia, Valencia and Andalucía. Given the nature of this tourist demand, it is all too easy to make the assumption that the literature of Spain has little to do with tourists' presence in that country.

Yet, alongside the 'sun, sea and sand' mass-tourism phenomenon, Spain is characterized by many other forms of tourism experience and that diversification has been a feature of recent years (Barke *et al.* 1996). Alongside the large numbers of foreign visitors an increasing number of Spanish people are exploring their own country more than ever before. Perhaps related to this is the fact that the diversification of tourism includes a much greater and explicit exploitation of the country's cultural heritage (Vera Rebollo and Dávila Linares 1995; Bote Gómez 1998). As part of that legacy, Spain does possess an undeniably great literary heritage (Priestley

1960) with early and highly original contributions to the development of the novel as a literary form, including what has been claimed to be the first European novel – *La Celestina* (1499) – (Brenan 1965; Chandler and Schwartz 1991), a rich dramatic tradition and a wealth of poetry in epic, narrative and lyrical styles, including the 3,731 verses of *Cantar de Mio Cid*, thought to date from 1140. Moreover, it has been claimed that Spanish literature has a distinctive character:

> ' ... this pungent national flavour [is] one of its chief charms. Behind every book we read, we feel not so much a new author as the pulse of a strange and peculiar society. For of all the European literatures Spanish is the most homogeneous. The popular poetry of the village, still being made and sung today, drifts like smoke into the brains of the cultured writers.' (Brenan 1951, quoted in Gathorne-Hardy 1992: 393)

The latter point may help to explain one of the curious features of the relationship of literature to tourism in Spain. Despite its rich literary heritage, much of it as we shall see 'place specific', there is little recognition of this resource by the tourist authorities and little is made of it in tourist promotion terms. For example, Spain has no real equivalent of Stratford upon Avon or Haworth, West Yorkshire. What makes this absence even more curious is the fact that the same observation does not apply to the visual arts where Spain possesses world-famous museums such as the Prado and numerous sites of artistic pilgrimage, ranging from Dali's museum at Figueras, El Greco's house in Toledo, and Gaudi's architectural creations in Barcelona. Spain has six cities which UNESCO has rated as World Heritage sites. A recent review of the rapid recent growth of cultural tourism in Spain makes no mention of the role played by literature or the literary heritage (Maiztegui-Oñate and Areitio Bertolín, 1996). One of the reasons for this is that what conventionally passes as 'literature' in other societies, and is usually associated with 'high culture', is accepted as the norm and in some senses as unremarkable in Spain. Authors as different in character and chronology as Augustus Hare (1873) and Gerald Brenan (1965) have commented upon this phenomenon. Some aspects of what elsewhere would be regarded as part of conventional 'literary' culture, especially poetry, are probably more 'alive' and part of a vernacular tradition than in most other parts of Europe. Poetry competitions and poetry readings at village fiestas are commonplace. Traditionally, the media has also played a different role in Spain than in many other countries and, in the past, it has been claimed that 'newspapers are the main organs of intellectual distribution and exchange' (De Madariaga 1942: 97). Important literary figures such as Azorín, Valle-Inclán, Benavente and Unamuno were central to this process in that they were major contributors who were widely read (De Madariaga 1942: 97). Thus, the fact that library usage is extremely low (Hooper 1995) does not mean that 'literature' plays no part in cultural or social life for the majority of people. One explanation for this is that some forms of 'literature' are actually more integrated into social life than in many other countries.

In addition to the distinctive national literature of novels, plays and, above all, poetry, Spain is one of the most written about countries in non-fiction. It has generated an immense 'travel literature', with contributions from both native Spaniards and, especially, from foreign visitors (Dendle 1996; Guerrero 1990; Rubow 1985; Vincent 1992). Therefore, another sense in which Spain may be argued to be 'different' concerns the way in which so many visitors feel impelled to write about it. Much of this writing is of rather indifferent quality but some of it is very good indeed. The output ranges from what many commentators regard as some of the best travel books ever written, for example, Richard Ford's *Handbook for Travellers in Spain* (1845), Laurie Lee's *As I Walked Out One Midsummer Morning* (1969), or Cees Nooteboom's *Roads to Santiago* (1997) through the many banal and frankly boring descriptions of yet another visit to the Alhambra Palace, Granada, to the self-consciously 'laddish' account of hedonistic pursuits on the Costa del Sol contained in Ritchie's *Here We Go* (1993).

But there is yet another sense in which Spain may be argued to be 'different'. Travel and exploration have always excited romantic notions about other cultures and environments. Spain is not alone in producing this effect but few other countries have persistently done so for so long, against the background of a rapidly changing socioeconomic climate and associated tourism structure. The origins and reality of 'romantic Spain' have long been debated by academics but such discourses are rooted firmly in literary criticism (Aymes 1983; Flitter 1992; Hoffman 1961; Peers 1940). However, a fundamental issue in this debate relates to the question of whether or not 'Spanish romanticism' was superimposed from 'outside' or generated from 'within'. V. S. Pritchett (1954), for example, has claimed that 'romantic Andalucía', at least, was an invention of the French, a view that has been widely accepted (Mitchell 1990). However, it will be argued here that the relationship between 'inside' and 'outside' writing is considerably more subtle than this 'superimposition' thesis and is manifest in the changing interactions between the two sources. For example:

> When foreign travellers approached Spain they perceived its traditionalism, producing an image of endurance, staticism, fixity and continuity which *seeped back into Spain* [my emphasis] through the ... descriptions by Byron and Gautier, and the first Romantic histories of Spanish literature ... (Saglia 1997: 141).

Spanish culture did then, come to be shaped, not only by its own 'internal' traditions but by its own reaction to the 'external' representation of that culture (Alvarez Junco and Shubert 2000). One such reaction is, of course, to attempt to reappropriate one's own culture, a continuing war waged by Spanish intellectuals such as Antonio Machado. Another reaction is to use such external representations for one's own ends. Arguably, this is precisely what happened when 'Spain is different', 'the tourism slogan devised by the Franco regime in the 1960s, made explicit reference to many of the characteristics of Spanish civilization generated by Romantic exoticism' (Ibid.: 127). At the same time, the slogan and campaign could be legitimized by references to the images of Spain popularized by Gautier, Mérimee, Victor Hugo, Washington Irving and many more. Although the superstructure of modern mass tourism in Spain was built around sun, sea, sand, ease of modern travel, the convenience of the 'package' and relative cheapness, the substructure relied heavily on a set of images which stretched back into Spanish literary history and external writings about Spain. Thus, literary images of Spain were used to support the view expressed by J. B. Trend (1928) that 'Spain is not only a geographical expression; it is a country of the mind' (p. 215).

Therefore, despite the easy assumption that the links between tourism and literature in Spain are, at best, tenuous and possibly of limited significance, such an impression cannot go unchallenged. This chapter will argue that only the most superficial of readings of the relationship between tourism and literature would lead one to conclude that the former has nothing to do with the latter. Although complex and subtle, such relationships do exist (Cohen 1979), and it will be demonstrated that literary images and communications, both factual and fictional, have had considerable impact upon the tourism phenomenon in Spain, albeit often in an indirect fashion. In this sense, as in many others, Spain may be argued to be, as yet, 'different' to many other countries. It is different in that, from the 'inside', its literary tradition is a 'live' and active one and this colours the way that tradition may be used for external purposes. It is different in that, from the 'outside', many of those who visit it feel impelled to write about it.

The chapter will begin by examining the relationship between tourism and literature at a theoretical level and this will lead into an identification of the various categories of literary representation that may be recognized. Some of the more significant sites of literary pilgrimage in Spain will then be identified and an account given of their development. This will be followed by an examination of a particular category of literature of especial significance in Spain – travel literature.

THE DIALECTIC BETWEEN 'TOURISM' AND 'LITERATURE'

In one sense the phenomena of 'tourism' and 'literature' may be defined as lying at opposite ends of a conceptual spectrum but, in another sense, that apparent gap helps to explain the close relationship that in reality exists between the two. Tourism is essentially concerned with consumption, including the means of travel, accommodation and sustenance. Over and above this, however, it is also concerned, in a variety of ways – some straightforward and some complex – with the consumption of place (Urry 1995). As tourism is a leisure activity, to be distinguished as much as possible from everyday 'work' and routine activity, the environments in which it is mainly pursued require specific characteristics, characteristics which signal to the individual or group that what is being experienced is different from the 'everyday' (Mannell and Iso-Ahola 1987). This difference may be manifest at a variety of levels, including the very obvious such as weather, scenery or 'exotic' cultures but may also be apparent in much more subtle and individualistic ways.

However, whilst tourism is about consumption, literature is essentially concerned with various forms of representation, including representation of place. In both fictional and non-fictional literature, the act of writing usually involves contextualizing what is being written, whether it be individual characters, relationships, action scenes or places themselves. So, not only is something being literally represented but, in order for the reader to make some sense of what is being written about, context is required. It would only be in the more extreme forms of surrealist literature, where the alleged beauty or other impact of the language used was an end in itself that such context would not be necessary. Place, either in terms of a specific description or in an attempt to convey a 'sense of place', forms one of the key, recurrent contexts for much literature, even for literature which ostensibly is not specifically concerned with 'place' as such. However, the very act of representation is also an act of production. In other words, an image – in this case a literary image – is being fashioned and in a sense, therefore, 'place' or a 'sense of place' is being produced. Whilst it is often the case that representations of 'place' may tell us more about the author(s) than about the place itself (Duncan and Gregory 1999; Said 1993), whether the literary output is an authentic representation of a 'real' place or not is beside the point as there is much about 'place' that has to be imagined anyway. Even the most detailed, factual written description of a place, whether it be in terms of climate, economic trends, architectural structures, quality of hotels, etc. requires an act of imagination on the part of the reader. Much literature does, of course, provide the reader with important signposts in order to assist the process of imagining, but there never can be an exact, one-to-one correspondence between the objective 'reality' of a place, how that 'reality' was experienced by the author, and how it is then conveyed to the reader. Even the most fact-based account of social realism is 'both revealing and transforming' (Herzberger 1991: 171). By conveying something in literary form an act of production has been engaged in, as that 'reality' is being conveyed in a more or less different form for the consumption of the reader, and is then still further subject to the interpretative skills and predispositions of the reader. Thus, whilst consumption and production are very different activities, the one obviously relates very closely to the other for, not only does production allow consumption to take place, but the nature of what is produced or represented is also significant for the nature of consumption.

Implied in the argument so far is the assumption that (amongst other things) literature (broadly defined) helps to 'create' tourism, in the sense that representation can create curiosity or demand for travel. But, quite clearly, the relationship could be the other way, as the tourist experience or the travel experience may stimulate the act of writing. One of the most famous British writers on Spain, Richard Ford, did not set out to write his *Handbook for Travellers in Spain* (1845) when he went there in 1830. In fact, he went to Spain because of his wife's delicate health and only came to write 'one of the best books of travel written in the English language' (Gilbert 1945: 151) over ten years later, when asked over dinner by the publisher John Murray who would be a suitable author to write on Spain to add to a series of travel handbooks for European countries (Okey 1906; Murray 1889). Ford jocularly replied that he could do it himself. Although some writers, V. S. Pritchett for example, have had specific commissions to write on Spain, there are many other examples of literary output which have been stimulated by the visit. One of the greatest of Hispanists, Gerald Brenan, did not set out to write about Spain but was impelled to write his major works out of perceived economic necessity (Gathorne-Hardy 1992; Price 2000).

We need to consider, therefore, the various forms of literary representation and production in order to tease out some of the ways in which these works may be of significance in the context of tourism in Spain. Three broad categories of writer may be identified as a starting point for this process. First there is a group of authors who do not, specifically, set out to write about 'place' at all but who, through their significance within the literary canon or their 'greatness', actually add meaning to place. This may be through the simple fact of being born in a particular place or, more likely, having lived there for a significant period of time. For this group, 'place' is an essentially passive entity and relates simply to an association between a specific location and an author. Others, of course, may wish to read into and attempt to find various meanings in the fact that author 'x' lived in place 'y' and seek to establish influences, especially of the latter upon the former's work, but the key point is that there has not necessarily been any self-conscious attempt on the part of the author to represent or 'produce' a specific place in her/his work. Despite this, the place associated with the author becomes a 'pilgrimage' destination because of such associations.

For a second category of writers, however, 'place' is central to their work in that they quite deliberately and specifically set out to represent place or to capture the spirit of place. This may be in the foreground of the literary output, for example, in a poem about a particular piece of landscape, or, as in the case of Hardy's Wessex novels or a book such as *Wuthering Heights*, an essential part of the background. In either case, the writer is seeking to create or capture an indelible memory for the reader in relation to a specific location. Such representations may be at a variety of scales, ranging from a specific and limited viewpoint, a street, village, town or city, a region or possibly even the whole of a country. The main point, however, is that in this category of literary output the writer's main, although not necessarily sole, purpose is to present a description or analysis, or even to create myths about one or more specific places (Shields 1991).

The third category of writer to identify relates to those authors whose output is concerned more particularly with travel, a journey or with several journeys. Frequently, such accounts also contain descriptions of specific places and therefore this group may overlap with the previous one and the difference in some cases may appear to be one of degree rather than kind. However, although the relationship may be close, describing travel or a journey is not the same as describing a specific place and there is no doubt that travel writing *per se* is a distinctive genre of literature (Duncan and Gregory 1999). As we shall see, this is particularly the case in the Spanish context. These three categories of literary output therefore provide a simple typology through which the relations of literature and tourism may be examined. However, two further elements need to be added to the typology in order to recognize additional and potentially important dimensions of the relationship. Each of these three categories may also take the form of fictional or non-fictional output. Although the difference between these two is fundamental in a literary sense, the distinction may be less important in its relation to tourism. Tourist motives may be stimulated by real or fictional events, people or places, and the end product is the desire to go somewhere to see, experience or associate with a phenomenon one has read about, whether it is 'real' or not. A rather more important differentiation relates to the nature of 'inside' or 'outside' writings, that is, the writers who excite interest may be indigenous or non-Spanish. This is important, as the two are likely to 'speak' to different markets and produce very different emotions. This, in turn, has important implications for the way in which the sites of such associations are handled and marketed.

SITES OF LITERARY PILGRIMAGE

We now turn to examine more directly the links between tourism and literature, firstly, through an examination of the process of creating literary 'shrines', sites and locations that have subsequently become 'tourist attractions'. Our first category of writers concerned those who, without specifically intending to write about 'place' have, through their fame and contributions to the literary canon, come to be associated with particular localities.

Although born in Bilbao in 1869, Miguel de Unamuno y Jugo spent most of his career in Salamanca (1900–36) where he became a professor of philosophy and rector of the university. Unamuno has become intimately associated with the city, not through any attempts to represent it in fictional or factual writings (although, of course, he did write about the city and especially Castile) but through his position as a leading European intellectual at one particular event. Unamuno was a philosopher, essayist, poet, dramatist and novelist and a leading figure of the group of young writers who came to be known as the 'Generation of 1898'. Although often working independently, they examined the contemporary condition of Spain and found it wanting. Their impact within Spain was heightened by the negative reaction to the nineteenth-century decay of their country and the humiliating war with the United States and Cuba (Shaw 1973). Although originally, if reluctantly, accepting the Franco uprising, in 1936 Unamuno launched a spectacular verbal attack on the nationalist militarism represented by General Millán Astray at a major public occasion at Salamanca University and lived under house arrest for the rest of his life (Thomas 1977). This episode added to his fame and is recounted in almost every travel-book's account of Salamanca, enhancing the association between the writer and the city and, in the post-Franco period, giving the latter a symbolic significance as the location of at least one intellectual's opposition to the regime.

Unamuno was a profoundly religious individual but was probably surpassed in this respect by St Teresa de Jesús (1515–82) who eventually took the very name of the Castilian town and province where she lived – Avila. St Teresa had no literary pretensions, wrote in an essentially autobiographical style and her output consists of mystical works, some poems and a large collection of letters. Yet, she is consistently acclaimed for the beauty and simplicity of her style, 'uncorrupted by the literary language' (Brenan 1965: 166) and, as a result of her impact upon the Catholic faith, has turned Avila (with all its other attractions, Plate 1) into a significant centre of tourist pilgrimage (Tomillo Noguero 1995) with a substantial impact upon other writers:

> No one should speak or tread loudly so as not to disturb the spirit of the sublime
> Teresa . . . everybody should feel weak in this city of formidable force . . . (García Lorca,
> *Avila*, 1987: 11)

The new drive to diversify tourism in Spain, and especially to promote the attractions of the interior, have inevitably led to specific promotional campaigns. Between September 1995 and May 1996, Avila was the location for a special exhibition on *Castillo Interior, Teresa de Jesús y el siglo XVI* specifically associated with the Cathedral and its connection with the life and work of St Teresa. This promotion is

Plate 1 Avila

estimated to have generated 250,000 visitors (Troitiño Vinuesa 1998) and produced an increase in hotel occupation levels in the province of between 75 and 100 per cent (Tomillo Noguero 1995: 645).

A recent literary guide to Spain (Caba 1990) has twenty-five main sections, twenty-four of them devoted to famous Spanish writers and the regions in which they lived. The twenty-fifth section is devoted entirely to a fictional character – Don Quixote – but is dealt with in exactly the same way as if he had been a living person, in that various routes and places associated with him are described. This does no more than acknowledge what many other authors have noted – that, for many people, Don Quixote *was* a real person (Azorín 1966; Wyndham Lewis 1962), 'and the figures of Don Quixote and Sancha Panza have attained a life of their own quite independent of the book they first appeared in' (Riley 1992: xii). Indeed, Nooteboom (1997) has observed of *Don Quixote* that 'The author is the one who is imagined, his characters are real' (p. 95). It is certainly the case that 'pilgrimages' to the various locations associated with the story – Alcázar de San Juan, Argamasilla de Alba, Campo de Criptana, El Toboso (Plate 2), Mota del Cuervo, Puerto Lápice, Ruidera and Tomelloso– have been made by many writers and others. In the light of the world-wide interest in Cervantes and his work, it is remarkable that the Don Quixote 'industry' remains so restrained within the region where the adventures were set, being restricted to a small museum at El Toboso. However, there is no doubt that the region holds a special significance for many people and not just for literary scholars. Many of the writings of those who have followed Don Quixote's footsteps demonstrate the influence of the story and the place in which it is set, both in prompting

Plate 2   El Toboso

meditations on the nature of reality and illusion and, often related, a process of self-examination (Azorín 1966; Jacobs 1994; Wollaston 1990).

Not all authors have been as consistently accepted as part of the Spanish genius as Cervantes. The Spanish Civil War saw the exile or death of many members of what had been one of the most brilliant of European cultural generations. The years since the death of Franco have seen revived interest in many of these individuals and, in the present context, one of the most significant is Federico García Lorca (1898–1936). As the fear engendered throughout the Franco years has gradually receded, the places associated with the poet and dramatist in and around Granada have come to be significant sites of interest for both Spanish and non-Spanish visitors. A small museum in Lorca's birthplace in Fuente Vaqueros in the Vega of Granada has recently been augmented by the opening of the rehabilitated Huerta San Vicente on the outskirts of Granada by the Fundacion Federico García Lorca (Plate 3). The refurbished former residence now forms a significant location in the Granada city authority's attempt to diversify cultural tourism away from its concentration on the Alhambra (Troitiño Vinuesa *et al.* 1998). The case of Lorca is particularly interesting in the context of 'inside' and 'outside' writings about Spain as it was the latter which resolved the mystery of his death, and which also added a sense of high drama and tragedy to the Lorca story. These features helped to popularize the story and generate what has almost become a 'Lorca-industry' including a popular guide providing a series of itineraries to the places within the city associated with the poet (Gibson 1992). The mystery of Lorca's death and the subsequent attempts to 'cover up' the truth have been brilliantly explored in Ian Gibson's *The Assassination of*

Plate 3 Huerta San Vicente, Granada, the residence of the Lorca family

Federico García Lorca (1979), although Gibson himself generously acknowledges his debt to Gerald Brenan who, on his return to Spain in 1949, set out to discover the burial place of Lorca and became convinced that, in contrast to the various 'official' versions, he had been killed and buried at Viznar in the hills to the north east of the city (Brenan 1950). Thus, although Spanish literary critics can complain with some justification that too many external writings on their country have served to perpetuate a series of romantic myths and 'fake' images of picturesqueness, here we have a case where external writings uncovered the truth and helped restore a great writer to his proper position in Spain's modern cultural history.

It is not just native Spanish writers who have, unwittingly, produced a tourist 'honeypot' simply through having lived in a place for a number of years. Amongst foreign writers, two residents of Mallorca, although with very different perspectives and resident for very different lengths of time, may be cited – George Sand (Baroness Aurore de Dudevant) and Robert Graves. George Sand came to Mallorca in 1838 and settled in the village of Valldemosa for two months with her subsequently rather more famous lover, Frederic Chopin. Their stay was not a happy one and Sand was extremely unpopular but, as we shall see below, in the next century this did not stop the creation of a series of myths for marketing purposes. Robert Graves moved to Deyá in 1929 and lived there until his death in 1986, with a ten-year period of 'exile' during and subsequent to the Civil War (Graves 1995). Graves was later to lament the massive impact of tourism upon the island but almost certainly never realized that his own legacy could become a part – albeit small and for a highly selective group – of the potential tourist experience, with readers keen to explore the site of literary inspiration: 'From the early Fifties on, Deyá gained a reputation for being an artist's colony, with Father as its doyen' (Graves 1995: 137). It was no coincidence that Dowling College's Mediterranean Institute, specializing in the humanities and creative writing, was located near the village, with Robert Graves giving occasional talks and poetry readings, and his son describes how day coach trips from Palma would slow down as they passed the village to be informed 'At your left is olive tree of one thousand years old, at your right is house of famous English writer, Mister Robertson, who wrote *Me, Claudio.*' (p. 136).

LITERATURE AND THE REPRESENTATION OF PLACE

The second group of writers, both native and foreign, concern those who quite deliberately set out to describe or analyse specific locations. The scale may vary considerably ranging from attempts to capture the essence of the nation, through the rather more common expressions of regionalism, specific cities and the numerous literary evocations of village and rural life. The relationship of this output to tourism may be direct, as described in the previous section, or – more frequently – indirect. Outcomes may also be quite different from those originally intended by the author. However, literary evocations of place, at whatever scale, may inspire the reader to explore or help to 'prepare' the tourist by providing a set of expectations or even an itinerary. The latter may relate to much more than travel routes and be concerned with an 'emotional' and 'experiential' itinerary. Quite obviously, not all representations of place lead to a desire to visit and some representations may be positive deterrents. However, in both factual and fictional writing, the description of particular incidents, of natural and man-made beauty, the skill of the author in conveying particular characteristics or romantic associations can all induce the desire to want to go and see. It may be that an atmosphere is created at the national scale as, for example, in the many writings on 'romantic' Spain, epitomized by Théophile Gautier's *A Romantic In Spain* and Prosper Mérimée's *Carmen and Other Stories* or the more sober and analytical tone of Angel Ganivet's elegant essay 'Idearium Espanol', written initially in 1897 (Ganivet 1946), exploring the 'Spanish condition', a task that has been frequently repeated although in more empirical fashion, by foreign writers such as John Hooper (1995).

However, we need to consider the extent to which literary representations of the world, or in this context Spain, are, in Roland Barthes's phrase 'agents of blindness' (quoted in Duncan and Duncan 1992). At one level the answer must be 'yes' as it would be naïve to assume that 'writing is the equivalent of doing and that words stand equal to the objects they name' (Herzberger 1991: 157). Yet, in many ways, this is rather a sterile debate as one of the purposes of literature is to throw a more intense light on the phenomena in question and, given the above quote from Barthes, somewhat ironically, this may mean quite legitimately ignoring part of 'reality', exaggerating another part, dramatizing specific events and so on. The key issues are the purposes of the literature and the critical faculties which the reader brings to it.

Intellectuals such as Barthes are perhaps too inclined to assert a monopolistic claim on the nature of 'reality' and, again ironically, make élitist assumptions about how literary representations will be interpreted. Thus, his objection that 'besides pictur-esque scenery, only monuments are extolled' (Duncan and Duncan 1992: 21) in the Hachette *Blue Guide* to Spain seems a little odd – the book is, after all, a tourist guide!

Nevertheless, some circumstances of Spanish history may lead to systematic ten-dencies in place representation, some of which may acquire mythical status. This is perhaps best seen in the context of Spanish regionalism which has tended to produce a creative tension – manifested in literature as much as in politics (and, indeed, the two are very often interlinked in Spain more than in any other European country (Kern 1995)) – between the regions and the centre, the 'centre' often being repre-sented as Castile. The specific forms of this regionalism are yet more important components of Spanish 'difference'. Yet, even here, and in spite of the complaints of critics such as Barthes, it is surely unrealistic to expect texts to be an exact mirror of the world as it is (Barnes and Duncan 1992) and, in any case, 'all discourse shapes and defines – rather than reflects – the nature of meaning' (Herzberger 1991: 165). In the celebration of Spanish regionalism there is an inevitable tendency to examine or present 'difference' at a heightened emotional level. This may produce great writing which also serves to excite interest and curiosity and whose purpose is to exacerbate 'difference'. A further key feature of this phenomenon in the present context is that such expressions of regionalism, although frequently censored in the past, are widely celebrated at public events such as festivals and poetry competitions. The late nineteenth-century revival of Catalan had a literary resurgence as a fundamental component and included specific cultural events such as poetry competitions, for example the *Jocs Florals* popularized by the writer Victor Balaguer (1824–1901). Influential Catalan writers such as Jacint Verdaguer (1845–1902) and Joan Maragall (1860–1911) participated in such events. In the north-west, two female writers are widely credited with evoking the spirit of Galicia and promoting the *Rexurdimento*, a regional literary revival with strong Celtic influences (Alvarez Junco and Shubert 2000). Rosalía de Castro (1837–85) wrote poetry in both Gallego and Castilian whilst Emilia Pardo Bazán (1851–1921), although writing in Castilian, brilliantly captured the essence of provincial Galician life in a series of novels as well as the non-fictional *Cuentos de la Tierra*. The essayist Blas Infante is often credited with being a central figure in the development of Andalucían regionalist sentiment and specifying a peculiarly Andalucían cultural heritage, including literature (Kern, 1995).

However, not all literary figures with origins in the regions of Spain felt it necessary to struggle against the centre. Antonio Machado was born in Seville in 1875 but 'came to incorporate in his verse, as no poet had ever done before, the ascetic spirit of Castile' (Brenan 1965: 430), especially in his *Campos de Castilla*:

¡Oh tierra ingrata y fuerte, tierra mía!
¡Castilla, tus decrépitas ciudades!
¡La agria melancolía
que puebla tus sombrías soledades!

¡Castilla varonil, adusta tierra,
Castilla del desdén contra la suerte,
Castilla del dolor y de la guerra,
tierra inmortal, Castilla de la muerte!

Machado was a provincial schoolmaster, working in Soria, Baeza and Segovia and the continuing popularity of his poetry has as much to do with his analysis of the ills of Spain in the early part of the twentieth century as with his evocation of the atmosphere and landscape of its central heartland although the two were often combined in his work. Although Machado was anything but a 'romantic' poet in the traditional sense, his use of landscape to 'exteriorize his own memories and hopes and the Spain of the late nineteenth and early twentieth centuries for which he grieves' (Hutman 1969: 38) together with his recurrent nostalgia and disgust with the present appear, to modern readers, to be essentially romantic concerns. This is one reason why the impact of the same writer may be quite different in different contexts. A writer who speaks as a 'realist' to one generation may speak as a 'romantic' to another, rather like *Don Quixote*, which 'has been read and re-read differently in every century since its first appearance' (Riley 1992: xvi).

Another Andalucían 'exile' for much of his life was Juan Ramón Jiménez (1881–1958) who won the Nobel Prize for literature in 1956. However, in his prose poem *Platero y Yo*, Jiménez captured the spirit of life in the small Andalucían village of Moguer in Huelva province and, by implication, life in a thousand similar villages. Moguer is 'an obligatory destination for anyone seriously interested in Juan Ramón's works' (Jacobs 1990: 208), quotations from his work are recorded on ceramics throughout the village and his house is much visited by Spaniards (Epton 1968).

Both Machado and Jiménez, in their different ways, captured the spirit of place of two areas varying considerably in size and character but, in some senses, their work has been appropriated and has become (albeit on a relatively small scale) central in local cultural tourism industries. Machado's brief, three-year marriage to Leonor was celebrated in his poetry after her death from tuberculosis. The sense of tragic romance was heightened by the fact that she was a sixteen-year-old girl when they met and he was thirty-four. In Soria especially, 'The associations with Machado have been exploited to the full, with the poet's name constantly linked to that of Leonor ... the "*Parador Nacional Antonio Machado*" ... looks out towards another hill crowned by the Hotel Leonor' (Jacobs 1994: 378). The early death of his wife has undoubtedly contributed additional romantic appeal to the association between poet and place. Similarly, in Segovia, where Machado spent his last years in Spain before fleeing to France at the start of the Civil War, his residence has been turned into a *Casa-Museo Machado*, although whether or not the museum is the actual site of his house is disputed, with some local residents claiming that the authorities simply chose the prettiest house in the street (p. 380). Although there is no such dispute over the Jiménez museum in Moguer (Patronato de Turismo de Huelva 1995), the poet actually spent most of his life in Madrid or abroad.

Not surprisingly, Madrid has functioned as Spain's main literary centre from its inauguration as national capital, and the city has been associated with many of Spain's great writers, from Lope de Vega (1562–1635), regarded as the founder of

Spanish drama, the poet/novelist Francisco Quevedo y Villegas (1580–1645), Pedro Calderón de la Barca (1600–81) who also helped to establish *zarzuelas* as a popular form of musical comedy, and the novelist Benito Pérez Galdós (1843–1920), sometimes compared to Dickens, who based many of his themes on Madrid life, most notably *Fortunata y Jacinta* and whose various accounts of the city and its districts have themselves turned into something of a tourist trail, the *Madrid galdosiano* (Esteban 1990). More recently, Arturo Barea (1897–1957) captured the atmosphere of the poorer areas of Madrid in his brilliant autobiography. Whilst it would be untrue to claim that this literary heritage matches the visual arts in making Madrid one of the most visited cities in Spain, it has at least two significant manifestations. One is the continuing role of the capital's legendary, intellectual 'café life' (Thomas, 1988), dominated by writers and ironically parodied but indirectly celebrated in Camilo José Cela's *La Colmena* (1951), a society to which aspiring writers and other intellectual 'hangers-on' wish to belong. The second is the continuous celebration of the lives and works of many writers, a phenomenon noted by James Michener (1968):

> Wherever I went I saw placards announcing grand assemblies of *Homenaje a . . .* Benito Pérez Galdós or Vicente Blasco Ibáñez or Pío Baroja. I attended three such *homenajes* to writers, and they were moving affairs at which men rose to give orations the like of which I had not heard for fifty years. All aspects of the life and writings of the man in question were reviewed and true homage was paid to him as a continuing cultural force. In the parks I found statues to these writers and in the newspapers a constant series of essays on their significance. (Michener 1968: 569–70).

This is just one of the many ways in which Spain is different, in that it emphasizes how literature and literary manifestations are perhaps more 'alive', and the 'gap' between so-called 'high' and 'popular' culture' is less pronounced than in many other European countries.

It is not only Spaniards, however, who have helped to communicate and represent different parts of Spain to an external audience. Many foreign writers have also done so and, in so doing, created curiosity and interest and acted as catalysts for travel and exploration and, arguably, for the more structured phenomenon of tourism. Many of these writers describe journeys and these will be introduced as a separate category below, but some foreign writers have essayed vivid accounts of specific places. Arguably, one of the most significant of these in the twentieth century was Gerald Brenan's portrait of 1920s life in the Alpujarran village of Yegen in *South from Granada* (1954), the book which 'finally confirmed him as the finest English writer on Spain this century' (Gathorne-Hardy 1992: 432). 'All other foreigners who write about Spain are outside; Gerald is inside' (ibid, p. 434). As we shall see below, although he almost certainly would not have wished it so, the development of tourism as a major alternative rural economic activity in the Alpujarras owes much to Brenan's writing. Although concerned with a period twenty years later, Norman Lewis's *Voices of the Old Sea* (1984), proceeds from a similar conviction that the true essence of Spain is (or was) to be found in the villages, a view that, according to Michael Jacobs (1994), was unlikely to have been shared by nineteenth-century writers on Spain or, indeed, despite his reputation as a 'poet of the people', by

Antonio Machado (Brown 1972: 74). Lewis provides a witty account of life in a Catalan village on the eve of mass-tourism development but the supreme irony, of course, is that his account of the place and the idiosyncrasies of its people help to provide the very foundation upon which a tourist industry can start to be built. Brenan in particular has had many would-be imitators on the autobiographical, 'going to live in Spain', or more particularly, Andalucía, theme. Shirley Deane provides an account of settling in Nerja just after the Civil War in *Tomorrow is Mañana* (1957), and Levy's *Spanish Mountain Life* (1950) is on the same theme in the Alpujarras. More recent descriptions of village life are Albert Rowe's *Untouched by Time* (1998) in the Almerian Alpujarras, Hugh Seymour-Davies's *The Bottlebrush Tree* (1988) on the Axarquía region of Malaga province, and Andrew and Lesley Grant-Adamson's Alpujarras-based *A Season in Spain* (1995). The recent remarkable success of Chris Stewart's *Driving Over Lemons* (1999) (set, yet again, in the Alpujarras, near Orgiva) on much the same theme, demonstrates the closeness of the relationship between a certain form of tourism and literature, although not necessarily great literature. However, the fact that no other region has the wealth of literature as the Alpujarras is indicative of the lasting impression created on successive generations by the writings of Gerald Brenan.

However, these influences are not confined to the relatively recent past. The development of the Costa del Sol as a major tourist destination did not happen by chance (Barke and France 1996). Important antecedents existed in the nineteenth century with the development of Málaga as a health resort, especially once attempts had been made to clean up the city (Pemble 1988; Castellanos 1998). Favourable impressions of the climate and other attractions (including the availability of English ale!) were reinforced by the writings of people such as Hans Christian Andersen (1862):

> In none of the towns and cities of Spain did I feel as happy and as comfortably at home as in Málaga. The customs of the people, nature, the open sea – each so rich and so indispensable for me – I found here. (Andersen 1975: 75)

However, echoing the common views of later, twentieth-century travellers who find too many tourists in their favoured destinations, just a few years later Augustus Hare complained 'Málaga is the dearest place in Spain, being the most Anglicised', and glumly noted 'There is very little to see' (Hare 1873: 139). But Hare appears to have been in a minority as successive generations of mainly English and German visitors praised the climate and other advantages of the city and region and so laid the foundations of what was to become one of the world's major tourist destinations with the advent of mass travel (Fitton 1971; Rubow 1985).

One of the clearest examples of 'reinventing' literary representations of place for tourist purposes concerns the island of Mallorca and the brief stay of George Sand and her lover Frederic Chopin at Valldemosa in 1838 and 1839. Despite the fact that they ended up hating the place, the weather (it was an appalling winter) and the people (Ferra 1961) – Sand vented her spleen in *Un Hiver á Majorque* (later translated by Robert Graves as *Winter in Majorca* (1956) – their sojourn in the island was used without shame in the Franco regime to promote Mallorca as the 'Isle of Love' (Whelpton 1953; Oppenhejm 1955). Initially aimed at Spanish honeymoon couples, supposedly reliving the entirely mythical and imaginary bliss shared by Sand and Chopin, this promotion established the basis from which the tourist industry on Mallorca began to mushroom into the massive concern it is today (Mitchell 1990).

Just as certain aspects of the reality of Sand and Chopin's visit to Mallorca needed to be overlooked in order to create the myth of their 'honeymoon', so in other locations a selective rendition of writings about place are used in promotional terms. The Alpujarras region of Granada province is one such area and is a region which has recently seen a spectacular increase in rural tourism (Barke and Newton 1995). Here, as elsewhere in the tourist industry, the process increasingly involves 'the manufacture and maintenance of preferred visions and sought images of people, places and pasts' (Hollinshead 1999: 47). The impressions of some early literary travellers to the region were less than promising. If Baron Davillier and Gustav Doré's initial doubts proved unfounded:

> In going from Lanjarón to Orgiva, we passed through a wild, hilly country, where the people we noticed on the way, while there was nothing hostile in their intentions, regarded us with an air of bewildered ferocity. (Davillier 1876: 206)

Augustus Hare made no secret of his dislike of the region:

> we were persuaded by glowing accounts of its scenery, to make ... the long excursion to Llanjaron (*sic*) ... But the distance is so great and the long diligence journey so fatiguing, that this expedition is not worth while ... the Alpuxarras (*sic*) are by no means the rich, verdant, smiling hills they are generally represented, but volcanic, bare, and arid in the highest degree ... We reached Llanjaron by a terrible road along precipices and through torrent beds, but it is an oasis in a hideous desert ... the village, chiefly frequented for the sake of its medicinal waters, contains few traces of its former occupants; the population is savage, the posadas miserable, and beyond bread, eggs and oranges, there is no food to be had. (Hare 1873: 171–2).

Suffice it to say that, in the promotion of the region, views such as Hare's are totally ignored and the somewhat idealized version of local traditions and culture represented by Brenan's *South from Granada* (1957) are the favoured 'interpretation'. Brenan's former village of residence, Yegen (Plate 4), is now rapidly becoming a tourist village with several hotels and rural holiday cottages to rent. *South from Granada* won acclaim in both the English- and Spanish-speaking world although, subsequently, Brenan has been criticized as an 'outside' writer with a rather romantic view of the Spanish past and especially of rural poverty (Rodríguez Monegal 1968). Yet his account appears to have been substantially true as several village inhabitants became hostile to Brenan especially because of his exposure of their past poverty, something which they wished to forget (Gathorne-Hardy 1992; Price 2000). Furthermore, more recent Spanish literary visitors to the area, producing 'inside' representations, have proved more than capable of closing their eyes to the excesses of more recent developments which Brenan would surely not have ignored (for example, Blanco Prieto 1991).

Although V. S. Pritchett (1954) claimed that 'romantic' Andalucía was an invention of the French there is no doubt that other writers, Hans Christian Andersen and the American, Washington Irving, for example, also made significant contributions to the formation of a specific image of the south of Spain (Calvo

Plate 4   Yegen, Alpujarras: Brenan's solitary walks are near a tourist route

Serraller 1978). The latter was particularly influential in popularizing the attractions of the Alhambra Palace and, arguably, raising the complex to iconic status within Andalucía and, by extension, Spain. His book is still on sale in every street corner, newsagents and tobacconists within the city of Granada. Ironically, at the time of Irving's residence in the 1820s the decoration and some of the structures were in a state of advanced decay (Mitchell 1990). The publication of *Tales of the Alhambra* in 1832 attracted other influential visitors such as Gautier and Ford who also took rooms in the palace despite the view of locals that it was 'little better than a *casa de ratones*' (Ford 1845). The influence of Irving is acknowledged in the work of Victor Hugo and, especially in Baron Davillier's account (1876) of his journey with Gustav Dore in 1872. The latter's drawings are, of course, frequently used as the epitome of 'romantic' Spain. Ford (1845) noted that 'Few *Granadinos* ever go there or understand the all-absorbing interest ... which it incites in the stranger. Familiarity has bred in them a contempt ... insensible to present as to past poetry and romance' (p. 545). It was largely due to the initial interest created by foreigners, especially Irving, that the Alhambra was eventually declared a National Monument and gradually underwent restoration (Castillo Ruiz 1994). But Trend (1928) argued that, far from being a monument to the former Moorish presence in Andalucía, 'the Palace, as I saw it, was the creation of Washington Irving and nineteenth century romanticism' (p. 140). In other words, this deliverance was based on the literary popularization of a series of myths and fairy stories about the Moorish occupation of the city and region. This may be thought, therefore, to represent a classic case of a place-related myth being created predominantly by 'outside' writings. Yet, if this is the case, then 'inside' writings have also helped to perpetuate it (Burgaleta 1998) and, in some early poems, Lorca 'could not avoid being seduced by the Romantic vision of Granada, to which foreign writers had contributed so signally' (Gibson 1992: xi).

LAS RUTAS: THE LITERATURE OF TRAVEL AND JOURNEYS

The final group of writings are, in many ways, the most prolific and influential in the present context and are concerned with accounts of particular travels or journeys within Spain. The list is a long and distinguished one and, although this form of literary endeavour may share some of the characteristics of the literary forms discussed above, travel writing often possesses its own distinctive qualities. The travel writer is, in a sense, a 'tourist' her/himself, albeit a very special one. The contact with places, events, and 'other' cultures becomes of special significance, as the likelihood of their being recorded for posterity and becoming part of a set of associations is considerable. It may well be, of course, that this recording becomes part of an invention or reinvention of a set of 'preferred' images (Hobsbawm and Ranger 1983), 'preferred' either by the author or by her/his readers. Beyond this, much travel writing – and this includes perhaps the best and the worst travel writing – has a sub-plot, of which the most common is the journey as part of a process of self-discovery. At best such writing can be extremely revealing, at worst it can be nothing more than the boring meanderings of an unbearably egotistical and not very interesting person.

Although most of these accounts are concerned with factual travel, there is one particular form of fictional Spanish literature to which travel, or at least movement is often central, namely the picaresque novel with its emphasis on 'poverty, delinquency, "upward mobility" (self-improvement of the pícaro), travel as an escape from despair, social satire of a system unresponsive to the needs ... of a growing community of "have nots"' (Sieber 1977: 9). *Lazarillo de Tormes* (1554) was the first important picaresque novel and deals with the adventures of a youth in his successive employments. The similar *Guzmán de Alfarache* (1599 and 1604) by Mateo Alemán and *La Vida del Buscón* (1608) by Francisco Gómez de Quevedo were both hugely successful. Although there is considerable academic debate on the subject (Close 1977; Forcione 1984) both novels are though to have influenced Miguel de Cervantes (1547–1616), the author of *El Ingenioso Hidalgo Don Quixote de la Mancha*, arguably Spain's literary masterpiece and, after the Bible, the world's most frequently published book. The novel appears to have several picaresque elements, not least because Cervantes parodies the chivalric novels which had been in vogue half a century earlier, and it is essentially the account of a journey, or journeys, and the adventures encountered in different, often identifiable places. These places have, of course, become sites of literary pilgrimage in their own right and have contributed their own, sometimes quirky, presence to the tourism infrastructure. They have also come to symbolize, rightly or wrongly, much that is 'romantic' about Spain's past.

Don Quixote has had many individuals who have sought to retrace his footsteps, creating almost a tourist trail in its own right. These include the American writer

August Jacacci in 1897 (Jacobs 1994), José Martínez Ruiz (better known as Azorín) in 1905 (Azorín 1966), Rupert Croft-Cooke (1959), Wyndham Lewis (1962) and Nicholas Wollaston who subsequently wrote his remarkable *Tilting at Don Quixote* (1990). The essentially allegorical nature of *Don Quixote* with its reflections on the state of Spain, on humanity, the nature of belief and the self has been parallelled in many works, not least in Graham Greene's *Monsignor Quixote* (1982) which itself was based on Greene's travels in Spain with his confessor, Father Durán.

Although it is the foreign traveller who has conventionally attracted most attention in literary accounts of the exploration of Spain, native Spanish writers have also made their sometimes unique contribution. In the English-speaking world, it is Gerald Brenan who is credited with 'discovering' the charms of the Alpujarras (although, as we have seen, for other writers such as Augustus Hare, the region possessed few charms), but it was the Spanish author, Pedro de Alarcón from Guadix, who first made the region famous in Spain (Castro 1992). Alarcón's account of his journey in the spring of 1872 emphasized the romantic wildness of the region and the manifestations of Moorish presence. Although it seems unlikely that Brenan was initially aware of Alarcón's writing on the region (Gathorne-Hardy 1992) their view of the region's uniqueness is a shared one. Interestingly enough, whilst recognizing Alarcón's role in making Spanish society aware of the region, much is now made of his failure to explore the 'High' Alpujarra (Gómez Montero 1971). The Brenan versus Alarcón debate on the 'discovery' of the Alpujarras for external readers provides a fascinating commentary on literary representations of Spain, especially in the context of 'inside' and 'outside' writings. On the one hand we have a native Spaniard with a partial account of a distinctive region but one that is claimed as a genuine 'discovery'; on the other hand we have a foreign writer – Brenan – who explored further, arguably understood more, and actually lived there.

A second significant account of 'travels in Spain' by a Spanish author, albeit one with English connections is Camilo José Cela's *Journey to the Alcarria* (1948), then a little visited region to the north east of Madrid:

> In the Alcarria I went along writing down in a notebook everything I saw ... (this book isn't a novel, it's more like a geography). Anything goes in a novel, so long as it's told with common sense; but in geography, naturally, it's not the same, and one must always tell the truth because geography is like a science. (p. 6)

Cela's view of travel (as of geography!) is very specific – it has nothing to do with physical exercise or recreation but is more a state of mind and a desire to comprehend the ordinary events of life. At first sight, therefore, it would appear to have little to do with tourism, which tends to be concerned with the 'different', the 'diverting' or the 'spectacular'. However, this is to overlook the 'difference' that is actually often present in 'everyday' things in different places and the fascination and curiosity they inspire. It is perhaps then not so surprising that Cela's journey has in itself become a specific tourist '*ruta*' for walkers and others. Cela's writing also reminds us that what is ostensibly 'inside' (in the sense that here we have a Spaniard writing about part of Spain) is actually fundamentally 'outside' in character. Cela always uses terms such as 'the traveller' to describe himself; in other words, he is an external and 'distanced' observer.

For the 'inside' writings on Spain, the clearest recognition of the links between literature and travel (if not, directly, tourism) in Spain may be found in *Rutas Literarias de España* (1990) edited by Rubén Caba. Although somewhat compromised by the desire to include all the major regions, the book provides an account of the places associated with twenty-five major Spanish writers and a travel itinerary for each one. Some of these, for example, that concerned with Pérez Galdós are at the intra-urban scale whilst others trace either the travels or the places providing inspiration for the writers under discussion. The purpose of the book is quite clearly to provide a set of itineraries for those who wish to explore the sites associated with some of Spain's greatest writers.

However, the genre of travel writing is dominated by contributions from 'outside' and it is primarily foreign writers who have provided the most influential accounts of their travels through and within Spain. Amongst the English-language writers the names of Richard Ford, Henry Swinburne, George Borrow, V. S. Pritchett, Gerald Brenan, Laurie Lee, Rose Macauley, Arthur Koestler, Count Tschiffely, Honor Tracey, Alastair Boyd (Lord Kilmarnock), Penelope Chetwode and James Michener are the most prominent and influential in generating a fascination with Spain but they have also their less-accomplished imitators. As noted earlier, one of the ways in which Spain is 'different' is the intense desire it seems to induce to want to write about it. Not all of this writing is complimentary but most of it is of high quality and needs celebrating more than it has been hitherto. It is, in many ways, a tourist resource in itself and, rather than contributing to any alleged conflict between 'inside' and 'outside' writings on Spain, it represents a distinguished contribution to the overall canon of travel writing and one that Spain can feel proud to have inspired.

CONCLUSION

In conclusion, we must recognize that in considering the relationship between literature and tourism, it would be simplistic and superficial to rely solely on physical manifestations as evidence for, or indicating the lack of, such relationships. Although such evidence exists, the links are predominantly, to found in less specific forms. The complexity of identifying these forms is exacerbated by the important differences which exist between different groups, and indeed individuals, in how they react both to place and to literary representation. The same place may therefore mean quite different things to indigenous Spaniards and to foreigners, or to indigenous Spaniards from different regions. We should not expect a uniform and consistent response from potential or actual tourists to any particular place or its literary associations. The absence of a Spanish equivalent of Stratford upon Avon does not necessarily signify minimal links between literature and tourism in Spain.

In his rather bitter expostulation 'wounded Spain, dressed up for carnival', Antonio Machado was reacting to the image of his country, an image that was largely a product of literary representations, those representations being, in turn, dominated by pervasive stereotypes of 'romantic' Spain. It has been widely accepted that most of the significant representations of 'romantic' Spain emanated from outside the country and were based on foreign models. This paradigm legitimized a tension between 'inside' and 'outside' writings on Spain and one that was particularly significant in the context of travel and tourism. It has been argued in this essay that this alleged tension is an oversimplification and that the relationship between 'inside' and 'outside' writings is a considerably more subtle one than is implied by such a crude distinction. The two interact in a variety of complex ways. Secondly, the very term 'romantic' Spain is not unproblematic. Conceptions of the 'romantic' as an idea and of its key components are themselves not static and have changed from one epoch to another. Furthermore, the 'romantic' as defined by literary criticism, for example, is not necessarily in full agreement with conceptions of the term in other contexts. These factors lend support to the view that Machado's pessimism was possibly unjustified. Although specific incidents may be cited, there is limited evidence that Spain's literary heritage has been systematically abused and exploited. There is equal evidence that, again, despite some misrepresentations, a considerable body of the foreign writing on Spain has served to illuminate and celebrate many aspects of Spanish society in a constructive way and to generate interest, curiosity and genuine affection for the country.

But it would be wrong to conclude that the only points of contact between literature and tourism are those concerned with the creation and dissemination of literary images. Although the notion of 'romantic' Spain represents one of the most significant aspects of the relationship between literature and tourism, other links also exist. The recent expansion of cultural tourism and the growing tendency of Spaniards to explore their own country, including their own cultural history, seems likely to lead to greater interest in literary heritage and what it means for particular places. The publication of Caba's *Rutas Literarias de España* is especially significant in this regard. Whilst literary culture lags significantly behind the visual arts as a tourism 'resource', we may expect in the future a considerable surge of interest in the former and an increased tendency to exploit or exhibit literary associations, be they real or fictional. The current emphasis on the strength of regional associations, the desire to exploit regional heritage and to stress regional distinctiveness, all seem likely to add significant impetus to this trend.

REFERENCES

Alvarez Junco, J. and Shubert, A. (2000) *Spanish History since 1808*. London: Arnold.

Andersen, H. C. (1975) *A Visit to Spain and North Africa, 1862*. London: Peter Owen.

Aymes, J. R. (ed.), (1983) *L'Espagne Romantique*. Paris: Métaillié.

'Azorín' (José Martinez Ruiz) (1966) *La Ruta de Don Quijote*. Manchester: Manchester University Press.

Barke, M. and France, L. A. (1996) 'The Costa del Sol', in M. Barke, J. Towner, and M. T. Newton, (eds) (1996) *Tourism in Spain: Critical Issues*. Wallingford: CAB International, 265–308

Barke, M. and Newton, M. T. (1995) 'The EU LEADER initiative and rural tourism development: applications in Spain', in N. Evans and M. Robinson (eds), *Issues in Travel and Tourism*, Vol. 1, Sunderland: Business Education Publishers, 1–40.

Barke, M., Towner, J. and Newton, M. T. (eds) (1996) *Tourism in Spain: Critical Issues*. Wallingford: CAB International.

Barnes, T. J. and Duncan, J. S. (1992) *Writing Worlds*. London: Routledge.

Blanco Prieto, F. (1991) *La Alpujarra: Notas de un Viaje*. Salamanca: Libreria Cervantes.

Bote Gómez, V. (1998) 'Turismo de ciudad y patrimonio cultural en España', in M. Marchena Gomez, (ed.), *Turismo Urbano y Patrimonio Cultural. Una Perspectiva Europea*. Seville: Diputacion de Sevilla, 37–53.

Brenan, G. (1950) *The Face of Spain*. London: Turnstile Press.

Brenan, G. (1951) *The Literature of the Spanish People from Roman Times to the Present Day*. Cambridge: Cambridge University Press.

Brenan, G. (1957) *South from Granada*. London: Hamish Hamilton.

Brenan, G. (1965) *The Literature of the Spanish People*, 2nd edn. Cambridge: Cambridge University Press.

Brown, G. G. (1972) *A Literary History of Spain. The Twentieth Century*. London and New York: Ernest Benn and Barnes & Noble.

Burgaleta, P. (1998) *La Poética de la Ciudad. La Imagen de la Alhambra*. Granada: Grupo Editorial Universitario.

Caba, R. (ed.) (1990) *Rutas Literarias de España*. Madrid: Aguilar.

Calvo Serraller, F. (1978) 'La imagen romántica de España', *Cuadernos Hispanoamericanos*, **332**, 240–60.

Castellanos, J. (1998) 'La promoción de Málaga y la idea de ciudad saludable', *Dynamis*, **18**, 207–31.

Castillo Ruiz, J. (1994) 'La valoración paisajistica de la Alhambra en los libros de viaje y su reconocimiento tutelar en la declaracion de ésta como Monumento Nacional en 1870', *Cuadernos de la Alhambra*, **29–30**, 1993–4.

Castro, E. (1992) *Guia General de la Alpujarra*. Granada: Caja General de Ahorros y Monte de Piedad de Granada.

Cela, Camilo Jose (1948) *Journey to the Alcarria: Travels through the Spanish Countryside*, New York: The Atlantic Monthly Press.

Chandler, R. E. and Schwartz, K. (1991) *A New History of Spanish Literature*, rev. edn. Baton Rouge: Louisiana State University Press.

Close, Anthony J. (1977) 'Don Quijote's love for Dulcinea: a study of Cervantine irony', *Bulletin of Hispanic Studies*, **54**, 107–14.

Cohen, E. (1979) 'A phenomenology of tourist experiences', *Sociology*, **13**, 179–202.

Croft-Cooke, R. (1959) *In Search of Don Quixote*. London: Putnam.

Davillier, C, The Baron (1876) *Spain*. London: Sampson Low, Marston, Low, and Searle.

Dendle, B. J. (1996) 'Algunos viajeros Franceses en España durante la decada de 1840', *Estudios de Investigacion Franco-Española*, **14**, 153–65.

Duncan, J. S. and Duncan, N. G. (1992) 'Ideology and bliss. Roland Barthes and the secret histories of landscape', in, T. J. Barnes and J. S. Duncan, (eds), *Writing Worlds: Discourse, Text and Metaphor in the Representation of Landscape*. London: Routledge, 18–37.

Duncan, J. and Gregory, D. (1999) *Writes of Passage: Reading Travel Writing*. London and New York: Routledge.

Epton, N. (1968) *Andalusia*. Weidenfeld and Nicolson.

Esteban, J. (1990) 'El Madrid de Galdós', in R. Caba, (ed.), *Rutas Literarias de Espana*. Madrid: Aguilar, 399–416.

Ferra, B. (1961) *Chopin and George Sand in Majorca*. Palma de Mallorca: Ediciones La Cartoixa.

Fitton, M. (1971) *Málaga; the Biography of a City*. London: George Allen & Unwin.

Flitter, D. (1992) *Spanish Romantic Literary Theory and Criticism*. Cambridge: Cambridge University Press.

Forcione, Alban (1984) *Cervantes and the Mystery of Lawlessness*, Princeton: Princeton UP.

Ford, R. (1845) *A Handbook for Travellers in Spain and Readers at Home. Describing the Country and Cities, the Natives and their Manners; the Antiquities, Religion, Legends, Fine Arts, Literature, Sports and Gastronomy: with Notices on Spanish History*, 2 vols. London: John Murray.

Ganivet, A. (1946) *Spain: An Interpretation*, London: Eyre & Spottiswoode.

García Lorca, F. (1987) *Impressions and Landscapes*. Lanham, New York: University Press of America.

Gathorne-Hardy, J. (1992) *The Interior Castle: A Life of Gerald Brenan*. London: Sinclair-Stevenson.

Gibson, I. (1979) *The Assassination of Federico García Lorca*. London: W. H. Allen & Co.

Gibson, I. (1992) *Lorca's Granada: A Practical Guide*. London: Faber & Faber.

Gilbert, E. W. (1945) 'Richard Ford and his Handbook for Travellers in Spain', *The Geographical Journal*, **CVI** (3, 4), 144–51.

Gómez Montero, R. (1971) *Ruta Alpujarreña: Los Pueblos Mas Altos de España*. Granada: Calle Elvira, Pregon Granadino.

Graves, W. (1995) *Wild Olives: Life in Majorca with Robert Graves*. London: Pimlico.

Guerrero, A. C. (1990) 'Illustrados y Romanticos: Viajeros Britanicos en España', *Ayeres*, **1**(2), 32–7.

Hare, A. J. C. (1873) *Wanderings in Spain*. London: Strahan & Co.

Herzberger, D. K. (1991) 'Social realism and the contingencies of history in the contemporary Spanish novel', *Hispanic Review*, **59**(2), 153–73.

Hobsbawm, E. and Ranger, T. (eds) (1983) *The Invention of Tradition*. Cambridge: Cambridge University Press.

Hoffmann, L. F. (1961) *Romantique Espagne: l'image de Espagne en France entre 1800 et 1850*. Princeton: Princeton University Press.

Hollinshead, K. (1999) 'Myth and the discourse of Texas: heritage tourism and the suppression of instinctual life', in M. Robinson and P. Boniface (eds), *Tourism and Cultural Conflicts*. Wallingford: CAB International, 47–93.

Hooper, J. (1995) *The New Spaniards*. London: Penguin.

Hutman, N. L. (1969) *Machado: A Dialogue with Time*. Albuquerque: University of New Mexico Press.

Jacobs. M. (1990) *A Guide to Andalusia*. London: Viking.

Jacobs, M. (1994) *Between Hopes and Memories: A Spanish Journey*. London: Picador.

Kern, R. W. (1995) *The Regions of Spain: A Reference Guide to History and Culture*. Westport, Connecticut: Greenwood Press.

Lee, L. (1969) *As I Walked Out One Mid-Summer Morning*. London: André Deutsch.

Levy, D. B. (1950) *Spanish Mountain Life: The Sierra Nevada*. London: Faber & Faber.

De Madariaga, S. (1942) *Spain: A Modern History*. London: Jonathon Cape.

Maiztegui-Oñate, C. and Areitio Bertolín, M. T. (1996) 'Cultural Tourism in Spain', in G. Richards (ed.), *Cultural Tourism in Europe*. Wallingford: CAB International, 267–81.

Mannell, R. C. and Iso-Ahola, S. E. (1987) 'Psychological nature of leisure and tourism experience', *Annals of Tourism Research*, **14**, 314–31.

Michener, J. A. (1968) *Iberia: Spanish Travels and Reflections*. London: Secker & Warburg.

Mitchell, D. (1990) *Travellers in Spain: An Illustrated Anthology*. London: Cassell.

Murray, J. (1889) 'The origin and history of Murray's handbooks for travellers', *Murray's Magazine*, **6**, 624.

Nooteboom, C. (1997) *Roads to Santiago*. London: The Harvill Press.

Okey, T. (1906) 'Introduction', in R. Ford, *Gatherings from Spain*. London: J. M. Dent & Sons, ix.

Oppenhejm, R. (1955) *Spain in the Looking Glass*. London: Macgibbon & Kee.

Patronato de Turismo de Huelva (1995) *La Provincia de Huelva: Guía Turística*. Huelva: Patronato de Turismo de Huelva.

Peers, E. A. (1940) 'A history of the Romantic Movement in Spain', 2 vols. New York: Hafner.

Pemble, J. (1988) *The Mediterranean Passion*. Oxford: Oxford University Press.

Price, K. (2000), personal communication, Álora, March 2000 (Along with Cucca Gross, Keith Price, brother of Gerald Brenan's long-standing companion, Lynda Price, helped to take care of Brenan in his last years at Alhaurín el Grande).

Priestley, J. B. (1960) *Literature and Western Man*. London: Heinemann.

Pritchett, V. S. (1954) *The Spanish Temper*. London: Chatto & Windus.

Riley, E. C. (1992) 'Introduction', in Miguel de Cervantes, *Don Quixote de la Mancha*. Oxford: Oxford University Press.

Ritchie, H. (1993) *Here we Go: a Summer on the Costa del Sol*. London: Penguin.

Rodríguez Monegal, E. (1968) *El Arte de Narrar: Diálogos, Colección Prisma*. Caracas: Monte Avila.

Rubow, A. (1985) 'La España del siglo XIX vista por viajeros Alemanes', *Aportes. Revista de Historia Contemporanea*, **1**, 195–200.

Saglia, D. (1997) ' "The true essence of Romanticism": romantic theories of Spain and the question of Spanish Romanticism', *Journal of Iberian and Latin American Studies*, **3**(2), 127–45.

Said, E. (1993) *Culture and Imperialism*. New York: Knopf.

Sand, G. (1956) *Winter in Majorca*. Mallorca: Valldemosa Edition (trans. Robert Graves).

Shaw, D. L. (1973) *The Generation of 1898 in Spain*. London and New York: Ernest Benn and Barnes & Noble.

Shields, R. (1991) *Places on the Margin*. London: Routledge.

Sieber, H. (1977) *The Picaresque*. London: Methuen.

Thomas, H. (1977) *The Spanish Civil War*. London: Hamish Hamilton, 2nd edn.

Thomas, H. (1988) *Madrid: A Travellers' Companion*. London: Constable.

Tomillo Noguero, F. (1995) 'Turismo cultural: Avila', in AECIT, *La Actividad Turística Española en 1995*. Madrid: AECIT, 623–45.

Trend, J. B. (1928) *Spain from the South*. London: Methuen.

Troitiño Vinuesa, M. (1998) 'Turismo y ciudades históricas: La experiencia Española', in M. Marchena Gómez (ed.), *Turismo Urbano y Patrimonio Cultural. Una Perspectiva Europea*. Seville: Diputacion de Sevilla, 89–105.

Troitiño Vinuesa, M., García Hernández, M. and La Calle Vaquero, M. (1998) 'Granada, un potente destino turístico dependiente del conjunto monumental de la Alhambra-Generalife', in AECIT, *La Actividad Turistica Espanola en 1998*. Madrid: AECIT, 605–25.

Urry, J. (1990) *The Tourist Gaze: Leisure and Travel in Contemporary Societies*. London: Sage.

Urry, J. (1995) *Consuming Places*. London: Routledge.

Vera Rebollo, J. F. and Dávila Linares, J. M. (1995) 'Turismo y Patrimonio Histórico y Cultural', *Estudios Turisticos*, **126**, 161–77.

Vincent, B. (1992) 'España vista por los viajeros Franceses', *Historia 16*, **17**, 103–07.

Whelpton, E. (1953) *The Balearics*. London: Travel Book Club.

Wollaston, N. (1990) *Tilting at Don Quixote*. London: André Deutsch.

Wyndham Lewis, D. B. (1962) *The Shadow of Cervantes*. New York: Sheed & Ward.

Chapter 4

'Frizzling in the Sun': Robert Graves and the Development of Mass Tourism in the Balearic Islands

John W. Presley

In a letter to W. K. T. Barrett, Robert Graves was quite dilatory about his choice of Majorca as his place to live and work:

> [W]e live here in perhaps the best place anywhere – these are the Classical Hesperides where it never freezes and never gets too hot and where it costs nothing to live if one is content to go native, and where the population is the most hospitable, quiet, sensible and well-being that you can imagine. We are near the sea and Palma a big town, is within reach for any European necessities ... We tried France and Germany first but of course though we knew the best parts it was no use; (the Germans are too serious and the French too false) it was just to confirm our previous choice of this island. (Graves (ed. Sarner) 1997: 34)

This was 20 May 1930. Graves, even at that early date, ended his letter with a warning:

> Don't advertise Majorca! You might want to come out here yourself some day. It's not overrun yet. (35)

But for contemporary Europeans, the Balearic Islands, including Mallorca and Ibiza, form the paradigmatic case study of mass tourism attacking landscape, culture and economy, transforming an agricultural society into a service-based, much more urbanized culture. One of the most complete of many analyses and descriptions of the tourist 'boom' in the Balearics may be found in R. J. Buswell's (1996) essay 'Tourism in the Balearic Islands'. Among the hundreds of statistics Buswell uses to illustrate the rapidity of change brought on by tourism in the Balearics, only a few are necessary to imagine the effects of commercial air travel and package tourism on the fragile resources of an arid island: in 1935, there were 43,000 (mostly Spanish) visitors to the islands, yet the number of visitors had risen to 3.6 million by 1973. At one point in 1964, a new hotel was being opened every 53 hours. In 1992, the Palma de Mallorca airport alone recorded 11,867,370 passengers arriving – up from 63,676 air passengers in 1960 – these were, of course, in addition to all those arriving by boat and ferry.

From 1929 until his death in 1985, Robert Graves lived in Mallorca, except for the years of the Second World War and the Spanish Civil War. Though never a travel writer *per se*, Graves did write essays about his experience living in Mallorca (in which he deals explicitly with the subject of increasing tourism), short stories with Mallorcan characters, poems describing the behaviour of certain types of tourists, and he even edited the early and infamous tourist report *A Winter in Mallorca* by George Sand. But in addition to his role as an early critic and witness of the tourism phenomenon, Graves was actually a participant or precipitating cause in the rise of Balearic tourism, however ambivalent or contradictory his participation may seem. In the 1930s, Graves and Laura Riding may have been the most famous literary couple in the world, drawing American and British writers, artists, musicians and like-minded intellectuals into a salon that did much to make the little village of Deià an international literary landmark. After the Second World War, that salon grew until it began to attract large numbers of rather unsavoury types drawn by what they had understood of *The White Goddess*. Moreover, though Graves was honoured for his work to preserve the northern coastline of Mallorca, he was also honoured for having brought so many tourists to Deià, and at various times in his long stay on the island, he too was even a speculator and at the least, a would-be developer.

So, the case of Robert Graves offers a rare opportunity to study a writer working in close observation of history's most notorious development of mass tourism.

Mallorca was famous as a destination well before the invention of the package tour. Thomas Cook first advertised Mallorca in 1903, as one stop for an organized tour of the Balearics. Clients were advised that 'the climate of Palma rivals that of Malaga and Algiers'. The sights listed included the Palma Cathedral, the bullring, La Lonja, the casino, and 'quaint 16th century houses'. Again in 1905 the island was promoted as one of the best viewing spots for the eclipse of the sun in August of that year (*Passport* 1995: 12).

Though wealthy travellers came to Mallorca in small numbers in the late 1800s, it was not until the years after the Second World War that tourists came in hordes. In 'Why I Live in Majorca', Graves sounded a worried note: 'Around 1951, British, French, and American travelers accepted the fantasy of Majorca as the Isle of Love, the Isle of Tranquility, the Paradise where the sun always shines and where one can live like a fighting cock on a dollar a day, drinks included.' During this period, Palma Nova and Magaluf, west of Palma, developed into the 'concrete jungle' – high-rise apartment and hotel blocks, restaurants, bars, souvenir shops – that 'still attracts a raucous element'. Despite Mallorca's reputation as resort for celebrities – film stars and royalty vacation on their own property on the island – it has a parallel reputation as the habitat of the *gamberros Ingleses* (English hooligans) and the classic tourist, 'wearing an oversize sombrero, carrying a donkey, and trailing a family of bad children. The place they are headed is a turbulent ocean of pink flesh and grey concrete' (Robert Elms, quoted in *Passport*: 26).

Even now, the figure of Robert Graves himself has become a sort of tourist attraction – just as before his death, he attracted artists (and later artistes) to the island. The Passport/Thomas Cook guide to Mallorca includes, in its brief section on

Deià, a paragraph of biography for Graves, noting that the village and the writer 'will be forever associated'. The guide goes on to say that 'Graves strove hard to stop Deià being ruined by the encroaching developments, and the town's unified and natural appearance is its greatest attraction.' However:

> Today the town lives in thrall to La Residencia, an idyllic mansion turned hotel that is partly owned by the British entrepreneur Richard Branson and attracts arty types from around the world. As the author Robert Elms puts it, 'Everything in Deià is taken slowly, except your money'. (*Passport*: 68)

Other attractions listed include 'several restaurants, a couple of art galleries, and a narrow, twisting road that leads down to the sea at Cala de Deià' (*Passport*: 68).

Of course, other artists and writers have made Mallorca their residence. Joan Miró kept his studio outside Palma; his wife and mother were Mallorcan. Miró was very conscious of Mallorca's influence on his work: 'As a child I loved to watch the always changing Mallorcan sky. At night I would get carried away by the writing in the sky of the shooting stars, and the lights of the fireflies. The sea, day and night, was always blue. It was here that I received the first creative seeds which became my work.'

The most famous artists before Graves to remain in Mallorca were George Sand and Chopin, who spent the winter at Valldemossa in 1838–9. Their experiences were not entirely pleasant, but Sand gave Mallorca credit for the maturity and sublimity of Chopin's *Preludes*. In editing Sand's *Winter in Majorca*, Graves' notes are a frequent counterpoint to Sand's scandalous references to Majorcans as thieves, monkeys and Polynesian savages. On her side of the argument, the locals had ostracized Chopin on the rumour of his tuberculosis, and Sand since she was a 'cigarette-smoking, trouser-wearing pioneer-feminist'. The 'lugubrious rain' and poor food didn't help matters any, but Sand later commented that things might have gone differently 'had they bothered to attend Mass' (*Passport*: 70, 78–9).

In his translation of *Winter in Majorca* (Sand 1956) Graves takes great pains in his notes and introduction to point out that Sand, the most well-known and vociferous critic of Majorca (until the tourist explosions of the 1960s) was entirely at fault in her relations with the Mallorcans. Typical is Graves' quotation from an 1839 traveller who reports that the local priest was 'mortified'.

> This French lady must indeed be a strange person! Just think of it: she never speaks to a living soul, never leaves the Cartuja and never shows her face in church, even on Sundays, and goodness knows how many mortal sins she is amassing! Furthermore, I have it from the apothecary, who also lives in the Cartuja, that *la señora* makes cigarettes like nothing on earth, drinks coffee all hours, sleeps by day, and does nothing but smoke and write all night. I beg you, dear sir, since you know her, to tell us what she has come to do here in midwinter. (116)

At the end of her stay on the island, as Sand was leaving on the French ship *Meleager* 'surrounded by intelligent, pleasant faces', she cries 'Vive La France' and summarizes her stay in Mallorca, 'We felt as if we had been round the world, and come back to civilization after a long stay among the savages of Polynesia.' Graves' annotation is direct, contradictory, and based on his loyalty to the Mallorcans – and his antipathy to the French: 'This remark will read most ironically to anyone who has studied the story of nineteenth-century French colonial enterprise among the noble Polynesians; even if he has not had the privilege of living among the generous, honest, and lovable Majorcans' (165).

Graves treats Sand's account of her winter on the island as yet another of his Gravesian puzzles. 'I find it difficult to square this account of the winter with Chopin's letters' (175). If Chopin felt 'poetic' in Mallorca, and was working productively, why was Sand so miserable? Graves imagines that the villagers 'will have described him [Chopin] among themselves proverbially as "a man who expects you to doff your hat from three leagues away"'. They would describe Sand as 'a shameless one who leaps out in anger like a stone from a crushed cherry'. As for Sand's children, Maurice 'hotly championed his mother', and his 'precocious sketches' made the Valldemosans uneasy, 'especially the Monastic Orgy, pinned up in the cell'. Solange comes in for a special bit of characterization; she 'offended their [Mallorcans'] sense of propriety by wearing trousers and playing the tomboy, instead of busying herself with the needle, the catechism, and other useful tasks' (178). And of course, Chopin's consumption was a physical threat to the villagers, consumption then being incurable. The Mallorcans believed, 'as they still do, that sickness is a divine punishment for ill-doing'. The Mallorcans would have considered Sand 'wicked' for exposing her children to consumption. 'They would think the same today', Graves writes, 'and with reason unless strict sanitary precautions were taken' (178).

Solange was 'no more than eight years old ... known only as rebellious, arrogant, lazy and a domestic tyrant who relied on violent displays of temper for getting her own way' (179). Graves, in fact, blames Solange for much of the misery of Sand and Chopin's visit. 'George spoilt and idolized Solange ... Solange repaid George with the cruelty, deceit and greed that [her father] had bequeathed to her' (179). Graves assumes that Chopin's obsession with the haunting of his cell by the ghosts of the original monks was intensified by Solange's stories of spectres in the cloisters. With little evidence but his own surmise, Graves solves this puzzle by imputing virtually all the mischief – spilled milk, fleas in bed and at table – to eight-year-old Solange, including serving even as her mother's conduit for learning the village gossip! Graves imagines that the villagers would have 'felt it their duty to enlighten Solange on the seriousness of her position' and would 'never have spoken directly to her mother or to Chopin on these subjects' (182). Moreover, Luis Ripolis' *Chopin: Su Invierno en Mallorca* 'supported [Graves'] theory by referring to a letter of Solange's' in which 'she gleefully describes how the chambermaid – presumably the *niña* – and herself dressed up in monk's habits, which they found in the monastery, and frightened Chopin out of his wits by creeping into the cell at dusk' (182).

George Sand blamed the villagers, Graves says, for Chopin's return to 'orthodox morality', and she 'revenged herself in this book on the Valldemossan villagers'.

She called them uncharitable, superstitious wretches, monkeys, cannibals, thieves and (most significant of the way in which her mind was working) the bastard children of lascivious and hypocritical Carthusian fathers, whose main pleasure lay in seducing the married women who came to their confessionals. (185)

Graves skewers Sand for her factual errors:

> [S]he devotes two chapters to denouncing the inhuman cruelties of the vanished
> Dominican Fathers, and extolling the noble rage of the people who had risen up and
> destroyed their monastery – though she is aware that this was the work of a demolitions
> contractor. Nobody could mistake hers for sober historical criticism. (183–4)

Graves gives the penultimate word to José María Quadrado, whose 'To George
Sand: A Refutation' appeared in *La Palma: A Weekly Journal of History and Literature* in May of 1841. Quadrado refutes Sand's 'doctrine' by the character of 'its
evangelist'. After quoting Sand's 'verdict'

> [T]hat the Majorcan is a savage who cheats, extorts, lies, abuses and plunders to his
> heart's content, and would eat his fellowman without a qualm were that the local custom;
> but who, despite his vices, is no more to be hated than an ox or a sheep because, like
> theirs, his spirit is lulled in animal innocence. (200)

Quadrado's retort, 'George Sand is the most unmoral of writers, and Mme. Dudevant the most obscene of women!' (200) is weak, frankly, as is Graves' observation
that 'the original manuscript of *Un Hiver a Majorque* is even cruder than the version
published' (200).

The essay central to understanding Graves' own attachment and loyalty to the
island is an essay written for *Harper's Bazaar* in 1953, 'Why I live in Majorca'. It
reads almost as a sentimental farewell to the island Graves first saw in the 1920s.

He chose Mallorca, Graves writes, 'because its climate had the reputation of being
better than any other in Europe ... I should be able to live there on a quarter of the
income needed in England ... it was large enough – some 1,300 square miles – not to
make me feel claustrophobic.' Graves chose Deià, then a fishing and olive-farming
village, because the village offered everything he needed as a writer: 'sun, sea,
mountains, spring-water, shady trees, no politics ... electric light and a bus service to
Palma, the capital'. Ever pragmatic, he does not fail to note 'it was also fairly
mosquito free, being some 400 feet above sea level'. Other 'desiderata' used to make
his choice included 'good wine, good neighbours, and not too great a distance from
the Greenwich meridian'.

Graves always claimed real affection and respect for his 'good neighbours', the
Mallorcan people themselves. He described them as 'excessively honest and friendly'.
Indeed, during his ten-year 'exile' from Mallorca, he certainly had reason to note
these two qualities. During the Spanish Civil War and the Second World War,
Graves could send neither money nor letters to Deià from Galmpton, England. Yet
when he returned – on what, ominously, was the first-ever charter flight to Palma –
he found the house he had built (on the best site for miles around Deià), 'unplun-
dered' by either side and, in fact, Graves was grateful to see that 'everything I had
left behind had been looked after – linen, silver, books and documents ... and if I felt
so inclined, could have sat down at my table, taken a sheet of paper from the drawer
and started work again straight away.'

In his own first seven years in Deià, Graves' life was, by English standards, primitive, but rewarding. 'Beef, butter and cow's milk were not easily obtained; but
there was plenty of fresh fruit throughout the year.' Graves provides a list of the

fruits, by season: 'oranges, loquats, cherries, apricots, peaches, plums, strawberries, apples, pears, first figs, grapes, pomegranates and oranges again'. The necessities were there, and were cheap. 'So with black coffee and cheap black tobacco, and a very sound heady wine from the village of Binisalem, and brandy at three pesetas a bottle, all was well.'

Even though Deià was a place where 'nothing of importance had ever happened ... no hunting, no racing, no yachting ... no ancient monuments ... not even village politics', the little fishing village had for years drawn a certain type of tourist, most of whom probably came for the same reason Graves came. His catalogue of the visitors during his first seven years in Deià includes 'painters, professors of literature, dipsomaniacs, pianists, perverts, priests, geologists, Buddhists, runaway couples, vegetarians, Seventh Day Adventists'. There were, according to Graves, seldom less than two painters renting cottages or staying at the inn 'during the season'.

For three years after the Second World War, 'the flow of tourists remained negligible'. Spain suffered under severe rationing of food, and a depressed economy. The slow increase in tourism was welcomed. 'There is this to say for tourists: their arrival in bulk tends to relax police regulations, encourage amenities in food and household utensils, and decrease unemployment.' In 1953 Graves was aware of the dangers that increased tourism presented, but felt that the island was little-spoiled except for the 'Golden Mile' west of Palma. 'And though an excess of visitors sends up prices and wages and fills the towns with ugly advertisements, souvenir shops, cheap-jacks, and shady adventurers from everywhere – and at the peak season can actually wear down the tempers of so patient and long-suffering a people as the Majorcans – still, the island has not yet been spoiled even by the massive influx of the recent "Majorca, Island of Love" period.' Graves perhaps reasonably did not fear for the island, because 'few Majorcan roads are capable of taking buses and taxis, so tourist traffic is canalized along a narrow grid'. (One could hardly have predicted that six buses at once might be parked at the first tiny restaurant outside Deià, or that on occasion one bus may have to squeeze off Deià's main street to allow two others to pass.)

Typically, Graves insists that previous writers on Majorca had not got it quite right. The flawed description of his predecessors Graves blames on 'the strange, hallucinatory power that Deià exerts on foreign visitors'. Writing in 1719, one such visitor named Campbell described 'the church and the country houses, but did not see the village; his successors saw the village, but neither the church nor the country houses'. Campbell describes a broad plain, but at Deià 'there is only a steeply terraced valley with nowhere a broad enough level place for a tennis court' (though one can see tennis courts now in Valldemosa, on the way to Deià). Writers after Campbell describe the 'trilling of wild canaries – there are none on the island – festooned barren precipices with foliage, crowned them with eagles' eyries, and credited the houses of Deià with nonexistent gardens'. Without providing specifics, Graves claims that 'Germans have written more extravagantly about the place', and since Deià is built on the site of a Moon-goddess shrine, Graves is willing to consider their 'derangement' the result of the Deià moonlight, so bright 'one can even match colors by it'.

Nor did the painters get it quite right. 'The painters splashed their canvasses with cobalt, viridian, vermilion, and a dirty olive-green, though the prevailing colours of the landscape are grey, smoke-blue, a translucent grey-green, blue-black, biscuit and rust; and the sea is never cobalt.' His severest criticism Graves saves for the painters who, for lack of attention, do not paint what is before them. 'They painted the crooked olive trees as though they were elms; and the harsh rocks as though they were cakes of castile soap.'

Graves describes Deià as 'a spectacular but not really beautiful place'. During his exile in England, Graves says he longed for 'the fruit in my garden, the smell of olive-wood fires; the chatter of card-players in the village cafe; the buoyant green waters of the cove; the sun-blistered rocks of the Teix mountain; my quiet whitewashed study; the night noises of sheep bells, owls, nightingales, frogs and the distant surf.'

In two graceful, central paragraphs of 'Why I Live in Majorca' Graves describes his village. Deià is evoked in specific, sensuous detail; typically, Graves' description is based firmly in the spatial, or geographical, arrangement of detail:

> But what was Deià *really* like? A village of some 400 inhabitants, and some 200 solid stone houses, most of them built on the landward side of a rocky hill which occupied the centre of a great fold of mountains. The coast-road encircled Deià but touched the outlying houses only. A church with a squat tower and a small cypressed cemetery crowned the hill; no houses at all were built between it and the sea, half-a-mile away. A torrent, dry during the summer, ran halfway round the village and down in a narrow gorge until it emptied into a cove, with a beach of sand and pebbles. Apart from the small port of Soller, six miles up the coast, this was one of the very few inlets along the island's ironbound north-western coast. No car could get down to the cove from the village, and the fisherman's path was a rough one indeed: a 400 foot descent from the coast-road, first through olive groves and then through a scrub of lentiscus, spurge, asphodel, caper and wild asparagus. (Robert Graves 1965)

The open vowels, repeated *I* sounds, the specificity of the diction describing both the landscape and the flora of northern Mallorca complement the purposeful syntax. Though the sentence patterns are quite varied, the sentences are dominated by nominals, absolutes, noun complements and by compound subjects and their modifiers. All in all, with the noun series which ends the paragraph, Graves uses very graceful, and standard, structures to pack a great deal of specific detail into these few sentences.

The attention to Mallorca's distinctive flora continues in the second of these paragraphs:

> The fisherman's huts in the cove were used only in the summer months. No refreshments could be obtained there and one got very hot climbing back after a swim. The mountains had been laboriously terraced all the way up from sea-level to about 900 feet. There were lemon and orange groves where irrigation was possible; but only three springs in the village ran all the year round, and the soil was everywhere poor and stony; apart from a few carob trees that provided wholesome fodder for mules, all the rest was olive orchard. And the olives were not the well-behaved, bushy-topped, stately variety that one finds in Italy, France, and California, but twisted, bossed, hacked-about grotesques, often growing from cracks in the live rock, never watered, never manured, once a year scratched around with a primitive mule-plough, and every seven years trimmed of their biggest branches. They were almost indestructible; a good many had been planted by the

Moors, more than 700 years before. 'Pamper an olive tree,' the villagers used to say, 'and spoil the fruit.' In the spring some of the olive terraces could be persuaded to raise a sparse crop of broad beans. These, with figs, served to feed the black pigs which were ceremoniously killed at Martinmas, and turned into red and black sausage; each household had its pig and the sausage must last until the following Martinmas. Above the olive-trees rose an unterraced belt of stunted evergreen oak, where charcoal-burners worked all summer, pigs rooted in the autumn, wild peonies flowered at Easter. And wild cats, martens, and civets maintained a precarious existence. Above that, towered sheer precipices streaked with rusty ochre, and above those the bald limestone brow of the Teix.

(Robert Graves 1965)

Here Graves displays in a beautifully organized paragraph (up the mountainsides from the cove to the 'brow of the Teix') the same attention to phonology and syntax as in paragraph one, and again, the specification is done with a profusion of nouns – note that only three colours are specified in this very lengthy passage. The overall effect is of a great tension between what should be a sparse, barren landscape and the profusion of crops which in fact the Mallorcan villagers can force the rocky land-scape to bear. And with his two asides about the cultivation of pigs and olives, Graves indicates that he both shares and respects the villagers' knowledge of agri-culture – wresting a life from stony mountainside.

Graves' regard for the Mallorcan people continued to remain high. 'I have now lived here under the Dictatorship, the Republic, and the present regime – but the people do not change.' Mallorcans, according to Graves, 'have always been liberty-loving, though staunchly conservative; highly moral, though confirmed skeptics of ecclesiastical doctrine; with a rooted dislike of physical violence, drunkenness, or any breach of good manners'. And Graves was particularly grateful that 'money-grub-bing' was considered a breach of good manners. 'In the villages, bills are presented neither weekly, nor monthly, nor quarterly, but at the end of the year.' Graves was noted for presenting his Deià baker with a cigar each time he paid his annual bill.

In his fiction, however, Graves is much less charitable about his adopted fellow citizens. All the stories of Mallorcan characters are replete with business swindles, family squabbles, death by witchcraft, even plagiarism.

In his 'Majorcan Stories', a separate section of the *Collected Short Stories* (1968), there is little evidence that Graves thought highly of the Mallorcan national char-acter. Perhaps for dramatic reasons, each of the stories revolves around a situation in which a Mallorcan behaves less than honestly ('The Whittaker Negroes', a non-story of which the less said the better, has no Mallorcan characters). In 'Valiant Bulls', the plot depends on a failed conspiracy to supply unenergetic bulls for the *corrida*. 'A Bicycle in Majorca' begins with a lesson on bringing an English bicycle into Spain without paying import duties, then proceeds by theft and re-theft of the imported bicycle, with an attempted suicide thrown in. 'Evidence of Affluence' exposes the ways in which Mallorcans are careful not to look too affluent, in order to avoid taxation. The most complex and most entertaining of the Mallorcan stories is 'The Viscountess and the Short-haired Girl', a tale of peasants conning a con. This story depends upon Mallorcan peasants willing to pretend to believe that a 'Bulgarian heretic' has kidnapped a 'short-haired girl' long enough to testify about her presence in the village; the joke around which the story revolves is that the peasants know as well as the lawyer and detective that the short-haired girl is having an affair with the Bulgarian and is not the niece of the Viscountess who will pay them to testify, but is in fact married to the Viscountess' lover – rather than a kidnapping trial, it is a divorce trial at which the peasants will testify. But first, they run up enormous expense accounts and squeeze the Viscountess for more and more pesetas in exchange for their testimony.

In 'To Minorca!' (collected in *Food for Centaurs*, 1960) Graves heaps criticism on the customs, food, architecture, even the climate of that neighbouring Balearic island. Little escapes his eye: 'Minorcans lack the enterprise of their Majorcan cousins', so they have never returned to olive growing. Their vineyards were destroyed by *phylloxer*, 'so that their staple drink is no longer wine, but gin – a word and habit borrowed from the British'. It is their British-derived customs Graves decries most, but he finds little about Minorca to recommend it, with the possible exception of their fresh seafood. The shopkeepers are complacent and far from accommodating: 'In these islands, storekeepers always believe that customers are trying to get rid of their money, it doesn't matter on what. You need a hammer; they haven't got one in stock, so they say brightly: "It will have to be a saw".' Indeed, almost the entire essay is a catalogue of the extreme nonchalance of the Minorcans: when told that the Pope has died, the confectioners' clerk shrugs, 'Indeed? I feel it deeply. So he has left us! But patience! What can we do? All things pass.'

Ironically, Graves may have had a model close at hand for the conniving and subtle Balearic businessmen of his fiction. At least one Mallorcan native may not have been so scrupulously honest as he appeared. Juan Marroig Mas, known locally as Gelat, became Graves' local adviser. It was Gelat who convinced Graves that he should buy 36,000 square metres of land to foil the building of a German tourist hotel between Graves' home and the sea. (He also convinced Graves to place his property in Gelat's name, since foreigners could not own land within five kilometres of the beach.) To pay for this purchase, Graves should build a road from his home to the cala – and recoup his investment by selling the road to the government. The road could be financed by selling plots of the 36,000 square metres to Graves' rich English friends. In the summer of 1931, Graves considered devoting the land, by then called 'Luna Land', to a university which would teach Laura Riding's views on life and society. Graves mortgaged his home to buy the land, eventually; this debt was a major factor in his decision to undertake the writing of *I, Claudius* (Seymour 1995: 204–05, 210–11). In September 1933, a rainstorm washed the new road away, and none of the land had been sold; in the fall of 1935 Graves was forced to explain the purpose of the road and to 'produce the appropriate authorizations' that would clear him of rumours of spying; sale to the government was impossible (Seymour: 219, 237).

In 1947, after his return from exile in England during the war years, Graves was anxious to settle ownership issues with Laura Riding, who had returned to America in 1939. Riding gave Gelat power of attorney, and the properties were transferred; Gelat would farm the land, providing olives and wood to Graves in rent payment. None of the transfers were legal, however: Graves was still a foreigner and still prohibited from owning land so near the beach. In fact, when Gelat died in 1949, he passed the properties on to his son. It was not until 1959 that Graves, finally realizing the duplicity, had a friend arrange for the village of Deya to 'annex' the property so his claim would be legal. He then had to repurchase his own properties from a trusted Mallorcan *émigré*, Ricardo Sicre, who acted as negotiator and go-between (Seymour: 325, 327). In fact, we know that Graves later based at least one conniving Mallorcan character on Gelat: on 4 December 1957 in a letter to James Reeves, Graves mentioned that 'a light story, as pleadingly asked for *New Yorker*' was based on 'Old Gelat and the Lady Carnarvon divorce case' (*Selected Letters* 1988: 172). This 'light story' eventually became 'The Viscountess and the Short Haired Girl'.

Mallorcan society and geography were being transformed rapidly in the years after Graves' return to the island. Before the Spanish Civil War, Mallorca had been the medically prescribed holiday for a 'rest in the sun'. With recently discovered penicillin, these visitors no longer came, and 'winter holidays in the sun went out of fashion' (William Graves 1995: 135). After the war, in the early 1950s, the Mallorcan Board of Tourism began advertising the island as a honeymoon destination; then the Ministry of Tourism in Madrid, a Franco project to develop the economy, took up the programme. State controls on room rates and the development of commercial airline routes made Mallorca cheap and convenient. 'Tourist complexes developed with little infrastructure and no consideration for the landscape. Planning permission in supposedly protected areas could be obtained, provided a high enough bribe was paid in the right place' (William Graves: 135).

When 'Why I Live in Majorca' was reprinted in *Majorca Observed* (1965), it was accompanied by a 'Postscript'. In this late addition, Graves brought his earlier ideas into the context of 'the brand-new phenomenon of mass-tourism'. By 1965, there were '5,000 planes a month' bringing tourists to 'over 1,000 new hotels'. Graves derides the worship of sun tanning, 'a new idea derived from D. H. Lawrence's German-inspired sun-cult'. Graves voices the criticisms of tourists which have by now become *de rigeur*, if not *passé*: food, behaviour, ignorance of geography or customs, guided tours of the Mallorcan countryside with bored and uninformed guides. 'Majorca is fortunate in its lack of exploitable historical attractions; mass tourism and individual travel need not get confused' (47). Graves then goes on to list the ways in which organized tours must exaggerate local history – such as Sand's visit to Valldemosa, or Archduke Ludwig Salvator's love life – simply to give tourists something to look at and think about, other than getting 'frizzled' on a beach. Already Graves was quoting the authorities' worries about the effect of 'the daily exhalation of carbon dioxide from the lungs of several hundred tourists ... rapidly flaking off the colours' (50) of not only the Mallorcan caves, but caves in Spain or France.

In 1965, Deià seemed relatively untouched in contrast to Palma, where 'the old Palma has long ceased to exist; its centre eaten away by restaurants, bars, souvenir shops, travel agencies and the like' (51). But, in contrast 'fortunately the rocks from which we swim at Deyá are inaccessible to the mass-tourist, nor is the village exploitable'. Graves, correctly as it turned out, predicted that Deià would remain relatively untouched as long as the roads were bad, 'but the still unexploited Majorcan hinterland is constantly shrinking as the roads improve'. Deià was, even in 1965, already touched by tourism of a different manner: 'of course, the usual German colonists have bought up the more spectacular sites on the coast nearby, and built houses in their own familiar domestic style' (51).

Graves' attitude may have become like that of the Count of Deià, a character in 'She Landed Yesterday', one of Graves' Mallorcan stories. The Count of Deià is heir to the family seat, the Palacio Deià in Palma, but chooses instead to live in the village of Deià, to take 'refuge from the enemy, here in the mountains'. When asked 'what enemy?' he replies,

> Those who smoke blond tobacco; those who strew our quiet Majorcan beaches with pink, peeling human flesh; those who roar around our island in foreign cars ten metres long; those who prefer aluminum to earthenware, and plastics to glass; those who demolish the old quarters of Palma and erect travel agencies, souvenir shops, and tall barrack-like hotels on the ruins; those who keep their radios bawling incessantly along the street at siesta-time; those who swill Caca-Loco and bottled beer! (*Collected Short Stories* 1968: 277)

If this series of characteristics attributed to tourists by the Count of Deià seems to come easily and be heartfelt, consider that for the Count 'the last straw came with the closing of the Café Figaro, which everyone of character in Palma used to frequent and the conversion of its premises into palatial offices for Messrs Thomas Cook and Son' (277). The Figaro was Graves' favourite cafe/bar in Palma.

William Graves' memoir, *Wild Olives*, is the story of his attempts to find a way both to earn an adult living (his original career was that of petroleum engineer) and to remain in Deià. His final chapter is an evocation of the changes that were wrought in Deià by tourist development between 1946 and the mid-1980s:

> [T]he village we returned to was not the one I grew up in ... There were now two luxury hotels ... an up market restaurant with its own swimming pool ... one could no longer walk to Canellún without being passed by a steady stream of cars and buses. Even Laura and Father's road to the Cala had been blacktopped by the Deyá Town Hall. The metamorphosis was complete. Deyá was an up-market holiday resort ... no longer did the fishwives bring the morning catch to the village; no longer did one hear the rattle of the carob beans being knocked down; no longer was the cafe filled with smoke and the cries of the *Truc* players on a Sunday morning. (William Graves: 258–9)

A horrible irony of this transformation is that, for five years, William Graves was himself a hotel-keeper in Deià, the solution to his career dilemma being one of the causes of Deià's move 'up market'.

When Bill Waldren, a friend of Graves' son, successfully remodelled an old mill in Deià to serve as a museum for his archaeological discoveries, Robert Graves bought two houses opposite the new museum and converted them into an apartment, a library and a laboratory. Thus, William became co-director of the 'Archaeological Study Centre' in Deià. In its last incarnation, it became known as the 'Deià Archaeological Museum, Library and Gallery Teix'. There were even plans to 'add a shop to the complex, to sell paintings, sculpture, photographs, ceramics and jewellery produced by *estrangers*' (William Graves: 178–207).

Robert Graves was recognized by the Mallorcan government in the spring of 1967 with a plaque honouring his contribution to the island. That same March, William Graves and his wife Elena opened their hotel Ca'n Quet for its second season. The first season had not been particularly successful but things changed in the second year.

> We were now listed as one of the special hotels in the Erna Low Travel brochure, and our clientele included doctors, architects, TV producers and writers. We were written up in glossy magazines such as *Cosmopolitan* and *Nova*. On my desk I found a flood of letters to answer and, by mid-June, we were fully booked. Erna Low charged £50 a fortnight, full board, including the flight; we had become the 'in' place to be. Girls wearing the latest Carnaby Street mini-skirts and white knee-high boots graced our *terraza* ... When Father was interviewed by the BBC, the crew stayed at Ca'n Quet ... We were discovered by young British actors ... Some even managed to pick up work on films being shot on the island. (William Graves: 233–4)

In 1962, Robert Graves had been instrumental – almost solely – in the decision to declare the northwest coast of Mallorca a National Park, with no high-rise hotels allowed. He suggested this solution to Don Manuel Fraga, the minister of Tourism (who had once been dispatched by Franco to visit Graves) as a way of halting a planned hotel and villa complex on the Deià cala. After this rather high-handed intervention on Graves' part, Deià and the other coastal villages were regulated by new building codes, and all new building had to win the approval of the Fine Arts Council in Palma. Many Deià villagers were angered both by this new restriction and by the loss of jobs that the hotel would have generated. Older villagers remembered that Graves had built the road to the beach, had planned a university campus between his home and the beach, and had even at one time considered building his own hotel on this land. 'The *senyor* plainly had double standards' (William Graves: 165).

By 1968, when Robert Graves was made an 'adoptive son of Deya', among the accomplishments for which the Mayor thanked Graves were his role in bringing electricity to Deià and for 'attracting so many *turistas*' (William Graves: 242).

One biographer, Miranda Seymour, believes that by the 1960s Graves was in fact tiring of village life in Deià, and especially of his role as a counter-culture guru for an alarming band of bohemians, 'hippies', and would-be artists, these last an element whom Graves satirized in his poem 'Wigs and Beards'.

After a first stanza describing how the 'bewigged country Squire' of the past would not pay his debts except for gambling losses, 'horsewhipped his tenantry' as he 'urged his pack through standing grain', how he 'snorted at the arts', 'blasphemed', and 'set fashions of pluperfect slovenliness', Graves introduces the modern version, the 'Beards', who,

> Latter-day bastards of that famous stock,
> They never rode a nag, nor gaffed a trout,
> Nor winged a pheasant, nor went soldiering,
> But remain true to the same hell-fire code
> In all available particulars
> And scorn to pay their debts even at cards.

At least the 'bewigged Squire'

Shot, angled . . .
And claimed seigneurial rights over all women
who slept, imprudently, under the same roof.

In contrast, the modern, loutish 'Beards' are first seen

Hurling their empties through the cafe window
and belching loud as they proceed downstairs.

. . . Moreunder (which is to subtract, not add),
Their ancestors called themselves gentlemen
As they, in the same sense, call themselves artists.

(*New Collected Poems* 1977: 270)

In a graceful and laudatory article in the June 1996 *Gravesiana*, Joan M. Fiol points out this essential contradiction. After Graves was duped into buying the land from his home to the cala – to forestall, Fiol maintains, the building of a German tourist hotel next to Graves' house – he built the famous road and attempted to sell plots along it.

The image of a land developer clashes noisily with that of the poet who so intensely loved that countryside and who later forcefully defended it against any danger of being spoilt. However, in those days the concept of balearization was not even an issue (Balearization is a word coined by French geographers to describe the systematic destruction of the coastline by indiscriminate and excessive building). Sadly, the scheme failed . . . (Fiol 1996: 65)

Fiol points out that the failure of the scheme at least led to Graves writing the *Claudius* novels to climb out of bankruptcy. Yet the road also led to rumours that Graves was a spy – who else would need a road to the water? (And his evacuation from the island by a British destroyer in 1934 kept this rumour alive well into the 1950s, even after an official inquiry cleared Graves.) In fact in 1967, the road was 'the sole point in the agenda of a special meeting held by the Town Council . . . when the poet was about to be named Adoptive Son of Deià'. The Mayor's final remarks about 'Mr. Graves' and his interest 'in matters related to his village, history, customs, folklore, etc.' contain this sentence: 'In 1934 he built at his own expense a road leading to the cove.' Finally in 1976 the local administration made the road public after repairing and paving it. Even Fiol writes, 'A happy end for an embarrassing business' (66).

Fiol can be more direct. Of Graves' mistakes about the Mallorcan language, his debunking of local legends used to 'attract tourists to his neighborhood', balanced with his debunking of Chopin's and Sand's harsh criticism in *Winter in Majorca*, Fiol says 'This is just another example of Graves' two different, sometimes contradictory, levels of expression when dealing with Majorcan matters' (71).

Nowadays, though Mallorca has its share of bohemians, artists and artistes, Ibiza is becoming the holiday destination for the bohemian class. Still, the Mallorcan tourism that led to the creation of the word *baléariser*, to describe the Mallorcan transformation from paradise to tourist development, (a transformation copied around the Mediterranean and a word not meant as a compliment) continues. Now, with the University of the Balearics running a degree programme in tourism, and with a private Escuela de Turismo in Palma, the Mallorcan government is consciously, however, following a strategy to move 'up market and green' with new beaches, hotels and roads (*Passport*: 16–17, 26, 56). The government is now following a policy of destroying hotels in order to reestablish 'greenbelts' around some of the larger hotel complexes, but all this may be too late. With a polluted and depleted aquifer, Mallorca now is brought potable drinking water by daily tankers that unload in Palma. Still, perhaps the enigmatic figure of Robert Graves, that so contradicts his works about the island he loved, can play a role in helping to develop a more sustainable tourism for Mallorca and the other Balearic Islands.

REFERENCES

Buswell, Richard J. (1996) 'Tourism in the Balearic Islands', in Barke, Mike, Towner, John and Newton, Mike (eds) *Tourism in Spain: Critical Issues*. Wallingford, UK: CAB International, 309–39.

Fiol, Joan. (1996) 'The perfect guest: the poet and the island – a lasting affair', *Gravesiana: The Journal of the Robert Graves Society*. June.

Graves, Robert (1960) *Food for Centaurs*. New York: Doubleday.

Graves, Robert (1965) 'Why I Live in Majorca', *Majorca Observed*. London: Cassell.

Graves, Robert (1968) *Collected Short Stories*. London: Penguin.

Graves, Robert (1977) *New Collected Poems*. New York: Doubleday.

Graves, Robert (1988) *Between Moon and Moon: Selected Letters of Robert Graves*, ed. Paul O'Prey. London: Moyer Bell.

Graves, Robert (1997) *Letters to Ken*, ed. Harvey Sarner. Cathedral City, CA: Brunswick Press.

Graves, William (1995) *Wild Olives*. London: Hutchinson.

Passport Illustrated Travel Guide to Mallorca (1995), Chicago: Passport Books and Thomas Cook Group Ltd.

Quadrado, José María (1841) 'To George Sand: a refutation', *La Palma: A Weekly Journal of History and Literature*, May.

Sand, George (1956) *Winter in Majorca*, trans. and ed. Robert Graves. London: Cassell.

Seymour, Miranda (1995) *Robert Graves: Life on the Edge*. London: Doubleday.

Chapter 5

Nevil Shute and the Landscape of England: An Opportunity for Literary Tourism

David T. H. Weir

1

Tourists visit 'places' and, in the case of 'literary tourists' it is the landscape of the writer that they seek to visit, pass through, and try to recover for themselves. In their own terms, they may come to inhabit these places, to own, and to value this experience which has become theirs. Thus it is plausible to describe these places as 'Cultural Property' in the sense used by Tomaszewski (1993). But the notion of 'landscape' is not incontestable. Landscape may on the one hand be taken as a given, a primordial element, a set of natural facts or a backdrop against which events occur, the result of processes which exist or pre-existed before the intervention of man. Writers in the geographical tradition like Stamp (1946) and Fleure and Davis (1951) explore the manifold, multiplex and historically evolving interactions between humans and the environment which shapes their actions and which, in their turn, they help to shape. But on the other hand landscape is treated as a construct irretrievably tainted by its human associations.

The concept of 'landscape' is quite frequently explained as a product of that specific and particular period of western civilization which we call 'the Age of Enlightenment' when, through the purposeful interventions of such pioneers of landscape gardening as William Kent and Lancelot (Capability) Brown the owners of country estates learned that a particular impression might be created within apparently 'natural' clusters of physical features, suitably altered and 'improved'. That this view, although popular, is a limited and partial one, is expressed by Hoskins, when he points out that 'it is the influence of Kent, Brown, and such later men as Repton, that has helped to give rise to the wholly inadequate view that the English landscape is "the man-made creation of the seventeenth and eighteenth century"' (1955: 135).

Most of the 'landscapes' with which we are familiar are indisputably human artefacts and as much a product of their time as the literature, music and other artistic creations of an epoch. Both landscape and writing about landscape may be treated equally as cultural productions.

With some writers indeed we tend to go further than this for they seem to 'inhabit' their landscape in a deterministic sense. Their writings are inextricably associated with specific locations, identified with particular places in a specialized and sometimes unique way. Thus, it is impossible to construe the novels of the Brontë sisters without locating them in the mid-Pennines of Western Yorkshire. Haworth and the 'Wuthering Heights' of the locationally real Top Withens thus enter the vocabulary of subsequent literature, both as unique identifiable locations and as a shorthand for a whole genre of literature. Specific vocabularies become associated with certain types of landscape – 'terrific', as in Turner's depictions of Gordale Scar. When Captain Scott wrote about the Antarctic wastes in his journal 'My God, this is an awful place' or when Stella Gibbons noted that there was 'something nasty in the woodshed' of Cold Comfort Farm , they touched some universal vein of empathy in their readers and these depictions have entered subsequent literature as emblematic of a certain second-hand but nonetheless real encounter with the physical world.

Drabble, in a sensitive and evocative review of a classic tradition in Literature, complemented by the photographic vision of Jorge Lewinski, enables us to see the 'landscape' of the world of these writers in relation to a whole vision of an English society in decline from some pre-existent mythical Golden Age. She claims that the 'Golden Age never existed, but by the same token it will never die, while there is a writer left to embody our desire' (1979: 277).

Ownership of the statement of proprietorial claims to inner and outer territory is clearly good for some sorts of business, among them the 'literary tourism industry'. This new industry is in good shape, and its representations are increasingly in evidence, cheek by jowl with older, more characteristic industrial structures. Writers were never so much read as they may be now and their supposed environments valued by people who may never read their books. Against the bridge on the A19 in Northern England, just after the entrance to the Nissan plant outside Sunderland, is a sign announcing the entrance to 'Catherine Cookson Country', and, in somewhat smaller signage below, doubtless reflecting commercial, if not literary or historical value, 'Bede's World'. Further south, outside Thirsk, the hopeful traveller encounters 'The World of James Herriot'. (This name itself is an artful construction: the real 'Jim Herriot' was a Birmingham City goalkeeper of the 1960s.)

The consequences of this kind of market positioning are reasonably clear for the tourist industry. In another example from the industrial North of England: if, as a tourist, you want to *do* England and *do* the Brontës, you have to *do* Haworth. It is a mean, cold place of no great intrinsic charm, yet on every day in summer you may see disciplined squads of bemused Japanese trudging up the steeply inclined cobbled streets of this small West Yorkshire place, bigger than a village but not by any means a town, past the souvenir shops and the tourist offices towards a glum foursquare parsonage on the edge of the moors, by a dark graveyard. And when they are 'there', what have they got? What is their experience? What is the landscape their journey passes through? What is the essence of this experience? Is it related in any way to the intentions of the authors thus commemorated or the reality of their separate artistic visions?

Some writers find themselves located by where they *happened* to be, which has obtained value long after in ways unanticipated by them. Thus the 'venomous' Bede's location in Jarrow hard against Jarrow Slake is in one sense an accident of the spread of the early Christian church and a testimony to the patronage of once influential local rulers. But 'Bede's world', which represents a modern attempt to create value retrospectively, has in a real sense rather little to do with the historical Bede and is certainly not to be found in his writings. He was a scholar, a sage, an historian, a saint. His location was a matter of indifference to *him*. His inner space constituted the infinity of Christendom, and the crescence of the English people. But Bede could have written his history from anywhere else in Christian England in that epoch. He had no idea that he was responsible for a 'world'. He would have been rather baffled by it all.

Celebrations of landscape occur in music and the pictorial arts also. To some locations literature or visual artefacts may be added as a bonus to satisfy other cultural needs. In a culture like that of Meiji Japan in need of unifying symbols, the unique and universally identifiable representation of Mount Fuji created its own literary, artistic and musical traditions. If the Mount Fuji we now 'see' is representational and symbolic, it is nonetheless real and we may climb to the top of it.

Such representations of place as these have a genuine power to move the minds and hearts of people. Some places and their representations have always been credited with special powers. Pomorski (1996) argues, 'Genius Loci is a cultural phenomenon. The conviction that a place can evoke unusual acts and events is deposited in the social structure of beliefs.' These locations can work wonders even in their absence or rather in the vicarious experiencing of them. In Communist Prague, under Soviet Russian suzerainty, Czech audiences would rise and stand in defiant silence as the playing of *Ma Vlast* or *Libuse* provoked evocations of Bohemia's woods and fields and Moravian mythological folk heroes. Some of these motivations may be explicitly celebratory as well. Respighi celebrated his own city, Rome, by creating a musical language of fountains, pines and festivals. These artistic representations, though destined to become iconic, badge the locational facts which are in themselves incorrigible.

Tourism sits well with what is obvious and physically visible in these cases. The place is a location, but becomes also a constructed representation. The 'landscape' exists, independent of its representation. Where it is, is what it is. What you see is what you get. It has been written about and that is another fact. As tourists, we consume the representation. Therefore we may be encouraged by those who have a commercial interest in the sale of this representation to visit, and to achieve visitor status as consumers.

We may thus, subsequently, assemble memories of events of which we have not in fact been part but wish to be associated with, and to participate in those representations. But these landscapes are still fixed in place, and we may revisit them and retest or renew our consumption and the consequential experiences of the mind. It has not been possible generally to move battlefields or to relocate cathedrals, so those who seek the shade of Oliver Cromwell will visit Marston Moor or Naseby, while those who wish to hear Quasimodo's bells must only seek them at Notre Dame de Paris. The place *is* the thing and becomes the experience. The representation is identifiable and traceable. It is corrigible by subsequent experience of its original source material.

Some writers have been associated with the creation of landscapes of the mind, rooted often in a highly descriptive and representational manner with particular historical places, but whose ultimate depictions are true works of art. While some of these still exist as physical entities, it is hard, if not impossible, to recover them as presented in the portrayals of the writer. So we search for them in vain, for while we may visit as tourists, places associated with Dickens' writings, it is not now possible to visit 'Dickens' London' and ever to find Dickens' England there, for that was rooted in the specifics of his observations, and these are relatable to historical reality. The natural effluxion of time has taken these places away.

Drabble, indeed, points to Dickens' essential ambivalence towards his own subject matter, and especially towards his concept of the city: 'Dickens is the great poet of pollution ... his London is dirty, but it is also wonderfully mysterious and dramatic ... the overall impression, despite the sordid detail and the social rage, is of intense exhilaration, of wonder at life's infinite variety, and of the infinite variety of the London scene' (1979: 209).

These considerations by no means relate only to the corpus of English literature: the classic Russian tradition provides many relevant examples. Turgenyev's *Notebooks of a Sportsman* (1950) for instance are located in an altogether distinct but nonetheless timeless and historically unchained landscape, populated by the eternal verities of emotion, affiliation, striving and failure, though positionally located in representations of the Russian landscape.

Jones (1995) claims that 'classic studies of literary geography were concerned with the equally classic rural and, often, spatially circumscribed novels of region and of landscape, such as Thomas Hardy's Wessex or Mary Webb's Shropshire.' But nonetheless these places and landscapes did exist in their time. Other writers while seeming to merely represent, in fact created their own landscapes from observed elements, but they exist nowhere, and it is only the representation which we can consume. For all his apparent fidelity to observed particulars, Nevil Shute was one of these.

2

Nevil Shute wrote much which could only have been written by one who had seen specific places and experienced particular journeys. But *his* Landscape of England is one in which the hand of the writer has carefully selected and recruited images of landscape to his fictional task in the light of his artistic vision.

Nevil Shute Norway was born in 1899 in west London. His father, Arthur Hamilton Norway, was a civil servant in the Post Office, who rose to become the Head of the Post Office in Ireland and consequently played a minor though significant part in the 1916 Dublin Easter Rising. Arthur Norway was also a topographical writer of some note and his books are still to be found in second-hand bookshops (A. H. Norway 1899).

The Norway family were long-established Cornish minor gentry, and the unusual name probably relates to the belief that the family's origins were due to the ship-wreck of Norwegian sailors on the cruel Cornish coast. Nevil Shute Norway's grandmother was also a writer. She wrote several children's adventure stories in the late nineteenth century.

His elder brother Fred, who fought in the First World War and died of wounds at Wimereux just outside Boulogne, had also started a writing career. Shute believed that his own talent could never be compared with the superior abilities of his much-loved brother. He wrote in his memoir *Slide Rule* (1958): 'If Fred had lived we might have had some real books some day, not the sort of stuff that I turn out, for he had more literature in his little finger than I have in my whole body' (1958: 24).

By the time of his death in 1960, Nevil Shute Norway had become, under his abbreviated *nom de plume* of Nevil Shute, the best-selling novelist in the English language of his time, as popular and as widely read in America and Australia as in his native country. He adopted the shorter version of his name to attach to his literary efforts because he had by then become a distinguished and successful aeronautical engineer and he did not want his reputation in that serious world to be risked by any association with popular fiction.

For his works did become very popular. Indeed, among Australian writers he holds an honoured place as one who created a successful stream of Australian novels, among which, *A Town Like Alice* (1950) and *The Far Country* (1952) came to symbolize the very aspirations of a new civilization in the process of establishment in an uncharted continent.

Many of his novels became films, and *A Town Like Alice* was the basis for two successful TV series. His stories translate well to visual modes of representation. He was above all, and like Simenon, a more or less precise contemporary, a highly commercial writer. He wrote books to sell, and they sold.

He eventually lived from his writing, giving up a successful career as an aeronautical engineer and aviation entrepreneur to do so.

So it would be tempting and plausible to suppose that Nevil Shute's talents derived from a family background of the literary kind, and that his career as a novelist owed much to his ingenuous facility at the description and representation of what had happened to him in his life. This, by historical chance, turned out to be an exciting period of history, encompassing among many crucial moments, two World Wars, a great depression, the birth of two new technologies in which he was intimately involved, that of airship and aeroplane construction, the collapse of the British Empire and the threat of the nuclear extinction of mankind. But this would be quite erroneous.

Nevil Shute's landscapes, while drawn from life, stand as close to experienced reality as does Sibelius' *Finlandia* to the historical experience of a small bitterly cold northern country. Nevil Shute created his landscape as much as he used it. His landscape moreover was one of *inner* experience, *post hoc* reflection, and speculation, which served as the inexorable counterpoint to experienced reality. His 'landscapes' are constructions of his craft as a novelist.

That is not to say that in any meaningful respect, Nevil Shute's Landscape, the essence of his fiction, is in itself fictional. He invented none of it. It is not a created world like that of Tolkien, Herbert or Rowling for instance. There are no Hobbits, no sand worms, no Hogwarts and Voldemorts, merely ordinary people, sometimes doing extraordinary things. Shute nonetheless often dealt with mighty themes. In *On the Beach* he wrote movingly of the end of the world of humankind. But his Göt-terdämmerung involved no biblical apocalypse, and his battle between good and evil requires no supernatural effects. His depiction of landscapes are in essence accurate, brief, and invariably correct down to points of detail. You may visit the places of which he wrote, if you can find them. You will be guided by a precise knowledge of his life and action because he 'never ever, wrote about places, which he had not personally visited', as his daughter, Shirley Norway (1999) has explained. But his landscape is not that of Mary Webb or of the Brontë sisters.

3

Nevil Shute was a boy at Shrewsbury School in 1918 when he heard that his brother had died. From that time on he was convinced that it was his destiny and duty to serve in the Armed Forces and it was with some surprise that he discovered at the end of the war that he was alive and had not in fact seen active service. He wrote in *Slide Rule*: 'For the remainder of my time at Shrewsbury I don't think I had the slightest interest in a career or any adult life. I was born to one end, which was to go into the Army and do the best I could before being killed' (1958: 24).

He went up to Oxford to read engineering. He was not a particularly outstanding student and in due course he achieved a third-class honours degree. But during his time at university he caught the aviation bug and never recovered.

The aviation industry was in its infancy and offered all the opportunities for adventure, risk-taking, and the application of the solid virtues of the personality seriously oriented toward engineering, which Shute saw in himself. He quotes more than once in his writings both fictional and straight, the maxim that 'there are old pilots and there are bold pilots but there are no old bold pilots'.

Shute recognized that the aviator who understood the nature of the engineering principles and practice on which this precision craft was based, owed a duty of care not only to himself but also to his machine. Shute rehearses this scenario many times in his life, and in his writings. The theme of several of his novels concerns the young man who has learnt how to take risks and survive. He understood the vital necessity of mastering one's craft before one forays into unknown territory. He was modest about his engineering also, noting many times that 'an engineer is a man who can do for five bob, what any damn fool can do for a pound'.

It is not quite clear when exactly Shute started to write, nor why he always, throughout a demanding, not to say, almost all-consuming career and in positions of increasingly onerous responsibility, felt the desire to write; nor of the extent to which he shared these aspirations with his parents. But he wrote carefully, meticulously, routinely and with forethought. Above all he wrote with the exactness and meticulous care that he learnt to apply to his engineering. Having being turned down by publishers for each of his first two novels he methodically put them back in the drawer and started again. They were never to be published in his lifetime. His judgement was correct. They are not bad but they are test pieces, apprentice works. He was learning his craft.

To the end his writing method varied little. Because of the demands of his professional life, and until he became a fulltime writer in the late 1930s, writing had to be restricted to evenings. He wrote regularly, tenaciously, professionally, precisely. He rewrote very little of the main body of a novel but always found it necessary, after a book was concluded, to rewrite the first chapter. It is as though a composer set out to compose a symphony and then only after the first performance decided to change the key signature. But for Shute, all had to be of a part. His craft was seamless as aeronautical engineers' aeroplanes had to be. Balance, precision, order and the tying up of loose ends are trademarks of the Nevil Shute novel.

It is, of course, a great mistake to suppose that the leading-edge developments in science and engineering in any era are matters of high excitement, or that fundamental scientific breakthroughs happen every day of the week. Shute begged himself a career in aircraft engineering after the First World War. This was a 'leading-edge' industry, but it was no Palo Alto or Science City. The aviation industry in post First World War England was an under-funded and hand-me-down affair taking place in temporarily rented factories, exiguously equipped with second-hand machines, and it was staffed by those whose enthusiasm for the industry and its prospects far outran the reality of monetary reward.

He described the premises of one of his companies thus: 'The new company was in a tiny way of business, and they were still glad to have my unpaid work, for money was very tight. The buildings consisted of one wooden hangar ... the head office was a little weatherboard building of three rooms ... the drawing office was an old army hut' (Shute 1958: 43). But Shute kept at his trade as others fell out. And he became one of the second generation of pioneers, among the company of those who made the new technology work, and created a new industry.

His craft initially was that of the stress calculator. This is a trade which has changed irrevocably since the advent of machine and subsequently electronic calculation. It is not high science. In the pre-computer 1920s, even pre-electromechanical calculators, it was a matter of dead hard sums, of minute meticulous calculation, of much reworking, under different and varying assumptions, and of the laborious checking of apparently obvious results. My own early career as a social researcher overlapped this era. Things are much easier now, and that is why egregious mistakes in scientific work are sometimes made, as in the case of the fatal miscalculations made in the design of the Hubble telescope. The calculations are delegated by the researcher to the software and the error is too easily masked within the black box. But each step in Shute's time was a new beginning because none of this had been done before by men better or worse qualified (Eliot 1944). It was handwork and brainwork. It was repetitive, and it had to be correct.

The 'science' was in no better state. Aerodynamics, the logic of airflow, the impending perils of metal fatigue, materials and sheer forces – all awaited their scientific resolution. This was an empirical craft based upon trial and error. And error meant death. So for the enthusiastic aviator there was every impulsion to get the sums right.

This reality was put with customary elegance by Saint-Èxupéry (1929), thus:

> I remember ... learning of the death of Lecrivain, one of those hundred pilots who in a day or a night of fog have retired for eternity ...
>   'Lecrivain didn't land at Casablanca last night.'
>   'Is that so? ... Couldn't he get through? Did he come back?'
>   And in the dead darkness of the omnibus, the answer came 'No.'
>   We waited to hear the rest, but no word sounded. And as the seconds fell it became more and more apparent that that 'No' would be followed by no further word, was eternal and without appeal, that Lecrivain not only had not landed at Casablanca, but would never again land anywhere.

Then (as now) many, if not most, of the victims of aviation disasters died not from the relatively good death of traumatic injury, but from the horror of being burnt alive. That was the reality of 1920s aircraft technology, and of the brittleness of its structures.

Airfields of that era typically carried among their rescue equipment a boatman's hook on an especially long pole. This had been found to be the ideal (indeed the only) way of hauling burning airmen from the wreckage of their vehicle without exposing the rescuers to an equally fiery fate.

The novels of Nevil Shute (and not merely those based on the world of aviation) often refer to the awful reality of death by fire. Indeed, the plot of one of his war novels, *Most Secret* (1945), is based on his actual experience as a member of the team of scientists, boffins and engineers who fought the 'Secret War' and in specific terms describes a plan to mount large flame throwers on small ships.

Death by fire and the purging of dross in the transmutation of base to noble metal may have had for Shute some mystical or religious significance as well as engineering reality. But it had strong personal connotations also.

Many of Nevil Shute's friends, professional competitors and former colleagues perished in the fiery inferno that followed the crash of the R101. Shute in a sense never got over this experience and his memoir of the events contains more than one outburst of uncharacteristic bitterness about the combination of political interference, technological arrogance and bureaucratic obfuscation which surrounded the R101 tragedy and put an instantaneous termination to the British Airship industry.

Other airships suffered a like fate, especially, and most spectacularly, the Hindenburg. Death by fire was the reality of failure at the leading edge of this technology.

The thread of aviation runs through all of Shute's work. He was an airman in the pioneer days of flying, and comfortably saw in the inception of the jet age. He died a few short years before man set foot on the moon.

In the logs of his own flights, as well as in the fictionalized journeys which form the heart of many of his novels, we catch the exuberance and emotion, as well as the respect for engineering and natural reality, that characterize the writings of St-Èxupéry.

4

So should we ascribe Shute's use of landscape to his experience as an aviator? Is Shute's 'Landscape of England' that of a country seen from the air, a topography surveyed from above? Does he, like the historian Maurice Beresford (1954), see the landscape as the sort of picture revealed by aerial mapping techniques? This approach, which had proven its utility in wartime in giving bomber crews a precise representation of the enemy terrain they were to find their targets among, was converted by Beresford and his team to rediscover the sites of long-lost medieval villages like Wharram Percy in North Yorkshire.

Or does he see the terrain as a cartographer, like Imhof (1951), who analyses the relationship of the map to the physical terrain, utilizing constructs from perceptual psychology and trigonometrical calculation? Is Shute's landscape that of the precise calculator of distances, heights and angles? To some extent this must be so and some of Shute's descriptions are indeed powerfully realized in this way. But the descriptions are always harnessed to his analysis and never simply imported for additional effect.

Some indeed of Shute's descriptions can be traced in their fictional form back to a particular flight. The terrain of Labrador and Canada flown over in the R100 and described in Shute's memoir *Slide Rule* is recreated in *An Old Captivity* (1940) and again in *No Highway* (1948*b*).

The terrain of the desert described in *Round the Bend* (1951) can be found in the actual flight log of his trip to Australia in 1948 (Shute 1948*a*).

Thus, when he flew from Rutbah to Habbaniyah, he records the landscape as 'rather beautiful'. And later on as he flew over northern Queensland he writes:

> A most beautiful flight up to Cairns. The coast is like the West Coast of Scotland, all mountains and the waters. Really lovely. Flew at about 1,500 to 2,000 feet to see it all better. Dunk Island has an airstrip and is owned by the honourable Hugo Brassey, who has just returned there with his new wife: flew out and circled it. There is a guesthouse there; it looked a charming retreat and I would like to land and spend a night there on the way down. Coral beaches and blue sea.
>
> South of Cairns the country is all sugar farms, in the valleys and this gives it an extraordinarily English appearance from the air. Sugar cane is cut by hand and only as much is cut each day as can be processed; for this reason a farm is arranged in small fields, all in varying stages, some in plough, some fallow etc., from the air this patchwork effect is just like England.

This passage indeed inescapably evokes Hopkins' celebration of *Pied Beauty* (1948) when he acclaims

> Landscape plotted and pieced-fold, fallow, and plough;
> And all trades, their gear and tackle and trim.

But it is apparent that Shute writes of landscape as no mere topographer and still less as a simple route follower. Even when writing up a log about flying from A to B and following a planned course, he is concerned not just with the visual effect, or the relation to the underlying land form and its structures, but with the patterns of settlement that tell of human life, of interaction, of work and family.

Flying – when Shute learned to fly just after the First World War, and even as late as 1948 in the kind of small plane which Shute revelled in – was not so much a matter of instrument-directed or of celestial navigation but of following landmarks.

Thus in India he writes: 'Refuelled and lunch and went on to Dumdum (Calcutta) following the railway line via Baya at about 2000 feet below cloud most of the way. About 500 miles as we flew, which took us a little over 4 hours. Circled over Benares and took photographs.'

Earlier he had complained while on the French leg of his flight: 'Flew via Lyon. The maps of France are very bad and many roads and railways are not shown on the map.'

Over the Lebanon and Syria he had to find a pipeline and follow it and his inability to do so caused annoyance:

> We got up at five and got out to the aerodrome soon after six, but formalities took a long time and it was not till 7.30 local time that we took off. The hills between Beirut and Damascus rise to about 7000 feet and the cities are only 50 miles apart, so we climbed over Beirut and set course at 2800 feet over the airport. Cleared the hills and passed over Damascus at over 7500 feet talking to them on the VHF and set course for H3. Country completely desolate, a rocky waste. Consumption at 7000 feet and full throttle was well down, a 10 gallon tank lasting 61 minutes and true air speed apparently about 130 miles per hour. Our course was set to hit the pipeline about 18 miles west of H3 but having run our time there was no sign of it so turned 20 degrees to the south and followed motor car tracks and found it all right – a huge great aerodrome in the middle of nowhere. The pipeline is not very obvious, but from H3 a tarmac road leads eastward through Rutbah to Baghdad 275 miles and this is very easy to follow.

It is clear that Shute was in many ways a literal writer. As we know, according to his daughter, he never wrote of anywhere he had not visited. It seems almost equally likely to infer that he never wrote of any people he had not met or of situations he had not experienced directly or at least had the opportunity of hearing about.

Shute was nonetheless not a merely descriptive writer, nor do his landscapes simply form the backdrop to action and the development of plot. In Shute, the life of the mind is implicitly woven in to the life of action, for Shute was a consummate artist in his use of sense data. It is impossible to understand his use of landscape unless one understands his method of working, of plotting, and of the underlying structures which underlie his apparently naïve representations.

5

Let us now try to define 'landscape' more precisely. Ucko (1994) writes:

> Landscape everywhere in the world is a construct of human beings – whether through human ascription to it through mythological creation, or to physical actions by the humans themselves ... whatever the difficulties of recognising such special sights ... all societies in the past would have recognised, as do all societies in the present, some features of their landscapes (if not all the earth) are special.

Knapp and Ashmore (1999) go further when they claim that 'the most prominent notions of landscape emphasise its socio-symbolic dimensions: landscape is an entity that exists by virtue of it being perceived, experienced, and contexualised by people'. It is in this sense that Shute's landscape is significant. He creates landscape from elements of perceived and experienced data in order to reflect and construct a different order of reality. His use of the representation of natural and man-made elements in his work accords well with much contemporary theory about the matter.

Sauer (1925) formulates a concept of a 'cultural' landscape as fashioned from the 'natural landscape'. It is this 'cultural landscape' that we as tourists subsequently seek to first deconstruct and then to reconstitute.

Tuan (1971) speaks of the landscape as 'a repository of human striving' and for post-modernists the landscape itself may constitute 'a cultural image' whose verbal or written representations provide images or 'texts' of its meaning or 'reading'.

Landscapes are constituted largely by humans growing and becoming fulfilled in them. This is what makes them special and gives them value. Landscape in this sense may be conceptualized as a set of potentials instantiated by human choice and action. This approach, in general terms, is, of course, as old as the hills of which men write. As Manzurul Islam (1996) says, 'Historically, space has been the most enduring trope of essential difference', (6).

Porteous (1985), quoted by Jones, argues that 'human experience of place is one major dimension, involving the fundamental distinction of existential insider/existential outsider ... '. Sometimes this has been related to wider conceptions of the spatial determination or culture as when Hegel (1956) concludes that '[the] Natural type of locality [is] intimately connected with the type and character of the people which is the offspring of such soil'.

For Urry (1999) the fact that landscape is primarily encountered visually is related to the 'hegemony of vision' in western culture, a phenomenon further noted by Slater (1995) when he speaks of the 'sanctification of vision'. But it is more than just vision that is at stake here: it is the whole range of human experience which can be evoked by visual means. The organization of space is logically prior to our perceptions of it.

Levinas (1969) ties the general significance of spatial differentiation to the uniquely human need for dwelling, and the need to relate human understanding to primordial locational reality when he says:

> Concretely speaking the dwelling is not situated in the objective world, but the objective world is situated by relation to my dwelling. (153)

But it is Heidegger (1962) who concisely positions our enquiry when he pronounces: 'The environment does not arrange itself in a space which has been given in advance; but its specific worldhood in its significance, articulates the context of involvement which belongs to some current totality of circumspectively allotted spaces' (138).

Social and cultural anthropologists require to define the boundaries of the entities they study. Usually this is based on a spatial definition of the objects of their discourse, and of the social relations which occur within that set of spatial constraints. There are, indeed, many ways in which this definition may be achieved, and we

(Lambert and Weir 1973) have previously attempted to describe and classify these as they have been used by British sociologists in their fieldwork.

But this endeavour in itself is problematic. As Descola (1992) complains, 'Conceptualising Society, the anthropologist confronts a paradoxical problem … ever since Malinowski, a strong tradition has encouraged ethnographers to describe small-scale and territorially circumscribed pre-literate groups as if they were perfectly coherent totalities, each endowed with a particular cultural logic which, properly decoded, offers a key for interpreting the observations recorded day after day.'

Descola correctly points out that a priori classification, no matter how subtle the taxonomic structuring, and mere enumeration, no matter how comprehensive, do not answer the case. He seeks 'principles of order rooted in overarching schemes through which each culture organizes its practices in an immediately distinctive pattern' (108).

Descola concludes that 'each specific form of cultural conceptualization also introduces sets of rules governing the use of and appropriation of nature, evaluations of technical systems, and beliefs about the structure of the cosmos, the hierarchy of beings, and the very principles by which living things function. The logic which informs these configurations is dictated both by the characteristics of the eco-systems to which each culture must adapt itself and by the types of practice through which these eco-systems are socialized' (110–11).

It is not stretching our evidence too far to claim that Shute's writing is informed by a similar need to explicate and to convey to the reader the same complex level of interpenetration of external features of the physical environment, not only with human action itself and to its external symbolization, but also with the inner journeys of psychic discovery, explication and justification undertaken by the protagonists of his fiction.

Shute's symbolization of landscape features are infinitely subtle and woven into the textures of his explanatory paradigms. They inform his characterizations and the logics of action which determine the life projects of his protagonists.

In this chapter we consider only a few of Shute's uses of his characteristic treatment of the Landscape of England, but enough, it is hoped, to illustrate his characteristic method, his apparently naïve but professionally artful manipulation of image, symbol and action into a duplicitous but seamless texture. And then we must consider whether the landscapes thus created are in any way a basis for tourism.

6

We first consider his use of landscape in the novel *Pastoral* (1944). It was a best seller of the late years of the Second World War.

The plotting of Nevil Shute's *Pastoral* is at first analysis simple enough. Indeed the theme and presentation seem almost to form part of a novel with purely propaganda intentions and of merely temporary interest. It was written in wartime. The subject is war. The main protagonists are English. The plot consists of a love story set on an aerodrome in wartime England. The hero is a young bomber pilot: the heroine a

WAAF. The love interest is predictable. Its treatment is apparently equally so. Set out thus, it appears to be merely the stuff of bog-standard romantic fiction of the Mills and Boon genre.

Peter Marshall, a young bomber pilot, in the intervals between sorties over enemy Germany to deliver the retribution of 'Total War' falls for a young WAAF. Boy meets girl. They fall for each other. He asks for her hand. She turns him down. Boy loses girl. The relationship surmounts a crisis. And in the last frame they walk off together into a golden sunset, or rather more immediately, into a less-dangerous posting to Coastal Command.

Shute plotted his books carefully and according to certain structural principles. Implicit in his depiction of character, details of incidents and the evolution of plot are some solid lines of construction. As the airships he designed supported a large mass and larger areas of lighter-than-air material crafted on a rigid framework of girders, with the load-bearing members each precisely calculated so that the structure remains stable no matter what the stresses imposed upon it, so Shute works out his themes in terms of polarities of meaning around which the action occurs. Strong, spare lines of construction, hard, skeletal struts, support extended nets of softer implication, and carry the narrative tissue.

In *Pastoral* the life on the ground, safe, relaxing, enjoyable and free is contrasted with the constrained, stressed, risky and threatened life in the air. Marshall is a man. His girl, Gervase, is clearly a woman. These polarities are clear and ineluctable. They frame the action. But each of them represents other polarities also. Marshall has come to service life from a job as an insurance salesman based in London's Holborn. In the England of the 1930s it was, if not a dead-end job, certainly not one with much potential for rising to becoming a captain of industry. Gervase is the daughter of a country doctor in Yorkshire. He is urban, commercial and southern. She is rural, professional and a girl of the North Country. Each of them brings certain elements to the relationship which are intrinsic to the view of England which Shute purposed.

It is not any old countryside which Peter Marshall learns about as this relationship develops. It is a specific set of locales, each precisely realized. It has not been, initially, the countryside of Gervase Robertson. The critical incident, which brings them together, is the catching of a giant fish in the millpond. Fishing for Marshall represents a unique form of solace from the rigours and tensions of life in the air. His regular fishing companion is his colleague and dependable co-pilot and navigator, Gunnar Franck, who is Danish.

Marshall has noticed WAAF Robertson around the station and he involves her in his life through offering her a share in his catch, when it is duly cooked and displayed in the canteen. Truth to tell it is not very tasty, but Section Officer Robertson understands the symbolism of the offer. Home is the hunter, home from the hill and the fisherman home from the pond.

Marshall had just made an attempt to involve in his celebration and feast of the giant fish, a colleague whose oppo had been lost in a recent raid. But his offer is turned down. (This officer subsequently perishes, losing his machine and his crew, unable to supervene the personal desolation caused by the loss of his comrade. The one death leads inexorably to the others.)

But something about the situation appeals to the young woman, who takes pity on

Marshall, empathizing with his need to have someone recognize his achievement in catching the fish, and his wish to share his spoils with his comrades.

> Section Officer Robertson looked up from *Punch* as he passed her. He looked like a little boy she thought, disappointed because nobody would play with him. It was too bad. She got up from her chair 'I'll come and see your fish' she said 'If I may? Where did you say it was?' (23)

Shute develops the relationship by taking Gervase to the country to involve her in his newly discovered world. It is not initially to the fishing pool but to the nearby woods to see a badger and a fox. He has been introduced to this landscape by another colleague. Out of the fusion of the polarities introduced in these initial, apparently artless descriptions, romance develops.

Shute has introduced the dynamic tension created by the balance of the forces of Man–Woman, Town–Country, Ground–Air, Day–Night, Life and Death to initiate the framework of his narrative journey. He has started to describe a landscape of the mind through which his characters will travel.

Later, Marshall, who is the captain of his crew and the pilot of his machine, makes a nearly disastrous error and almost loses his plane and crew through failing to accept feedback from Gunnar Franck in a desperate situation over the target. There is tension and lack of trust between the crew and the pilot as they start to lose faith in his ability, on which they have all previously been able to count, to get it right on the night. Marshall is going through a dark night of his own soul, but the lives of others depend on his retaining control of his emotions.

They lose their way, run out of fuel, and crash in Yorkshire, miles off course, but close to Gervase's home territory. But she is not there in the flesh and he has to bypass this unfriendly territory to get back to his base. A long train journey, which the captain shares with his crew, brings them back to the reality of the aerodrome and a critical enquiry into the nearly catastrophic events of the night. His superior recognizes that this has been a failure which very nearly turned into a disaster and considers splitting the crew up for something has clearly gone wrong and even worse could happen if they stay together. But his crew are willing to trust Marshall again, realizing that he needs nonetheless to resolve the conflicts in his emotional life, or they may all perish. This requires the woman in the case to move her ground. In an engineering sense she has become the fulcrum of the stresses that have built up and in order to prevent catastrophic failure she has to readjust, to reposition this fulcrum, to take up the necessary weight in the pattern of stresses which has developed.

She recognizes that it is her move and the resolution of all of the themes occur as Gervase creates an opportunity of team building by obtaining access to a private lake well stocked with fish to which the whole crew are invited. Her offer of reconciliation is a present of time and space – an outer landscape with inner symbolization. Marshall knows that he, personally, is being offered his life. It will be a new chapter, framed in a synthetic meaning, constructed from thesis and antithesis.

One of the important and fascinating aspects of Shute's writing is that because of his detailed grasp and specific knowledge of people and events and mainly, of course, of the underlying technologies, both of hard and tangible and of human structures, he often appears to anticipate events which only occurred in real life later on.

Thus the plot of a later novel, *No Highway* (1948*b*) is based on a detailed account of the scientific and engineering importance of metal fatigue and appears to predict the subsequent crashes of the Comet airliners in flight.

The plot of *Round the Bend* (1951) predicts almost precisely the rise a decade later of Gulf Airlines and Emirate Airlines in the Persian Gulf. Shute was no mere apocalyptic or visionary prophet though. These anticipations of the future were based on state-of-the-art knowledge and good judgement about how economies and technologies developed.

Fortunately so far the predictions of the end of the human world in *On The Beach* (1957) due to an all-encompassing nuclear world war have not yet come to pass.

In *Pastoral* the theme which links the action in the bomber itself and on which the incidents bear is that of team work and what was subsequently identified as 'morale'. The seminal report *Morale Among Bomber Crews* (1946), drafted by T. T. Patterson (later to become Head of the Business School at the University of Strathclyde), was not commissioned until two years after the publication of Shute's book and not published officially until some years after that. But Shute knew the significance of the phenomena we now understand as 'morale' without having to read the social psychologists' report, because he understood how men in aeroplanes need to work together and the factors which sustain and, in their absence, corrode human trust.

The landscape of Shute's novel is nonetheless not simply a matter of description and analysis. Shute wishes his work to be construed as true art, and much as composers quote phrases and themes from other and earlier composers in order to demonstrate their different handling of them, so each sector of *Pastoral* is headed by sometimes quite extensive quotes from the corpus of English poetry.

Shute's taste in poetry is not exotic. It is very English and leans heavily on the Romantic tradition. It is the poetry of the pre-1914 England of Nevil Shute Norway's youth, probably the poetry of the school curriculum he had studied as a boy, first at Lynam's and later at Shrewsbury school. In *Pastoral* he references Housman, Herrick, Keats, Rupert Brooke and Newbolt, but he also knew well what the popular music of the era had to say about these matters and his final quotations are from the wartime hit song 'A Nightingale Sang in Berkeley Square'.

Let us examine more closely the use Shute makes of this thematic material. The initial point of contact between Peter Marshall and the girl with whom he is later to fall in love is occasioned by the pike, which Marshall has caught in the millpond. Alone among the people in the mess, this WAAF officer has expressed an interest in seeing the fish . . . his fish.

Marshall took the girl through into the deserted dining room. The fish lay recumbent on its dish, its sombre colours dulled. Death had not improved it: it leered at him with sordid cruelty, and was smelling rather strong.

Section Officer Robertson said brightly, 'I say, what a lovely one! How much does it weigh?'

'Eleven and a quarter pounds.'

'Did you have an awful job landing it?'

'Not bad, I had it on a wire trace; I was spinning for it.'

'In this river here?'

He nodded. 'Up at Coldstone Mill.'
'Oh, I know that', she said, 'A great tall building in the fields.'
'That's the place,' he said, 'I got it in the pool below the mill.'
'It must have been lovely out there this afternoon', she said, 'It's been such a heavenly day.' (Shute 1944: 24–5)

This passage is typical of the way Shute introduces landscape in his writing. There are no long detailed, adjectival depictions, parenthetical to the flow of the action, framed by and framing dialogue. Shute counterpoints dialogue with staccato bursts of exact specification. He had introduced the mill in the previous chapter. He avoided redundancy in description. The mill is 'a great, tall building' with a pool below, on 'the River Fittel, that ran southwards to the Thames through the pleasant farms of Oxfordshire' (9).

Coldstone Mill was a tall, factory-like building set in the countryside along the river Fittel. A lane crossed the river on a stone bridge of two arches: a hundred yards below the bridge the mill stood by the weir, and below that again was the mill pool. It was a broad, gravely pool, scoured wide by the mill stream and the weir, overhung by trees at the lower end. It stood in pasture fields, very sunny and bright. (16)

Shute uses words economically, sparingly and with no exaggerated emphasis. The style is plain, aiming, like the typical engineer 'to do for five bob, what any damn fool can do for a pound'. But it does not lack detail. It is exact in its specification. The pool is 'broad and gravelly'. The bridge is stone with two arches. We could draw that mill by that pond beyond that bridge and could recognize it if we came upon it. This is precision engineering in the written word.

Later Marshall talks to a 'civilian from the district' in the pub about the pike he has caught. He finds that the man has been, like himself in civvy street, a salesman in London. His new acquaintance 'has been in the motor trade, Great Portland Street, . . . now in tractors'. Marshall enquires whether he does not find it 'a bit quiet after London?' The man replies that he 'loves it down here'.

[Marshall retorts] 'I should have thought it would have bored you stiff.' The man said: 'Well, you might think so. But – what I mean is, up in London you arse around and go to the local and meet the boys and perhaps take in a flick, and then when you go to bed you find you've spent a quid and wonder where in hell it went and what you got for it. Down here there's always something to do . . . shooting for example. I know most of the farmers because I keep the tractors turning over for them . . . any time I want to take a gun and shoot a rabbit or a pigeon, they like to have me do it round the farm.' (29–30)

Marshall enquires if the man knows the people at Coldstone Mill and whether he could 'have a go at the pigeons in the trees below the mill'.

The conversation turns to foxes and badgers and his new acquaintance offers to take Marshall to the moonlit woods where he would 'show him a fox and a badger within a quarter of an hour'. They plan to go out at four in the morning:

Marshall walked back to the station with his companions and went up to bed. Lying in bed before sleep, he thought that he had had a splendid day. He had got up in the middle of the morning, and it had been fine and bright and sunny. He had gone fishing with his new rod. He had caught one of the biggest fish in the river and landed it without net or gaff. He had showed it to a girl, quite a pretty girl, and she had been nice to him about it. He was well on the way to a day's pigeon shooting, and he had contracted to be shown a wild fox and a wild badger both within a quarter of an hour. A splendid day. Quite a pretty girl. He wondered how he could find out her Christian name without calling attention to his curiosity. (31)

The 'quite pretty' girl hears about the proposed moonlight expedition. She understands that it would not be appropriate for her to accompany the men. She is a WAAF; Peter Marshall is a pilot officer. Their fraternization would bring trouble for both of them.

She was deeply disappointed. She was a country girl from the North Riding: her father was an auctioneer in Thirsk. Her uncle was rector of Thistleton, a little village in the hills near Helmsley: she knew country matters very well. She had a considerable knowledge of foxes: she had followed the hunt on various farm ponies, and she had crept out several times into the woods to stalk a vixen playing with her cubs before the earth; for one of these expeditions she had a blurred Brownie photograph to show. In all her experience of the country she had never seen a badger. This expedition in the moonlight night before the dawn was in her line exactly: she ached to be going with Marshall in the morning. The very suggestion had been like a breath of fresh air to her, a reminder of a sane, decent, country world that she had left behind her in the North. (36)

Gervase Robertson had herself tried to explore the surrounding countryside but 'all she had managed so far was to go for rides upon her bicycle and since the country was flat and she came from the hills, she didn't think much of that'.

In due course Peter Marshall makes his 4.00 a.m. assignation:

They rode off down the main road leading north. The sky was practically clear; the half moon was rising, making it light enough to see the detail of the countryside ... they found the gate and left their bicycles inside it, and went on up a muddy track that wound slowly up hill through the woods. The leafless branches made a fine tracery over their heads, screening the white clouds drifting past the moon. There was little wind; the woods were very quiet. From time to time a rabbit shot away before them; once an owl swooped low over their heads with a great whirr of wings.

When they get down to the clearing they wait to see the badger:

They settled down upon a log to wait and watch motionless. The silvery radiance of silver clearing, ebbing and flowing with the passing clouds was nothing novel to Marshall; he knew moonlight very well. For many hours he had sat patterned in black and white within the moonlit cockpit, uneasy and vigilant for night fighters: home to him was the appearance of a moonlit landfall seen through gaps of cloud, faint, silver, ethereal cliffs and fields. He had seen so much moon in the past fifteen months that he had absorbed a little of its serenity, perhaps. At the beginning of his career as a bombing pilot he had been confused and distressed and bewildered by the casualties, by the deaths of friends that he had known and played with in their leisure hours. The casualties had less effect upon him now: they were things that happened, that must be accepted as they came. One day he would probably go too: the thought did not distress him very much. Life in the RAF was real, and exciting, and great fun – better by far than the life he had known in his insurance office before the war. Everything had to end sometimes, it was undesirable to be killed, but it was also undesirable to go creeping back into the office when the war was over. (41–3)

In these few paragraphs apparently consisting mainly of dissociated description we see the Spartan elegance of Shute's craft. All of the main themes that are to engage the action are described in these confrontations with physical reality. The inner landscape of Marshall's mind, his 'musings', contrast with and provoke an understanding of the nature of life, and of the life of nature, of his journey through it and of his project for his own life. Shute's method is simple, as a good engineer's analysis has to be.

He takes a limited number of elements and out of them creates structure. The structure is itself economical and aims to hang a greater weight upon it. As the members of the frame of the airships on which Shute had worked had to support, economically and efficiently, a massive area of canvas containing a large quantity of lighter-than-air gas, so Shute's structural elements have to control and support his argument.

The primary method is that of binary opposition. Some of these oppositions are obvious enough. Marshall is a man, Gervase Robertson a woman. They themselves represent opposites. Marshall is urban and from the South, Robertson's origins are rural and in the North. He travels on a perilous journey two or three nights a week. Her activity is responsible and occurs within a disciplined framework, takes place in relative safety and during normal daylight hours.

There is an opposition within Marshall's life space also. The primary tension is that between the ground and the air. The countryside is revealed intimately and in detail on the ground as it is revealed in large and at a distance from the air. Within Marshall's terrain we find the opposition of the station contained, controlled, ordered and hierarchical, contrasted with the freedom and availability of the countryside. But the countryside itself contains a delicate and finely balanced ecology, which Shute as a countryman well understood. There is no sentimentality in Shute's *Pastoral*. This is not a countryside of lovely views observed from a safe distance. Within the countryside, death and the end of things contrast with the ongoing life which is reborn out of the death of living things.

Above all, the master frame of *Pastoral* is of the landscape of England itself, of 'small rivers flowing down into the Thames' and of 'the rapid rushing streams of the North Country hills'. It is the great canvas of war and of the defence of this silver sceptred isle that frames and forms the thesis of Shute's novelization.

Shute understood both war and peace. He had survived war and had pursued a career as a successful engineer and businessman in time of peace.

What and where are the landscapes depicted in Shute's writings? Can we visit them and is there a possibility of creating a value in the sense of a business opportunity for tourism in these places?

Perhaps the formative influences on his developing perception and involvement in landscape came in his youth as a boy at Shrewsbury School. Three years before Shute's birth A. E. Housman (1896) had published *A Shropshire Lad*, perhaps the most significant evocation of English landscape of the late nineteenth century. It falls well into the 'Golden Age' mythologizing of which Drabble writes, as far as readers and critics of our era are concerned, but, in its own day and read in the light of its own period, it responds to a far darker tempo.

It is in many ways a bitter and despondent saga that Housman sings, a celebration of the transient nature of life and the betrayals of glory. As J. B. Priestley (1960) writes of the twentieth century in his wide-ranging summary of *Literature and Western Man*: 'the vital seeds, flowering eventually into their own kind of literature, was sown earlier and at a depth inaccessible to whatever comes from political events', (375). Housman was for several generations of English writers, certainly for Shute (and probably later for Dennis Potter (1979)) one of those seeds.

Shute had been a teenager at Shrewsbury School when his much-loved older brother Fred had been wounded by a shell-burst in the Western Front. He died of gangrene at the hospital at Wimereux, about three weeks after he was wounded,

> with my mother by his side ... He was only 19 when he died, and after nearly 40 years it still seems strange to me that I should be older than Fred ... For the remainder of my time at Shrewsbury I don't think I had the slightest interest in a career or any other life. I was born to one end, which was to go into the army and do the best I could before being killed. The time at school was a time for contemplation of the realities that were coming as a spiritual preparation for death. (Shute 1958: 24)

This is the atmosphere of Housman. In penning these reflective phrases in *Slide Rule*, Shute catches exactly the mood of early death and frustrated promise that infuses Housman when he writes, of an athlete dying young,

> Smart lad to slip betimes away,
> from fields where glory does not stay,
> and early though the laurel grows,
> it withers quicker than the rose.
>
>   (Housman 1896: stanza xix)

Shute, throughout all his writings, was conscious of the debt owed by the living to the dead and his landscape is infused with the call to activity symbolized by Housman in 'Reveille':

> Up lad up, 'tis late for lying,
> Hear the drums of morning play,
> hark the empty highways crying,
> who will be on the hills away,
> play lies still but blood's a rover,
> breath's a ware that will not keep
> up lad when the journey's over,
> there'll be time enough to sleep.
>
>   (Housman 1896: stanza iv)

Not all of Shute's structures are inorganic. He understands the elemental relations of bone structure to softer flesh. Housman too uses this conceit in his celebration of 'The Immortal Part':

> before the fire of sense decay
> the smoke of thought blow clean away
> and leave with ancient Night alone

the steadfast and enduring bone.

(Housman 1896: stanza xciii)

In his engineering and in his writing alike, Shute pursues the steadfast and the enduring under-structures of life and relationships. His plotting is exact, his characterization to an extent limited, but all is pinned on a steadfast and enduring framework.

The great polarities in Shute's writing are those that have engaged writers down the ages, youth and age, life and death, north and south, boy and girl, and above all country and town and in *Pastoral* England against the world. He writes for his generation of a sceptred isle set in a silver sea openly, straightforwardly and without fuss. Shute's landscape is painted on a sturdy canvas with bold colour, his tapestry is woven on a robust texture with strong thread.

His landscapes of the mind endure in the reader's memory, counterpointing his narrative in which ordinary people summon their strengths in order to achieve extraordinary things.

It is this feature which perhaps explains his wide appeal to readers in the New Worlds of America and Australia. Nevins and Commager (1942) write of Andrew Jackson that he 'had the Western faith that the common man is capable of uncommon achievement'. Nevil Shute understood this principle implicitly. It imbues all his writing and his perceptions of physical reality. But his heroes and heroines have to respect both natural and technical constraints.

To deconstruct the landscape of Nevil Shute's England as revealed in his novels is one thing; to recover, locate and seek to visit it is quite another.

Probably only *aficionados* of his works will take the trouble to do so. Yet most of it is physically still available. You may find the millpond, the woods, streams, rivers and woods in which the action of *Pastoral* occurs, and I have commenced this task. Once you understand the principles on which he worked, and his precision of description and accuracy of recall it is quite possible to make these places accessible and to become, for a while, a tourist among them. They are widespread, though, and cover most of the continents of the world, and much of the landscape of England.

You may also find the mooring-ring of the R100 and the club in which he lived while a bachelor in York (1958: 138).

You may follow the track of the fictional clubman, another, older bachelor, as he treks through the Jura and on through Occupied France, with his party of refugee children, as described by Shute in *Pied Piper* (1942).

Shute's depictions are locationally precise and rooted in real places. Above all his distances and dimensions are accurate. Many of these places are, nonetheless, still to be found, and doubtless they will be and may form the object of some literary tourism.

Probably these journeys of discovery will be of interest to the social historian also. To my generation, which grew up during the Second World War and the years immediately following, it is the landscape of our childhood, which we will recover in these exploitations.

It is this England which made us. These are our Blue Remembered Hills. But

Shute's landscapes are not only to be found in England. He depicted other places, and in a sense his reach was global. His landscapes of the mind are far-reaching.

Shute epitomizes them significantly in the title of one of his Australian novels *The Far Country* (1952), a direct quote, of course, from Housman.

In this novel he tells the story of landscapes recovered in a new country, Australia. The hero is a refugee from war-torn Europe, a Czech doctor, practising his skills illegally, but using them in an emergency to save a man's life, as he awaits the slow workings of Australian medical bureaucracy to recognize the medical qualifications he had already obtained in his homeland. The heroine is a London girl, escaping the austerity of post-war Britain to find a new life in the open spaces of an empty continent. (Now they might both be characterized unkindly in 'New Labour Speak' as 'Economic Migrants'.)

Shute's vision is essentially an optimistic one. His landscape is of a Europe of the mind, to which an earlier generation of migrants had already aspired a century earlier. But at the book's end, hero and heroine decide to return to England, where Carl can resume his medical training. She is fearful of losing the hut in the hills where their romance had blossomed, as they return to a cold, deprived post-war England. Shute writes:

> They turned into the bleak, shabby, covered cab way of the railway station ... she paused, and looked around her at the stained and dirty brickwork, at the antiquated building, at the wet streets in the blustering windy night ... (335)

But the girl shares her lover's assurance that they will get back to those 'blue remembered hills', now on the other side of the world. 'We'll get back to it all right,' she said. 'Some day, some how, we'll get back there again.' And Shute's novel ends on an upnote, like the Australian accent itself.

But Shute's vision is not of some idyllic, pastoral Utopia, recoverable only in nostalgic imaginings. He pines for no 'Land of lost content happy highways where I once went and cannot come again' (335). Shute has a clear awareness of the 'unchanged and changing places', as Drabble (1979: 277) puts it. But his antitheses do not result in the conflict identified by Drabble, between 'a far country' of a rural Golden Age and a polluted and decadent city, nor of the intrinsic tension of which Sylvia Plath complained, even if, as Drabble writes 'in the twentieth century the conflict is, perhaps deeper than it has ever been' (1979: 277).

The focus of Shute's concerns, the actions of his characters and the direction of his sentiments are strictly in the present, in his characters and in the dilemmas they face. These are undoubtedly rooted in the social and political realities of his time, but more significantly in the elemental choices of humankind. He is by no means a narrow 'Little Englander' and he writes in other novels with insight and empathy of other places, races and agendas. He foresaw the multiracial society that his England has become; and the liberal tolerance of belief systems other than those contained in the England which formed him, are well outlined in *The Chequer Board* and *Round the Bend*. He embraced the new worlds of a nascent Australia and a vibrant America as warmly as he celebrated his native sod. Jones identifies *The Far Country* as a classic of Australian migration literature. He shows how Shute handles Australia as a 'Land of plenty where success, particularly material success, is possible for those who work for it', and as a 'land flowing with steak and wool cheques'. (Jones 1995: 252–3).

The writings of Nevil Shute were best sellers, wherever in the world English was the language of communication. But he never became a member of any literary establishment and remained to the end a provincial, colonial, marginal and in a deep sense a critical figure in relation to the contemporary prejudices of the rich, famous and powerful. His life took him from Cornwall, a peninsular attachment of England, to the Mornington peninsula, a peripheral location of Australia, an antipodean continent on the margins of Empire, via Ireland. Whatever he was, in the words of Prime Minister Thatcher, he would hardly have rated as 'one of us' in the eyes of the British Establishment.

While as an engineer in an evolving industry in a leading-edge technology, he had been distrustful of the artistic streak, exemplified by such great figures as his boss and mentor Barnes Wallis, as an artist, himself, and in his productions he celebrated the plain lineaments of the engineer.

But his landscapes become 'Art' in a way undiscerned by the vacuous effluxions of such celebrants of 'landscape' as Kenneth Clark (1949), because their accessibility masks both their artful, spare, efficient constructions and their centrality to the life-purposes of the ordinary men and women of his time, who saw their landscapes effectively and succinctly portrayed in his writings. But we shall have to undertake some personal research to rediscover Shute's landscapes and make them the basis of an offer to the tourism industry. Their very ubiquity creates many diverse opportunities but their artfulness makes them evanescent

The terrains purposed by Shute constitute an opportunity for an inescapable journey for those who wish to understand the landscape of England in the mid-twentieth century, its streams and fields, its grim cities and smiling meadows, its technology, its social relations, its ordinary men and women, and above all in their personal moral and practical choices, the awful ethical dilemmas of a society trembling on the brink of technological mastery, or conclusive and self-willed annihilation.

This is a landscape of importance, a journey worth taking. For some of us, of my generation, it is a journey through the landscapes of our childhood, from the rough upland terrain of total war to the apparently sunlit pastures of New Labour content.

But these journeys are still perilous in retrospect and prospect, and tourists may find there no lands of lost content, only the reflections of their own terrible anxieties.

As Michelin would have advised 'Vaut bien le détour'. But how to make the trip? To start with, you have to read the books, then do some research, then think a lot, then test your understanding, then work it out: your itinerary will be as much mental as physical, but what a journey into the fabric of twenty-first century technologically based consciousness may be in store! And when you finally arrive, after travelling hopefully, you will find it because, as we recall, 'he never wrote about places he had not been to'. But will you find anything resembling Disneyworld or even Haworth ? Hopefully not.

It would certainly have intrigued Nevil Shute to think of his works as the stimulus for a new non-locationally specific approach to tourism. In the age of the internet, of e-maps and data-bases, the post-modernist researcher will have to roll his or her own. The opportunity is a tantalizing one and the rewards, in England, Australia, North America, the Middle East and Myanmar could be spectacular: but locate this prophet of high-tech globalization once and for all in a fixed location? Never!

REFERENCES

Beresford, M. W. (1954) *The Lost Villages of England*. London: Lutterworth.

Clark, Kenneth (1949) *Landscape into Art*. Harmondsworth: Penguin.

Descola, P. (1992) 'Societies of nature and the nature of society', in A. Kuper (1992) *Conceptualizing Society*. London: Routledge, 107–26.

Drabble, Margaret (1979) *A Writer's Britain, Landscape in Literature: Photographed by Jorge Lewinski*. London: Thames & Hudson.

Eliot, T. S. (1944) *Four Quartets*, 'East Coker'. London: Faber & Faber.

Fleure, H. J. and Davis, M. (1951) *A Natural History of Man in Britain*. London: Collins.

Hegel, G. W. F. (1956) *The Philosophy of History*, trans. J. Sibree. New York: Dover Publications.

Heidegger, M. (1962) *Being and Time*, trans. J. MacQuarrie and E. Robinson. Oxford: Basil Blackwell.

Hopkins, G. M. (1948) 'Pied Beauty' in *Poems of Gerard Manley Hopkins*. Oxford: Oxford University Press.

Hoskins, W. G. (1955) *The Making of the English Language*. London: Hodder & Stoughton.

Housman, A. E. (1896) *A Shropshire Lad*. London: Kegan Paul, Trench, Trubner and Co.

Imhof, E. (1951) *Terrain et Carte*. Erlenbach-Zurich: Eugen Rentsch Verlag.

Islam, Syed Manzurul (1996) *The Ethics of Travel: from Marco Polo to Kafka*. Manchester: Manchester University Press, 6.

Jones, R. (1995) 'Far cities and silver countries', in R. King, J. Connell and P. White. *Writing across Worlds: Literature and Migration*. London: Routledge.

Knapp, Bernard A. and Ashmore, Wendy (1999) 'Archaeological landscapes: constructed, conceptualized, ideational', in Wendy Ashmore, and Bernard A. Knapp. (1999) *Archaeologies of Landscape: Contemporary Perspectives*. London: Blackwell. 1–30.

Lambert, C. and Weir, D. T. H. (1973) 'Locality' in Gittus, E. (ed.) *Key Variables in Social Research*. London: Heinemann and British Sociological Association.

Levinas, E. (1969) *Totality and Infinity*, trans. A. Lingis. The Hague: Martinus Nijhoff.

Nevins, A. and Commager, H. S. (1942) *America: The Story of a Free People*. Oxford: Oxford University Press.

Norway, A. H. (1899) *Highways and Byways in Yorkshire*. London: Macmillan.

Norway, Shirley (1999) Personal discussion with the author at the Nevil Shute

Centennial Conference, Albuquerque, New Mexico, January 1999.

Patterson, T. T. (1946) *Morale Among Bomber Crews: Report to the Air Ministry, London*.

Pomorski, J. M. (1996) 'The city and its Genius Loci', in *The Historical Metropolis*, ed. J. Purchla. Krakow: International Cultural Centre, 21–36.

Porteous, J. D. (1985) 'Literature and humanist geography', *Area*, **17**, 117–22.

Potter, D. (1979) *Blue Remembered Hills*. Play for Today: BBC: 30/01/79.

Priestley, J. B. (1960) *Literature and Western Man*. New York: Harper & Row.

Sauer, C. O. (1925) *The Morphology of Landscapes*. University of California Publications in Geography: **2**, 19–54.

Shute, N. (1940) *An Old Captivity*. London: Heinemann.

Shute, N. (1942) *Pied Piper*. London: Heinemann.

Shute, N. (1944) *Pastoral*. London: Heinemann.

Shute, N. (1945) *Most Secret*. London: Heinemann.

Shute, N. (1947) *The Chequer Board*. London: Heinemann.

Shute, N. (1948*a*) *Flight Log*: (unpublished log of Nevil Shute's visit to Australia in 1948. Kindly made available by Dan Telfair, organizer of the 1999 Nevil Shute Centennial Conference in Albuquerque, New Mexico, and John Henry, president of the Nevil Shute Society, to whom grateful thanks are due).

Shute, N. (1948*b*) *No Highway*. London: Heinemann.

Shute, N. (1950) *A Town Like Alice*. London: Heinemann.

Shute, N. (1951) *Round the Bend*. London: Heinemann.

Shute, N. (1952) *The Far Country*. London: Heinemann.

Shute, N. (1957) *On the Beach*. London: Heinemann.

Shute, N. (1958) *Slide Rule*. London: Heinemann.

Slater, Don (1995) 'Photography and modern vision', in Duncan Jenks (ed.) *Visual Culture*. London and New York: Routledge, 218–37.

St Èxupéry, A. de (1929) *Wind, Sand and Stars*. Paris: Editions Galimard (quotation taken from the translation published by the Travel Book Club, 1946).

Stamp, Dudley L. (1946) *Britain's Structure and Scenery*. London: Collins.

Tomaszewski, A. (1993) 'An international strategy for the cultural heritage', in *Heritage Landscape*. Krakow: International Cultural Centre, 101–13.

Tuan, Y. (1971) *Geography, Phenomenology, and the Study of Human Nature. Canadian Geographer*, **15**, 181–92.

Turgenyev, I. (1950) *Notebooks of a Sportsman*. London: The Cresset Press.

Ucko, P. J. (1994) 'Foreword', to D. L. Carmichael, J. Hubert, B. Reeves and A. Schanche, (eds) (1994) *Sacred Sites, Sacred Places, One World Archaeology*. xiiii–xxiii. London: Routledge.

Urry J. (1999) 'Sensing the city', in D. R. Judd and S. Fainstein, *The Tourist City*. New Haven: Yale University Press.

Chapter 6

Tourism Comes to Haworth

Robert Barnard

The origins

The date when tourism arrived at Haworth can be pinpointed with some accuracy. On 5 March 1850 Charlotte Brontë wrote to her friend Ellen Nussey: 'Various folks are beginning to come boring to Haworth on the wise errand of seeing the scenery described in *Jane Eyre* and *Shirley*,' (Wise and Symington 1933). Her scorn was especially sharp because *Shirley* was set in the Gomersal/Birstall districts, and *Jane Eyre* had no Haworth settings either. But beyond that, she seemed to find it ridiculous that they should come at all.

Gentry and professional people on a visit to a strange town at that date could be expected to make a courtesy call on the minister of the place, and in this case the convention gave them an ideal opportunity to catch a glimpse of the woman who rumours said was 'Currer Bell', author of the best-selling novels. In the same letter, Charlotte Brontë describes two such visitors, Sir James and Lady Kay-Shuttleworth, who had signalled their visit by a letter in advance, and compounded their offence in Charlotte's eyes by pressing on her an invitation to visit them, an invitation which her father insisted that she accept. Charlotte was unimpressed: 'Sir James is very courtly, fine-looking; I wish he may be as sincere as he is polished. He shows his white teeth with too frequent a smile; but I will not prejudge him.' She already had. It went for nothing with her that he was, by marriage, a considerable landowner in Lancashire, or that, by his own talents and energy, he was virtually responsible for the establishment of state education in Great Britain. She distrusted his manners, his Branson-like teeth, his pushy insistence on furthering his acquaintance with her. She also distrusted the impulse that incited him to come there.

Thus began an acquaintance that brought more embarrassment and irritation than pleasure to Charlotte, and thus began, too, her experience of the phenomenon of tourism. For the rest of her short life visitors were to arrive in Haworth and knock at the Parsonage door, drawn there by the fame of her novels and the mystery of their authorship. Occasionally the visitors were received with good grace, particularly if they were young, aspiring authors. More often they aroused in this shy, intensely private person annoyance and panic. It did not help that her proud, lonely father was more often than not delighted at the intrusions.

The Brontës' lives become public property

The process thus started was inflamed rather than dampened by Charlotte's death in 1855. Already rumours were in circulation about her schooldays at Cowan Bridge school, her drunken brother, the deaths in close succession of all her siblings. When, shortly after her death, Mrs Gaskell was commissioned to write her biography to scotch sensational stories that had appeared in the press, she determined to write a life not of Currer Bell but of Charlotte Brontë, and with that decision the *lives* of the Brontës entered the tourist equation, having a fascination equal to their writings. Mrs Gaskell was determined to make her *Life of Charlotte Brontë* (1857) a monument to her friend's *goodness* – her selflessness and long-suffering; and in this she was enthusiastically abetted by her principal informant, Ellen Nussey. The more the central figure on the tapestry had to shine, the more the background had to be darkened to throw it into relief: Patrick Brontë became eccentric to the verge of madness: Branwell's drunken decline was advanced in time to account for Charlotte's unhappiness in the mid-1840s, which in fact was due to her frustrated love for her Brussels teacher Constantin Heger; Emily Brontë was dismissed with a judgement whose inadequacy is almost comic: 'all that I, a stranger, have been able to learn about her has not tended to give either me, or my readers, a pleasant impression of her', (Gaskell 1857). So much for Emily. But the main darkening was not of a person but of a place. Haworth became an antechamber to Hell.

Gaskell recreates Haworth

That second chapter, in which Haworth is described, has fixed Haworth in the minds of readers to this day: remote, inhospitable, the very steepness of its main street making a sort of barrier to the outside world. Haworth is depicted as if it were on the very edge of the civilized world and its people – brutal, surly, avaricious, vengeful – seem as near as makes no difference to animals. It is a brilliant snapshot, a series of sharp *aperçus* from an outsider, whose visits never stretched longer than a couple of days. Yet thus was Haworth imprinted on the popular imagination for a century and more to come: a populous small town, within easy reach of Keighley and Bradford, was transformed into an outpost of darkness. Not all her readers remembered that Mrs Gaskell brought to the writing of the biography the instincts of a writer of fiction.

And her picture did not stop the tourists coming. Quite the reverse. The sort of tourist who wanted sun and sybaritic luxury certainly gave it a wide berth, but the sort who got a *frisson* from going back in time to a less civilized, more passionate age found in Haworth a Mecca. Here one could lodge at the Black Bull and be shown

Branwell's special chair; here one could take the paths to the bleak moorlands stretching across to Lancashire, Emily's particular love; here one could be taken round the church and graveyard by the sexton who perhaps, if the visitor was not a man of a straightlaced kind, might show him Branwell's obscene letters to that earlier sexton, John Brown. And perhaps, if he talked widely to Haworth folk, he might pick up a particular Brontë story, something new to him. For Haworth itself, it should be remembered, features in none of the Brontë novels. Its appeal is as the setting of the Brontës' *lives*.

Haworth gears up for tourism

It sometimes comes as a shock how many well-loved Brontë stories depend on Haworth sources. The story of Branwell, bleating like a calf, having a fit in the Black Bull when he has just been brought the news that Mrs Robinson can never see him again, was told to Mrs Gaskell, and is the origin of the idea that he was an epileptic; the story of Emily dying on the sofa in the parlour first appeared in Mary Robinson's biography of 1883, and may have been from a Haworth source. It is the task of the biographer to decide which of the stories are credible and consistent with other accounts, and which probably sprang into existence at the glint of a shilling.

If stories from those who knew them were one easy way of slaking the tourists' thirst for things Brontë, there were other possibilities, too. Brontë memorabilia – little pictures, manuscripts, china even – were distributed among the village people, particularly those who had been servants of or tradespeople to the family. John Greenwood, the village stationer, on whose paper the poems and the novels had been written, was a general port of call, and he produced postcards of the Parsonage and the church, even notepaper with a photograph of the Parsonage at its head. And of course he had copies of the novels available. Haworth folk, with Yorkshire canniness, were gearing themselves up, scenting a nice little earner.

But the Parsonage itself was less accessible than in the Brontës' time. Patrick Brontë's successor, John Wade, was a man with no particular interest in the literary family of his predecessor. He had himself a large family and a liking for privacy. The wing of the Parsonage which abuts on Church Street was built by him – understandably, since by 1880 his household numbered eleven – and he was instrumental in the destruction of the Brontës' church, all but the tower, and the building of the present one. The nickname 'envious Wade' and the idea that he resented the fame of his predecessor's children may be a piece of Haworth iconoclasm, but he certainly repelled invaders in the form of tourists wanting to see round his home, and he felt understandably bitter about people who came to peer through his windows. The fact that the visitors at that time were mainly bookish middle-class people does not seem to have been any guarantee of seemly behaviour.

This was the pattern of tourism in the latter part of the nineteenth century: sporadic visits by intrepid people of a literary turn, who came to see places and things associated with the Brontës, and who were prepared to be mildly exploited on the process. The sporadic nature of the tourism was at least partly due to a dip in the popularity of the Brontë novels in the 1860s and 70s. Then in 1893 came the Brontë society and things began to change.

The Brontë Society

The last decades of the nineteenth century were a time when literary societies were founded. Many of them had the doubtful privilege of numbering among their members or officials Thomas J. Wise, collector, bibliophile and forger – many, indeed, sought it as a guarantee of respectability, for his exposure as a forger was decades away. The Brontë Society may well have been the first such society devoted to novelists, for the Dickens Fellowship was not founded until 1913, the Jane Austen Society not until as late as 1940. Right from the earliest deliberations about a possible society, a museum was stated as one of its main aims: 'to consider the advisability of forming a Brontë Society and Museum', (Lemon 1993) said the circular which called the meeting that formed it. It is worth noting that when the museum was opened in 1895, the inaugural address, written by Charlotte's second biographer Wemyss Reid, who was too ill to deliver it himself, wedded life and writings as the concern of the fledgling museum in a particularly nineteenth-century way:

> Fame, even the highest literary fame, like riches, may take wings and disappear, but virtue will endure. We believe that the fame of the Brontës, as stars in the firmament of our literature, will long abide; but whatever may be the actual result so far as their place among the writers of our tongue is concerned, we know that the heroic example of their lives will remain an inspiration and encouragement for ever. (Lemon 1993)

The speech suggests that Wemyss Reid felt a definite uncertainty about the merit of the Brontë novels, perhaps born of the years of their unfashionableness, so he was hedging his bets by backing them for virtue. Mrs Gaskell's Angel of the Barren Moors was still very much alive, though her sisters were by now allowed some share in the brilliant light.

The first museum and the origins of the collection

And so the relics of the Brontës, which had been given by admirers and bought from Haworth people and others, were collected in a room above the Penny Bank next to the Old White Lion, now the Tourist Office. In its first summer the museum had on display the manuscripts of *Jane Eyre* and *Villette*, today unimaginably valuable. During its second season of April to September 1896 the display boasted important loans from Thomas J. Wise and Clement Shorter.

Wise never, so far as we know, forged Brontë manuscripts. Manuscripts were not his line – fraudulent pamphlets were. Nevertheless the 1890s had been a good decade for both Wise and Shorter. Wise had got hold of well over a hundred of Charlotte's letters to Ellen Nussey, paying her something over one pound for each of them, and promising to give them, as had been Ellen's dearest hope, either to the British Museum or the 'museum at Kensington' after they had been used by his friend

Clement Shorter to write his biography of Charlotte. Shorter himself had been to Banagher in Ireland, the home of Charlotte's widower, and – probably acting as Wise's emissary – had taken away almost his entire collection of childhood writings, as well as other mementoes. How that intensely private man Arthur Bell Nicholls was persuaded to this can only be guessed at, but it is possible that a similar promise about their eventual destination was made to him too.

So at the very time that the Brontë Society was beginning the process of collecting material for its museum, Wise and Shorter were setting about dispersing what they had wrested from the rightful owners for their own profit. For as Ellen began to find out shortly before her death, profit was the name of Wise's game. One of his cleverest ruses was to stitch up a few pages of Charlotte's tiny juvenile writing (valuable) with many pages of Branwell's (not valuable) and sell the whole as a youthful story of Charlotte's. He was helped by the fact that the writing of the two was almost indistinguishable and almost undecipherable. Collectors, in any case, were not necessarily experts. Some were not even enthusiasts, just collectors. Mr Wise, as usual, was on to a good thing.

The beginnings of Brontë country

Meanwhile the museum and Society were going from strength to strength. By the turn of the century, the museum was getting about three thousand visitors a year, and the Society's membership was approaching three hundred. In 1899, the Society had begun to run an annual excursion, thus beginning a tradition which was to form a strong strand in Brontë activities, and one which the early tourist trade took advantage of. There had always been, as we have seen, a strong topographical component to the interest in the Brontës' works and lives. It had been encouraged by the first illustrated edition of the novels in the 1870s, for which the artist Wimperis had received advice from Ellen Nussey as to which buildings had been the inspiration for buildings in the novels (hence, for example, the identification of Top Withens, the moorland farmhouse near Stanbury, as the original Wuthering Heights). In 1902, the Brontë Society published H. E. Wroot's *Sources of Charlotte Brontë's Novels: People and Places*, and a new secondary industry was well under way – one which may be thought to be based on a misapprehension, because all novel-places are places of the mind before they are bricks and mortar or stone and soil. Still, the bicycle and the motor car had arrived, and so had the charabanc, and thus Cowan Bridge, Norton Conyers, Scarborough and Law Hill joined Haworth and the *Shirley* country as places of pilgrimage for Brontëans. The Brontë Society, in its excursions, showed the way, and the tour operators followed behind. The path was already pointing to signposts in Japanese leading to Top Withens.

For the Brontës' period of diminished popularity was well and truly over. The books and the lives were once again part of Britain's literary culture. Clement Shorter's two books on Charlotte (containing of course, extensive quotation from her letters to Ellen) helped fan the interest, and as the twentieth century got under way the novels consolidated their classic status. For people of judgement, *Wuthering Heights* was beginning to overtake *Jane Eyre* as the favourite and the most-admired

Brontë novel. Lord David Cecil's *Early Victorian Novelists* (1934) crowned this revaluation, its essay on Emily one of the most influential and persuasive she had so far been the subject of. But even before that there had been a silent film version. By 1939, the book had been made into a Hollywood box-office success, all romantic music, waving studio heather, and the brylcreamed anguish of Laurence Olivier.

The Parsonage becomes a museum

But influential though films were for decades in luring people to Haworth, the most important event in the inter-war years was the decision of the Church of England authorities to build a new vicarage for the incumbent of Haworth, and to offer to the Society for the sum of three thousand pounds the 150-year-old building that had been the Brontës' home. It was 1927, and the Society was still operating on a shoestring budget. As has so often happened since, though, the Brontës were news, their names a magnet to reporters. Sir James Roberts was sent newspaper reports of the offer while he and his wife were abroad. He was an industrialist and Haworth-born, and as his wife said to him when she read the report: 'Now you have the opportunity of doing something for your native Haworth,' (Lemon 1993). It is a remark resonant with the tones of Victorian philanthropy, the tradition in which Sir James grew up. The negotiations took no time. The inadequate little room above the Penny Bank was about to be transformed into the Parsonage Museum.

The opening on 4 August 1928 is remembered by all the older people of Haworth as the town's greatest day. Local politicians and dignitaries, literary figures and hundreds of Brontëans attended the ceremony, making Main Street and Church Street look as if they were part of a Coronation route. There are not many museums whose opening have caused such mass enthusiasm. The crowd's instinct was sound. The gift of the Parsonage to the Society changed everything. Before, one came to see the Brontës' home. Now one could visit it. The psychological difference was immense. From now on Haworth was a place of literary pilgrimage, on a par with Stratford-on-Avon and Abbotsford. One might be forgiven, looking at the pictures of the Parsonage rooms in its early days as a museum, for thinking that little had changed. In the dining-room, bookcases and display cases rub shoulders with Emily's piano and a reproduction of Richmond's well-known chalk-drawing of Charlotte. The feel is still of a museum. The desire to display was no doubt augmented by the magnificent legacy to the Society from H. H. Bonnell (both expert and an enthusiast, unusually), who bequeathed his collection of manuscripts, first editions and memorabilia – the bedrock of the superb collection the Parsonage has today.

The museum becomes a 'home'

It seems likely that in the minds of some of the Society's Council there was the idea that eventually parts, at least, of the old house would be made into something as close as possible to what the Brontës knew. Butler Wood, a former chairman and president of the Society, was a pioneer of modern ideas of presentation and display in art galleries and museums. He complained that in a typical overcrowded Victorian gallery, 'exhibits crouch and jostle each other', and believed that pictures and other objects should 'wear the air of being at home in a ... natural combination', (Royal Academy of Arts 1998). Prophetic words, in that they seem to sum up the aims and objectives of most of the museum's directors in our own time.

The 1930s and 40s consolidated the museum's position as a centre of literary tourism, but it took time, and some diligent collecting, before any idea of making parts of the museum into a 'home' could reach fruition. Brontë scholarship flourished in those decades, however, with the first comprehensive edition of the letters (the ubiquitous Thomas J. Wise again, as joint editor with another dodgy character called J. A. Symington); the first (and some would say the best) scholarly edition of Emily's poetry edited by C. W. Hatfield, and early work on the mass of juvenilia. The crucial work of changing the Parsonage into something resembling the Brontës' home was done in the 1950s, when the country was starting to recover from war and austerity. The rethinking coincided with the building of an extension on to the back of the Parsonage – initially intended as a flat for a resident custodian, later turned into a shop and offices as the staff expanded in the 1970s.

It was when the Parsonage reopened in 1959 that the changes were most apparent, particularly so in the downstairs rooms. Patrick's study, to the right of the front door, was now a nineteenth-century clergyman's study again, and the parlour/dining-room to the left was now the room where the Brontës not only ate but imagined, played and wrote, with furniture they knew, pictures and objects they had owned. Behind Patrick's study the kitchen was reconstructed, largely with Brontë relics, sometimes with comparable objects to those they would have known – though this attempted reconstruction is marred to my mind by the fact that the Wade extension robbed this area of an outside window looking out on the moors, so it has a closed-in, artificial feeling. But is there any palace or stately-home kitchen that has the feel of a working kitchen? The upstairs rooms were still basically the exhibition area, though over the years Patrick's bedroom and the tiny bedroom beside it have moved closer to what they were in the Brontës' time.

Haworth is taken over by tourism

All these changes, and the ideals behind them, made it ever more possible for the imaginative visitor to transport himself back to the years of the Brontës' occupancy of the house. Some might say that a rude awakening awaited him when he went outside into the village itself. Even in the 1960s, on my first visit to the town, shops and teashops on Main Street were trading under a variety of Brontë and tourist-Yorkshire names, and the shops which were the stuff of normal village life were being forced out of Main Street (which is still the only street, apart from Church Street, that the vast majority of tourists visit).

It is easy to cluck disapproval of this, and the newspapers regularly raise the dust about the tacky nature of the shops and their wares (as if they were quite above any suspicion of tackiness themselves). But the determined exploitation of visitors is only part of a continuum stretching back as we have seen to the more random fleecing that went on in the nineteenth century. And if the Brontës would have been horrified and disgusted by today's Haworth, they would have been no more so than Wordsworth by today's Grasmere or Shakespeare by today's Stratford – one could imagine the dramatist borrowing the language of his own Thersites. At least Haworth has a museum worthy of the object of the pilgrimages there, which cannot be said of, for example, the Austen museum at Chawton or the Mozart museum in Vienna.

The changing face of Haworth tourism

But though Haworth has remained since that time basically a tourist village, definite changes have taken place in the type of incomer it attracts, and the changes date back to the early 1970s. It is not too fanciful to attribute the major change to the film of the *Railway Children* – not a book with any Brontë or Haworth connections. However, E. Nesbit's classic story of early this century was filmed around the privately owned and run Worth Valley Line, with other scenes outside and inside the Parsonage. The success of the film with children of all ages was augmented by Christopher Fry's television series *The Brontës of Haworth*, a sensitive and intelligent retelling of the family's story. The explosion of tourism was spectacular. In 1969, admissions to the Parsonage had for the first time risen above 100,000. By 1974, they exceeded 200,000 – the sort of figure that is easily accommodated in a Blenheim Palace or a Windsor Castle, but in a modest domestic structure could be seen as destructive both of the fabric and of the atmosphere. The admission charge at the time was still tiny, and this was felt to be in accordance with the aims of the Brontë Society: to spread love and knowledge of the Brontës and their works.

However, this visitor explosion marked a real change in Haworth as a tourist venue. It was becoming not a place for Brontë-lovers to come to, but a tourist centre *tout court*. People came to travel on the steam trains, coaches brought parties of pensioners to the mill shops, people came for the tearooms and the souvenir shops in Main Street, and some came to say that they had been. The Parsonage was still very much an attraction, and as long as admission prices remained low many of the new visitors went round, but tourism to Haworth had a momentum now which was independent of the Brontë story and the Brontë novels. Occasionally one even heard local tradespeople expressing resentment at the Parsonage and its shop, as if it represented unfair competition That said, it was obviously beneficial to the local economy, granted that Haworth had ceased to be any kind of industrial centre, for visitors to be drawn by a variety of attractions.

The appeal of a Haworth visit

This is perhaps an opportune moment to pause and consider the special elements in Haworth's appeal as a tourist venue, some of them strengths, some weaknesses. The phenomenon I have just mentioned, the growth of Haworth from a place of literary pilgrimage to a tourist venue independent of its associations, probably would not have happened if the Brontës had not been popular classic writers. Their novels were and are usually encountered first in adolescence, and the meaning and value of the books grow with the growth to maturity and beyond of their readers. In addition, non-readers have some idea or impression of the novels, and of their authors' lives as well. Just as people 'know' the elements of the Othello story or the Shylock story without having read the relevant plays, so people have heard of the mad wife in the attic, the terrible girls' school, the love of Heathcliff and Cathy and the fact that it is played out on the Yorkshire Moors. Popular affinity to the novels that falls short of reading them has been strengthened in the case of the two most popular by film, stage and television versions, and in the case of *Wuthering Heights* by a musical, a Kate Bush song, and comic parodies. *Cold Comfort Farm* is often thought to have Emily Brontë's classic in its sights as one of its satiric targets.

The popular impression of the Brontës' lives tends to centre on 'those poor, sick, miserable girls', a supposed 'tyrannical father', self-suppression, consumption and early death. Though it was accepted in the first decades of the Parsonage Museum that a rough knowledge of the lives could be taken for granted, since 1982 the upstairs of the Wade Wing has been devoted to an exhibition chronicling each stage of the story and correcting or modifying popular myths. In other words, the new audience brought in by, among other things, *The Railway Children*, demanded new strategies if they were to be brought into the Brontë orbit.

Another point that is special about Haworth's rise as a tourist destination is that it was not already a place with plenty of things to attract tourists irrespective of the Brontës, as, say, Mozart's Salzburg or Grieg's Bergen were. Nor can it, except superficially, be compared to Grasmere and Dove Cottage. The Lakes were an area of popular resort before the Romantic poets, and this has continued independently of them. The stream of cars and coaches that make Cumbria intolerable in the summer months contain only a tiny proportion of people who know or care about Wordsworth beyond a vague notion about daffodils. The Lakes were always the English beauty spot *par excellence*. The Brontës created the taste for the Yorkshire Moors, and with it a taste for a beauty that was harsh and bleak — what Hardy, about another area of the country, described as 'singularly colossal and mysterious in its swarthy monotony', (Hardy 1878).

Translations to other media

The plethora of film and television versions of the novels certainly have had a strong immediate effect on the Parsonage and Haworth tourist numbers in the past. Though no version of *Wuthering Heights* has come near to encompassing the book, the Hollywood version of 1939 was without doubt popular. A few years later, *Jane Eyre* with Joan Fontaine and Orson Welles, though many felt it should have been called *Rochester*, was equally popular and more successful as a version, and over the years that novel has proved particularly successful in adapted form – film, stage and television. Its strong lines clearly respond well to adaptation into another medium.

Recent years, however, have told another story. The latest film versions of

Wuthering Heights and *Jane Eyre* (the former, admittedly, a disaster, but the latter an interesting attempt by Zeffirelli) have had little appreciable effect on visits to the Parsonage, and the TV boom in classic adaptations (an excellent *Tenant of Wildfell Hall*, a middling *Jane Eyre* and a feeble *Wuthering Heights*) have similarly had little or no effect on visitors numbers. Possibly, *Tenant of Wildfell Hall* would have bucked this trend if it had not been screened in the dead month of November: by the time that the popular visitor months had come round again it had been forgotten, as everything on TV except a really good sitcom is forgotten. Maybe the Brontë books are by now so accepted and absorbed (as *Pride and Prejudice* is not) that adaptations no longer send people off to the spring's source. In any case, the temporary blips caused by adaptations have been a small factor in the museum's visitor figures, though perhaps the viewers sent to the books for the first time, thence to the lives, even perhaps to joining the Brontë Society, are a more enduring and important legacy of classic serials.

The present-day role of the literary society

One thing that marks the Brontë Parsonage Museum off from most other museums devoted to a literary or artistic figure is that it is owned and administered by a literary society. A recent director, Mike Hill, commented on the difference soon after his appointment: for example, where in museums and galleries in the local government sector it is often quite difficult to bully together a quorum of the administrative body to come to decisions, the Brontë Society Council – 24 elected members meeting in full session five times a year – often has 100 per cent attendance. Where the members of the local government body often have no particular interest in the attraction it is supervising or its context, the Brontë Society – not just the Council, but its members too – have a vivid interest in the building, its collection, what is on show, how it is displayed, what image of the Brontës it projects, and so on. Some directors and curators may have found them too interested by half, but even when this interest takes wrong-headed forms, it is arguably better, and more stimulating, than apathy.

The extent of the commitment and passion of the governing organization was well shown in the row over the proposed extension to the Parsonage Museum in the early 1990s. The plan was to build on to the back of the Parsonage a large extension, neo-Romanesque in style, to house a visitor centre, conference hall, staff offices, exhibition room and so on. The scheme was described in very general terms to members, but when plans began to circulate, including an artist's impression, and when it was realized how the Parsonage itself would be dwarfed by its monstrous offshoot, anger erupted. After the stormiest AGM in its history the seven Council members up for election were voted off. A year later a further seven were ejected. By then the heritage bodies to whom the plan had been referred had given it the thumbs down in no uncertain terms, one of them summing up the general feeling by saying that it was a classic case of killing the building the visitors had come to see. On this matter, the Council had got way out of step with the membership, and it was the membership that showed the better judgement.

This incident was a turning-point in the make-up of the Society. Before it, Council consisted of local worthies and dignitaries, scholars and enthusiasts, and workhorses – in varying proportions. When vacancies occurred on Council someone deemed suitable was approached, and it was very rarely necessary to have an election. Since 1990, there has been an election every year – so there have been more in the last decade than in the entire nine decades of the Society's earlier history. In other words, the rank-and-file members have begun to take an active interest not just in how the Society is run, but in how the Museum is run. They vote for people who seem to represent best *their* feelings about the Brontës and their home.

This can mean problems for the staff, because there are a great number of different and often contradictory feelings about the Brontës and how their memory and achievements are best honoured. So we find that, among those elected to Council there are people who are only interested in the books, people who are only interested in the lives, people who are passionately for or passionately against the education programme, people who have a warm and personal investment in *one* of the six Parsonage figures to the exclusion of the rest, and so on. Often the older Council members sigh for the Museum 'as it was', which usually means when they made their first visits. Then, as like as not, one staff member would serve as money-taker on the door, guide when necessary and postcard-seller at the exit. One has to say that times have changed, standards have risen: care of the collection has a much higher priority, knowledge has increased on how, for example, light can damage exhibits, labelling has to be done with sensitivity and scholarship, sale-room catalogues have to be scrutinized and the claims of auction houses looked at with a beady eye. If the times are not, to a degree, moved with, the Museum ceases to be one of the jewels in Yorkshire's crown. Backwaters are sometimes tempting places to be, but the 'promotion of interest in the life and works' of the family, as laid down in the Society's memorandum of Association, is not best done from a side stream.

The current situation

The Brontë Parsonage Museum, as the foregoing should have made clear, has always been a scholarly place by the standards of the time. Its exhibited artefacts have never included items such as 'Window Through Which Bill Sikes Is Reputed to Have Pushed Oliver Twist When Robbing the Maylies', an item which still disfigures Dickens House in London. Confusion between fiction and real life often afflicts Brontë biographers, but not the Parsonage Museum. When a traditional story becomes questionable, the doubt is likely to be reflected in the labelling.

This may seem to militate against it in an age when museums are adopting a more populist approach. I suspect on the contrary such scholarly precision is part of its appeal, not just to its core audience but generally to any reasonably literate and historically aware visitor. So is the range of its exhibits. Having studied the tiny writings in which the Brontës narrated the passionate and bloody events of their imaginary kingdoms of Angria and Gondal, the visitor can go into the room where those writings were done, very much as it was in their time; she can see the pictures they painted of each other and of their animals, their clothes, the spiked overshoes they donned to get down Haworth Main Street in icy conditions. From there the visitor can go on to a wider view: the terrible death rate in Haworth due to the insanitary conditions there, the industrial unrest in the area, women's education, and so on. As well as showing the Brontës' lives, the museum presents suggestive hints of life in the first half of the nineteenth century, particularly women's lives.

In the last few years, visitor numbers have fallen, first as a matter of policy, but more recently probably as a result of the enormous increase in the number of museums both in the region and the country at large. We are competing in the market-place for our share of a limited customer base. Figures for 1999 suggested that our drop in attendance had levelled out, but subsequent years have showed continuing decline, the situation not helped by an unnecessary and mishandled dispute between Council, director and staff. Now more than ever, it is vital to look at marketing, shared initiatives with other museums and galleries in the area, indeed at the whole question of trying to regain for West Yorkshire the prominent position in British tourism that it had a few years ago. Interest from Japan, France and the Low Countries remains strong, but many other European countries are comparatively untapped, as is China. It is all a far cry from Charlotte's scorn of the 'wise errand' of those early tourists, yet tourism must be counted as an important factor in establishing and maintaining the eminent position which the Brontë novels now have in the annals of British, and indeed world, fiction.

REFERENCES

Gaskell, E. C. (1970) *The Life of Charlotte Brontë* (1857). London: J. M. Dent, Everyman Edition, 277.

Hardy, Thomas (1958) *The Return of the Native* (1878). London: Macmillan, 6.

Lemon, Charles (1993) *A Centenary History of the Brontë Society 1893–1993*. Haworth: The Brontë Society, 3, 9 and 25.

Royal Academy of Arts (1998) *Art Treasures of England: The Regional Collections*. London: Royal Academy of Arts, 45.

Wise, T. J. and Symington, J. A. (eds) (1933) *The Brontës: Their Lives, Friendships and Correspondence*. Oxford: Blackwell, vol. 3, p. 81.

Chapter 7

Tourists and the Cultural Construction of Haworth's Literary Landscape

Sarah Tetley and Bill Bramwell

LITERARY LANDSCAPES

Through their work or lives, writers of various forms of literature can endow places with a distinct literary landscape. Notable examples in the UK include Shakespeare's birthplace of Stratford, and Hardy's fictional Wessex that has strong links with the English county of Dorset (Newby 1981). In the USA, Mark Twain's childhood days in Hannibal, Missouri, which is also the setting for his book *Adventures of Tom Sawyer*, have made it 'a symbol of lost childhood and small-town America' (Curtis 1985: 8).

It has been suggested that 'To the leisure traveller, literary associations are as much a part of the landscape as country houses or historic buildings or beauty spots' (Ousby 1990: 22). Previous research on literary tourism suggests several reasons why tourists may choose to visit an area because of its literary landscape. First, visits can be encouraged by a writer's use of an area as a specific backdrop or setting for their work, or even as a more indirect or vague inspiration. Newby (1981) argues that the growth of a summer season in the Mediterranean was encouraged by Scott Fitzgerald's description of the French Riviera in the novel *Tender is the Night*, published in 1934. Similarly, some of the visitors to Prince Edward Island in Canada are attracted by L. M. Montgomery's novels about the fictional Anne of Green Gables, set on a Prince Edward Island farm in the late nineteenth century (Squire 1992). Second, an adaptation of a book or play for another medium, such as for a film or television series, may encourage visits to the area that formed its original setting or to the area used for filming. Adaptations can help to popularize some 'classic' literature, so that they enter the realm of popular culture as well as of literary heritage. In the case of *Anne of Green Gables*, Squire (1992: 8) suggests that 'As much as they are shaped by literary associations, images of Prince Edward Island may today be drawn from many sources ... Television has appropriated the literary texts and transformed them into different contexts, adding new layers of meaning.'

A third influence on visits to literary landscapes is interest in the life of writers, such as to see where they were born, lived or worked. In the UK many visitors go to Chawton, which was home to the author Jane Austen, and to Dove Cottage, which was the Lake District home of the poet William Wordsworth (Herbert 1995). Visitors to Hannibal, USA can go to Mark Twain's restored boyhood home, a museum (housing his desk, first editions of his books, original letters and photographs, and his famous white suits) and the restored home of his childhood sweetheart (Curtis 1985). Some writers draw on the areas where they lived or worked as an inspiration for their work, and then visitors may be attracted by both 'real' and fictional elements of the literary place. According to Herbert (1995: 33): 'Heritage tourism based on literary places can use both the real lives of the writers and the worlds created in their novels. Visitors can be attracted to houses where writers lived and worked and also to the landscapes which provided the settings for their novels. The lines blur as imagined worlds vie with real-life experiences.' Hence, tourists may be drawn to literary destinations by both respect for the author and their work, and also by a desire to transcend the medium, to anchor in reality the dramas and characters that are fictional. Fourth, the biographies of literary figures, as well as travel writing that draws from those figures and their work, can add further layers of meaning and encouragement to visit a literary site (Daiches and Flower 1979).

Finally, Butler (1986) notes that tourism businesses and marketing organizations are prone to capitalize on the name of a writer associated with an area in order to develop tourism activities in the area and to sell specific products or services. For example, on Prince Edward Island there is an amusement park called 'Rainbow Valley', itself named after one of Montgomery's novels, which includes an 'Anne of Green Gables Land' featuring miniature representations of her fictional places and buildings. Squire (1996: 126) explains that 'While vestiges of Montgomery's literary landscape remain, they are juxtaposed in certain places with an encroaching landscape of mass tourism. While much of this tourist development does not mirror literary heritage, literary images have shaped visitors' impressions of place and serve as the currency for a range of tourist sites, attractions and promotional activities.'

Literary landscapes are a particular form of cultural landscape. Ringer (1998: 6) describes cultural landscapes as the 'manner in which the visible structure of a place expresses the emotional attachments held by both its residents and visitors, as well as the means by which it is imagined, produced, contested and enforced'. There are two elements to his interpretation of cultural landscapes. First, cultural landscapes are images or myths of place that are produced, contested and enforced by various actors, such as residents and tourism promoters. Second, they are the visible structures associated with people's emotional and cultural attachments to place. It is helpful to use Ringer's concepts to examine the elements of literary landscapes as they relate to tourists.

The first element is the myth of place. With literary landscapes it is writers who help to form the 'place myths' that become the symbolic images and meanings that are broadly shared by many people. These 'place myths' can be reinforced and altered by tourism businesses and promoters in a place with a literary association, and they are also interpreted and changed by the tourists that visit it. The second element of literary landscapes is the visible structures connected with people's attachments to a place. These structures may take the form of the buildings or landscapes associated with a writer's life in an area, or else the backdrop or setting depicted in their literary work. Other physical or visible structures associated with an area's literary connections include the activities of tourists, such as the sites they visit, and of the tourism industry, such as the attractions that draw on the area's literary links. According to Shields (1991), people's actions or practices can materially 'spatialize' the myths of place: hence, the activities of tourists and of the tourism industry can 'spatialize' the myths of literary place.

The tourism industry tends to simplify and represent places associated with literature within a relatively small number of place myths. It would be a mistake, however, to see the commoditized myths of these places as wholly hegemonic, saturating and dominating the expectations and practices of the tourists who visit them. Too much tourism research has assumed that people are not in active negotiation with their material and symbolic environment, but are passively shaped by it. It is contended here that when people visit a literary destination they make their own sense and value, their own knowledge, albeit negotiated within a myriad of influences. Hence, the 'literary landscape' is a shell of place myths and practices in which people make their own meanings within social contexts.

Squire's work on literary tourists is important as she examines how people negotiate and refigure their own meanings to make sense of the prevailing values and meanings surrounding a literary site. She argues that 'As visitors make sense of their encounters with literary places, private meanings are likely to interact with public forms and images' (Squire 1994: 107). Similarly, McIntosh and Prentice (1999: 607) assert that tourists at heritage sites 'assist in the production of their own experiences through their imaginations, emotions, and thought processes, and imbue objects in the setting provided with their own personal meanings'. Crouch (1999) also argues that in tourist activities people actively negotiate their own meanings, but within socialized contexts. This conclusion leads him to contend that there is a need for more research in tourism on the 'lay' or 'popular geographical knowledge' based on people's reflexive and ongoing encounters in everyday social life.

The present chapter examines the features of a literary landscape that visitors consider enable them to experience its literary connections during their visit. Based on the ideas already outlined, it is suggested that these features are likely to draw on the myths of place, including those based in a writer's literary work or life and also those promoted by the tourism industry. They are also likely to be affected by physical or visible structures, possibly including the buildings and landscapes connected with a writer and the associated activities of visitors and of the tourism industry. These elements are potentially key influences on how visitors negotiate or construct in their social contexts their own meanings, values and knowledge of literary landscapes. The intention here is to examine for visitors to a literary destination what it is that forms their 'popular geographical knowledge' of its literary landscape. The case study used here is Haworth in West Yorkshire in the North of England, which is well known for its connections with the Brontë family and their novels. Notable among their novels are Emily Brontë's *Wuthering Heights* (1847), Charlotte Brontë's *Jane Eyre* (1847), and Anne Brontë's *The Tenant of Wildfell Hall* (1848). The case study is also used to examine the characteristics of visitors to this literary destination. One reason for evaluating visitor characteristics is that information on visitors to other literary places tends to be fragmentary.

HAWORTH AND BRONTË TOURISM

Much of Haworth's reputation as a tourist destination is based on its associations with the Brontë family. Reverend Patrick Brontë moved with his six young children and wife into the parsonage in this large village on the edge of the Yorkshire moors in 1820, with family members living there until 1861. It is remarkable that one family produced three, if not four, talented writers, and the extraordinary closeness of the family was a key to their achievements. Patrick Brontë's children lived together for long periods and they created an elaborate fantasy world in the many stories they wrote for each other. Their unusually intense lives in the Haworth parsonage, and the bleak and wind-swept landscape of the surrounding moors, were important influences on their writing (Daiches and Flower 1979; Wilks 1982). Charlotte Brontë's preface to the 1850 edition of Emily Brontë's *Wuthering Heights* suggests the novel drew on Emily's acquaintance with 'the inhabitants, the customs, the natural characteristics of the outlying hills and hamlets in the West-Riding of Yorkshire' (Brontë 1968: 27). As well as the surrounding sweep of moorland, today there are several other physical remnants of the Brontës' Haworth, including some stone-built properties on Main Street that snake up a hill to the parsonage, the churchyard and tower of the original church, and the National Church Sunday School that Patrick Brontë had built. Formal interpretation of the Brontë links is provided by the Brontë Society, originally founded in 1893, with its own shop situated on Main Street. A Brontë museum was also opened in 1895, transferring in 1925 to the parsonage where the family had lived (the Brontë Parsonage Museum) (Pocock 1987).

While previously there had been a trickle of tourists to Haworth due to the Brontë connection, this increased substantially in 1857 after the publication of Mrs Gaskell's biography, *The Life of Charlotte Brontë*. In 1857, photographs of the Reverend Patrick Brontë, his church and the parsonage were displayed for sale in a chemist's shop window on Main Street, these probably being the first Brontë tourist souvenirs (Barker 1995: 810). Today, the tourist industry in Haworth is concentrated along Main Street. Here numerous attractive old buildings are now tourist shops, selling Brontë souvenirs ranging from Brontë soaps and jams to T-shirts and writing paper, as well as tea-rooms selling Heathcliff sandwiches and Brontë biscuits. At the top of Main Street is the Tourist Information Centre. Haworth bustles with tourists during the busy tourist season. Brontë Country Tourism, a division of Keighley Business Forum, uses the 'Brontë Country' theme to promote the region's diverse tourist attractions and businesses to visitors and the travel trade (Brontë Country Tourism 1998).

Barker (1995: xviii), a recent biographer of the Brontë family, argues that 'The Brontë story has always been riddled with myths'. These are likely to be mirrored in the place myths promoted by Haworth's tourism industry. Barker contends that one Brontë myth is that every location and incident in their novels must have a counterpart in reality. In her view this idea was influenced by Mrs Gaskell's widely-read biography, the *Life of Charlotte Brontë* (1857). Mrs Gaskell sought to defend several of the Brontës' novels against contemporaries who were shocked by the passion of the writing and by their disregard for social niceties at the time about violence, brutality and vulgarity. Her explanation for the supposed 'coarseness' of the novels, following suggestions by Charlotte herself, was that this was simply a product of the innocence of the Brontës, leading them to write accurate representations of the harsh realities of life in and around Haworth. Barker also suggests that Mrs Gaskell's *Life of Charlotte Brontë* popularized a myth that Haworth was a remote and obscure backwater in the early nineteenth century. She explains that in Mrs Gaskell's biography ' "Isolated", "solitary", "lonely" are the epithets on every page. But in reality, Haworth was a busy, industrial township and not some remote rural village of *Brigadoon*-style fantasy' (Barker 1995: 92).

Visitors to Haworth

The characteristics of visitors to the village of Haworth may differ from those to a specific site dedicated to the Brontës within the village. Such variation might be due to the Brontë site drawing 'literary tourists' with an evident interest in the literary connection. Alternatively, visitor characteristics could vary between the two locations because the village appeals more to 'general' visitors interested in its scenically attractive and historic qualities, its other visitor attractions or its tourist shops, rather than in its Brontë links. As Herbert (1996: 78) claims of places with strong literary or artistic links: 'Such places are commonly very attractive settings which, even without the literary or artistic connection, might draw visitors; the duality of general and specific attraction has to be recognized.' Hence a survey of visitors in the village of Haworth was analysed separately from a survey of visitors who had just been round the Brontë Parsonage Museum. The Brontë Society cares for this intimate museum in the small Georgian parsonage that was the former Brontë family home. It has rooms furnished as in the Brontës' day, with displays of their personal belongings, including their pictures, books and manuscripts. The first survey sought a sample of visitors to the village, so it retains visitors interviewed in the village who had been to the Brontë Parsonage Museum.

The survey involved face-to-face structured interviews with visitors who had travelled more than 15 kilometres to reach Haworth and were visiting for the day or as part of an overnight stay for leisure purposes. Every fifth visitor was approached at three survey sites within Haworth and they were interviewed if they met the criteria outlined previously and they agreed to respond. Interviews in the village were conducted at two sites selected because they were busy with visitors walking by. First, at the top of Main Street, which is near the Tourist Information Centre, the parsonage and two of the biggest car and coach parks; and, second, at the bottom of Main Street and near Haworth's steam railway station, which is a busy visitor attraction. A total of 330 visitors were interviewed at these two locations. The findings reported here relate to all 330 visitors or just to the 230 visitors interviewed at the top of Main Street – when it is the latter, this is indicated. A further 150 visitors were interviewed outside the Brontë Parsonage Museum, immediately after they had completed their visit and left this well-known Brontë attraction. The survey was conducted on a sample of weekdays and weekends between April to July, 1996, to include a shoulder period and part of the main tourist season. Estimated non-responses at all sites were just under 10% of people approached, and, although this is small, this reduced, for example, the proportion unable to respond in English.

The two sample populations included a mixture of local day visitors and tourists: 41.5% of visitors in the village, and 51.3% of those questioned after leaving the Brontë Parsonage Museum, were on a visit involving an overnight stay in the area or elsewhere. This also indicates that slightly more visitors in the museum sample were tourists. As many as 89.4% of the village sample, and 84% of the museum sample, normally lived in the UK. The proportions living in the North of England were 69.1% of the village sample and 61.3% of those interviewed after leaving the museum. In the village sample, 4.8% came from the USA or Canada, 2.7% from Australia or New Zealand, 2.1% from the rest of Europe and 0.9% from Japan. In the museum sample, 6% came from the USA or Canada, 2% from Australia or New Zealand, 6% from the rest of Europe and 2% from Japan.

The age range of visitors in both samples was quite wide. Among visitors in the village, 40.9% were aged under 35, 37.6% were 35 to under 55, and 21.4% were aged 55 and over. However, visitors questioned after leaving the museum tended to be more middle aged (48% were aged 35 to under 55 years, compared to 37.6% in the village) and fewer (12.7%, compared to 21.4%) were aged 55 years or more. Professional and managerial workers appear over-represented in the village sample (39.1%) and particularly so among visitors in the museum sample (58.7%), while manual workers appear under-represented (17.6% of those in the village and 10% of those leaving the museum). There may be some distortion, however, to higher socioeconomic groups as respondents assigned themselves to a socioeconomic category. Yet the trend here lends some support to Herbert's (1996: 81) suggestion that 'Literary and artistic places ... can be expected to have a stronger appeal to higher-income and more educated groups.'

Were visitors to Haworth mainly 'general' tourists who happened to be visiting this village, or were they more focused 'literary tourists' who had been drawn there because of its specific Brontë associations? One approach was to establish whether visitors had read at least one Brontë novel or seen one dramatized for the television, cinema or theatre. This was claimed to be the case by 62.6% of the 230 visitors interviewed at the top of Main Street and for 76.7% of visitors questioned after leaving the museum. Although the latter percentage is higher, the difference is not very large, especially as the experience of visiting the museum might prompt greater recall of prior exposure to the Brontës' work. Hence, while the majority of visitors stated they had read or seen a dramatization of a Brontë novel, quite large numbers replied that they had not.

Visitors were also asked how interested they were in the Brontë family before their visit. Care should be taken when interpreting responses to this question and the next, however, because of the prevalence of the Brontë name in association with the village and in its promotion. Among the visitors in the village, 60% stated they had been 'moderately' or 'very interested', and this applies to 62% of visitors questioned after leaving the museum. Quite modest proportions in both samples claimed they were 'very interested' in the Brontës before their visit (16.1% and 15.3% respectively). It is also evident that significant proportions of both samples considered that the Brontës were not of particular interest to them before their visit. Among visitors in the village, 29.1% had 'little interest' and 10% 'no interest' in the Brontës before their visit, and even among visitors interviewed after leaving the museum, 32.7% had 'little interest' and 5.3% 'no interest'.

A further question asked respondents to indicate the degree of importance of the Brontë family in their decision to visit Haworth. Large proportions of both samples claimed that the Brontës were at least of 'moderate importance' in this decision. This was the case for 62.8% of visitors in Haworth and for 82% of visitors interviewed after leaving the museum. However, the proportions claiming the Brontës were 'very important' for their visit is quite modest, with this being claimed by 16.4% in the village sample and by 28% in the museum sample. Despite the village's well-known Brontë connections, there were also still many visitors in both samples who stated that the Brontës were of 'little' or 'no importance' in their decision to visit. This was the case for 36.1% of visitors in Haworth and for 17.3% responding after leaving the museum. Hence, more than a third of visitors to the village indicated that the Brontë link had 'little' or 'no importance' for their visit.

Visitors in the village were also asked about the general purpose of their visit. In response, 11.5% said that they came to learn about the village or the Brontës, 21.2% to have 'a fun day out', and as many as 67.3% for both. When the same question was put to visitors after leaving the museum, 12.7% said that they had come to learn, 7.3% to have a fun day out, and 80% for both. Hence, visitors in the museum sample were less likely simply to have sought a fun day out, but the majority wanted both a fun day out and also to learn. In both samples, it seems most visitors sought to have an enjoyable day out and to learn at least something.

Taken overall, these findings suggest that only a small proportion of visitors were very interested in the Brontës, although most were moderately interested. The number with little or no interest in them also appears broadly similar to the number with a very strong interest. Visitors leaving the museum were more likely than those in the village to have been influenced to visit by the Brontë connections, but there was relatively little difference between these two groups in their prior interest in the Brontës.

TOURISTS AND THE CULTURAL CONSTRUCTION OF HAWORTH'S LITERARY LANDSCAPE

The rest of this chapter examines the features of Haworth that visitors considered enable them to experience its literary connections. As discussed earlier, within this literary landscape there are likely to be physical or visible structures, including the activities of tourists and the tourism industry, and also place images, with these features being used by visitors to establish their own meanings from the literary connections, albeit within their social contexts. Some features in Haworth are connected with events or characters in the Brontë novels, poems or juvenilia, and others are more associated with the lives of Brontë family members. The analysis of the views of visitors in the village is based on the sample of 230 visitors interviewed at the top of Main Street.

First, these 230 visitors were questioned about whether they had gained a sense that Haworth is where the Brontë family had lived. As many as 83% replied positively, suggesting that the great majority were satisfied with this aspect of their visitor experience. Second, these visitors were asked if they had gained an insight into the lives of the Brontës from the village, with 34.8% replying positively. Hence, relatively fewer felt they had gained an appreciation of the Brontë' lives, as distinct from gaining a sense that Haworth was the home of the Brontës. This response might be less positive because the question was restricted specifically to the village. But it is also likely to be more difficult for visitors to gain insights into specific aspects of the lives of the family. Hence, several respondents made comments such as 'I could sense that they lived here, but I didn't gain much of an insight', and 'You don't get much of an insight, but a sense that they lived there because of the names of the shops.'

Third, the 62.6% of visitors who had read a Brontë novel or seen one dramatized for television cinema or theatre, were asked about the extent to which their images from these sources were evoked by the village. Among these respondents, 82.7% stated their images were evoked at least 'to a small extent', although only 38.9% considered them evoked 'to a large' or 'to a very large' extent. Hence, among these visitors a majority did not consider that their images had been evoked in a substantial way, although most considered they had been evoked, if to a lesser degree.

If respondents replied positively to any of the three questions, they were asked in an open-ended question to explain what prompted that response. Their replies are shown in Table 7.1.

The sense of Haworth as the place where the Brontës had lived

The 83% of visitors who had gained a sense of Haworth as where the Brontës had lived were asked what helped them gain this sense. Table 7.1 shows that as many as 52.9% of responses relate to the built environment, 17.2% to the rural environment, 16.8% to the general ambience, and 10.9% to formal interpretative provision.

Many responses were about the historic built environment, with its many old stone-properties, and with the Brontë Parsonage Museum prominent among them. The parsonage is categorized as built environment because of its physical prominence in the village centre, and respondents had not necessarily been in the museum to experience its interpretative provision. When the content of the museum was mentioned specifically, this was included in the interpretation category. Visitors who mentioned the parsonage often also identified the adjacent church, parts of which date back to when Patrick Brontë was minister. Eighteen people mentioned the shops; typical comments were that 'Every shop has Brontë souvenirs and books' and 'all the shops sell things with Brontë on'. Main Street was identified as connected with the Brontës by three respondents. One explained that they felt this connection 'when I arrived this morning when it was quiet and not many people were on Main Street', and another commented that 'Main Street is like in the film.' The Black Bull

Table 7.1   Features of Haworth helping visitors to make connections with the Brontë family, their life and their novels

	Mentions of features helping visitors:		
	gain a sense of Haworth as the place where the Brontë family lived*(%)	gain insight into the life of the Brontës from the village**(%)	evoke images from the novels or dramatizations[#](%)
General ambience	*(16.8)*	*(14.6)*	*(3.0)*
Brontë connection everywhere	12.0	4.9	0.5
Atmosphere	4.5	9.7	0.5
Weather (e.g. mist or wind) or bleakness	0.3	0	2.0
Built environment	*(52.9)*	*(51.6)*	*(52.4)*
Brontë Parsonage Museum	30.8	11.7	14.2
Shops	5.8	6.8	1.0
Church	5.2	3.9	5.1
Cobbled or narrow streets	3.2	3.9	10.2
Main Street	1.9	2.9	4.1
Buildings	1.9	4.9	4.1
Whole village	1.6	11.7	4.6
Pubs, notably 'The Black Bull'	1.3	2.9	6.1
School	0.6	0	1.0
Architecture	0.6	0	2.0
Rural environment	*(17.2)*	*(1.0)*	*(40.6)*
Moors or countryside	8.1	1.0	36.0
Top Withens	8.1	0	3.6
Brontë Falls	1.0	0	1.0
Interpretation	*(10.9)*	*(30.1)*	*(3.0)*
Signs or plaques in the village	6.8	18.4	0.5
Brontë Parsonage Museum interpretation	1.6	2.9	2.5
Tourist Information Centre	1.3	2.9	0
Information leaflets	0.3	1.0	0
Brontë Society shop	0.3	3.9	0
Other interpretation	0.6	1.0	0
Souvenirs	0.3	2.9	0
Other	1.3	2.9	1.0
Total percentage	100	100	10
N =	308	103	197

* Mentions of features by 191 respondents who indicated that they had gained a sense that Haworth is the place where the Brontë family lived.

** Mentions of features by 80 respondents who indicated that they had gained an insight into the life of the Brontës from the village itself.

[#] Mentions of features by 119 respondents who had read a Brontë novel or seen one dramatized for television, cinema or theatre and also indicated that their own images from the books or dramatizations had been evoked by the village of Haworth.

and other pubs were probably mentioned as Branwell Brontë may have drunk there, although some visitors explained that in some pubs there were photographs and pictures of the Brontës.

Aspects of the rural environment were the next most frequently mentioned as providing a sense that Haworth was where the Brontës had lived. Twenty-five respondents identified Top Withens, a ruined farmhouse on the moors that has been associated with the Earnshaw home in Emily Brontë's novel *Wuthering Heights*. However, a plaque at the site notes that the building, even when complete, bore no resemblance to the house she described, although the situation may have provided some inspiration for her description of the moorland setting for the novel. The moors were also often commented on. One respondent explained how 'when we drove in over the moors, I imagined seeing Wuthering Heights'.

Many comments related to the area's general ambience, notably to the ubiquity of the Brontë name and motif. A typical response was one of appreciation of 'the whole atmosphere of the village' and of 'just being here and enjoying the atmosphere'. But many more simply observed that 'the Brontë name is splashed all around', and 'everything is Brontë – it's very commercialized on the Brontë front'. One visitor even stated that they gained a sense of visiting where the Brontës had lived, but 'only because the Brontë name is everywhere – it could be transferred to another village and it would be exactly the same'.

Insights into the lives of the Brontës from the village

The 34.8% of visitors who had gained an insight into the lives of the Brontës from the village were asked what had helped them gain this. Table 7.1 shows that responses were broadly similar to the previous question about gaining a sense that the Brontës had lived in Haworth. However, comparatively more insights into the Brontës' lives were gained from the interpretative provision (30.1% of responses compared with 10.9% for the previous question), probably because this provision often presents details of aspects of their lives. This question asked specifically about the village, so there were few responses concerning the rural environment.

Many responses concerned the interpretative provision, with the many signs or plaques in the village often being noted. The source of insight for one visitor was 'the signs around the village on the walls and above shops', and for another it was 'all the signs on the walls that tell you what happened in the building, and all the information in the Tourist Information Centre'. The information provided could be described as a 'marker' or 'signifier' explaining to visitors why Haworth is a tourist 'sight'. Culler (1988) argues that 'A marker is any kind of information or representation that constitutes a sight as a sight: by giving information about it, representing it, making it recognizable.' These responses by visitors to Haworth suggest it is possible that 'the markers themselves quite explicitly become the attraction, the sight itself' (Culler 1988: 165; Leiper 1990).

Four respondents gained insights from the Brontë Society Shop. This literary society was formed specifically to encourage appreciation and understanding of the Brontës' achievements, and visitor reaction to it and to the Brontë Parsonage

Museum suggest these features promote perceptions that the village has authentic connections to the Brontës. This reaction supports Macdonald's (1997: 156) suggestion that the existence of such establishments celebrating the heritage or culture of a place 'is in itself a generalised sign of "being" or "having" a culture'.

Many people claimed that their insight into the Brontës' lives came from the village as a whole, including its general historic character. Typical comments were that their insight came from 'the general atmosphere of the village' or from 'the general feel and look of Haworth'. One commented that 'by looking at the village it is easy to imagine how they lived with no transport', and another felt inspired by 'the quaint village. It's easy to imagine the Brontës still living here.'

Images evoked from the novels or dramatizations

The 52% of visitors who were familiar with at least one Brontë novel or dramatization and also indicated that their images had been evoked by the village were asked what had evoked these images. Table 7.1 shows that compared with responses to the previous two questions, these images were influenced much more by the rural environment and much less by the general ambience. This finding probably reflects the influence of the moorland scenes in Emily Brontë's novel *Wuthering Heights*. Indeed, for many visitors the surrounding moors were specifically mentioned as evoking the Brontës' literary work. Typical comments were that this occurred when 'driving in over the moors from Colne' or during 'the drive over here, over the moors'. Specific descriptions included 'the bleak moors' and 'the mist over the moors in the early morning'. Some visitors provided explanations such as 'I read the books at school – the moors and the town show the books' feelings', 'the moors – Heathcliff and *Wuthering Heights*' and 'the windy moors and the fact that the area is so hilly. The novels dictate that the area is hilly, so it's wonderful to see it actually is' Many of the comments associating the books with the built environment were about the cobbled streets. One visitor claimed to have related to the novels through 'the cobbled streets, although there's too much traffic'.

Responses to tourist shops

The findings already reported suggest that the frequent use of the Brontë motif in Haworth's tourist shops might help some visitors to connect the village with this literary family. It is possible that some visitors could consider these shops to be essential tourist facilities that also remind them of the Brontë connections, and hence the shops may simply add to their overall experience. Others, however, might regard their presence as a commercial intrusion, perhaps based on them disturbing their images of an appropriate or even 'sacred' landscape which ought to be separate or elevated from the realities of our profane lives (Tresidder 1999). Hence, tourist shops may be a source of ambiguity and tension in how people react to a literary landscape. Such tension could influence tourist behaviour and be important for the tourist's own literary landscape.

In order to examine these issues, the visitors in the survey were asked 'Would you be happier if there were fewer tourist shops, and Haworth was more of an historic village?' As many as 70.9% replied negatively, only 20.4% replied positively, and 8.7% were unsure. This suggests that most of these visitors were not unduly concerned by the presence of the tourist shops, or at least were prepared to accept them. This response might be affected by a trading-off of concerns about the shops with the advantage of them being convenient within the village, or by a recognition that such shops are found in other tourist centres. To explore these issues further, the respondents were asked why they replied positively or negatively to the idea of there being fewer tourist shops. The responses are shown in Table 7.2.

Table 7.2   Reasons given against and for Haworth having fewer tourist shops and being more of an historic village

Reasons against (%)		Reasons for (%)	
Tourist shops are acceptable;	35.2	It is too commercialized;	26.6
The balance is right between history and shops or between types of shops	18.8	Tourist shops spoil authenticity;	25.0
Tourist shops are needed to make it worth visiting;	16.4	Replace tourist shops with traditional or craft shops;	17.2
Tourist shops needed to attract visitors;	11.7	Tourist shops sell identical items;	14.1
Tourist shops needed to make a living;	8.6	It is too busy;	9.4
Tourist shops needed for souvenirs;	7.0	It is too modern;	4.7
Other.	2.3	Other.	3.1
Total percentage	100		100
N =	128		64

Among the majority who replied negatively, many explained that they considered there is a good balance between the village's shops and its historical features. For example, one visitor commented that 'the blend of history and shops is good, although the buskers are quite annoying', and another explained that 'my wife likes to browse around the shops as well as visit the museum'. A common justification was that the shops are required to make the village worth visiting. The usual argument was that there has to be something else to do other than visit the Brontë Parsonage Museum: 'apart from the museum there's not a lot else to do except shop'. A few people related the shops to a requirement to offer several visitor activities: 'I think you need them otherwise there wouldn't be much else to do, because, lets face it, you couldn't stay here longer than a day when you've been in the museum and to the waterfall.' But many simply stated that 'people wouldn't come here if there wasn't the shops'. A related observation was that the shops are needed in order to attract tourists. Typical comments were that 'The shops are good to look around. I don't think a lot of people would come if there were no shops,' and 'I don't like all the tourist shops, but the village needs them to attract lots of people.' There was also occasional recognition that the shops help the village to secure economic returns from its literary associations. It was even claimed that 'The village won't survive without the shops – tourism is a big part of the economy.'

Although still a significant proportion, only a minority (20.4%) wanted fewer shops in Haworth. Many explained this is because the shops reduce the village's 'authenticity'. The shops were claimed to 'detract from the real Haworth – the one the Brontës lived in – especially in Main Street'. Another response was that 'There are too many people and too many shops: the village is too busy. I don't like it. It should be like it was when the Brontës were alive.' Another concern was that the shops are commercializing the village and contributing to the village losing its character. The type of goods on sale to visitors in the shops was another cause of unease. Some complained that many shops sell almost identical souvenirs, and others viewed the souvenirs as often of low quality or lacking in taste. A few were disappointed that there are not more traditional shops or shops selling local crafts.

Conclusions

The precise degree to which the Brontë factor is a separate motivation in visits to Haworth probably cannot be determined because the village's connections with the Brontës are so widely promoted. But Haworth does appear to attract some 'literary inspired' visitors who have a genuine and strong interest in the Brontës, while others are 'generalist' visitors who have little or no interest in this literary family. Probably the majority, however, go there for a relaxing day out in the context of a moderate interest in seeing for themselves the village where the Brontës lived. The edges between these groups may well be indistinct (Craik 1997).

The study has examined visitors' 'lay geographical knowledge' of Brontë Haworth. It has focused on the features of Haworth that visitors consider enable them to experience its literary connections during their visit. Visitors create their own specific knowledge or literary landscape by identifying and responding to these features. According to Crouch (1999: 3), this type of knowledge 'is wholly different from learnt, expert knowledge or of knowledge by reading representations. It is instead a knowledge that incorporates all of these, and is perhaps incoherent, certainly "incomplete" and uneven.' While visitors to Haworth draw on the wider social context, they each experience and interpret the literary landscape in a unique way. This knowledge is influenced by the 'place myths' and by physical or visible structures found in the village or its surroundings. The influences include prior awareness of the novels and the lives of the Brontës, images promoted by the tourism industry, and also their perceptions of landscapes and buildings and of tourist activities in the village.

The majority of visitors gained some appreciation during their visit of Haworth's links with the Brontës. A range of features triggered this appreciation. The village's attractive, historic built environment, and particularly the Brontë Parsonage Museum, helped many visitors to make associations between the village and the Brontës. It was an important influence on visitors gaining a sense of Haworth as the place where the Brontës lived, on gaining insights into the lives of the Brontës, and also on them evoking their images from the novels or dramatizations. It may also have helped visitors to feel that such places 'are almost timeless, they have (it seems) not been ravaged by time, or at least not by instantaneous or clock times' (Rojek and Urry 1997: 15). It should be noted, however, that aspects of Haworth's built environment are a pastiche of the past, such as its antique-style street furniture, and may evoke a sense of the past that never was (Hughes 1992; Teo and Huang, 1995).

The moorland scenes in *Wuthering Heights*, perhaps the most famous Brontë novel, help to explain why the rural environment often evoked visitors' images from the novels or their dramatizations. Many of the insights of visitors into specific aspects of the lives of the Brontë family were gained from the interpretative provision, notably the signs and plaques around the village. This interpretation provided for conservation and tourism reasons appears to have enhanced visitor appreciation of the village's links with the lives of the Brontës, although it did not help much in evoking images from their novels.

Most visitors did not agree that they would be happier if there were fewer tourist shops and Haworth was more of an historic village. Visitors often found these shops to be convenient, provided them with more choice of activities, or else considered them inevitable features of a busy tourist centre. Some visitors even commented that the shops and the souvenirs in them had provided them with reminders of the village's Brontë associations. Only a fairly small proportion had found these shops sufficiently 'inauthentic', 'over-commercialized' or otherwise inappropriate that they wanted fewer of them in the village. However, while most visitors accepted or did not seriously question the presence of these tourist features, it is likely that they saw them as distinct and separate from more 'authentic' aspects of the village's literary landscape.

Many visitors appear to have distinguished in their own minds the more contemporary features of the village from those they took to have 'special' qualities because they conformed to their images of how it was at the time of the Brontës. Similarly, Squire (1994: 117) suggests that at the English Lake District home of the author Beatrix Potter 'visitors were consciously indulging in escapist fantasies, filtering out those elements that did not conform to the dictates of popular mythology'. Visitors to Haworth seem often to have sought and also to have gained at least some appreciation of what was perceived to be a 'special' place. At a deeper level this might be interpreted as reflecting desires to reaffirm their individual place within a collective cultural heritage. Further research is needed to examine how visitors use the features they recognize as Haworth's literary landscapes as a starting point for various kinds of introspection and hence for exploring their reflexive and reflective selves.

REFERENCES

Barker, J. (1995) *The Brontës*. London: Phoenix Orion.
Brontë Country Tourism (1998) *The Brontë Experience, 1999*. (Promotional Brochure) Bradford: ADVentura Publishing.
Brontë, E. (1968) *Wuthering Heights*. London: Collins.

Butler, R. W. (1986) 'Literature as an influence in shaping the image of tourist destinations: a review and case study', in J. S. Marsh (ed.), 'Canadian studies of parks, recreation and tourism in foreign lands', Occasional Paper 11. Department of Geography, Trent University, Canada.

Craik, J. (1997) 'The culture of tourism', in C. Rojek and J. Urry (eds), *Touring Cultures: Transformations of Travel and Theory*. London: Routledge, 113–36.

Crouch, D. (1999) 'Introduction: encounters in leisure/tourism', in D. Crouch (ed.), *Leisure/Tourism Geographies. Practices and Geographical Knowledge*. London: Routledge, 1–16.

Culler, J. (1988) *Framing the Sight*. Oxford: Blackwell.

Curtis, J. (1985) 'The most famous fence in the world. Fact and fiction in Mark Twain's Hannibal', *Landscape*, **28**, 8–14.

Daiches, D. and Flower, J. (1979) *Literary Landscapes of the British Isles: A Narrative Atlas*. London: Bell and Hyman.

Herbert, D. T. (1995) 'Heritage as literary place', in D. T. Herbert (ed.), *Heritage, Tourism and Society*. London: Mansell, 32–48.

Herbert, D. T. (1996) 'Artistic and literary places in France as tourist attractions', *Tourism Management*, **17**(2), 77–85.

Hughes, G. (1992) 'Tourism and the geographical imagination', *Leisure Studies* **11**, 31–42.

Leiper, N. (1990) 'Tourist attraction systems', *Annals of Tourism Research*, **17**, 367–84.

Macdonald, S. (1997) 'A people's story. Heritage, identity and authenticity', in C. Rojek and J. Urry (eds), *Touring Cultures. Transformations of Travel and Theory*. London: Routledge, 155–75.

McIntosh, A. J. and Prentice, R. C. (1999) 'Affirming authenticity. Consuming cultural heritage', *Annals of Tourism Research*, **26**(3), 589–612.

Newby, P. T. (1981) 'Literature and the fashioning of tourist taste', in D. C. D. Pocock (ed.), *Humanistic Geography and Literature*. London: Croom Helm, 130–41.

Ousby, I. (1990) *The Englishman's England. Taste, Travel and the Rise of Tourism*. Cambridge: Cambridge University Press.

Pocock, D. C. D. (1987) 'Haworth: the experience of literary place', in W. E. Mallory and P. Simpson-Housley (eds), *Geography and Literature. A Meeting of the Disciplines*. New York: Syracuse University Press, 134–42.

Ringer, G. (1998) 'Introduction', in G. Ringer (ed.), *Destinations. Cultural Landscapes of Tourism*. London: Routledge, 1–13.

Rojek, C. and Urry, J. (1997) 'Transformations of travel and theory', in C. Rojek and J. Urry (eds), *Touring Cultures. Transformations of Travel and Theory*. London: Routledge, 1–19.

Shields, R. (1991) *Places on the Margin*. London: Routledge.

Squire, S. J. (1992) 'Ways of seeing, ways of being: literature, place and tourism in L. M. Montgomery's Prince Edward Island', in P. Simpson-Housley and G. Norcliffe (eds), *A Few Acres of Snow. Literary and Artistic Images of Canada*. Toronto: Dundurn Press, Chap. 11, 1–11.

Squire, S. J. (1994) 'The cultural values of literary tourism', *Annals of Tourism Research*, **21**(1), 103–20.

Squire, S. J. (1996) 'Literary tourism and sustainable tourism: promoting *Anne of Green Gables* in Prince Edward Island', *Journal of Sustainable Tourism*, **4**(3), 119–34.

Teo, P. and Huang, S. (1995) 'Tourism and heritage conservation in Singapore', *Annals of Tourism Research*, **22**(3), 589–615.

Tresidder, R. (1999) 'Tourism and sacred landscapes', in D. Crouch (ed.), *Leisure/ Tourism Geographies. Practices and Geographical Knowledge*. London: Routledge, 137–48.

Wilks, B. (1982) *The Brontës*. London: Hamlyn Publishing.

Chapter 8

Cultural Gatekeepers in the L. M. Montgomery Tourist Industry

Patricia Cormack and Clare Fawcett

Everywhere I have gone this summer I have heard fulminations against Uncle John for tearing down the old home. The Charlottetown people were especially indignant. They said it was the only 'literary shrine' the Province possessed and it was a shame to destroy it ... I am well content that it should be torn down.

It would not please me to think of it being overrun by hoards of curious tourists and carried off piecemeal.

(L. M. Montgomery, 1923)

As the setting for Lucy Maud Montgomery's novels, the Island plays a large role in her stories of turn-of-the-century rural life. Its **pastoral beauty** and the fascinating local characters are important elements of stories like *Anne of Green Gables*™ and *Emily of New Moon*™. Visitors who come to see 'where Anne grew up' are not disappointed. Many of the farmsteads and villages have changed little, and the local folk you may **meet at an auction** or a lobster supper could have walked straight out of a Montgomery story.

Literary visitors to the Island can follow 'Anne tours,' see *Anne of Green Gables, The Musical* and visit the sets of the new *Emily of New Moon* TV show.

(*Prince Edward Island 1998 Visitors Guide*, bold in original)

As these quotations demonstrate, the literary tourist industry established in Prince Edward Island (PEI), Canada, around author Lucy Maud Montgomery (1874–1942) and her most famous novel, *Anne of Green Gables*, has long been the site of competing and conflicting efforts to create meaning. In the first quote, taken from Montgomery's own autobiographical reflections, local Islanders are outraged when the author's uncle tries to control the incursion of visitors onto his property by destroying the house where Montgomery penned *Anne of Green Gables*. The second quote, taken from the official Tourism PEI guidebook, shows that while the titles of Montgomery's novels have become property, legally protected through trademark, provincial tourist officials attempt to entice tourists to PEI by advertising the folksy, friendly and 'pastoral' aspects of the Island described in the novels. Taken together these quotations point to themes that must be considered when examining the Montgomery literary tourist industry:

(1) the relationship between high culture and 'literature';
(2) the link between mass culture and the commercial production and consumption of images, objects and themes for 'hoards of curious tourists'; and
(3) folk or popular culture as celebrated in Montgomery's novels and as presented on PEI as a central element of tourism.

The following is a case study of two organizations that give shape to the Montgomery tourist industry: the L. M. Montgomery Institute (hereafter, 'the Montgomery Institute') and the Anne of Green Gables Licensing Authority (hereafter, 'the Anne Authority'). The Montgomery Institute is an academic body housed at the University of Prince Edward Island. Its mandate is to nurture and enhance scholarly appreciation of Montgomery's work and promote the author as both a popular and academically recognized literary figure. The Anne Authority, made up of Montgomery's heirs, provincial government officials and appointees of the heirs and government, controls the use of the names and images of 'Anne' and other Montgomery characters in the commercial and non-commercial sectors. We characterize these organizations as 'cultural gatekeepers' within the industry because they claim the authority to make judgements about and control the generation of ideas, themes, objects and practices associated with Montgomery and her works. Although tourists are usually not aware of the actions of the Montgomery Institute or the Anne Authority, both organizations influence what tourists will encounter when they visit PEI. They do this by endorsing, and thus allowing to exist publically, some representations and interpretations of Montgomery and her works and actively excluding others. Moreover, these organizations gain legitimacy and amass resources by creatively and strategically presenting themselves as adjudicators of appropriate representations of the author and her works as these are located at particular conjunctions of high, mass and folk/popular cultures.

HIGH, MASS AND FOLK/POPULAR CULTURES

Any claim to cultural judgement is also a claim to legitimacy and resources, and perhaps the most obvious site of such cultural differentiation and resource allocation is literature. The literary is, by definition, about cultural exclusion, as demonstrated by the existence of and critical acrimony over what is and what is not to be included in various literary canons. Typically, literary critics, academics, political élites and writers have deemed particular works to be literature or even great literature worthy of celebration. These players, furthermore, have chosen the works to be included under the rubric of 'high' culture by examining them for qualitites such as 'formal complexity', 'moral worth', 'critical insight' (Storey 1993: 7), 'timelessness', and 'universality'. Contemporary theorists have come to highlight the social and political context within which evaluation takes place and challenge such taken-for-granted criteria. They have argued that social and political differentials are inherent, if sometimes hidden, in the process of criticism. Analysed from such a perspective, 'high culture' does not simply exist, but is a complex set of practices that actively distinguishes a small élite of highly educated and powerful individuals from ordinary people. By defining what is and what is not included in 'high culture', this élite perpetuates itself by teaching only certain individuals – often its own biological or intellectual offspring – to recognize, appreciate and create 'high culture'. In the words of Pierre Bourdieu, 'taste' is 'one of the most vital stakes in the struggles fought in the field of the dominant class and the field of cultural production' (1984: 13). Outside the 'field of the dominant class', the mainstream cultural consumer either fails to understand or has no interest in understanding high-cultural products and practices. Literary tourism, because it is associated with literature, at least partially resides in the realm of 'high culture'. Like art galleries and museums, the contents and artistic value of literary tourist sites and artefacts are subject to arbitration and interpretation by experts with academic, artistic or professional credentials. Moreover, while this mediation on the part of such cultural gatekeepers between the literary text and the tourist can have a quite profound influence on what tourists encounter, the presence of such mediation is not always apparent.

While 'high culture' is delineated by educated élites and their arbiters of taste (individuals we might generously imagine to be beyond the crass consideration of the profitability of the cultural objects and practices they evaluate), 'mass culture' is associated with what Horkheimer and Adorno have disparagingly called the 'culture industry' (1972), that is, the large-scale, industrial production and undiscriminating consumption of inexpensive homogeneous goods. According to this view, 'mass culture' is practiced and perpetuated in a cultural field where tastes are necessarily 'unrefined' and 'undiscriminating'. Critics of 'mass culture' have argued that because it is fully inclusive and, therefore, generates ideas, products and activities immediately accessible to all, 'mass culture' inevitably promotes an ethos of immediate gratification and uncultivated desires. From this perspective, the 'masses' demonstrate agency only by choosing to purchase or refusing to purchase any particular product, activity or lifestyle (MacDonald 1957: 59). In other words, the 'masses' neither create nor arbitrate taste; they simply consume what advertisers and social trends direct them to want. Early studies of modern large-scale tourism applied this understanding of mass culture and portrayed tourists as cultural philistines consuming 'staged' experiences created by tourism producers and operators (Boorstin 1961).

In contrast to 'mass culture', popular culture is often defined as that which resists the hegemony of mass cultural production (Fiske 1989). While mass cultural products are indiscriminately consumed by an uncultivated public, popular culture is actively produced by ordinary people. In other words, popular culture, while often unrefined, uneducated and naïve, at its base involves production rather than consumption. Furthermore, in some cases, this production actually consists of reshaping the meaning of mass-produced goods through local interpretations and applications. Many observers of tourism have suggested that tourist industries characterized by a nostalgic longing for 'the folk' represented by images of the pre-industrial and premodern past, and the craft production that represents this past, are premised on a celebration of popular culture (McKay 1994). For this reason, we have joined popular culture and folk culture in our schema (Table 8.1).

Table 8.1   Characteristics of high, folk/popular and mass culture

	High culture	Folk/popular culture	Mass culture
Production	By 'artists'. Limited quantities.	By locals and/or craftspeople. Relatively limited, particular, slow production.	By unskilled, anonymous labourers. Large-scale, fast, industrial production of homogeneous goods.
Consumption	By knowledgeable and educated élites with economic resources.	By locals and discriminating consumers.	By the undiscriminating masses.
Judgement of value	By experts and élite who are educated and discriminating. Judgement of aesthetic value.	By locals who generate meaning and may resist mass cultural meanings.	By any and all consumers. Associated with unrefined and undiscriminating taste and passive consumption.
Exclusivity	Exclusive.	Exclusive of non-local only.	Fully inclusive.

Some critics argue that because these cultural distinctions are saturated with political and social meaning, and therefore perpetuate inequality, they should be rejected as analytical concepts. Fredric Jameson, for example, suggests that the very distinction of cultural levels or spaces 'tends to function in some timeless realm of absolute aesthetic judgment ... ' (1979: 133), rather than in the real world of lived cultural practices. In opposition to Jameson, we suggest that the tripartite distinction of high, mass and folk/popular cultures remains an effective analytical tool. Far from being solely derived from a theoretical or ideological model overlaid on to concrete situations, these distinctions explicitly reside (for better or worse) in the language, ideas and policies articulated by members of the Montgomery Institute and the Anne Authority. In other words, these cultural distinctions inform the attempts of these two organizations to generate respectful, legitimate and resilient representations of Montgomery, her characters and her work.

Viewed in terms of such distinctions, even the most cursory inspection of the Montgomery tourist industry reveals a culturally complex situation. For example, almost all products and practices now associated with Montgomery and Anne are mass-produced for a large consumer market. Nevertheless, as we shall demonstrate, local, craft and non-academic, that is, popular cultural interests, are still a crucial part of this industry. Members of the Anne Authority, especially, struggle with the need to promote modern, mass production, while protecting what they see as an inherently folk/popular culture associated with the author. Finally, people associated with the Montgomery Institute and those involved with specific tourist sites and heritage societies have made efforts to promote Montgomery as simultaneously culturally-weighty, unique and valuable, as well as popular and accessible. Both the Montgomery Institute and the Anne Authority display the difficulties inherent in any attempt to promote Montgomery within the contexts of high, mass and folk/popular cultures. More importantly, as we shall show, both organizations rely on these distinctions to shore up their claims to legitimacy and resources.

MONTGOMERY LITERARY TOURISM

L. M. Montgomery was born in Clifton (now New London), PEI in 1874. For most of the first 36 years of her life, Montgomery resided with her maternal grandparents on a homestead in Cavendish, PEI. When her grandmother died in 1911, Montgomery married Ewan Macdonald and left PEI for Ontario where she lived as a Presbyterian minister's wife until her death in 1942. As evidenced in her journals, letters and fictional writing, Montgomery remained tied to PEI all her life. Not only did she visit frequently, but she set all but one of her 20 novels on her beloved island. Montgomery penned her first and most famous novel, *Anne of Green Gables*, in Cavendish. The novel describes the adventures of Anne, a talkative and imaginative young orphan, adopted by the taciturn Marilla Cuthbert and her shy brother Matthew. Matthew and Marilla live in a house called Green Gables in the village of Avonlea, PEI. One of the most distinctive features of the novel is its detailed and romantic depictions of the natural beauty of rural PEI. When describing Anne's view from her bedroom window, for instance, Montgomery writes:

> Below the garden a green field lush with clover sloped down to the hollow where the brook ran and where scores of white birches grew, upspringing airily out of an undergrowth suggestive of delightful possibilities in ferns and mosses and woodsy things generally. (L. M. Montgomery, *Anne of Green Gables*)

This novel and other Montgomery works detail the personal quirks, character traits and lives of ordinary people of rural PEI. For example, Montgomery describes one of the characters in *Anne of Green Gables* in this way:

> She was a notable housewife; her work was always done and done well; she 'ran' the Sewing Circle, helped run the Sunday-school, and was the strongest prop of the Church Aid Society and the Foreign Missions Auxiliary. Yet with all this Mrs. Rachel found abundant time to sit for hours at her kitchen window, knitting 'cotton wrap' quilts – she had knitted sixteen of them, as Avonlea housekeepers were wont to tell in awed voices – and keeping a sharp eye on the main road that crossed the hollow and wound up on the steep red hill beyond. (L. M. Montgomery, *Anne of Green Gables*)

Montgomery's fictional writing has been characterized as 'late nineteenth-century Canadian pastoral idyll' (Squire 1992: 139). Her romantic descriptions of simple, rural life, ecstatic communes with nature and strong civic and familial bonds are central to the enduring success of Montgomery's works and Montgomery tourism. The non-fictional reflections found in her journals, letters and autobiographies also make an explicit idyllic connection between places, people and nature and set the tone for tourism in Montgomery's early home of Cavendish, PEI.

Soon after the 1908 publication of *Anne of Green Gables*, visitors began to come to Cavendish. Some of these early tourists sought out the abandoned homestead where

Montgomery had written the novel. Eventually, the removal of 'souvenirs' from the house and property provoked the owner, Montgomery's Uncle John Macneill, to tear down the old house. Early tourists also visited the farmhouse which Montgomery used as a model for the setting of Anne Shirley's fictional home, Green Gables. In the 1920s, Ernest and Myrtle Webb the owners of Green Gables House, as this property came to be known, began taking in summer visitors for farm vacations. This practice ended in 1936 when the Webb's land and house were expropriated for inclusion in the newly established Prince Edward Island National Park. Ever since, Green Gables House, Prince Edward Island National Park has been the central focus of a vibrant and growing literary tourist industry (De Jonge 2000; Fawcett and Cormack 2001).

Since the 1960s, Montgomery tourism has expanded in Cavendish and elsewhere on PEI to include: public and private Montgomery heritage sites; shops, hotels and restaurants using the Anne/Montgomery theme; products related to Anne and other Montgomery characters; and, since 1965 and 1999 respectively, productions of *Anne of Green Gables: The Musical*™ and *Emily of New Moon*™ at Charlottetown's Confederation Centre of the Arts. While limited numbers of Montgomery tourists had been accommodated in Cavendish since at least the 1920s, by the 1960s Montgomery tourism had begun to spread along PEI's north shore. For example, in 1965 the 'Lucy Maud Montgomery Birthplace' heritage site was established in New London, and in 1971 'Silver Bush and the Story Girl House' was developed in Park Corner. This site was renamed 'Anne of Green Gables Museum at Silver Bush' in the late 1970s.

Many attractions and accommodations bearing Montgomery-related names are located in and around Cavendish: 'Shining Waters Country Inn', 'Rainbow Valley Family Fun Park', 'Green Gables Golf Club', 'Kindred Spirits Country Inn and Cottages', 'Anne Shirley Motel and Cottages' and 'Green Gables Bungalow Court'. One of the most recent Montgomery-related enterprises in Cavendish is 'Avonlea Village', an open-air commercial venture comprising relocated and replica nineteenth-century buildings containing shops and restaurants. Montgomery-related businesses also thrive in other parts of PEI as shown by the success of the 'Anne of Green Gables Store', a retail outlet opened in Charlottetown in 1993, selling souvenirs, books and other products related to Anne. A second 'Anne of Green Gables' store was opened in 1995, and a third in 1999.

Montgomery literary tourism was affected by two important cultural events that occurred in 1985: the publication of the first of Montgomery's edited journals (Rubio and Waterston 1985) and the premier broadcast of Sullivan Entertainment's *Anne of Green Gables* television miniseries. Public access to edited versions of Montgomery's journals enhanced scholarly and non-specialist knowledge of the author's life, inspired her descendants John and Jennie Macneill to create a new tourist site ('The Site of L. M. Montgomery's Cavendish Home'), and provided information that allowed Parks Canada to make a stronger thematic link to Montgomery and reduce its previous emphasis on Anne in the redevelopment of Green Gables House. After 1985, the Montgomery tourist industry shifted its thematic emphasis to include, not only 'Anne' and 'Green Gables', but also the marketing of other Montgomery characters such as Emily, and the promotion of Montgomery herself. Sullivan

Entertainment's television miniseries productions *Anne of Green Gables* (1985), *Anne of Green Gables: The Sequel* (1987) and *Anne of Green Gables: The Continuing Story* (2000) as well as their television series *Road to Avonlea* (1990–96) have introduced a new generation of viewers to Montgomery's characters and have been immensely popular overseas. In 1998, Salter Street Films began *Emily of New Moon*, a second television series based on Montgomery's lesser-known *Emily of New Moon* trilogy.

THE L. M. MONTGOMERY INSTITUTE

At the millennium, the Canadian Broadcasting Corporation polled Canadians about their favourite authors of fiction: L. M. Montgomery was the most popular Canadian fiction writer of all time. While Montgomery has enjoyed a broad readership for generations, bringing her into the 'Canadian literary canon' has not been easy. As Gans notes, a literary work that enjoys a broad and inclusive audience can be granted low artistic status, since critics assume the general public cannot discern excellence or make sophisticated cultural judgements and that anything with broad appeal must necessarily be bad (1974: 21). This has been particularly true in the case of authors such as Montgomery, whose readers have consisted primarily of women and girls. As Rubio points out, in the early decades of the twentieth century, 'She became increasingly marginalized when academics professionalized reviewing and literary study, defining the canon of "great books." Her domestic subject matter, colloquial style, and use of female protagonists worked against her' (1994: 5). For years, scholars continued to denigrate Montgomery as a sentimental writer who produced children's books of no literary merit. Nevertheless, by the late 1980s academics were challenging Montgomery's secondary status and urging her inclusion in the canons of Canadian literature (Epperly 1988; Gerson 2000).

Toward this end, the L. M. Montgomery Institute was established at the University of Prince Edward Island (UPEI) in 1993. The Montgomery Institute was created by scholars working on PEI who recognized the need for an academic institution on the Island where Montgomery could be publicly acknowledged as a major Canadian writer. When the Montgomery Institute was founded, Montgomery's diaries and journals and many of her papers were already housed off-Island at the University of Guelph, although some of her book manuscripts were at the Confederation Centre of the Arts in Charlottetown. Dr Elizabeth Epperly, the founder of the Montgomery Institute, argued strongly for situating the hub of Montgomery scholarship at the author's alma mater, UPEI (Montgomery graduated from Prince of Wales College which, in 1969, united with St Dunstan's University to become the University of Prince Edward Island). As Epperly states: 'We have all … the physical manifestations, we have the family, and we have all the ties. So this university must declare itself as the centre for Montgomery studies' (personal communication, 4 August 1998). Initial funding for the Montgomery Institute came from a three-year grant from the Social Sciences and Humanities Council of Canada (SSHRC), the leading academic granting agency for the humanities and social sciences in Canada. Additional funding came from the MacDonald Stuart Foundation, with SSHRC continuing to lend its support. Key principles of the Montgomery

Institute include dedication to academic scholarship on Montgomery, commitment to public education about Montgomery, promotion of a feminist perspective, and the generation and maintenance of links with the community. These principles guide the work of the Montgomery Institute and are reflected in the Montgomery Institute's organizational structure, promotional information and projects.

The Montgomery Institute's position as part of UPEI, the province's most prestigious academic institution, places it comfortably within the domain of high culture. In addition to giving serious and scholarly consideration to Montgomery and her literary works, however, the Montgomery Institute also seeks to expand the author's popular audience. In short, the Montgomery Institute tries to prevent the scholarly encoding of Montgomery and her literature from over-shadowing the popular enjoyment and celebration of the author's work. In fact, as we will show, the Montgomery Institute carefully uses academic arguments, especially those rooted in feminism, to legitimize Montgomery despite her popular appeal. And it uses the inclusiveness and accessibility of Montgomery to the ordinary reader to authorize the academic study of her life, times and work.

Montgomery's fictional and autobiographical texts have fascinated feminist critics just as they have entertained generations of female readers. Within the Montgomery Institute, scholars have argued that the academic value of Montgomery and her works is partly based on her broad popular appeal. This position is rooted in a number of feminist assumptions about the relationship between literature and women's experiences. Feminist scholars were among the first to treat literary canon-making as a political action rather than a mere aesthetic and intellectual judgement. By asking why so many female writers had been left out of the canons of important literature, feminist scholars were able to begin isolating and articulating the implicit criteria for canonical inclusion and exclusion. This feminist critique of literary canon-making sometimes produced a tension within academic circles as scholars asked for the inclusion of women writers in extant literary canons while simultaneously denouncing the practice of canon-making as élitist and exclusionary. Feminist scholars studying Montgomery have dealt with this tension in two ways. First, through research on Montgomery's texts – works filled with detailed descriptions of the lives, challenges, joys and sorrows of ordinary women – they have explored the lived experiences of all women, that is, of women writers and of women readers. In doing so, they have tried to lessen the cultural distance between the 'artist' and the 'non-artist'. Second, feminist scholars have turned their academic gaze on women who read Montgomery's books to ask how these readers generate meaning from the novels. In other words, the Montgomery Institute has used feminist theory to expand the literary cannon so that it includes a popular author like Montgomery while simultaneously critiquing the politics of canon-making.

The Montgomery Institute's organizational structure shows that its legitimacy and access to resources depend on its location in a recognizable academic institutional setting as well as its links to local organizations and to a broad popular base of Montgomery enthusiasts. The Montgomery Institute was originally made up of two sections – a Research Section and an English Language School – both of which reported to a Committee comprising the UPEI Dean of Arts, a member of the Department of English, a member of the Women's Studies Programme and an appointee from within or outside UPEI interested or involved in Montgomery scholarship. The mandate of the English Language School, which held sessions each summer from 1994 to 1999, was to use books and stories written by and about Montgomery, and other English-language materials, to teach English as a Second Language to young Japanese students. The mandate of the Research Section is to facilitate and conduct research on the life and works of L. M. Montgomery. As of 2000, this mandate had been fulfilled by the hosting of four biennial Montgomery conferences (in 1994, 1996 and 2000, and a day-long panel on Montgomery in a co-hosted UPEI conference on the 'Literature of Small Islands' in 1998); the establishment of a credit course on Montgomery at UPEI; the organizing of three L. M. Montgomery lecture series; the posting of an internet site about the Montgomery Institute; the provision of Montgomery workshops for Island school children; the collection of Montgomery books and artefacts; the moderation of a 500-member Kindred Spirits e-mail list serve; working with other Montgomery heritage organizations to create the L. M. Montgomery Heritage Society; and the response to approximately 800 annual research requests from students, members of the general public, and scholars (L. M. Montgomery Institute 1998: 3).

The Montgomery Institute's website shows that its creators have carefully managed and balanced the sometimes contradictory interests of Montgomery scholars and non-academic readers. The site opens with the Montgomery Institute's broad mandate that 'The L. M. Montgomery Institute is dedicated to helping students and scholars learn about and study L. M. Montgomery's life, works, and influence' (www.uP.E.I..ca/~lmmi/). Although this mandate stresses the academic rather than the popular nature of the Montgomery Institute, it includes a reference to non-specialists under the guise of 'students' who 'learn about' rather than 'study' Montgomery. Further into the website the Montgomery Institute's attempt both to popularize and study Montgomery becomes more apparent. For example, the website tells us that the goals of the Research Section are 'to initiate and participate in projects that expand our knowledge of Montgomery, her works, and the impact she has had as an author, journal writer, woman, and native of Prince Edward Island' (www.uP.E.I..ca/~lmmi/). This statement points to dual interests by clearly saying that the aim of the Montgomery Institute is: (1) to make Montgomery better known and acknowledged on the world stage as an important literary figure ('to *expand* our knowledge of Montgomery … and the impact she has had') and (2) to reinscribe Montgomery as a local Island author, i.e. as a home-grown talent with all the particularities this brings to her work ('woman and native of Prince Edward Island'). In other words, the website suggests that, as a signifier, Montgomery is universal and particular, international and local, specialized and general.

By including dedicated enthusiasts, local residents, Montgomery heirs and descendants, as well as conventional and postmodern scholars in one cultural space, the Montgomery Institute invites a plethora of readings of Montgomery's work generated from various positions. The Montgomery Institute's website obliquely addresses this issue of multiplicity by stating that people from all over the world leave messages in the Montgomery Institute's on-line guest book (www.uP.E.I..ca/~lmmi/addguest.html), that the Kindred Spirits Mailing List is open to 'scholars and regular folks' (www.uP.E.I..ca/~lmmi/listserv.html), that Montgomery's work is read by 'general readers' as well as scholars, and that 'her writing appeals to people who love beauty and to those who struggle against oppression' (www.uP.E.I..ca/~lmmi/about-lm.html). In short, the website constructs an image of the Montgomery Institute as multicultural, populist and committed to principles of respect for both nature and human dignity.

The Montgomery Institute's fourth biennial conference, open to both general readers and Montgomery specialists, was held at UPEI in June 2000. This SSHRC-sponsored event provides an excellent example of how the Montgomery Institute acts as a cultural gatekeeper defining the Montgomery heritage by deftly mixing the academic and popular. The theme of the conference – 'L. M. Montgomery and Popular Culture' – dealt with the popular appeal of Montgomery, but more specific questions found in the conference's promotional literature were couched in academic language: 'Is there an aesthetic of the popular? Is popular culture subversive of mainstream culture? How does popular culture transcend national boundaries?' (www.uP.E.I..ca/~lmmi/conference.html). Cultural products derived from Montgomery's books and other writings – such as adaptations of Montgomery's novels for stage, television and video and tourist sites linked to Montgomery – were treated as 'translations' to be understood and analysed in terms of how ordinary people use and make sense of Montgomery. As Epperly explained, in the planning stages of the conference: 'popular culture, you notice that is what we're looking for in that conference ... We'll be talking about *all* of the translations, because that's what they are, [translations] of Montgomery's work into other media. So songs and plays and videos and even board games and all of the things that she's found her way into. And that's the way people understand or try to interpret and try to translate the most powerful impulses in their own lives' (Epperly, personal communication, 4 August 1998).

Popular and folk translations of Montgomery appeared throughout the conference: registrants were greeted by women in period costume and straw hats with freckles drawn on their faces; an artisan exhibited and discussed the quilt she had made to represent Montgomery's life and works; Montgomery's granddaughter, Kate Macdonald Butler, gave a keynote address written in the style of a letter to her dead grandmother; and participants were encouraged to attend the musical, *Emily*^{TM}. Nevertheless, the core of the conference involved academic interpretations of such popular translations and events which placed the conference firmly in the realm of high or élite culture. The opening reception of the conference, held at Government House, was hosted by 'Their Honours Gilbert R. Clements and Mrs Clements' and was attended by 'Her Excellency, Adrienne Clarkson, Governor General of Canada' and member of the Montgomery Institute's International Advisory Committee. Welcoming speeches were given by Dr Wade MacLauchlan, president of UPEI, and Dr Irene Gammel, co-chair of the L. M. Montgomery Committee. Dr Gammel acknowledged the size and importance of the vast popular culture industry that has grown up around Montgomery but then pointed out that the conference brought together 'prominent scholars' from 'all corners of the world' for an international symposium. Finally, a large majority of the people invited by the International Advisory Committee to present papers or give keynote addresses were affiliated with universities or colleges. The audience, however, was constituted by everyone from international enthusiasts to family, local residents and prominent and less-prominent scholars. At times, this meant that highly specialized and esoteric talk appeared to be misinterpreted by audience members, while very particular and concrete questions from the enthusiasts could not be satisfactorily answered by the academic presenters who seemed lacking in the kind of knowledge that make them 'experts'.

Perhaps the most successful moment of the conference, in terms of a meeting of the academic and the popular, was the launching of a thoroughly researched and graphically beautiful CD-ROM titled *The Bend in the Road: An Invitation to the World and Work of L. M. Montgomery*. Created by UPEI academics Drs Elizabeth Epperly and Anne-Louise Brooks and co-chair of the Montgomery Institute's Committee, author and part-time UPEI lecturer, Ms Deirdre Kessler, this work is aimed at both scholars and non-academic Montgomery enthusiasts.

Throughout the CD-ROM the academic/high cultural motifs are intertwined with those of popular culture. For example, the section titled 'Work' contains numerous excerpts from the author's novels, journals, letters and photographs. Significantly, the feminist authors of 'The Bend in the Road' have also included in this section information about Montgomery's gardens, cooking recipes and scrapbooks – parts of her lived experience as a woman. Throughout the CD-ROM, short commentaries are presented by renowned Montgomery scholars such as Drs Elizabeth Epperly, Mary Rubio and Elizabeth Waterston. Legitimacy is also leant to the project, however, through the inclusion of interviews, comments and photographs by non-academics including Montgomery's grandchildren, cousins, other relatives and Island friends. The CD-ROM contains a bibliography of works by and about Montgomery, some academic and others from newspapers and other journalistic sources. A final excellent example of the CD-ROM's merging of academic and popular is the reading, by Elizabeth Marsdan, the actress who for decades played the part of Marilla in the Charlottetown Festival's production *Anne of Green Gables: The Musical*, of excerpts from Montgomery's original works. Nevertheless, despite the embedding of the popular in the CD-ROM, its authority and legitimacy are principally derived from its association with academic authors and the Montgomery Institute at UPEI.

For the Montgomery Institute, the inclusion of the popular is a necessary element in the continued academic study of Montgomery. 'Ownership' of Montgomery reaches far beyond the confines of the academy to the many non-academic Montgomery enthusiasts who possess invaluable information about Montgomery's life and times. Furthermore, the diversity of the Montgomery Institute's activities and audiences means that a unified vocabulary and normative agreement about the standards of knowledge are not as easily assumed as they are in many other academic settings. This is particularly noticeable when one considers that part of the Montgomery Institute's implicit mandate is to rescue Montgomery from the status of secondary literary talent and the author of books aimed at children. Clearly, the Montgomery Institute does not find a threat to the author's reputation in the general community. Rather the Montgomery Institute members work hard to ensure that academics as well as the general public acknowledge the importance of Montgomery. The Montgomery Institute respects Montgomery's broad appeal and treats the popular appreciation of Montgomery as an advantage rather than as an impediment to improving the author's reputation.

Indeed, by sliding between and sometimes mixing university-based research on Montgomery with the public's appreciation of the author's work, the Montgomery Institute gains access to resources from two sources, the academic and the popular, and maintains legitimacy in the eyes of two constituencies – scholars and Montgomery readers and fans. Its focus on scholarship and academic excellence makes it eligible for financial support from such high cultural sources as SSHRC and provides it with a base at UPEI. Its openness to inquiries from the public and outreach into the community give it access to support from key non-academic players on the Montgomery scene, such as the Montgomery heirs, creators of popular cultural renditions of Montgomery's work, guardians of Montgomery historical sites and Montgomery readers. Clearly, the benefits of this relationship between people associated with high culture and those associated with folk/popular culture go both ways. On the one hand, by staying open to popular interpretations and translations of the author's life and works, the Montgomery Institute can present itself as a relevant academic organization and, in this way, gain access to people and information as well as obtain funding from sources such as the MacDonald-Stewart Foundation. On the other hand, the Montgomery Institute acts as a cultural gatekeeper which legitimizes the popular by recognizing and promoting Montgomery's works and folk/popular translations of Montgomery's works. Elizabeth Epperly points out that her academic credentials and work as a Montgomery scholar vindicate popular readings. Many readers respond to her scholarly work and public talks by exclaiming : ' "I knew there was something good there!", they'd say "I knew that was good!" ' (Epperly, personal communication, 4 August 1998). By cultivating this open, but controlled relationship with the popular, the Montgomery Institute justifies its own political stance *vis-à-vis* literary judgement and canons, while maintaining access to power, resources and information.

Despite its symbiotic relationship to the popular, the Montgomery Institute is fundamentally an academic cultural location. While it does honour, appreciate and, when applying for funding and community support, use motifs drawn from non-academic sources, popular culture often takes second place to high/academic culture. In other words, as a cultural gatekeeper, the Montgomery Institute works to situate popular cultural products by using academic analyses to decide which of these products are valuable, legitimate and worthy of study and endorsement.

THE ANNE OF GREEN GABLES LICENSING AUTHORITY

The Anne of Green Gables Licensing Authority (Anne Authority), established in 1994, holds the right to license 'products, services and events using images of Anne and controls use of the Anne trademarks in Canada, the United States, and elsewhere' (Anne of Green Gables Licensing Authority news release, January 1995). The Anne Authority has an eight-person Board of Directors: three of these members are appointed by the Province of Prince Edward Island, three are appointed by the Montgomery heirs and two are jointly appointed by the Province and the heirs.

Decisions about the licensing of Anne products, services and events are made by one of two five-person committees. The Prince Edward Island Licensing Committee screens products, services and events on PEI and the Family Licensing Committee deals with all other products, services and events.

The creation of the Anne Authority was not without conflict and acrimony between the Montgomery heirs, the Province of PEI, local Island producers, and off-Island producers. In 1983 a lawyer representing the Montgomery heirs established that the family legally controlled the rights to the Anne books. In 1984, the Province of Prince Edward Island Development Agency applied for a copyright for an 'Anne of the Island' tourism trademark (Beazley 1992: 1; MacAndrew 1989: 14). In the meantime, Montgomery's heirs established a trademark for Anne merchandise and, in July 1988, in return for royalties, gave a small Ontario marketing company, Avonlea Traditions Inc., 'exclusive licensing rights to all products, events and services based on Montgomery's books except for the right to the musical, the 1985 movie and to the publications of the books themselves' (Corelli 1989: 40). This move angered craftspeople on Prince Edward Island who, for the previous two decades, had been producing Anne crafts and merchandise for a rapidly growing tourist market. Island craftspeople were disturbed that an off-Island company now had the legal right to screen their work and collect a 5 per cent royalty on sales. As one member of the Anne Authority licensing committee said, 'There's an attitude here on the Island ... of proprietorship for Anne ... people here don't feel that they should have to pay royalties.' Prince Edward Island government officials told Island manufacturers to ignore Avonlea Tradition's demand for royalties and disputed 'Avonlea's claim that they are the sole licensor's of Anne products' (Gordon Campbell quoted in Corelli 1989: 40). In 1989, Montgomery's heirs filed an application for a copyright to 'Anne of the Island', effectively scuttling the provincial government's attempts to win this trademark (Beazley 1992: 1). Despite their disagreements, the Montgomery heirs, Avonlea Traditions and the Province continued to talk, through the late 1980s and early 1990s, about coming to an agreement about who would control the name and image of 'Anne'. These discussions were interrupted in 1992 when the Province used Section Nine of the federal Trademarks Act to win the Canadian copyright to the names 'Anne of Green Gables' as well as various images of Anne and Green Gables (Beazley 1992: 1; Moulton 1995: 14). This use of Section Nine, which gives 'public authorities' the power to have an application granted immediately without the usual five-year waiting period, disappointed the Montgomery heirs as they had thought negotiations between their lawyer and the Province were going smoothly (Beazley 1992: 1). By 1992 negotiations did resume and, in 1994, the Anne of Green Gables Licensing Authority was established to oversee licensing and quality standards (Moulton 1995: 14). The Montgomery heirs and the Province of Prince Edward Island began to work together to control the marketing of Anne.

This brief history of the creation of the Anne Authority may give the impression that the organization is concerned only with regulating the capacity of various competing parties to profit from the lucrative Montgomery industry. While this aspect of the Anne Authority is undeniably real, the organization also plays a central role in regulating the cultural manifestations of Montgomery and her characters. It does this by deeming some products, places and events appropriate to Montgomery's legacy and others as unworthy. Those products, places and events which the Anne Authority deems appropriate receive a license and become part of the Montgomery tourist industry; those deemed inappropriate are denied a license and cannot be produced or distributed for public consumption.

The Anne Authority's goal is 'to protect the integrity of Anne images – word and visual depictions – as they appear on or in connection with craft or manufactured products and other items such as books, pictures and photos, as well as in connection with services and events and to preserve the memory of Lucy Maud Montgomery and the integrity of her legacy' (Anne Authority news release, January 1995). To accomplish this goal, the Anne Authority uses property rights and litigation.

The Anne Authority is inherently conservative since it limits and regulates the production and distribution of commodities and, in this way, prevents the unfettered proliferation of Montgomery-based images and artefacts. The Anne Authority's claim to protect and preserve assumes that what needs to be protected and preserved is already self-evident. Its mandate does not invite debate about cultural value, but only enforces an unstated version of this value. There is a certain 'snob value' to the products licensed by the Anne Authority since these licenses 'give exclusivity and legitimacy to products' (Epperly, personal communication, 4 August 2000).

The Anne Authority website sets out the following 'general guidelines' which govern the decision to grant a license:

1. They must be appropriate to the image of Anne (or other characters, e.g. Diana Barry, Marilla, Matthew, or place, e.g. Green Gables House) as depicted by L. M. Montgomery.
2. They must be of high quality and meet standards specified by the Anne Authority.
3. They must be appropriate to the use or purpose for which they were intended.

The first guideline suggests that Montgomery's fictional descriptions limit what Lynes has called the 'thematic range' of producers (Lynes 1998: 10). This is demonstrated by one Anne Authority licensing committee member's response when asked how committee members decide which images are appropriate and which are inappropriate for licensed products. She said: 'We wouldn't license a topless Anne T-shirt. We wouldn't license an Anne of Green Gables beer mug. We wouldn't license an Anne of Green Gables ash tray.' What seem to be 'appropriate to the image of Anne' are products that fit into the novel's temporal setting and moral ethos. This informant thought that the products mentioned above were inappropriate because, in Montgomery's novels, Anne is a girl-child who would neither smoke nor drink and who would show extreme modesty. Moreover, the products themselves often suggest a pre-industrial, domestic setting or childhood. Included in the list of products licensed by the Anne Authority are tea and tea pots, salt fish boxes, raspberry cordial, honey, jewelry, book jackets, candles, soap, picture frames, organic potting soil, wildflower seeds, aprons, cross stitch, sewing baskets, pin cushions, quilts, dolls and school supplies.

The second guideline speaks to the material condition of the product rather than what it represents. The Anne Authority's licensing application form and list of currently licensed products show that the Anne Authority defines quality in terms of both productive process and materials. Applicants for licenses are required to indicate how their product is made, that is, they must tell the Anne Authority whether the 'type of operation' used to make their product is 'craft' or 'manufacturing or processing'. An examination of the Anne Authority's list of licensed products shows that it tends to license objects made using pre-industrial manufacturing processes, such as the 'hand carved', 'handmade', 'handcrafted', or 'hand painted'. Although the Anne Authority never directly asks producers what materials they use, the list of Anne Authority licensed products makes no mention of items made of plastic – a material which suggests industrial mass-production – but does mention items made of china, pewter, porcelain, wood, cotton, straw, resin, earthenware, rag, stained glass, tin and clay. The list suggests that the Anne Authority is particularly willing to license self-described craft products because their mode of manufacture and materials connote the historical period and productive practices discussed in Montgomery's novels. Montgomery's fictional and autobiographical works are peopled by rural PEI girls and women who sew, quilt, preserve food, and run households in the late nineteenth and early twentieth centuries. Twenty-first century PEI craftspeople create products which reference Island folk traditions and perpetuate this tradition of folk production. Nevertheless, not all products manufactured at home using local materials are licensed. As another member of the Anne Authority licensing committee notes, craft products made without care and skill may be denied a license: 'when you get mud balls with braids and it's called an Anne doll, obviously ... neither the family nor the province is going to license that to be sold'. Clearly a 'craft' is not merely something made at home. Furthermore, while the Anne Authority's licensing guidelines imply that, in terms of materials used in production and objects produced, the Anne Authority promotes an industry characterized by craft products central to folk/popular culture, the Anne Authority does license mass-produced products as long as they are durable, tasteful, thematically appropriate to Montgomery and not obviously mass-produced.

The third guideline stipulates that products be useful and dependable, that is, 'appropriate to the use or the purpose for which they were intended'. The Anne Authority tries to protect consumers from experiencing frustration because of products that do not work properly. Presumably, they do not want consumers to associate unreliability with Anne or Montgomery. As one Anne Authority licensing committee member pointed out, people 'get sick of cheap and shoddy goods. And they then associate them, as people, do with ... Montgomery and with the characters and not with the producers.'

In her discussion of the commodification of Montgomery, Lynes points out that: 'commodifiers of the Avonlea mythology allow for, indeed engineer as part of their marketing tactics, a certain amount of slippage. It is clearly in the interests of those who manufacture Avonlea products to expand their thematic range and thus, profit range, as much as possible' (1998: 10). It is just this 'slippage' and 'thematic range' that the Anne Authority seeks to control through its licensing procedures. Nevertheless, while the Anne Authority has created licensing guidelines, these guidelines themselves allow Anne Authority committee members to make subjective judgements about what should and should not be licensed. How, for instance, do committee members decide whether a particular product is 'appropriate to the image of Anne (or other characters, e.g. Diana Barry, Marilla, Matthew, or place, e.g. Green Gables House) as depicted by L. M. Montgomery' as required by Guideline 1? Where does the Anne Authority define what constitutes 'high quality' and where does it elucidate its 'standards' as required by Guideline 2?

The Anne Authority grants licenses for craft and mass-produced products on the basis of whether these products adhere to certain unstated themes that denote pre-industrial productive techniques and materials. As long as mass-produced products adhere to these themes they will be licensed. A license will be denied to products that do not meet these criteria. An excellent example of the failure of a product to meet the unspoken criteria of the Anne Authority is that of a pair of Anne eyeglasses. During an interview, an Anne Authority licensing committee member told us that: 'I recently had an application for Anne of Green Gables eyeglasses ... I just couldn't let myself, I couldn't wrap myself around this.' She explained that the rejected eyeglasses had a 'little image of Anne in the corner' and said that she would have accepted the eyeglasses had they been of the style worn during the late nineteenth or early twentieth century or if the name 'Anne of Green Gables' had been printed on them. She rejected the eyeglasses because they had no relationship to Montgomery's Anne novels, nor to the Anne character since 'Anne of Green Gables didn't wear glasses'.

Perhaps it is the quality of the process of mass production that helps explain why this Anne Authority licensing committee member could intuitively reject eyeglasses bearing an image of Anne. Mass production threatens the limits that inherently exist in craft culture. Mass production is not limited by local or traditional materials, conventional styles of production, or shortages of skilled craftspeople. In other words, mass production references no limit and no particularity to the productive process or the producer. Products may be produced anywhere by anyone with minimal training or skills and no interest in the product other than the wages associated with its production. Of course, these qualities give mass-produced products a competitive edge over craft products in terms of their retail price.

Critics like Walter Benjamin (1969) and Jean Baudrillard (1983) have argued that mass production destroys cultural ideals like uniqueness and particularity because the continual production of copies eradicates the original to which they once may have referred. Mass production 'uses up' the original (in this case Anne) by putting it everywhere. The image, in other words, gets in front of the original and determines (in most cases, diminishes) the original's cultural value. In the context of Montgomery and Anne, the Anne Authority implies that, if no controls were applied to create standards, Montgomery products, images and events would cease to be tied to and limited by the 'original' Montgomery novels, Montgomery's autobiographical texts, or PEI interests. The Anne Authority limits and controls the proliferation of Montgomery referents by defining some as appropriate and others as inappropriate to the legacy of Montgomery. In this way, they clearly act as cultural gatekeepers maintaining the cultural value of 'Anne' and 'Montgomery' by delimiting their meaning.

And yet there is an unease in the Anne Authority's stance that is betrayed in decisions like the one described above involving the eyeglasses. The eyeglasses were not dismissed because they were poorly made, tasteless, or impractical. That Anne did not wear eyeglasses seems an incomplete explanation for their rejection because other Montgomery characters wore eyeglasses and because other products not explicitly mentioned in the novel have been licensed. Perhaps a fuller explanation why Anne Authority licensing committee members rejected the eyeglasses lies in the glasses' inability to reference any process of manufacture – they simply appear on the scene. Mass-produced objects that the Anne Authority has licensed reference themes of childhood and pre-industrial rural PEI. For example inexpensive rag dolls which were licensed, even those not themselves made of rags, reference the theme of childhood and pre-industrial rag doll craft production which, in turn, links to ideas like care, love and local pride. Because these latter ideas are core themes of Montgomery's novels and the Montgomery/Anne tourist industry, any product which elicits them, whether made at home or in a factory, will receive a license. The Anne Authority's reluctance to license products which have obviously been mass-produced and its willingness to license those which seem to have been manufactured using craft methods and local materials defend traditional motifs in the Montgomery industry and preserve the industry itself. Nevertheless, the Anne Authority's willingness to license some mass-produced products and reject some craft products shows that it defends general material and thematic codes rather than a strict mass- production/ craft-production distinction.

Members of the Anne Authority – the heirs and representatives of the provincial government – legitimate their claim to regulate and limit the commercial and popular appearance of Anne and other Montgomery characters by reference to their status as blood kin or as local officials. The themes defended in their judgements of products and activities to be licensed are the same themes that lend them legitimacy as culture gatekeepers – ties to the past, local particularity, the willingness to make judgements of value. In protecting a particular version of Montgomery heritage they are also preserving a particular cultural scene in which their authority makes sense and is reinforced. Ordinary Islanders, Montgomery scholars, and tourist operators generally accept the authority of this organization and assume that it is defending Island interests and identity.

CONCLUSION

We began this discussion by suggesting that any study of literary tourism should analyse the differing and often divergent cultural resonances of the 'literary' as they are played out within any particular literary tourist industry. The idea of the literary is often associated with high cultural claims about taste and value, but tourism as an industry includes mass and folk/popular cultural claims. Cultural gatekeepers work with these sometimes contradictory claims to give shape to literary heritage, legitimize themselves, and gain resources. In the preceding case study we have shown how two cultural gatekeeping organizations – the L. M. Montgomery Institute and the Anne of Green Gables Licensing Authority – use the resonances of high, mass and folk/popular culture towards these ends.

The Montgomery Institute carefully balances its promotion of Montgomery as a valuable and distinctly Canadian author with its promotion of Montgomery as popular and accessible. This allows high academic culture to justify popular culture, and it allows the popular to justify the high. The mutual legitimization of high and popular culture is rooted in the Montgomery Institute's feminist epistemology and politics. The Montgomery Institute both challenges the exclusion of women from the literary canons and argues for the inclusion of Montgomery in that canon because of her broad popular appeal and her ability to write about the lives and concerns of ordinary women.

The Montgomery Institute encourages diverse and inevitably conflicting readings of Montgomery's texts generated in disparate cultural locations. In doing so, it risks losing minimal normative agreements that make discussion and dialogue possible. The Montgomery Institute manages this problem of an infinitely dispersed text by allowing the author's own celebration of place – a celebration central to Montgomery's fiction and non-fiction writing – to root her in Prince Edward Island. The Montgomery Institute encourages multiple readings of the texts at its conferences and it allows geographically unmoored debates and conversations to occur in cyberspace. Nevertheless, for the Montgomery Institute, the place where Montgomery scholarship and enthusiasm must be grounded is PEI or, more specifically, the University of Prince Edward Island. As Elizabeth Epperly says:

> one of the greatest charms of the books is that Prince Edward Island sounds like a mythical place and yet it's geographically undeniable. There it is. And so the Institute should be the same. It should be for everybody and it should be global and it should be accessible through the internet and what have you, but it should be geographically located in the place that also was her fixed point of reference. (Elizabeth Epperly, personal communication, 4 August 1998)

In this statement Epperly suggests that Montgomery's literary value is tied to her tourist value, that is, the tourist's search for and celebration of a 'geographically undeniable' 'fixed point of reference' actually increases the relevance and hence the importance of Montgomery's work. Indeed, when the literary and tourism are linked, the particularities of a celebrated literature are associated with the distinctiveness and value of a nation, region, town or people. Literary tourism often implies an intimate and natural connection to the essence of a place and its people, almost to the extent that a local literature is seen as capturing and articulating a local identity. That Montgomery Institute committee members and staff recognize this connection attests to their savvy as intellectual promoters of Montgomery and of the Montgomery Institute. By linking Montgomery's texts so closely to PEI, the place the texts celebrate, the Montgomery Institute ensures that it will be considered relevant and answerable to local interests and concerns, attractive to Montgomery enthusiasts who visit the island, and legitimate to scholars. In doing so, it ensures its own ongoing vitality and a broad-based interest in Montgomery.

The Anne Authority balances mass production with local and craft production by limiting the production and distribution of Anne commodities and events. This does not, however, entail giving exclusive rights to craft producers. Rather, it means that the Anne Authority licenses products which in some way – through productive process, materials used or the artefacts produced – evoke the theme of traditional craft production while meeting standards of durability. The Anne Authority licensing committee's unarticulated and implicit licensing guidelines allow producers of Montgomery tourist commodities to sell mass-produced items which may or may not be locally made, or involve traditional craft skills. Nevertheless, these unspoken guidelines control the deracinating tendency of mass production by licensing only products which fit certain themes, for example, girlhood, nineteenth-century rural PEI, the domestic, or the handmade. This preserves Anne and other Montgomery characters and places as signifiers and commodities without exhausting their meanings. As the judgements made by the Anne Authority preserve productive practices and values that are celebrated in Montgomery's novels and still held by many people who live on PEI, the legitimacy of the Anne Authority is re-inscribed each time its committee members limit and demarcate the boundaries of Montgomery heritage.

The L. M. Montgomery Institute and the Anne of Green Gables Licensing Authority ground the Montgomery literary tourist industry in a particular geographic place and time. Each of these cultural gatekeepers controls the interpretive breadth of Montgomery and her characters by rooting them in Prince Edward Island and in the pastoral, pre-industrial past. Each gatekeeper has found subtle and relatively inclusive ways of achieving this goal; the Montgomery Institute consciously allows multiple, yet often segregated or layered readings of Montgomery's texts and the Anne Authority permits relatively diverse commodification of Anne while protecting essential elements of the industry – particularly modern-day interpretations of Montgomery, her characters or her fictional world – from being exhausted and ultimately destroyed through industrial production and mass- marketing.

REFERENCES

Anne of Green Gables Licensing Authority (1995) *Anne Authority News Release.*

Baudrillard, Jean (1983) *Simulations.* trans. Paul Foss, Paul Patton and Philip Beitchman. New York: Semiotext(e).

Beazley, Doug (1992) "Province and Anne heirs square off over copyright 'Agreement' ", *Journal Pioneer,* 5 December, 1.

Benjamin, Walter (1969) *Illuminations.* trans. Harry Zohn, ed. Hannah Arendt. New York: Schocken.

Boorstin, Daniel J. (1961) *The Image: A Guide to Pseudo-Events in America.* New York: Harper & Row.

Bourdieu, Pierre (1984) *Distinction: A Social Critique of the Judgement of Taste,* trans. Richard Nice. Harvard: Harvard University Press.

Corelli, Rae (1989) 'Anger on the Island', *MacLean's,* **102**(28), 40.

De Jonge, James (2000) *The Real and the Imaginary: Popular Culture and the Commemorations of L. M. Montgomery's Cavendish.* Paper presented at L. M. Montgomery and Popular Culture, University of Prince Edward Island, Charlottetown, 29 June–2 July 2000.

Epperly, Elizabeth (1988) 'L. M. Montgomery and the Changing Times', *Acadiensis*, **17**(2), 177–85.

Fawcett, Clare and Cormack, Patricia (2001) 'Guarding authenticity at L. M. Montgomery tourist sites', *Annals of Tourism Research*, **28**(3), 686–704.

Fiske, John (1989) *Understanding Popular Culture*. London: Unwin Hyman.

Gans, Herbert, J (1974) *Popular Culture and High Culture: An Analysis and Evaluation of Taste*. New York: Basic Books.

Gerson, Carole (2000) *L. M. Montgomery and Academic Culture: Bridging the Gap*. Paper presented at L. M. Montgomery and Popular Culture, University of Prince Edward Island, Charlottetown, 29 June–2 July 2000.

Horkheimer, Max and Theodor W. Adorno (1972) *Dialectic of Enlightenment*, trans. John Cumming. New York: Continuum.

Jameson, Fredric (1979) 'Reification and Utopia in Mass Culture', *Social Text*, 1.

L. M. Montgomery Institute (1998) *L. M. Montgomery Institute Newsletter*, **1**(1).

Lynes, Jeanette (1998) 'Consumable Avonlea: the commodification of the Green Gables mythology', *Canadian Children's Literature*, (**24**:3/4), 7–21.

MacAndrew, Barbara (1989) 'Who owns Anne?', *Islandside*, **1**(10), 13–15.

MacDonald, Dwight (1957) 'A theory of mass culture', in B. Rosenberg and D. Manning White (eds), *Mass Culture: The Popular Arts in America*. New York: The Free Press, 59–73.

McKay, Ian (1994) *The Quest of the Folk: Antimodernism and Cultural Selection in Twentieth-Century Nova Scotia*. Montreal and Kingston: McGill-Queen's University Press.

Moulton, Donalee (1995) 'Green Gables grows greener: the settlement of a rights dispute changes the retail character', *Marketing*, **100**(41), 14, 16.

Rubio, Mary and Elizabeth Waterston (1985) *The Selected Journals of L. M. Montgomery: Volume I*. Toronto: Oxford University Press.

Rubio, Mary (1994) 'Introduction: harvesting thistles in Montgomery's textual garden', in M. Rubio (ed.), *Harvesting Thistles: The Textual Garden of L. M. Montgomery*. Guelph, Ont.: Canadian Children's Press, 1–13.

Squire, Shelagh J. (1992) 'Ways of seeing, ways of being: literature, place, and tourism in L. M. Montgomery's Prince Edward Island', in P. Simpson-Housley and G. Norcliffe (eds), *A Few Acres of Snow: Literary and Artistic Images of Canada*. Toronto: Dundurn Press, 137–47.

Storey, John (1993) *An Introductory Guide to Cultural Theory and Popular Culture*. Athens, Georgia: University of Georgia Press.

Acknowledgment

The authors would like to thank Maureen Moynagh for her insightful comments on an earlier draft of this paper. Thanks also go to named and anonymous informants associated with the L. M. Montgomery Institute and the Anne of Green Gables Licensing Authority. Research for this paper was funded by a grant from the Centre for Regional Studies, St Francis Xavier University.

Chapter 9

The Two Mark Twains as Tourists

Lawrence I. Berkove

Mark Twain was one of America's most travelled authors. During the course of his lifetime he travelled widely in the United States; crossed the Atlantic twenty-nine times; lived for months on end in rented quarters in various European countries; and circled the globe once with stopovers in Australia, New Zealand, India and South Africa (Salamo, Smith and Browning 1998). He travelled widely in books also. Although mostly self-taught, he read extensively and often selected reading that prepared him with detailed information on the history, culture and geographical features of the places he visited. A notion of Twain as a diamond in the rough, a native but largely unlearned and unpolished genius, would be exactly wrong. On the contrary, he is one of the world's most sophisticated literary artists as well as one of the most popular, and is also an extraordinarily skillful ironist.

Most of Twain's books contain evidence of his travels, but the 'official' travel books are *The Innocents Abroad* (1869), in which Twain recounts his experiences in Europe and the Near East; *A Tramp Abroad* (1880), his impressions of a pedestrian tour of Europe, mostly Germany, Switzerland and France; and *Following the Equator: A Journey Around the World* (1897), his report of tours of Fiji, Australia, New Zealand, Ceylon, India, Mauritius and South Africa. To these standard travel books may be added *Roughing It* (1872), his adventures in Nevada, California and Hawaii; and *Life on the Mississippi* (1883), his recollections of his youth and later years on that river. And to these may be further added 'Extract from Captain Stormfield's Visit to Heaven' (1907–08), an unusual trip to a place everyone wishes to go to, but which, even yet, is barred to tourists and is (said to be) highly selective about immigrants. Each of these books incorporates two reflections of Twain: a surface narrator who is sometimes naïve and credulous, but usually humorous; and also an ironic and more private narrator who avoids centre stage but is introspective, sceptical and often critical.

The travel books are of uneven literary value. None achieves the stature of either *Huckleberry Finn* (1884–5) or *A Connecticut Yankee in King Arthur's Court* (1889).

Each has indebtedness to various contemporary travel books with which Twain was familiar; but even the least of them has sparks of Twain's fire. Twain early developed a unique layered style whose surface level is typically pleasant, loosely organized and humorous, but whose deeper levels are thematically organized and constitute a virtual counterplot. The surface level derives mainly from situation and obvious humour; the deeper levels derive from the themes embedded in textual ironies. These thematic values are often at odds with what he seems to praise. What keep them from being readily recognized are the dazzling brilliance of the surface level, and the subtle and unexpected audacity of the ironies. Twain wanted, after all, to sell books, so his surface level is rich in entertainment value. But he also wanted to be honest, so he compromised by including his controversial truths but using subtle artistry to make them inobvious.

Innocents Abroad; or, The New Pilgrim's Progress (1869) was Twain's first significant travel book. It was a financial success and established his reputation. It is loosely based – with considerable fictionalizing – on a five-month tour of the Mediterranean he joined in 1867. Using the steamship *Quaker City* as their floating home, a group of largely affluent and mostly middle-aged or elderly and devoutly Protestant Americans set out on a variation of the Grand Tour of famous places in Europe, North Africa and the Holy Land (Ganzel 1968). As the full title suggests, the allusive model is Bunyan's *Pilgrim's Progress* and its narrative of how Christian finally reached the Celestial City after coping with the dangers and snares of the world. It therefore intimated to be somewhat of a burlesque of American pilgrims (whose furthest destination would be the Holy Land and Jerusalem), encountering the jaded sights and venalities of the Old World with their New World innocence. The book, fortunately, is more sophisticated than that, for Twain recognized good as well as bad in the Old World, and bad as well as good in the 'innocents'.

Wherever the Americans went, they had to cope with the frustration of 'doing' a place on a tight schedule. For example, Paris in five days (where they 'galloped' through the Louvre in two hours), Venice and Florence in two days each, Rome in less than a week, a surreptitious one-night visit to the Acropolis, four days in the Crimea, four days in Constantinople, a week in Lebanon and Syria, twelve days in the Holy Land, and a week in Egypt, plus incidental stops in the Azores, Gibraltar, Tangiers, Sardinia, Algiers and Malaga. The Americans also often had to cope with unreliable and officious guides, and with a good deal of phony history – pieces of the true cross and other holy relics were scattered from the Azores to the Holy Land, legends of miracles were often represented as truth, and paintings of martyrs that fancifully embellished the manner of their deaths adorned the walls of churches and museums.

Whereas the pilgrims and other tourists looked forward to admiring the Old World, the narrator and a small group of irreverent rebels on the tour persisted in observing things realistically. A great part of the book's delight results from their refusal to feign awe or to swallow myths. They notice the filth, squalor and decrepitude of the places they visited, and are even critical of the Holy Land. They sometimes turn the tables on their guides, as in Rome (ch. 27) when they pretend not to know who Columbus was or to accept that he discovered America, and frustrate the guide with questions such as 'is – is he dead?' They also mock pious frauds, such as the tomb of Adam in Jerusalem, where the narrator ironically claims to have burst into tears. 'I deem it no shame to have wept over the grave of my poor dead relative. (. . .) Noble old man – he did not live to see me – he did not live to see his child. (. . .) Weighed down by sorrow and disappointment, he died before I was born – six thousand brief summers before I was born' (ch. 53).

Interspersed with these conflicting currents are sarcastic observations about the ignorance, cheap piety and crassness of the pilgrims themselves, as well as other Americans in Europe. One member of the tour is outraged in the Azores at being charged 21,700 'reis' for ten dinners until he eventually realizes that 'reis' are not the same as dollars, and that with the currency exchange, the bill comes to only $21.70 American (ch. 5). Another pilgrim is fond of chipping off pieces of statuary for souvenirs. Because some of the pilgrims did not want to travel on the Sabbath, they insist on making a normally three-day trip to Damascus in two days, though it meant cruelly abusing their very tired horses (ch. 43). The narrator criticizes some resident Americans in Europe for their affectations in Europeanizing themselves (ch. 23). In the penultimate chapter, Twain allows himself to indulge in some overt criticism of the tour. 'The pleasure ship,' he says, 'was a synagogue, and the pleasure trip was a funeral excursion without a corpse.' The book's conclusion slightly softens its criticism of the pilgrims by ambiguously stating that '[t]ravel is fatal to prejudice, bigotry, and narrow-mindedness, and many of our people need it sorely on those accounts'. It never, however, implies that all of the pilgrims learned these beneficial lessons of travel. While *Innocents Abroad* was mainly appreciated for its refreshingly humorous and sceptical view of the Old World, also present in the book is its cold undercurrent of criticism of the tourists for their sanctimoniousness, hypocrisy and small-mindedness, and of Americans as well as Old World people for their common venality and parochialism.

Although the real-life experiences behind *Roughing It* (1872) occurred before those for *Innocents Abroad*, *Roughing It* was written later. Hence, it benefited from many of the lessons learned during the composition of *Innocents Abroad*. Without a doubt, *Roughing It* is one of Twain's most brilliant and delightful works as well as the best of the travel books. In fact, *Roughing It* is difficult to classify as only a travel book. Insofar as it dwells on the character development of the narrator, for example, it may have more in common with the genre form of the novel than with that of the travel book. It is also a virtual compendium of nineteenth-century techniques of American humour, such as the tall tale, local colour, the use of vernacular and the hoax. In Twain's time, the West was still a barely explored territory, and tales of its wonders made it an exotic place where a traveller might acquire riches as well as adventures. The first chapter lays out these prospects along with its introduction of a very young-sounding narrator who has never been anywhere, for whom 'travel' has a 'seductive sound', and who envies his brother and covets his distinction, for he is about to leave for Nevada where he

would see buffaloes and Indians, and prairie dogs, and antelopes, and have all kinds of adventures, and maybe get hanged or scalped, and have ever such a fine time, and write home and tell us all about it, and be a hero. And he would see the gold mines and the silver mines, and maybe go about of an afternoon when his work was done, and pick up two or three pailfuls of shining slugs, and nuggets of gold and silver on the hillside. And by and by he would become very rich, and return home by sea, and be as able to talk calmly about San Francisco and the ocean, and 'the Isthmus' as if it was nothing of any consequence to have seen those marvels face to face.

Hence, when his brother offers to take him along, 'it appeared to me that the heavens and the earth passed away, and the firmament was rolled together as a scroll! I had nothing more to desire. My contentment was complete.'

The breathless recitation of the marvels of being a traveller to the Far West marks the narrator as being naïve and unsophisticated, as does his incongruous inclusion of being 'hanged or scalped' in the list of benefits of travel. The narrator's pose is so well maintained throughout most of the book that readers cannot fail to be amused by his experiences and observations. On a diverting side excursion during the stagecoach trip across the Great Plains, for example, a fellow traveller named Bemis is rescued from a tree in which he had taken refuge from a buffalo he had been hunting, which turned upon him (ch. 7). Bemis blames his predicament on his horse which, he claims, was so frightened by the buffalo that he became a 'raving distracted maniac'. As Bemis tells it, 'I wish I may die if [the horse] didn't stand on his head for a quarter of a minute and shed tears (. . .) and then for the next ten minutes he would actually throw one hand-spring after another so fast that the bull began to get unsettled, too.' Other fantastic details follow, including the buffalo trying to climb the tree after Bemis. The absurdity of these claims is obvious to readers, but the credulous narrator appears not to be completely convinced that he has heard a tall tale. 'I made up my mind that if this man was not a liar he only missed it by the skin of his teeth.'

A great deal of *Roughing It* is characterized by the humour of exaggeration. The preceding event is clearly one example, but so is the first chapter. Although Twain did go out West with his brother, that grain of truth is buried under the author's skillful but fictitious characterization of the narrator. Twain was neither as young, untravelled, nor as unsophisticated as he made himself out to be. He had actually done a great deal of travelling before he went West. He had been to Cincinnati, Philadelphia, New York and Washington, DC and had been for several years a pilot on the Mississippi River between St Louis and New Orleans. Furthermore, what motivated him to go out West was not so much its allurements as his desire to flee from the Civil War, which had just begun. Finally, almost all readers of *Roughing It* slight it by treating it as a loosely strung series of mainly humorous episodes, and underestimate the consideration that it is 'written' by the disillusioned narrator of its last chapter who knows from the first chapter that the youngish-sounding narrator is not reliable and that his exaggerated expectations of achieving fame and fortune with work would be doomed to disappointment.

As a writer, however, Twain shrewdly capitalized on the reputation of the West as an attractive place full of wonders, noble Indians and riches for the taking, and a territory which was being settled and developed by heroic adventurers. He knew his readers were primed for stories about these myths, and he knew from experience that they were also receptive to his kind of humour, exaggeration and self-deprecating irony. By casting himself as a humourless and gullible tenderfoot, he could recount preposterous narratives which his readers would doubly enjoy: for the hyperbole, and for the fun they could have at his expense when he was so frequently and easily hoaxed. What very few of them understood, however – and what few readers today fully appreciate – is that Twain continually hoaxes his readers for being even more gullible than his narrator because they prefer romance to realism, and myth to truth.

The basic theme of the book, at least of its counterplot level, appears in chapter 36, disguised as a momentary complaint. Resentful of his job doing hard physical labour, the narrator says: 'It is a pity that Adam could not have gone straight out of Eden into a quartz mill, in order to understand the full force of his doom to "earn his bread by the sweat of his brow." ' The comment is really a studied and quite serious key to the book. Its point is a surprisingly conventional affirmation that the human race is sinful, the expulsion from Eden is permanent, and that God's doom cannot be evaded. The main reason why this comment has to be taken seriously is because it organizes and explains the book, whose Far West part consists of narratives of men who attempt to escape the need to work by striking it rich, but instead condemn themselves to long years or lifetimes of solitary wandering, frustration, deceit, hard work and terrible working conditions. Most of the few men who do become rich are preyed upon or get little satisfaction from their wealth because either they remain ignorant or do not know what to do with their money. The sixteen chapters that deal with Hawaii similarly contrast occasional humorous episodes and recurrent allusions to the Edenic appearance of the islands to Hawaii's unpleasant realities: scorpions and other noxious insects, a brutal native religion that was ridden with superstition and human sacrifice, which was supplanted by an oppressive Christianity that brings the message of hell, and the hellish features of the islands' volcanoes.

Even though the book abounds in choice episodes of humour, in every chapter are subtly ironic hints to readers that they share many characteristics with the human victims of their own romantic self-deception. Chapter 28, for instance, deftly accomplishes contradictory purposes. Its surface level recounts with many brilliant strokes of humour the humbling adventures of the gullible narrator in his efforts to become rich. Literally believing that all he has to do is clamber among the hills and pick up shining bits of gold, he 'guiltily' sneaks out of camp, crawls about the ground, and loads himself up with bright fragments of rock, believing with a 'delight that was more pronounced than absolute certainty itself could have afforded' that they are valuable. The ridiculousness of the picture has another side to it, however; it is also tinged with extreme naïvete verging upon foolishness, and with guilt. These touches may be regarded as clues which unwary readers will not recognize, as they also probably will not the hyperbole of a delight 'more pronounced than absolute certainty itself could have afforded'.

Next, the narrator confesses to readers that '[o]f all the experiences of my life, this secret search among the hidden treasures of silver-land was the nearest to unmarred ecstasy. It was a delirious revel.' Not until the end of the chapter can some of the irony of these sentences be realized, and not until the end of the book is the rest made clear. Readers are pulled in by the strong language to share in the narrator's emotional high, and do not suspect that they are being tricked. The chapter ends, however, with the revelation that all the bright fragments of rock are just 'granite rubbish and nasty glittering mica that isn't worth ten cents an acre!' So much for romantic expectations of the 'hidden treasures of silver-land', and so much for sensations of 'unmarred ecstasy'. Amid the abundance of romantic wishful thinking and hyperbole, it is easy to miss the literal accuracy of 'delirious' as a coldly precise diagnosis of the narrator's condition. Also, the fact that the passage is written in what might be called the 'misleading past tense' leads readers to think that the description is the narrator's final evaluation of the event. It is not; the narrator knew when he wrote it that he was only recording the conclusion of his younger self *up to that moment* in his life, but he also knew that in light of subsequent events his youthful ecstasy was fundamentally misguided, a case of being self-deceived. In the last chapter, the narrator ends with an explicit moral: 'If you are of any account, stay at home and make your way by faithful diligence; but if you are "no account", go away from home and then you will *have* to work, whether you want to or not.' In miniature, therefore, this episode characterizes not just the younger narrator but also the great majority of gold and silver hunters who are just as deliriously irrational about striking it rich as the narrator, and also, probably, the readers who, had they been there, would have been doing the same thing, hoping against all odds to find a trove of riches for which they do not have to labour.

Chapter 28 also ends with a moral. The chagrined narrator extends from rocks to men his bitter lesson that '*nothing* that glitters is gold'. But, he adds, 'like the rest of the world, I still go on underrating men of gold and glorifying men of mica'. If the narrator had really learned that lesson at the end of chapter 28, there would be very little left to say in *Roughing It*. But chapter 29 immediately plunges into further schemes for quick and easy wealth. The narrator and his partners stake a claim, but get tired of labouring on it after just one week and decide to look, instead, for a claim that was already developed. Again, Twain's text is at odds with the situation. 'We were *stark mad* with excitement', says the narrator, '*drunk* with happiness', for all believed the '*frenzied cant*' about being in the midst of the 'richest mines on earth' (italics mine). All about them are mining claims with grandiloquent names that promise wealth – but '[t]here was nothing doing in the district – no mining – no milling – no productive effort – no income – and not enough money in the entire camp to buy a corner lot in an eastern village'. So the lesson of chapter 28 was intellectually recognized but not assimilated. In *Roughing It*, both the narrator and the majority of gold and silver prospectors keep having the same lesson – that they must earn their bread by the sweat of their brow – replayed for them, and yet they keep falling for the lure of unearned wealth. Thus, on its surface, *Roughing It* is a collection of delightful anecdotes hilariously told of the escapades of men under the influence of 'silver fever' or a dream of Eden. At a deeper level, however, the very same escapades can be identified as fevered or romantic delusions (Berkove 1998).

A Tramp Abroad (1880) is a lesser book but still one that works on two different and opposing levels. With the exception of several chapters that contain digressive narratives, and six appendices, the great majority of the book's fifty chapters are set in Germany and Switzerland; the last three chapters include mere glimpses of Italy, Paris, Holland and England. The book's title is deliberately ambiguous. One of the meanings of 'tramp' is a hike, or a journey made afoot. In this sense of the term, the book is about a proposed walking tour of parts of Germany and Switzerland. Another meaning of 'tramp', however, is a vagrant or a vagabond who is not successful in the practical workaday world, and this sense also applies ironically to the narrator (Kersten 1998; Melton 1998).

The surface level story is the travelogue, in which Twain takes the reader from place to place, describing the scenery, inns, stores and people. Although the book deals entirely with Europe, it is worth noting that while Twain was composing it he was also writing material that would later be used in another travel book, *Life on the Mississippi*. As with *Innocents Abroad*, Twain's humour enlivens these descriptions by his droll style and his narratives of the misadventures he and his hired agent, Mr Harris, experience. Twain often adds additional colour to the travelogue by recounting historical or legendary incidents associated with some of the locations, and he several times digresses entirely from the journey by telling a tale that has nothing to do with Europe or the journey. The most famous of these is 'Jim Baker's Blue Jay Yarn', a delightful tall tale about a California miner who understands jay language and overhears some of the birds talking. It occupies part of chapter 2 and all of chapter 3, and, like 'The Awful German Language', the hilarious send-up of German which is an appendix to the book, it is often reprinted by itself in collections of Twain's works. Twain also occasionally quotes long excerpts from guide books, so that readers depending upon him for information about the locales he visited are thereby referred to what he considers better sources.

Careful readers will also notice Twain's sly humour in the way the narrator always promises but somehow avoids doing much foot travel. For example, in chapter 11 the narrator and Harris determine to walk from Heidelberg to Heilbronn and set out early on a perfect day, dressed in the very best hiking gear. But when they get as far as downtown Heidelberg, they learn that a train going within five miles of Heilbronn is about to leave, so they change plans and take it. In chapter 30, learning that no pedestrian tour of Europe is complete without experiencing the Furka Pass, the Rhone Glacier, the Finsteraarhorn and the Wetterhorn, the narrator promptly orders Harris to climb them and report back to him. A week later Harris hands him a detailed report written in a mixture of vivid language, foreign words and phrases, and imaginary words like *gmwkwllolp*, *hogglebumgullup* and *Kahkaaponeeka*, which Harris illogically justifies as coming from such foreign languages as Chinese, Eskimo and Choctaw. In chapter 31, the two men plan to walk from Lucerne to Interlaken but instead hire a carriage, and fall asleep for an hour and half while passing through lovely scenery. This routine is repeated, with variations, throughout the book, including situations in chapters 34, 36 and 41, where famous and well-written accounts of climbs convince the narrator that he could not do better than skip the climbs himself and just use the narratives in place of his own first-hand reports. What keeps these tricks from being too obvious is the deadpan style of the narrator, who appears unaware that he is failing to live up to his resolutions, and the skillful placement of the abundant illustrations in the book whose factual nature sometimes tones down the implausibility of the humorous narrative.

Perhaps the most hilarious incident in the book is the actual ascent of the Riffelberg by the narrator and Harris (chs 37–39). This time they do not prevaricate or evade the climb. Wearing formal evening dress they set out with an expedition of 154 people, including 17 guides, 15 barkeepers, 4 surgeons and 3 chaplains. They also bring 51 mules and cows, tons of equipment, and two miles of rope. It takes seven days to make the climb, during which time they blast one rock with nitroglycerin and another with dynamite, only to discover later that a chalet had been built upon it. Finally, they reach the top and march proudly into the dining-room of the Riffelberg Hotel. The grandeur of the accomplishment is somewhat diminished but its humour is vastly increased when we later learn that most people are able to walk up the Riffelberg in three hours.

A mixture of the ludicrous and the factual, *A Tramp Abroad* is entertaining but not gripping. Its organization is loose to begin with and is further weakened by individual episodes having little or nothing to do with the pedestrian tour. Occasional hints of distinctively Twainian interests flicker unexpectedly. Chapter 19, for example, with its story of a dream that replaced reality looks forward to both *Huckleberry Finn* and *Connecticut Yankee*. The Nicodemus Dodge digression in chapter 23 ends with a reference to Jimmy Finn, the town drunkard – a character who was to be revived as Pap Finn, Huck's father. And chapter 24 begins with an animadversion on Sunday, an attitude which appears in Twain's early and late works and in some of them achieves ominous significance.

A deeper purpose in the book may be found in its satire of the American tourist narrator, who undertakes a pedestrian tour but prefers to travel by train, by carriage and by proxy; and who eschews original first-hand experience in his intention of gathering material for a book by duplicating what has already been done well before. Despite the patina of patriotic sentiment in the last chapter, *A Tramp Abroad* is an anti-travel book with an anti-hero narrator who would rather be in America than Europe and who would rather read about the challenges of travel than experience them. The book is in effect a longer version of Hawthorne's short story, 'The Celestial Railroad' (1843), an ironic update of Bunyan's *Pilgrim's Progress*. The story teaches that pilgrimages are more than physical travel. Unless pilgrims prepare themselves mentally and spiritually, only their bodies move from one place to another and no deeper benefit is earned. What is true of pilgrimages, Twain implies, is also true of travel.

Life on the Mississippi (1883) was composed in two stages. Chapters 4–17 were written in the winter of 1874–5 and were published as 'Old Times on the Mississippi', a seven-part series in the *Atlantic Monthly* magazine of 1875 that recalls Twain's early experiences, first as an apprentice and then as a full-fledged river pilot. The first three and the last 43 chapters were completed between then and 1883. Chapters 1–3 are introductory, chapters 18–20 and one paragraph in 21 contain additional recollections of Twain's cub-piloting years, and the rest of the book derives from Twain's 1882 trip as a steamboat passenger and reflect on the country and culture traversed by the Mississippi River. Although uneven in quality and organization, *Life on the Mississippi* contains some of Twain's most memorable writing and is a major source of information about his life and attitudes.

The most beloved part of the book is the 14-chapter segment of the original 'Old Times on the Mississippi'. Twain's river years, his childhood in Hannibal, and his early adulthood as a newspaper reporter in the Far West of Nevada, California and Hawaii, were the three most richly formative periods of his character and literary material. Apart from their literary and biographical value, the chapters on his cub-piloting experience are also valuable as history for their incomparable evocation of the colourful details and piquant flavour of life on one of the world's greatest rivers just as civilization began to harness its mighty natural force.

Those chapters are a Midwestern counterpart to the series of 'factual' chapters in *Moby Dick* that lead to chapter 82, 'The Honor and Glory of Whaling'. Just as it epitomizes the process of raising whaling and whalers to an epic level, so does Twain's chapter 14, 'Rank and Dignity of Piloting', do the same for piloting and river pilots. Twain awesomely describes the pilot in those frontier days as 'the only unfettered and entirely independent human being that lived in the earth'. The great authority that pilots enjoyed derived from their ability to memorize the river, every bend, channel and shallow in it, and understand it so well that they could imagine its continuously changing shape and navigate it even in total darkness just from its image in their minds.

This impressive feat, Twain notes, had an unfortunate cost. In one of the book's most pregnant and magnificent passages, the last three paragraphs of chapter 9, he grants readers an insight into his double vision of life that led to his layered style of writing. At the end of the long process of his learning to master 'the language of this water', Twain realizes he had lost something. 'All the grace, the beauty, the poetry had gone out of the majestic river!' He then recounts a majestic sunset scene on the river, apprehending it as a romantic artist might see it, 'bewitched' and drinking it in in 'speechless rapture'. Next, he contrasts that impression to the way a professional pilot had to see it, as full of ominous signs. Then he sums up the meaning of this double vision:

> No, the romance and beauty were all gone from the river. All the value any feature of it had for me now was the amount of usefulness it could furnish toward compassing the safe piloting of a steamboat. Since those days, I have pitied doctors from my heart. What does the lovely flush in a beauty's cheek mean to a doctor but a 'break' that ripples above some deadly disease? Are not all her visible charms sown thick with what are to him the signs and symbols of visible decay? Does he ever see her beauty at all, or doesn't he simply view her professionally, and comment upon her unwholesome condition all to himself? And doesn't he sometimes wonder whether he has gained most or lost most by learning his trade?

Twain the artist was able to see the apparent loveliness and marvels of life, but as a truth-seeker he also saw critically, and came to believe, with Melville's Ishmael, that 'earthly hues ... are but subtle deceits', that they are cosmetic gildings, and that 'all deified Nature absolutely paints like the harlot, whose allurements cover nothing but the charnel-house within'. Twain might have been a happier man if he had been able to rest in one or the other of these two visions, but he saw both and his greatest artistry, as exemplified by this passage, reflects his sense of the tensions and pulls between the beauties and the deceits of surfaces.

After chapter 21, the rest of *Life on the Mississippi* continues to have some excellent chapters, but such unity as the book has derives from their common association: all chapters either describe incidents and places on Twain's sentimental journey in 1882 or are near digressions suggested by them. As Twain recreates the downstream trip of a Mississippi River steamboat he describes the cities on the river: Memphis, Tennessee; Napoleon, Arkansas; Vicksburg, Mississippi; and Baton

Rouge and New Orleans, Louisiana, and tells stories he associates with those once familiar stops. In the hands of a lesser writer, the book might seem too loosely connected, but with Twain, only a purist can object to its discursiveness.

Life on the Mississippi has a number of connections to other of Twain's works and, for that matter, to Twain's sources. The rafting episode in chapter 3 was written for *Huckleberry Finn* but was extracted from the novel before it was published, and has only recently been re-inserted in chapter 16 of the authoritative Mark Twain Papers edition. Chapters 31 and 32 with their setting in Germany obviously have close ties to *A Tramp Abroad*. Chapter 31, 'A Thumb-Print and What Came of It', also anticipates *Pudd'nhead Wilson*. Chapter 38, 'The House Beautiful', is a reverse image of chapter 17 of *Huckleberry Finn*, in which Huck describes in detail the appointments of the parlour of the Grangerfords' home. In the novel, Huck is impressed by the room, but *Life on the Mississippi* makes it clear that Twain is highly critical of the standardized and predictable tastes of Southern gentry. Astonishingly, in chapter 46, 'Enchantments and Enchanters', Twain puts much of the blame for the Civil War on Sir Walter Scott! On a literal level, this is absurd, but once it is understood that to Twain Scott epitomized romanticism (which Twain considered false by definition), then this chapter explains a great deal about Twain's writing. Scholarship has recently revealed that parts of chapter 14 were appropriated by Twain from sketches written earlier by his Nevada colleague Dan De Quille (Berkove 1988), that the description in chapter 42 of a New Orleans cemetery may have been at least partly influenced by a published travel letter written from Paris by his friend and editor Joe Goodman (Goodman 1997), and that the references in chapters 44 and 47 to George Washington Cable are to the excellent Louisiana author whose novel *The Grand-issimes* (1880) supplied critical ideas to the germinating *Huckleberry Finn* (Berkove 1980).

A wealth of information exists in *Life on the Mississippi* about Twain's biography, values and art. Readers find in it charm, delight, variety, entertainment – as well as serious food for thought. Considered aesthetically, it may fall short of his very best works, but there can be no doubt that *Life on the Mississippi* is essential Twain.

Following the Equator (1897) is the last of the travel books and the one that seems most like a travel book. But it is not a typical travel book. It was conceived as a money-making venture to restore Twain's financial losses from disastrous business ventures. Twain was additionally troubled by illnesses and fatigue during the trip, and his daughter Suzy died while it was being written. It is not surprising, therefore, that the book has little of the choice humour, spirited invention and enthusiasm of his earlier travel books. Instead, the book is largely patterned after a chronological diary of the places he visited with his wife Livy, their second daughter Clara, and (later) his Australian tour agent and his son, on an 1895–96 round-the-world lecturing trip. Twain sailed to Hawaii (where he could not disembark because of quarantine), Fiji, Australia, New Zealand, Ceylon, India, Mauritius and South Africa. Where the other travel books often display delicate and complicated irony, *Following the Equator* is characterized by blunt and pungent irony. Even when down, Twain could still write memorably and valuably.

Earlier in his career, Twain went to some lengths to conceal or at least be subtle about his true views about the places and people he described, and about life in general. In *Following the Equator*, however, it is as if Twain knew he no longer had a reputation to make and could afford to be more direct about his opinions. Accordingly, the book is unusually and explicitly critical about a number of topics. Western civilization's impact on other areas of the world is a common target, but he also recognizes the shortcomings of indigenous cultures, and he has some harsh things to say about Nature. He does not attempt to create a fictionalized persona/narrator but speaks in his own voice. It is obvious that he despises and detests slavery and oppression in every form, is a bitter opponent of racism, and has contempt for lawlessness and for immoral laws. In this book, instead of writing only amusing or fanciful anecdotes about his itinerary, Twain frequently records his ire and also his horror at some of the things he sees, and quotes substantially from historical records and guide books that document the events that affect him. Much of the tone of the book is reflected in the acerbic apothegms, ascribed to '*Pudd'nhead Wilson's New Calendar*', at the head of each chapter. As a consequence, *Following the Equator* is almost as much about Twain's social criticism and philosophical outlook as it is about travel.

While the ship is anchored off Hawaii, Twain in chapter 3 is already recollecting things he said in *Roughing It* about the barbarities of Hawaiian religion and upon the devastating effect on the native population of Westernization. Once it is realized that Twain feels that Christian civilization brought more unhappiness to Hawaii than its savage indigenous beliefs, the irony of the following statement is evident. 'All intelligent people praise Kamehameha I. and Liholiho for conferring upon their people the great boon of civilization. I would do it myself, but my intelligence is out of repair, now, from over-work.' In a shorter replay of 'The House Beautiful' chapter of *Life on the Mississippi*, Twain also recalls the unimaginative 'universal' decor of typical American homes in the Honolulu of his 1866 visit.

Before his ship arrives at Fiji, Twain contemplates the deceit and ruthlessness of French and English 'recruiters' of native Pacific islanders for work in colonial plantations. Although Twain seldom had a good word to say about missionaries, in this matter he credits them with being the main opposition to the near-enslavement conditions arranged by recruiters. 'But for the meddling philanthropists, the native fathers and mothers would be fond of seeing their children carted into exile and now and then the grave, instead of weeping about it and trying to kill the kind recruiters.'

Twain was well-received and well-treated in Australasia, and the book has many compliments for the people he met and what they had accomplished. He gave a total of forty-eight performances in the fifteen weeks he spent in Australia and New Zealand (Shillingsburg 1995). It was the most profitable segment of his trip. Clearly he especially liked Australia, and Australia liked him. He gave multiple performances in Melbourne, Adelaide, Ballarat and Bendigo and ten performances in Sydney alone. His agent claimed that the success of his tour was 'phenomenal' and that his receipts established a record.

But he was also aware of problems in the colony. For example, he notes that although the Aboriginals practiced infanticide as a method of population control, the whites introduced vastly superior methods – including poisoning – which reduced Aboriginal numbers 80 per cent in twenty years. He reports that the indigenous Tasmanians had been cruelly and systematically wiped out, that recruited labourers are financially exploited in Queensland and have a high death rate. He visits the gold fields of Bendigo and Ballarat and compares them favourably to the mines he knew in Nevada and California. But he also observes that Ballarat was the site of a successful miners' revolt against an arbitrary tax by the colonial government, and compares the revolt to the American colonists' stands against the British at Lexington and Concord.

Twain finds New Zealand a place of sharp contrasts. It has lovely countrysides and towns and natural wonders, but it also has a bloody history. The Maoris, he learns, 'often met and slaughtered each other just for a lark, and when there was no quarrel'. The whites, also, killed each other for trivial reasons, as he notes in chapter 33, where he quotes at length about the cold-blooded and pitiless Maungatapu murders. Twain implies by this even-handedness that it is human nature at work rather than some cultural aberration. He is more partisan toward the Maoris when he notices that the white immigrants set up a monument to settlers who were killed in the Maori wars 'in defense of law and order against fanaticism and barbarism'. He agrees that the settlers deserve praise but objects to the wording because it one-sidedly compliments the whites for lofty ideals and detracts from the dignity of the cause of the Maoris who, from their point of view, were defending their homes and country from invaders. Another monument, to Maoris who died fighting with the whites '*against their own people*', he objects to as teaching 'treachery, disloyalty, unpatriotism'.

Twain reveals an early sensitivity to environmental issues in his awareness that Australasia has a number of unique life forms but that the human alteration of the habitat has been upsetting the natural balance. He notes that a parrot whose supply of food grubs was destroyed by cultivation has adapted to eating meat and fat scraps from the skins of commercially killed sheep, and that the introduction of rabbits to the area has become a plague. He regretfully records that the moa, a native ostrich-like flightless bird, was first decimated by the native peoples and then rendered extinct by Westerners. And he reacts bitterly to 'a ghastly curiosity – a lignified caterpillar with a plant growing out of the back of its neck'. This phenomenon, he recognizes, is not by accident but by Nature's design. 'This caterpillar was in the act of loyally carrying out a law inflicted upon him by Nature – a law purposely inflicted upon him to get him into trouble – a law which was a trap.'

The visit to Ceylon is brief, highlighted mainly by Twain's lyrical praise of the lovely costumes and dark skin of the natives – 'that radiant panorama, that wilderness of rich color, that incomparable dissolving-view of harmonious tints, and lithe half-covered forms, and beautiful brown faces, and gracious and graceful gestures and attitudes and movements, free, unstudied, barren of stiffness and restraint'. In contrast, Twain finds Western clothing '[u]gly, barbarous, destitute of taste, destitute of grace, repulsive as a shroud'. Twain's sympathies for people of colour is inclining to a preference.

Twain originally intended to stay in India for only a month, but remained instead for sixty-eight days, during which time he gave eighteen performances in twelve cities with large English populations (Ahluwalia 1996). He was often in ill health during his tour but nevertheless enjoyed himself greatly. Twain compliments the English on what they have done with the country and recounts admiringly their energy and resolve during the time of Clive and the Great Mutiny of 1857. But toward India itself, 'the most extraordinary country that the sun visits on his round', Twain feels something akin to awe, and uncommon warmth toward its people and its spirituality.

> You soon realize that India is not beautiful; still there is an enchantment about it which does not pall. ... Of course, at bottom, you know in a vague way that it is *history*; it is that that affects you, a haunting sense of the myriads of human lives that have blossomed, and withered, and perished here, repeating and repeating and repeating, century after century, and age after age, the barren and meaningless process; it is this sense that gives to this forlorn, uncomely land power to speak to the spirit and make friends with it; to speak to it with a voice bitter with satire, but eloquent with melancholy. The deserts of Australia and the ice-barrens of Greenland have no speech, for they have no venerable history; with nothing to tell of man and his vanities, his fleeting glories and his miseries, they have nothing wherewith to spiritualize their ugliness and veil it with a charm. (Ch. 49)

Twain's criticisms of caste, suttee, the Thug sect, snakes and the fragmentation of India into a Babel of languages make manifest that he both read and observed thoughtfully, but there is little of condescension in most of his remarks. He wonders at the rich spectacle of human myriads in India and the range of religious beliefs, and in chapter 53, set in Benares, meets Sri, a 'living god' – one of two, he says coyly, that interest him overwhelmingly. His discussion of this human god verges on the humorous but is really mainly contemplative, for it returns Twain to his life-long questioning about the nature of God. And for the god's disciple, a man who was a success in the world but renounced everything to 'meditate upon virtue and holiness and seek to attain them', Twain feels sincere reverence. In the next few years, Twain will begin a number of reflections on God, e.g. *The Mysterious Stranger* manuscripts (including 'No. 44') and 'Letters from the Earth', and it would be surprising if Twain's encounters with religion in India did not influence those works.

After the intensity and depth of these experiences, the rest of *Following the Equator* is anti-climactic, and Twain shows signs of a letdown. On the voyage to Mauritius, Twain reflects that Nature has been generous to all of her creatures – except man, and notes with irony how hard man has to grub to 'keep him alive and provide kings and soldiers and powder to extend the blessings of civilization with. Yet man, in his simplicity and complacency and inability to cipher, thinks Nature regards him as the important member of the family – in fact, her favorite. Surely, it must occur to even his dull head, sometimes, that she has a curious way of showing it.' Twain finds 'reposeful' the tranquillity of an empty sea and the experience of being cut off from mail, news and worldly turmoil. Others are eager to arrive at a destination, but not he:

> I myself am wholly indifferent as to when we are going to 'get in' (...) If I had my way we should never get in at all. This sort of sea life is charged with an indestructible charm. There is no weariness, no fatigue, no worry, no responsibility, no work, no depression of spirits. There is nothing like this serenity, this comfort, this peace, this deep contentment, to be found anywhere on land. If I had my way I would sail on forever and never go to live on the solid ground again.

It is tempting to speculate if this mood reflects some influence of the Hindu belief in Nirvana, but in the next few years, Twain was to contradict it in such gloomy unfinished works as 'The Great Dark' and 'The Enchanted Sea-Wilderness', which contemplate terrifying endless voyages. (The latter story, originally intended for *Following the Equator* (Rasmussen 1995), alludes to South Africa and Australia, and features a ship named the *Adelaide*.)

On Mauritius itself, Twain briefly describes its lush vegetation, but mainly uses the stop at the island as an excuse to indulge anti-French sentiments, and to predict a 'frenzy' of further seizures of backward African and Asian territories by 'claim-jumping' and land-robbing imperialistic Christian European governments. Then he professes to be 'glad' of this eventuality because the 'savages' may fare better under 'the mercies of alien rulers' than they did under the oppressions of their own rulers. His unconvincing conclusion, 'Let us hope and believe that they will all benefit by the change,' is desperate cold comfort, and belies the ending of *A Connecticut Yankee* as well as the final, South African, section of the book.

In these last chapters is the book's strongest statement against imperialism (Philippon 2001). Despite some perfunctory treatment of the Rand gold-fields, the Kimberley diamond deposits, and the scenic highlights of Cape Town, most of what Twain has to say about South Africa relates to the looming conflict between the British and the Boers. He is sharply critical of Cecil Rhodes and the abortive Jameson raid, which helped precipitate the Boer War. But he also observes that both white camps exploit native Africans and treat them as a pool of cheap menial labour. Twain does not use the phrase 'the damned human race' in *Following the Equator*, but the idea is there.

The last two lines of the book may seem anti-climactic, but they actually sum up the author's dismal view of the human race all around the globe. Twain relates that astronomers recently reported that 'another great body of light had lately flamed up in the remoteness of space which was traveling at a gait which would enable it to do all that I had done in *a minute and a half*. Human pride is not worth while; there is always something lying in wait to take the wind out of it.' The lesson of *Roughing It* is repeated: travel takes us to different places, but human nature is the same, and has more of hell in it than of heaven.

The 'Extract from Captain Stormfield's Visit to Heaven' (1907–08) was the last book Twain published in his lifetime. As the title suggests, it is a fragment of an unfinished work. Like the just-mentioned body of light which flamed up in the remoteness of space, Captain Stormfield, thirty years dead, whizzes through space like a comet, heading straight for the Hereafter. Delightful though the story is, Twain put a good deal of sobering thought into it – forty years of thought, for it was begun in 1868 (LeMaster and Wilson 1993). Although Twain professed determinism in his latter years, religion was a dominant interest of his during his entire life, and this story as well as some posthumously published works such as 'Letters from the Earth' represent his serious grappling with conventional Christian conceptions of God and the afterlife.

'Captain Stormfield's Visit' both satirizes Biblical religion and honours it. The opening section that conveys a sense of the vastness of space and the immensity of heaven are complimentary to the Creator. Heaven itself, however, Stormfield discovers once he arrives there, is not the place described to most believers. First of all, it is not restricted to humans. Beings from unknown galaxies greatly outnumber earthlings. Next, heaven is infinitely varied. 'Did you imagine the same heaven would suit all sorts of men?' a clerical angel asks Stormfield. The captain also quickly learns that it is a mistake to take the figurative language of the Bible literally. Harps, wings and white robes are available to those who ask for them, but they serve no practical purpose in heaven. Nor would anyone in his right mind wish to spend eternity singing 'Hallelujah!' with a harp or without it. Further, heaven is not exclusively for Christians. It is for *everyone*: all races, all colours, all creeds. 'God cares for all kinds', Stormfield is told; 'He doesn't leave anybody out in the cold.'

The rest of this short but pithy narrative continues to erode narrow, exclusive and severe conventional Christian teachings about God and heaven. There are rules in heaven, but they are not the rules of any single sect. In the final analysis, 'Captain Stormfield's Visit to Heaven' cannot be taken as Twain's last word on God and the afterlife, but it may be regarded as his serious and sincere idea of how he would design an ideal God and an ideal heaven. Of course, not even Twain conceived of heaven as a place open to tourists, inasmuch as the price of admission was mortality. But as his last published work on travel, 'Captain Stormfield's Visit to Heaven' recasts as a projected heavenly ideal what he much earlier proclaimed as an established fact of life in *Innocents Abroad*: 'Travel is fatal to prejudice, bigotry, and narrow-mindedness, and many of our people need it sorely on those accounts.'

Modern-day tourists will profit by *studying* Twain's themes and not just merely *reading* his works either for travel tips or humour. As Twain demonstrates in all his books, the true traveller must prepare himself or herself spiritually as well as mentally to be honestly open to new insights as well as sights. Otherwise, one merely travels with a list of sights to be seen and checked off, sees only surfaces, and experiences quantity rather than quality. One need not be as pessimistic as Twain was about life and the human race, but Twain's message that human nature is universal is a valuable antidote to credulous beliefs that in some other part of the world people either are better or worse than they are at home, and to tendencies to stereotype people from other countries or cultures. And, of course, a distinctive part of any lesson from Twain is to cultivate a sense of humour, a readiness to laugh at one's own myths as well as those encountered abroad. The laugh may derive from the rueful realization that we know less than we thought we did, and are not as important or as superior as we would like to believe, but in this risible diminishment of our egos is the possibility for wholesome growth that is the main point of travel.

In retrospect, it can be seen that Twain's travel books continue the themes and strategies he uses in his great works of fiction. An advocate of justice and freedom, he was pained and enraged to see their opposites prevail the world over. Cherishing human nobility, he was profoundly depressed by the prevalence of hypocrisy, deceit, cruelty and mediocrity. How to represent this in literature was the problem he faced in all of his writings. In order to sell books he had to be entertaining. But for his own soul's sake, he resolved to tell the truth. His solution, a compromise made possible by high artistry, was to develop a layered style. At the surface he posed an engaging persona who entertainingly depicted places, people and events; below the surface he veiled the private conflicted humanist: sensitive, compassionate, sceptical, critical and angry; seemingly two different Twains, but really two different aspects of the same man. The link between them is irony, often surpassingly brilliant irony. 'Every one is a moon, and has a dark side which he never shows to anybody' is the maxim which heads chapter 66 of *Following the Equator*. Everyone can see Twain's bright side, but the dark side is also there and can be seen by readers who track his layers of irony. Whoever follows Twain on his journeys through the world will become a better tourist by learning to recognize both sides and how to value each.

REFERENCES

Ahluwalia, Harsharan Singh (1996) 'Mark Twain in India', *Mark Twain Journal*, **34**(1), 1–48.

Berkove, Lawrence I. (1980) 'The free man of color in *The Grandissimes and Works by Harris and Mark Twain*', *Southern Quarterly*, **18**(4), 60–73. Rpt. Thomas J. Richardson, (ed.) (1981) *The Grandissimes: Centennial Essays*, pp. 60–73. Jackson: University Press of Mississippi.

Berkove, Lawrence I. (1988) 'More information on Dan De Quille and "Old Times on the Mississippi"', *Mark Twain Journal*, **26**(2), 15–20.

Berkove, Lawrence I. (1998) 'The Trickster God', in *Roughing It. Thalia*, **18**(1 & 2), 21–30.

Bridgman, Richard (1987) *Traveling in Mark Twain*. Berkeley: University of California Press.

Ganzel, Dewey (1968) *Mark Twain Abroad: The Cruise of the 'Quaker City'*. Chicago: University of Chicago Press.

Goodman, Joseph T. (1997) 'An irregular correspondent', *The European Travel Letters of Mark Twain's Editor and Friend Joe Goodman*. Ed. w/intro. Lawrence I. Berkove. *Mark Twain Journal*, **35**(2), 1–44.

Hirst, Robert H. (1975) *The Making of The Innocents Abroad: 1867–1872*. Ph.D. thesis, University of California-Berkeley.

Kersten, Holger (1998) 'Mark Twain: The Tramp Abroad', *Literatur in Wissenschaft und Unterricht*, **31**(1), 45–54.

Kruse, Horst H. (1981) *Mark Twain and 'Life on the Mississippi'*. Amherst: University of Massachusetts Press.

LeMaster, J. R., and James D. Wilson (eds) (1993) *The Mark Twain Encyclopedia*. New York: Garland.

Melton, Jeffrey A. (1998) 'Adventures and tourists in Mark Twain's *A Tramp Abroad*', *Studies in American Humour*, **3**(5), 34–47.

Philippon, Daniel J. (2001) '*Following the Equator* to its end: Mark Twain's South African conversion', *Mark Twain Journal*, **39**(1).

Rasmussen, R. Kent (1995) *Mark Twain A to Z*. New York: Facts on File.

Robinson, Forrest G. (1995) 'The Innocent at Large: Mark Twain's travel writing', in Forrest G. Robinson (ed.), *The Cambridge Companion to Mark Twain*. Cambridge: Cambridge University Press, 27–51.

Salamo, Lin, Smith, Harriet Elinor and Browning, Robert Pack (1998) 'Mark Twain at large: his travels here and abroad', *An Exhibition [Catalogue] from the Mark Twain Papers of The Bancroft Library, University of California, Berkeley.*

Shillingsburg, Miriam J. (1988) *At Home Abroad: Mark Twain in Australasia.* Jackson: University Press of Mississippi.

Shillingsburg, Miriam J. (1995) 'Down under day by day with Mark Twain', *Mark Twain Journal*, **33**(2), 1–41.

Twain, Mark (2001) *Adventures of Huckleberry Finn*, ed. Victor Fischer, Lin Salamo, with Harriet Elinor Smith and the late Walter Blair. Berkeley: University of California Press.

Chapter 10

Matthew Arnold's Guerilla in the Glade: The Politics and Poetics of Tourism

Donald Ulin

In 1851, the British census registered what must be considered one of the world's great watersheds: Britain had become the first nation in which residents of towns and cities outnumbered those still living in the country. And yet, in a paradoxical twist familiar to any student of British literature and history, that newly urban citizenry had begun to identify itself as quintessentially rural. 'Over the whole face of our country', wrote William Howitt in 1838, 'the charm of a refined existence is suffused, there is nothing which strikes foreigners so much as the beauty of our country abodes, and the peculiarity of our country life' (1.4–5). If the national wealth derived from the activity of the cities and seaports, the national identity, it seemed, had to come from the rural regions.

As Benedict Anderson has argued, a national identity requires a collective act of imagination and a social and cultural life capable of sustaining that act (1991: see esp. 22–6, 32–9). Along with the rise of a mass readership, identified by Anderson as key to the emergence of national identity, tourism must be included among the principal activities through which large numbers of strangers could engage collectively in imagining a nation. Writing about twentieth-century American tourism to sites such as Mt Rushmore and the Grand Canyon, Gregory Ulmer notes that 'The tourist ... will travel to see what is to be seen in order to reinvent our national identity' (Ulmer 1993). Unlike the American West, however, whose relatively powerless inhabitants could be easily displaced or exterminated, the English countryside remained the site of powerful, if residual, social and economic forces. 'When I go through the country', Matthew Arnold wrote, 'and see this and that beautiful and imposing seat of theirs crowning the landscape, "There," I say to myself, "is a great fortified post of the Barbarians"' (1932: 104). Middle-class reformers and promoters of tourism often looked to the English countryside for the mythopoeic power they believed could reconcile disparate classes and interests around a common national identity.[1] What they often failed to appreciate or at least acknowledge was the powerful predisposition of the countryside as a signifier of aristocratic values.

As the poet of the ancients – often contrasted to the self-consciously modern Arthur Hugh Clough – Matthew Arnold might seem an unlikely representative of the effort to appropriate the landscape in the interest of middle-class tourism. Indeed, conventional readings of Arnold have emphasized his affiliation with Pastoral – a mode of experience associated more with aristocratic privilege than with middle-class tourism.[2] Certainly Arnold's Cumnor Hills poems are characterized less by engagement than by flight: the narrator of 'Thyrsis' flees the fox-hunters just as in the earlier poem he had urged the scholar-gipsy to 'Fly hence, our contact fear!/Still fly, plunge deeper in the bowering wood!' (LL.206–7) (all references to Arnold's poems are to *The Poems of Matthew Arnold*: 1979); even the scholar-gipsy's goal is a '*fugitive* and gracious light' ('Thyrsis': L.201; emphasis added). The scholar-gipsy's 'bowering wood' or the 'screen'd ... nook' where the narrator reposes with his copy of Glanvil suggests a kind of *locus amoenus* familiar to readers of pastoral – a 'pleasant place', marked by a natural harmony unavailable in the busy world of the city or court. Like Wordsworth, burdened with 'the weary weight of all this unintelligible world' ('Tintern Abbey': 40–1), Arnold depends on some form of rural experience to steady him 'Mid city-noise ... [and] the great town's harsh, heart-wearying roar' ('Thyrsis': LL.232–4). However, to a greater extent than we see in Wordsworth or earlier versions of the pastoral, access to the *locus amoenus*, or to the feelings of renewal one might expect there, is frequently contested or even barred completely.[3] The success of the rural experience in Arnold's poetry, therefore, depends ultimately on its capacity, not to replicate some classical pastoral emotions (although it often evokes those emotions at the outset), but to sustain a wholly new set of terms through which landscape can be made accessible to the modern, urban visitor. There is no indication that Arnold understood his own poetry or prose as any kind of promotion of tourism. Indeed, to read him as I propose requires that we refuse Arnold's own desire to be read as addressing only those 'great primary human affections ... which are independent of time' (1960b: 4). What we gain in doing so, however, is an understanding of the power of poetry to contribute to the constitution of a distinctly modern countryside.

BEYOND PASTORAL

While the classicist in Arnold believed in following the ancient models, the modern man saw all too clearly the great distance between classical antiquity and his own 'unpoetical age'. Unlike the Sicilian shepherds who could 'make leap up with joy the beauteous head/Of Proserpine', the modern poet faced a landscape barren of such divinities: 'of our poor Thames she never heard!/Her foot the Cumnor cowslips never stirr'd! / And we should tease her with our plaint in vain' ('Thyrsis': LL.87–8, 98–100). In the same volume that introduced 'The Scholar-Gipsy', Arnold wrote that '[i]n the sincere endeavour to learn and practise, amid the bewildering confusion of our times, what is sound and true in poetical art, I seemed to myself to find the only sure guidance, the only solid footing, among the ancients' (1960b: 14). And yet, as Honan points out, Arnold was never able to compose successfully in a classical vein.[4] Often, as we see most dramatically in 'Stanzas from the Grande Chartreuse', this dilemma takes the form of an ambivalence toward pastoral uses of landscape. What might otherwise have been imagined as a *locus amoenus* is clearly tainted here with a sense of paralysis and even death:

> We are like children reared in shade
> Beneath some old-world abbey wall,
> Forgotten in a forest-glade,
> And secret from the eyes of all.
> Deep, deep the greenwood round them waves,
> Their abbey, and its close of graves!
>
> But, where the road runs near the stream,
> Oft through the trees they catch a glance
> Of passing troops in the sun's beam –
> Pennon, and plume, and flashing lance!
> Forth to the world those soldiers fare,
> To life, to cities, and to war!
>
> (LL.169–80)
>
> 'Fenced early in this cloistral round
> Of reverie, of shade, of prayer,
> How should we grow in other ground?
> How can we flower in foreign air?
>   –   Pass, banners, pass, and bugles, cease;
> And leave our desert to its peace!'
>
> (LL.205–10)

The world of the abbey, at first imagined as an oasis and a 'forest-glade' becomes by the end a desert, haunted by the sounds and sights of the world outside. Even with the first reference to the forest-glade, the sense of pastoral security seems moribund by virtue of its association with the 'close of graves', an association strengthened by the near-rhyme of 'glade' and 'grave'. Whereas earlier pastoral retreats allowed for at least an imaginative escape from the busy world, Arnold's allow no such escape – only a thicket from which to watch the world pass by.

In lamenting the death of poetry as a necessary accessory to the loss of traditional rural ways, Arnold might seem to be echoing the lament of Oliver Goldsmith, whose elegy to English rural life in 'The Deserted Village' ends with a farewell to 'sweet poetry, thou loveliest maid ... Unfit, in these degenerate times of shame,/To catch the heart or strike for honest fame.'[5] However, Arnold's sense of the difficulties of poetry in the modern landscape differs significantly from Goldsmith's in at least one very important way. While Goldsmith imagines the problem in terms of a fall from an idyllic past, Arnold is haunted by the *persistence* of a past that is neither idyllic nor so completely departed as Goldsmith's 'rural Virtues'. In spite of Arnold's advocacy of a notion of culture that would transcend the specifics of time and place, Arnold's own sense of both culture and landscape is inevitably coloured by a deep understanding of social history and of the residual power of landed interests.[6] It is, after all, those same 'barbarians' returning to their 'fortified posts' from a fox-hunt, who put Arnold's narrator to flight in 'Thyrsis'.

MAPPING A NATIONAL HERITAGE

One thing that distinguishes tourism from earlier modes of travel and distinguishes touristic representations of rural life from pastoral representations is the mediating role tourism plays between work and leisure. Unlike the gentry on a Grand Tour of the Continent or at home in the country, the tourist is most typically one who *has* worked and will work again, making the vacation a respite from, but also a justification for, one's daily work and a reward for work well done. Dean MacCannell has noted the fascination tourists display for any exhibitions of work, what he calls the 'work display' (1976: 36). And certainly tourism itself might well be described as a kind of work, with an impressive list of responsibilities: sights to see, trains to catch and postcards to be written, not to mention the mental work of processing and assimilating all the new impressions. Modern tourism with its strict scheduling requirements (akin to the time discipline associated with capitalist labour), its dialectical relationship to the tourist's regular work, and its fascination with labour, sets it at odds with the pastoral valorization of '*otium*', defined in the OED as 'leisure or freedom from business'. Indeed, the appearance of the derogatory term 'otiose' in the middle of the nineteenth century, just as record numbers of middle-class tourists were availing themselves of their newly gained wealth and leisure, points to this devaluation of the idea of *otium*.[7] Although independent wealth may allow the upper classes to spend more time than the middle classes in tourist-like activities, the structure of modern tourism derives ineluctably from the structure of modern work.

It should come as no surprise, therefore, that Arnold's experience of the English countryside reflected his own mobile professionalism. When he wrote 'The Scholar-Gipsy', Arnold had recently been appointed one of Her Majesty's Inspectors of Schools, a career which would make him among the most well-travelled Englishmen of his day. Moving from school to school, Arnold examined the students and 'pupil-teachers', took note of conditions in the facilities, interviewed teachers and administrators, and reported his findings to the Education Secretary in the Council Office. Arnold was a kind of professional tourist in so far as his job was to travel, observe and record.

That is not to say that Arnold enjoyed his work as he might have enjoyed a vacation, but that his own experience of the English landscape seems to have synthesized touristic and professional elements. Writing to his new wife, Fanny Lucy, about the prospects of their new life together, Arnold predicted, 'We shall certainly have a good deal of moving about ... but we both like that well enough' (1996: I. 227). Later, his letters home suggest that he was able to combine a good deal of touristic pleasure with his business. Shifting easily from one mode to the other, Arnold reported to his wife,

I have had a hard day. Thirty pupil teachers to examine in an inconvenient room and nothing to eat except a biscuit. ... The schools are mostly in the hands of very intelligent Unitarians, who abound here, and belong to the class of what we call ladies and gentlemen. This [Birmingham] is next to Liverpool the finest of manufacturing towns: the situation high and good, the principal street capital, the shops good, cabs splendid, and the Music Hall unequalled by any Greek building in England that I have seen. (1996: I. 227–8)

Touristic and professional travel combine interestingly in the composition of 'Haworth Churchyard', written to commemorate the death of Charlotte Brontë. Although the poem's visual and imaginative engagement suggests a distinctly touristic experience, the errors in the poem (the Brontës were not buried in the churchyard) indicate that Arnold's closest connection to the actual site was his professional visit to the Wesleyan school in Haworth (1979: 422).

Symptomatic of that characteristically touristic synthesis of business and pleasure was Arnold's love of maps. Park Honan notes that maps were 'one of his lasting passions' and that before starting on a new business trip, Arnold routinely

> filled his pockets with them and must have pored over them when sitting alone, on the edge of his bed, in a lodging house. As a child he had spent mornings with 'dissected maps' and as a poet he had brought beautiful, topographical features into his imagery to render complex moods and blends of feelings and ideas. (L. 248)

As an adult, Arnold's daily work entailed a survey of the landscape of national education very much akin to the work of the Ordnance Survey's goal of producing a graphic representation of the national countryside.[8] Indeed, a great deal of middle-class reform work entailed some mode of survey through which the state of sanitation, education, criminal activity or some other arena of modern life could be mapped onto the landscape of Britain.[9] Arnold's love of maps, and his use of them in connection with his work as an Inspector, suggest a thoroughly professional approach to the English landscape. And yet, as Honan suggests, Arnold also derived from his maps an experience that was seemingly more pleasurable than professional. To read a map is to read the landscape in a distinctly modern way, as the map becomes a surrogate for that landscape, even offering many of the same pleasures. John Jakle cites one twentieth-century tourist whose experience of trip planning is perhaps not atypical: 'We wouldn't have missed that year of planning. The pleasure it gave us, poring over guidebooks, maps and catalogues almost equalled the pleasure of the trip itself' (1985: 11). In his essay on 'Ordnance Maps', Arnold praised the modern map over the ancient map for its ability, not only to provide basic travel information, but to reproduce the actual experience of travel through the landscape: 'By its shading a good map becomes, to the lover of maps, almost a picture; it shows him all the relief and configuration of a country. He can trace, in those finely graduated lines, mountain and valley, slope and plain, open ground and woodland, in all their endless variety' (1960a: 41). According to Arnold, the most recent Ordnance Survey maps fail the 'lover of maps', for '[t]hey give him indeed ... the Great Western and the London and North Western Railways; but where, he sorrowfully asks, is the Cumnor hill country on the right bank of the Thames, as the original map gave it? Where is Bredon Hill, with all its beautiful staging from the plain to its summit?' (41). While we might infer that Arnold derived two distinct benefits from his maps – one pleasurable, the other vocational – I would argue instead that Arnold's reading of maps and his notion of what a good map should accomplish demonstrate the imbrication of work and pleasure in the modern experience of the countryside.

Arnold's questions, 'where ... is the Cumnor hill country? ... Where is Bredon

Hill?' suggest the powerful role of a national survey-style mapping in constructing an English or British countryside: absent from the maps, these landscapes disappear from the national landscape. Insofar as the landscape was increasingly identified as 'national heritage', the existence of properly produced maps was essential to the construction of that heritage, and here Arnold's attitude regarding maps neatly parallels the attitude regarding literature we find in 'The Literary Influence of the Academies'.[10] In France, Arnold writes, 'the Academy serves as a sort of centre and rallying-point to [educated opinion], and gives it a force which it has not got here' (241). Isolated genius may thrive without the existence of an academy (which is why, Arnold believes, English poetry is better than French), but without 'the influence of a supposed centre of correct information, correct judgement, correct taste', provinciality will predominate over urbanity, 'fixed and familiar notions' over 'intellectual action', local half-truths and falsehoods over general truths (245, 253). As an ideal representation of the nation, Arnold believed, the state, or government, was naturally suited to be the organ for elevating the national culture.[11] Similarly, in 'Ordnance Maps', Arnold takes issue with those who would leave map-making to private entrepreneurs. Instead, he argues, precisely because 'a government is not a tradesman', it is its duty 'to provide a good map of its country, and to keep that map in good order ... it is not its duty to provide cheap maps for the millions. ... The cheapness or dearness is a secondary consideration for it; the first consideration is excellence' (42–3). As an ideal rather than a descriptive representation of the political or physical nation, the state would naturally be better able to represent the national landscape in maps than could the tradesmen, governed as they would be by the interests of self and class – by their 'everyday self' as Arnold called it, rather than their 'best self'.

As in his discussion of culture, Arnold's discussion of excellence in map-making assumes a decontextualized standard by which maps are to be measured, while in fact, map-making is historically and inevitably charged with political interests and consequences. Until the middle of the eighteenth century, cartography had been largely the province of the military; coastal towns were mapped in the greatest detail as a defence against foreign enemies, while rebellious regions of the country were closely mapped in order to prevent or quell insurgency.[12] The founding of the Ordnance Survey in 1791 and the production (between 1801 and 1867) of a complete, standardized set of maps for Great Britain marked a new approach to map-making consistent with new uses of the English (and British) countryside, including popular tourism (Vaughan 1974: 84). Indeed, the efforts of the Ordnance Survey to produce a uniform mapping of the entire nation represent nothing less than an effort at representing the nation to itself as a coherent and unified whole.[13] Like the Liberal vision of the state-as-organism, which was to gain popularity later in the century, the Ordnance Survey maps constructed the nation as a collection of perfectly interlocking components, since each map could be joined seamlessly with its neighbours to create one great map of the British Isles. Equally important, as Arnold suggests, was the ability of the map to represent the quintessential and natural Englishness of that landscape: 'the open ground and woodland, in all their endless variety'. Thus map-making not only supported the rise of tourism by providing tourists with the tools of their 'trade'; it was clearly addressing on its own terms the same problem being addressed by both tourism and poetry, namely how to give coherent meaning to a rapidly changing landscape.

GUERILLA IN THE GLADE

The cultural and historical content of that entity, however, was the subject of an ongoing struggle, a struggle which focused increasingly on the right to assign meaning to England's rural areas. As Arnold realized, the effort of imagining the countryside as a space apart from class conflict and class interest required that it be wrested from the hands of the aristocracy and remade to correspond with middle-class interests and desires. Maps, like any texts, can be made to serve not only the interests of the state but those of subversive movements as well. In countries threatened with revolution, maps are frequently classified as military secrets, since they make possible the kinds of stealth and covert movements necessary to take control of any territory. Deleuze and Guattari point out the tactical value of a map's plasticity when they write that '[t]he map is open and connectable in all of its dimensions; it is detachable, reversible, susceptible to constant modification. It can be torn, reversed, adapted to any kind of mounting, reworked by an individual, group, or social formation. It can be drawn on a wall, conceived of as a work of art, constructed as a political action or a meditation' (1988: 12). It is for this reason that campaigns are first executed on maps before being carried into the landscape itself.

Arnold would perhaps not have been one to take up anything as Hebraistic as armed struggle, but if we recall his ongoing battle, not just with the philistines, but with the much more deeply entrenched culture of the barbarians, we gain a new appreciation for those frequent images of flight, retreat or hiding in Arnold's poetry. Those retreats into forest glades or into a 'high-field's dark corner' or some other sequestered nook become, not instances of surrender, but of a provisional, tactical retreat to new positions with new vantages on the world. The passages I quoted earlier from 'Stanzas from the Grande Chartreuse', for example, locate the narrator in a spot where, 'secret from the eyes of all', he nevertheless looks out on the procession of life around him. At the opening of 'The Scholar-Gipsy', Arnold, on a visit from Oxford, has occupied the shepherd's nook, in which he is hidden ('screen'd') but nevertheless able to look and listen to the world around him from the nearby vegetation all the way 'down to Oxford's towers'.

A 'tactical retreat' implies a deeper, long-term motive. For Arnold, that motive is the possibility of some new, and typically middle-class engagement with the landscape or its inhabitants. The 'Tyrian trader' at the end of 'The Scholar-Gipsy' shuns the 'merry Grecian coaster' just as the narrator of 'Thyrsis' runs from the boisterous hunters. Both threats represent throwbacks to a barbarian age, threats which must be resisted as incompatible with the narrator's and poet's more serious interests.[14] It is by no means a flight from the responsibilities of the world, but an attempt to establish a more fluid and mobile form of engagement with that world – an engagement based on the distinctively middle-class sphere of commerce. By contrast, the Grecian coaster, the hunters, and others come to seem frivolous, atavistic barbarians. Arnold's position is more effective, more powerful, because it is more tactical. Insofar as the Gipsies represented to Arnold's audience a threat to 'precisely those Hebraistic middle-class values (industry, wealth, pragmatism, respectability) that Arnold attacks as Philistine', Anthony Harrison finds in Arnold's valorization of Gipsies an attempt 'to resist ideological constituencies and commitments, and to wrest cultural power from the hands of his middle-class opposition' (1991: 374, 368). Yet the middle class can hardly be imagined as Arnold's principal opposition; if he sometimes chose to attack its more philistine elements, his interests and sympathies are more aligned with theirs than opposed. Neither the scholar-gipsy's nor the Tyrian Trader's relationship to the landscape is really subversive of middle-class values, for each performs a union of work and leisure. At times, the scholar-gypsy may seem to offer a fantasy of perpetual leisure,

Trailing in the cool stream thy fingers wet,
As the punt's rope chops round;
And leaning backward in a pensive dream,
And fostering in thy lap a heap of flowers
Plucked in shy fields and distant Wychwood bowers,
And thine eyes resting on the moonlit stream.

(LL. 75–80)

However, it is a leisure joined to the middle-class Victorian passion for fieldwork and documentation: the scholar-gipsy, it turns out, is engaged in a project redolent of ethnography (a field also connected to middle-class dreams of empire).[15] His intention among the gipsies, we are told, was to learn 'the secret of their art, [which] / When fully learned, [he] will to the world impart' (LL. 48–9). The image of the Tyrian Trader is nostalgic and anti-modern in its own way, as it looks back to an earlier mode of trade characterized by perfect trust and unsullied by 'the great town's harsh, heart-wearying roar'. And yet the poem itself operates against pastoral convention by opening in a secluded nook and concluding in the realm of commerce, however removed that realm may be from the realities of life in the English city. The 'Grecian coaster', from which the Tyrian Trader flees, represents not so much an active life as an unreflective and therefore unproductive one.

Arnold's tactical and circumspect manoeuvres in the landscape are revealingly distinct from what Mary Louise Pratt calls 'the monarch-of-all-I-survey scene' typically located on a high promontory, and frequent in mid-century imperial narratives.[16] The aim of such scenes is to display a 'mastery of the landscape' presented as a 'broad panorama anchored in the seer' (1992: 209). That such a perspective should have been available to the African explorer on a foreign continent but not to the Englishman on his own soil points to the uncertainty of middle-class access to the English landscape. Whereas in 1860 Richard Burton (Pratt's primary example) could imagine the landscape of Lake Tanganyika displayed prostrate at his feet, Arnold in this same period is less able to ignore the reminders of formidable claims already laid on the landscape he would like to make his own. In another contrast, Wordsworth's more panoramic visions of the countryside a generation earlier, as in the opening chapter to the *Guide to the Lakes* or the view from Mt Snowden in *The Prelude*, demonstrate his greater affiliation with an earlier, agrarian relationship to the landscape and a time when the contest for control of that landscape had not reached the pitch it had by the middle of the century. Arnold is simply not comfortable with the broad vista or 'prospect' that characterized so much landscape painting and poetry of the eighteenth and nineteenth centuries.

Michel de Certeau's distinction between 'strategies' and 'tactics' defines more precisely both the difference between Burton's and Arnold's perspectives and the middle-class anxiety that runs through Arnold's landscapes. 'Strategies' he associates with the maintenance of existing power, while the term 'tactics' refers to the work of marginal groups to undermine that power: a strategy, he writes, 'postulates a *place* that can be delimited as its *own* and serve as the base from which relations with an *exteriority* composed of targets or threats (customers or competitors, enemies, the country surrounding the city, objectives and objects of research, etc.) can be managed'. The knowledge produced by strategies is 'sustained and determined by the power to provide oneself with one's own place' (1984: 36). 'By contrast to a strategy', de Certeau continues,

> a *tactic* is a calculated action determined by the absence of a proper locus.[17] . . . The space of a tactic is the space of the other. Thus it must play on and with a terrain imposed on it and organized by the law of a foreign power. . . . It operates in isolated actions, blow by blow. It takes advantage of 'opportunities' and depends on them, being without any base where it could stockpile its winnings. (36–7)

Representing the tremendous power of European imperialism, Burton's 'strategic' perspective commanded a fixed position, or 'base' from which his panoptic vision could 'manage' the surrounding landscape. Whereas imperialist narratives frequently imagine foreign landscapes as fully available for appropriation, Arnold is always aware that, as a bourgeois in a landscape still redolent of aristocratic privilege and power, he is operating in 'the space of the other', an awareness that gives his movements and his perspectives a more tactical quality. This mobile and provisional occupation of a series of small but prominent spaces indicates a relationship to the landscape very different from the confident vistas of Wordsworth in an earlier English landscape or of Burton in Africa, or perhaps of today's tourist in a landscape more fully assimilated to a bourgeois order.

ARNOLD AND THE *RUS IN URBE*

If the middle-class poet or tourist in the countryside felt himself in 'the space of the other', he could nevertheless claim his own 'proper locus' in the form of the modern city, and it is – perhaps paradoxically – that base from which the modern countryside will be conceived. Jean-Paul Hulin analyses what he calls the *rus in urbe* 'motif' or 'philosophy' characteristic of Victorian writing on the city. As Hulin describes it, this 'mode of evasion' represents 'an anti-urban strategy' and a refusal on the part of Victorians to accept their urban reality (1979: 17). The *rus in urbe* philosophy took both a sociopolitical form and a literary form:

> [t]he socio-political strategy usually consists in *restructuring urban society or the urban environment, on specifically rural patterns* [e.g. city parks, suburbs]. The more 'literary' approach, though not totally unconnected with the preceding one, will rather consist in

exploiting to the utmost, for sentimental or aesthetic reasons, those natural elements that
have managed to survive among the city's artefacts. (16–7; emphasis in original)

However, while Hulin follows Martin Wiener in equating an idealization of rural life
with a rejection of modernity, we might more accurately interpret the *rus in urbe*
philosophy as a strategy for *reconceiving* landscape itself to accord with the interests
and circumstances of an urban middle class.

'Lines Written in Kensington Gardens' enacts just such a strategy by situating a
pastoral grove, or *locus amoenus*, 'amid the city's jar', belying his complaint in
'Thyrsis' of the 'town's harsh, heart-wearying roar'. This poem demonstrates precisely the sentiment Hulin identifies as Victorian *rus in urbe*, but the motives are
clearly different insofar as the poem displays a progressive rather than a purely
nostalgic view of rural life. In sharp contrast to the Cumnor Hills, which are characterized by change and loss beyond the narrator's control, Kensington Gardens is a
place of peace and permanence even though it is surrounded by, and very much a
product of, 'the city's girdling hum':

> Yet here is *peace for ever new*!
> When I who watch them am away,
> Still all things in this glade go through
> The changes of their quiet day.
>
> (LL. 29–32; emphasis added)

The rhetoric of pastoral is there, but it is a sturdy, urban pastoral undisturbed by –
even comfortable with – the constant, seemingly anti-pastoral interruptions of the
surrounding city. The idea of 'peace for ever new' is tellingly ambiguous: while it
might refer to a mythical prelapsarian eternity, it might just as easily be taken as
heralding a new *form* of peace consistent with the continual novelty of urban life.
Arnold's experience of the glade echoes those Wordsworthian 'spots' of rural
memories called into action as a defence against the meaninglessness (the 'jar', 'hum',
or 'roar') or the city. Yet, as Roper notes, Arnold 'has brought the city's jar into the
glade instead of leaving it behind' (1969: 53). Far from being a desperate and
hopelessly inadequate re-enactment of rural life, as Hulin's argument would suggest,
Arnold's experience in Kensington Gardens is wholly satisfactory on its own terms –
terms that borrow from the conventions of pastoral while adapting those conventions to an urban setting:

> Scarce fresher is the mountain-sod
> Where the tired angler lies, stretched out,
> And, eased of basket and of rod,
> Counts his day's spoil, the spotted trout.
>
> (LL. 17–20)

In this glade, nature and the life of the city blend insensibly into each other; 'Birds
here make song, each bird has his, / Across the girdling city's hum' (5–6). The
individuality of the birds, each with its own song, offers a natural correlative to the
individualism and even isolation by which urban life is so often characterized. And
yet, the preposition 'across' introduces an ambiguity that saves them from full
immersion in that life: like Arnold in his urban glade, the birds are neither excluded

from the city nor consumed by it, but move tactically through it or across it as they will.

Outside the city, Arnold's landscapes are more distinctly rural, but even they are conceived and experienced in a way that calls into question the conceptual boundaries of rural and urban. Indeed, for the *rus in urbe* to be effective, the notion of '*rus*', or 'country', has to be radically redefined. Taking seriously a visit to Kensington Gardens as a substitute for rural experience requires that the true countryside be imagined in similar terms; there is, after all, no opportunity for the broad panorama or the sublime mountaintop view in a city park. Thus, even where such a panorama might be available, Arnold's most satisfying rural experiences invariably involve a small space – a 'nook' or 'glade' – which can be easily entered or exited, very much like a city park. Thus the comparison by which he anchors Kensington Gardens in the larger experience of the countryside involves a similarly limited experience: the 'tired angler ... stretch'd out' on the 'mountain sod', not the sublime vistas of a Romantic countryside.

In short, the emergence of a *rus in urbe* must be understood not merely as an urban expedient, but as an expression of a more general change in the relationship of the middle class and the countryside generally. When Charles Cherbery in 1822 invoked 'that deep-seated rurality which is at the centre of every Englishman's heart' (quoted in Hulin 1979: 37n), he was already speaking of something associated only symbolically or metonymically with any genuine rural area – something recognizable in the city park, the garden in the suburb, the weekend in the country, the sentimental engraving in the *Illustrated London News*, or the keepsake edition of Tennyson or Wordsworth on the drawing-room table. As an urban idea, that 'rurality' no longer required a strictly rural location: portable and transferable, it could operate with equal effectiveness in London or Manchester as well as Sussex or Cumberland. It is this portable 'rurality' that attracts Alton Locke to the London picture galleries, where, 'shut out from every glimpse of Nature', he could nevertheless 'taste her beauties, even on canvas, with perfect relish and childish self-abandonment' (Kingsley 1983: 96). It is a very different manifestation of the same phenomenon, one based in memory this time, that gives the Lake Isle of Innisfree its value for W. B. Yeats even though, 'standing on the roadway, or the pavement gray' his access to it is perpetually deferred by the repetition of 'I will arise and go now'. What is important now is not the actual presence of the 'small cabin ... in the bee-loud glade', but that 'I hear it in the deep heart's core'.

The relevance to tourism of this construction of the countryside is best understood with reference to Dean MacCannell's structural analysis of tourism. The touristic experience, he observes, requires an interplay of sites (signifieds) and markers (signifiers). The tourist recognizes the authenticity of his experience in Paris (the signified) by reference to Eiffel Tower (signifier). Signifiers become signifieds, however, as prints and miniature castings of the tower proliferate to document (or signify) the authenticity of tower itself. The construction of 'Paris' or any other geographical space as a meaningful site for tourism therefore requires two steps. First, isolated and recognizable sites within the city must be made to signify the city itself: they may be unique sites like the Eiffel Tower or the Tuilleries, or multiple, like the Parisian café. Only then can tourists recognize their experience of 'Paris' as authentic, making possible the second step in the process, namely the proliferation of second-level markers pointing to the individual sites which, in turn, point to the idea of Paris itself. In Arnold's poetry, attention to geographical detail helps to take the English countryside through the first of these two steps. The detail with which he describes the Cumnor Hills – themselves a distinctive landmark outside of Oxford – turns a generalized landscape into one that invites comparison with the site itself: a reader might reasonably assume that some traipsing would turn up the 'signal tree' and perhaps even the glade from which the narrator looks down to Oxford's towers. What sets Arnold's glades apart from physically similar spaces in the pastoral mode (even as recently as Keats' Romantic 'bowers') is that those glades may be imagined as existing in a real landscape which they can be made to represent synechdochally just as the Eiffel Tower has been made to represent Paris or the Golden Gate Bridge San Francisco.

ARNOLD, POETRY AND THE AIMS OF TOURISM

Superficially at least, the intimate and sophisticated experience offered by poetry might seem antithetical to the experience of tourism, with its crowds and trains. 'To a Gipsy Child by the Seashore', for example, an early autobiographical account of a family vacation to the Isle of Man, might be characterized as anti-touristic in spite of its subject matter on the grounds that its power derives from the intensity of the solitude in which the speaker and the gipsy child are wrapped. And yet, if this experience is far removed from the world of the Thomas Cook package tour, it is exemplary of what John Urry calls the 'romantic gaze'. With its emphasis on 'solitude, privacy and a personal, semi-spiritual relationship with the object of the gaze', the romantic gaze is at least on one level opposed to the unashamedly public 'collective gaze', which 'necessitates the participation of large numbers of other people, as ... for example in the seaside resorts' (1995: 45–6). On another level, however, the romantic gaze can be understood as simply one available stance, or attitude, within a fundamentally collective practice of tourism. As James Buzard points out, 'anti-tourists or practitioners of the "romantic" gaze *required* the crowd they scorned and shunned, for they built their travellers' identities in opposition to the crowd' (1993: 153). Indeed, if there is any question as to the participation of the seemingly solitary romantic gaze in a fundamentally collective activity, we have only to remember that, paradoxically perhaps, 'the authentic sight', so highly valued by the Romantic tourist, nevertheless 'requires markers, though part of our notion of authenticity is the marked' (Culler 1981: 137). In Arnold's poetry, we are never far from that 'city's girdling hum', a welcome reminder of the value of our solitude. The early poems are especially remarkable in this dialectic of solitude and crowd: 'To a Gipsy Child by the Seashore', 'The Forsaken Merman', 'The Strayed Reveller'. Yet even in a very late poem, in that seemingly perfect romantic moment recorded nostalgically in 'Thyrsis', Arnold locates his own solitude as temporally and spatially adjacent to the crowd, '*Above* the locks, *above* the boating throng' (L. 122).

Poetry and tourism both display a concern for loss and for a redemption of that loss (what else, after all, are those popular tourist sites, the tombs to the unknown soldiers?), a concern expressed most poignantly in 'Stanzas from the Grande Chartreuse' – one of Arnold's most explicitly touristic poems about an episode from his honeymoon in France. There, in 'the Carthusians' world-famed home', the speaker's nostalgic and spectatorial enjoyment is interrupted by 'whispers pierc[ing] the gloom: / *What dost thou in this living tomb?*' The standard explanation for the final exam would be that Arnold is registering the *angst* of the Victorian mind confronting the decay of faith before the march of rationalism. But it is also the *angst* of the tourist, 'condemned to look elsewhere, everywhere, for his authenticity', and yet unavoidably alienated from that authenticity by virtue of the otherness on which his notion of the 'authentic' is based (MacCannell 1976: 41).

Fortunately, Arnold's poetry suggests, tourism also provides the means by which that loss can be in some measure redeemed and the alienated modern tourism can be assured of some meaningful place in the otherwise alien landscape. In 'Salisbury Plain', the 'Ruined Cottage' incident from *The Excursion*, and elsewhere, Wordsworth suggested that a sensitively elegiac representation of loss could confer a therapeutic value capable of redeeming the loss itself. However, if for Wordsworth, the redemption associated with mourning is always largely personal, Elizabeth Helsinger points to a more collective redemption to be found in the representation of rural decay and loss. In her analysis of Gerard Manley Hopkins's 'Binsey Poplars', she argues that such representations may call 'into being a new collectivity of those who share both the loss and responsibility' for the destruction (1997: 5). There is no history of violence or opportunity for blame in 'Thyrsis' as there is in Hopkins's poem, but the sense of loss, even so romantically imagined, opens the door to a similar sort of collectivity:

> Where is the girl, who by the boatman's door,
> Above the locks, above the boating throng,
> Unmoored our skiff when through the Wytham flats,
> Red loosestrife and blond meadow-sweet among
> And darting swallows and light water-gnats,
> We tracked the shy Thames shore?
> Where are the mowers, who, as the tiny swell
> Of our boat passing heaved the river-grass,
> Stood with suspended scythe to see us pass? –
> They all are gone, and thou art gone as well!

(LL. 121–30)

In good elegiac tradition, the death of Thyrsis/Clough is echoed in the decay of the landscape and in the absence of the girl who tended the locks and the mowers who 'stood with suspended scythe'. Memorialized in their arrested positions, however, these figures achieve a permanence in the scene that could not be imagined if they were really still visible: they cannot, like the uprooted wanderers in *Lyrical Ballads*, threaten to disrupt the spectatorial experience or challenge the interpretation of the observer. Furthermore, what may be most important for our purposes is the interpellation of the figures as visual souvenirs (literally, as 'memories') of the narrator's own experience. Simply by watching and acknowledging the passage of the poet's boat through the landscape on an earlier occasion, the mowers and the girl reaffirm the status of the tourist as the central and organizing figure in the scene, while their own stasis underscores the power of the tourist's movement as the legitimate basis for narrative.[18] Their absence at the time of this later visit – presented as a problem in the poem – actually allows the poet to identify nostalgically with the natives and their landscape in a way that would only have been made more difficult by their continued presence *in* the landscape.

Going to visit the Grande Chartreuse, strolling in the Cumnor Hills, or boating on the upper Thames, Arnold not only participates in that collectivity of mourning, but also demonstrates its affiliation with the mobility of the detached observer. As Roper has pointed out, Arnold's poetry frequently 'endeavors to convert the spatially observed scene into a temporal record by means of physical movement through the scene' (1969: 41). By the same process, however, the landscape and any human figures in it become fixed spatially in a way that lifts them out of the temporal reality altogether. More to the point, the mobile gaze of the Arnoldian poet, very much like that of the tourist, isolates the landscape and its inhabitants from any existing 'temporal record' and reinscribes them in a new temporal record organized according to the tourist's own itinerary. Like a series of snapshots in a photo album, the newly organized landscape always recognizes the tourist as the focal point of its composition. However, if this movement through the landscape looks forward to the rise of tourism, it also looks backward ironically to the figure of the genteel family pivotally positioned in the foreground of so many eighteenth-century landscapes. If in the earlier landscapes the authority of the genteel family is (to quote de Certeau again) 'sustained and determined by the power to provide [themselves] with [their] own place', the authority of the Arnoldian poet/tourist is emphatically mobile and provisional: 'it operates in isolated actions ... without any base' other than the subjectivity of the observer.

Among mid-Victorian poets, Clough engaged most overtly with the concerns of tourism in his long 'mock-pastoral', *The Bothie of Toper-na-Fuosich*[19] and *Amours de Voyage*. The first of these earned him the most undisguised contempt from Arnold, who wrote in disgust that he might break with all his Oxford friends, including Clough, rather 'than be sucked for an hour even into the Time Stream in which they and he plunge and bellow' (1968: 95). Unlike Clough, Arnold invariably distanced himself from the 'multitudinousness' of modern life, and yet what he perhaps unwittingly demonstrates is the effectiveness with which that gesture – on the part of the poet or the tourist – may contribute to the collective production of the very landscape of modernity itself.

NOTES

1. This gesture toward the countryside is evident at least as early as Hannah More, whose tracts (e.g. 'The Shepherd of Salisbury Plain') invoked pastoral simplicity and hard work as an admonishment to the urban working classes. William Howitt's fiction and non-fiction of rural life makes a similar effort. Thomas Cook's first public excursion carried workers from the manufacturing town of

Leicester to the village of Loughborough in 1836, and a few years later William Wordsworth objected famously to similar plans to bring large numbers of working-class excursionists to the Lake District. Even today in the United States, the 'Fresh Air Fund' seeks to ease urban tensions by arranging for inner-city children to spend their summers in the country.

2. In a dated but still influential study, Dwight Culler understands Arnold's 'forest glade' as representing 'the freshness of the early world' (from Arnold's 'Memorial Verses') and a respite from the 'burning plains' of modernity (1976: 10: 1–17 passim.)

3. In a reading of 'Resignation', Morgan notes that, although the narrator and his sister Fausta 'mimic the speaker in "Tintern Abbey", who positions himself on the hill in order to obtain a glorious "prospect on nature", Arnold's characters are distinctly bound within the Wordsworthian landscape they see below them' (1986: 437).

4. Even his most classical composition, *Merope*, Arnold acknowledged was 'not a bit Greek', though he added that 'it is *very* beautiful' (Honan 1983: 287).

5. Roper believes that 'Thyrsis' fails because the landscape cannot stand in for immortality; it cannot sustain the symbolic burden it is forced to carry. ... The poem buckles beneath the weight of its own philosophical pretensions. To hold together it must find something, preferably in the landscape, to mediate between the literal world of the Cumnor hills with all its emotional associations and the idyllically unchanging world of the antique pastoral (1969: 228–9).

    Yet even within the poem there is a sense of the inevitability of that failure, and Arnold's elegy includes a lament for the loss of the landscape's capacity to sustain the meanings it might have sustained in earlier times.

6. In using the term 'residual', I am intentionally invoking Raymond Williams' formulation of the 'residual, dominant, and emergent' in *Marxism and Literature*. Williams complicates the more conventional Marxist dialectical historiography by arguing for the existence of multiple social formations at any given moment in history. Residual and emergent formations, while not (or no longer) fully realized, nevertheless influence culture and society in important ways.

7. In *Pendennis* (1849), for example, Thackeray pokes fun at the phrase *otium cum dignate* when he notes that 'Mr. Morgan was enjoying his *otium* in a dignified manner, surveying the evening fog, and smoking a cigar.'

8. J. B. Harley notes that the first comprehensive 'survey' of Great Britain begun in 1765 'did not apply [the term] solely to maps; it was a generic word referring to the whole process – written and graphic – of inspecting and reporting on fortifications' (Seymour and Andrews 1980: 7). Although the Survey focused increasingly on maps, the goal was nevertheless a comprehensive representation of the English landscape.

9. E. J. S. Parsons documents the affiliation between Edwin Chadwick's sanitation movement and the work of the Ordnance Survey, noting that sanitation work placed such a burden on the Survey that other efforts by that agency had to be postponed (Seymour and Andrews 1980: 113–4).

10. 'Since the early nineteenth century', writes Lowenthal, 'national identity has required having a heritage and thinking it unique', and in England the principal

'icon of heritage' is landscape: 'nowhere else does the very term suggest not simply scenery and *genres de vie*, but quintessential national virtues' (1991: 206, 213).

11. Catherine Gallagher's insightful analysis of Arnold and Mill concludes that the legitimacy of the state's authority as arbiter of national culture is predicated on an understanding of the ideal state as an embodiment of a people's 'best self'. Arnoldian culture, she writes, 'is the process that scrapes away economic, sectional and class identity, social identity itself, leaving the pure and disinterested kernel of the best self behind. It is this self that the State should represent. And what is this self? The knowledge of the best that has been thought and said. It follows that the state should represent culture' (1984: 127).

12. J. B. Harley notes that a complete mapping of Scotland between 1747 and 1755 in response to the 1745 uprising was 'the most extensive survey of its kind to be made in eighteenth-century Britain, and it had no real precursor or successor' (Seymour and Andrews 1980: 4). Later, these maps of Scotland were to form the basis for similar efforts in 'response to the same perceived needs of underdeveloped "colonial" territories' in India, Ireland and North America (Seymour: 6).

13. The biggest issue facing the Ordnance Survey during this time was the choice and implementation of a single scale for the several hundred maps that would cover the British Isles.

14. As E. K. Brown notes, 'The Tyrian trader's flight before the clamorous spirited Greeks is exactly analogous to the scholar-gipsy's flight before the drink and clatter of the smock-frocked boors or before the bathers in the abandoned lasher or before the Oxford riders blithe' (quoted in Arnold 1979: 368n).

15. Interest in ethnography and folklore had been growing rapidly in recent decades and clearly informed the ways in which tourists viewed rural life. See Dorson (1968) for an overview of this movement, (though not its affiliation with tourism).

16. Pratt's phrase comes presumably from Cowper's 'Verses, Supposed to be Written by Alexander Selkirk During his Solitary Abode in the Island of Juan Fernandez':

I am monarch of all I survey,
My right there is none to dispute,
From the centre all round to the sea,
I am lord of the fowl and the brute.

(1992: 1–4)

17. De Certeau uses the term 'proper' to include a sense of ownership or belonging, as in the French '*propre*'.

18. The memorial value of these figures for Arnold is clear from his preference for this particular stanza as one of those most able to 'bring certain places and moments before me' (quoted in Tinker, Lowry and Wylie 1980: 218).

19. This poem was later renamed and republished posthumously as *The Bothie of Tober-na-Vuolich*. For more on this poem in relation to the concerns of domestic tourism, see my article on 'Tourism and the Contest for Cultural Authority in Clough's *Bothie of Toper-na-Fuosich*', (Ulin 1999).

REFERENCES

Anderson, Benedict R. (1991) *Imagined Communities: Reflections on the Origin and Spread of Nationalism*. London: Verso

Arnold, Matthew (1960*b*) 'Preface to First Edition of Poems (1853)', *On the Classical Tradition*, ed. R. H. Super. Ann Arbor: University of Michigan Press, 1–15.

Arnold, Matthew (1932) *Culture and Anarchy* [1869] ed. J. Dover Wilson. Cambridge: Cambridge University Press.

Arnold, Matthew (1960*a*) 'Ordnance Maps', *Essays, Letters, and Reviews*. Cambridge: Harvard University Press, 20–4.

Arnold, Matthew (1962) 'The literary influence of academies', *Lectures and Essays in Criticism*, ed. R. H. Super. Ann Arbor: University of Michigan Press, 232–57.

Arnold, Matthew (1968) *The Letters of Matthew Arnold to Arthur Hugh Clough*, ed. Howard Foster Lowry. New York: Russell & Russell.

Arnold, Matthew (1979) *The Poems of Matthew Arnold*, ed. Kenneth Allott and Miriam Allott, 2nd edn. London: Longman.

Arnold, Matthew (1996) *The Letters of Matthew Arnold*, ed. Cecil Y. Lang. Charlottesville: University Press of Virginia.

Brendon, Piers (1992) *Thomas Cook: 150 Years of Popular Tourism*. London: Secker & Warburg.

Buzard, James (1993) *The Beaten Track: European Tourism, Literature, and the Ways to Culture, 1800–1918*. Oxford: Oxford University Press.

de Certeau, Michel (1984) *The Practice of Everyday Life*. Berkeley: University of California Press.

Culler, Dwight A. (1976) *Imaginative Reason: the Poetry of Matthew Arnold*. Westport, Conn.: Greenwood Press.

Culler, Jonathan (1981) 'Semiotics of tourism', *American Journal of Semiotics*, **1**, 127–40.

Deleuze, Gilles, and Félix Guattari (1988) *A Thousand Plateaus* [Milles Plateaux], trans. Brian Massumi. London: Athlone Press.

Dodd, Philip (1986) 'Englishness and the national culture', *Englishness: Politics and Culture, 1880–1920*, ed. Robert Colls and Philip Dodd. London: Croom Helm, 1–28.

Dorson, Richard Mercer (1968) *The British Folklorists: A History*. Chicago: University of Chicago Press.

Gallagher, Catherine (1984) 'The politics of culture and the debate over representation', *Representations*, **5**, 115–47.

Harrison, Anthony (1991) 'Matthew Arnold's gipsies: intertextuality and the new historicism', *Victorian Poetry*, **29**(4), 365–83.

Helsinger, Elizabeth K. (1997) *Rural Scenes and National Representation: Britain, 1815–1850*. Princeton, NJ: Princeton University Press.

Honan, Park (1983) *Matthew Arnold, a Life*. Cambridge, Mass: Harvard University Press.

Howitt, William (1838) *The Rural Life of England*, 2 vols. London: Longman, Brown, Green and Longmans.

Hulin, Jean-Paul (1979) 'Rus in Urbe: a key to victorian anti-urbanism?', *Victorian*

Writers and the City, ed. Jean-Paul Hulin and Pierre Coustillas. Lille: Publications de l'Université de Lille III, 11–40.

Jakle, John A. (1985) *The Tourist: Travel in Twentieth-Century North America*. Lincoln: University of Nebraska Press.

Kingsley, Charles, and Cripps, Elizabeth A. (1983) *Alton Locke, Tailor and Poet: An Autobiography*. New York: Oxford University Press.

Lowenthal, David (1991) 'British national identity and the English landscape', *Rural History*, **2**, 205–30.

MacCannell, Dean (1976) *The Tourist: A New Theory of the Leisure Class*. New York: Schocken Books.

Morgan, Thais E. (1986) 'Rereading nature: Wordsworth between Swinburne and Arnold', *Victorian Poetry*, **24**(4), 427–39.

Pratt, Mary Louise (1992) *Imperial Eyes: Travel Writing and Transculturation*. New York: Routledge.

Roper, Alan (1969) *Arnold's Poetic Landscapes*. Baltimore: Johns Hopkins Press.

Seymour, W. A., and Andrews, John Harwood (1980) (eds), *A History of the Ordnance Survey*. Folkestone: Dawson.

Tinker, Chauncey Brewster, Lowry, Howard Foster and Wylie, Francis James (1940) *The Poetry of Matthew Arnold: A Commentary*. New York: Russell & Russell.

Ulin, Donald (1999) 'Tourism and the contest for cultural authority', in *Clough's Bothie of Toper-Na-Fuosich*. *Victorian Poetry*, **37**(1), 71–98.

Ulmer, Gregory L. (1993) 'Metaphoric rocks: a psychogeography of tourism and monumentality', *Postmodern Culture*, **4**(3). (http://muse.jhu.edu/journals/postmodern_culture/v004/4.3ulmer.html (12 April 2002). (http://muse.jhu.edu/journals/postmodern_culture/v004/4.3ulmer.html) 4.3.

Urry, John (1995) *Consuming Places*. New York: Routledge.

Vaughan, John Edmund (1974) *The English Guide Book, c.1780–1870: An Illustrated History*. Newton Abbot: David & Charles.

Williams, Raymond (1977) *Marxism and Literature*. Oxford: Oxford University Press.

Chapter 11

Literature, Tourism and the Grand Tour

John Towner

INTRODUCTION

On Good Friday, in the year 1778, James Boswell turned into Bolt Court just off Fleet Street in London. He was on his way to breakfast with his friend and hero Dr Samuel Johnson. During the meal Boswell mentioned that he wanted 'to publish an account of my Travels upon the Continent of Europe, for which I have a variety of material collected'. The Doctors' reply was not encouraging:

> I do not say, Sir, that you may not publish your travels; but I give you my opinion, that you would lessen yourself by it. What can you tell of countries so well known as those upon the Continent of Europe, which you have visited?

'But', persisted Boswell, 'I can give an entertaining narrative, with many incidents, anecdotes, *jeux d'ésprit* and remarks, so as to make very pleasant reading.' This was to no avail, however: 'Why Sir, most modern travellers in Europe who have published travels have been laughed at; I would not have you added to their number,' (Boswell 1791: Vol. 1, 215).

These exchanges between Boswell and Johnson make a number of points about the Grand Tour and literature. The Tour was a major cultural institution, much discussed in fashionable and literary circles; even over breakfast. Many travellers felt it was highly desirable that an account of their tour should appear in print for the benefit of themselves and a wider audience. However, by the later eighteenth century, few of these works could pretend to have any literary merit and were, instead, a cause for some mockery. In the event, Boswell did not publish his Grand Tour (he had already written an account of his stay on Corsica (1768)). On the other hand, we get a very much better idea of what his tour was really like from another form of literature: his private papers (Pottle 1952–5).

This chapter develops a number of these themes. After briefly discussing the institution of the Grand Tour and the prevailing 'Culture of Travel', the various forms of literature produced by the Tour are outlined. We then move on to a consideration of the differences between the 'public' face of the Grand Tour which emerges from the published literature and the 'private' face of the Tour occasionally glimpsed through unpublished material. Finally, the legacy of the Grand Tour is considered, both in terms of the literary output and the extent to which its authors left any literary shrines for future tourists to venerate. Much of the focus of this chapter is on the British experience, although it should be remembered that the French, Germans and Russians also had their versions of the Grand Tour and produced their own travel literature.

THE GRAND TOUR AND THE CULTURE OF TRAVEL

Much has been written about the Grand Tour of Europe (Black 1992; Mead 1914; Schudt 1959; Towner 1985, 1996) and so its complex origins and various forms will not be discussed here. In essence, it was a circuit of Western Europe undertaken by the wealthy, especially from Britain. The principal aims of the tour ranged from education and culture to the pursuit of health and pleasure. The practice of visiting the major cultural centres of Europe, particularly those in Italy and France, developed in the sixteenth century and reached its zenith in the eighteenth century. From then, Grand Touring survived in various modified forms into the nineteenth century but was fragmenting by the 1840s. Its coherent form and nature had gone, as the wealthy élite sought out new destinations and as middle-class tourists visited the Continent in increasing numbers and for far less time. To some extent, the Americans continued the cultural traditions of lengthy journeys in Europe (Baker 1964), but for the British the days of the Grand Tour were over. At its height, the wealthy sons of the landed classes would go abroad for journeys lasting from three to five or six years, sometimes longer. Often accompanied by a tutor and servants, this élite would study art and architectural treasures, admire scenery, mix with their social equals at grand houses and courts, acquire languages and manners and enjoy the leisure which their position provided in such ample quantities.

To understand the relationship between the Grand Tour and literature, it is important to understand the central position that travel played in the culture of the élite. Travel was the process through which many of the most critical aspects of their thought, education and taste were transmitted. From the Renaissance onwards, gaining knowledge through travel underlay much philosophical and scientific thought; to be travelled was to be educated, and there were many books of advice which outlined 'theories of travel' for the serious visitor (Adler 1989; Frantz 1934). In addition, touring the Continent was desirable for the gentlemanly ideal of the 'virtuoso'; the wealthy amateur who united an interest in science with the collections of antiquities as works of art (Houghton 1942). Above all, however, the Grand Tour confirmed status in society and access to the best circles in the land. This 'travel culture' was cemented through a number of networks. One was the social intercourse of visits to London, the watering places and the country estates of the landed classes. But literature was another part of this process. London and provincial booksellers were centres of culture as well, whilst circulating libraries serviced the gentry in remoter parts. The great houses also had their extensive libraries (Dent 1974). Thus, theories of travel, experiences and ideas and opinions were transmitted in published books, diaries and journals, whilst guidebooks conveyed the practical information on how and where to travel, which places to visit and where to stay. Travel literature was also hugely popular amongst a wider audience. In fact, it formed the main diet of secular reading for the British in the eighteenth century (Curley 1976; De Beer 1955; Dent 1974). The surviving records of borrowings from the Bristol library, 1773–84, show that the middle- and upper-class subscribers were devoted to accounts of tours, many of which were of the Grand Tour (Kaufman 1960). Little wonder that Boswell was keen to get his travels into print.

THE LITERATURE CREATED BY THE GRAND TOUR

The Grand Tour produced a number of different forms of literature, each in their own way communicating the experience of travel. First, there were the diaries, letters and journals kept by the tourists during their journey. These either remained in manuscript form or were subsequently published (Batts 1976; Cox 1935–49; Matthews 1950; Pine-Coffin 1974). Even in their unpublished form, however, there is evidence that these records could be widely circulated amongst family and friends both in Britain and in France (Broc 1974; Dent 1974; Harder 1981; Nichols 1812–15; Nichols and Nichols 1817–58). In published form, hundreds of travel accounts were produced. The Grand Tour was also continually being discussed in the magazines and literary journals that appeared in the eighteenth century such as *The Spectator, The Tatler, Critical Review, Monthly Review* and the *Gentleman's Magazine* (Fussell 1962; Golden 1977; Towner 1984). Here, there was a lively debate on the merits of the Tour and the merits of its literature. Thus, whilst in 1794, *The British Critic* felt that: 'Books of Travels as constituting an agreeable medium betwixt works of mere amusement, and those of abstract literature. have always been secure of a favourable reception from the public' (1794, iv: 391). *The European Magazine* considered: 'We begin to apprehend that the Public will, in a short time, be sated with travellers who pass over the same ground as their predecessors, without adding anything of importance to the stock of intelligence already known' (1974, xxv: 283).

For communicating basic information, the most obvious literary form was the guidebook. However, a neat division did not exist between a travel account and a guide as many of the former were used as the latter. Thus, manuscript diaries might be circulated as guides amongst acquaintances. Thomas Potter, on a Grand Tour in 1737, wrote home asking to be remembered to a friend, 'and let him know that I am now upon the scene of his travels and am likely to find his diary of great service to me' (Nichols and Nichols 1817–58, iii: 690). Other tourists might use well-respected publishers' travel accounts such as Addison's *Remarks on Several Parts of Italy* (1705) to help direct them. Nevertheless, the expanding market for travel books encouraged the production of specialized guidebooks devoted to the Grand Tour (De Beer 1955). The earliest English guidebook to Italy was Andrew Boorde's *The Fyrst Boke of the Introduction of Knowledge* in 1542, but this was very sketchy. More directly useful books came in the seventeenth century with works such as Lassels's

The Voyage of Italy (1686) and Misson's *A New Voyage to Italy* 1691). In the eighteenth century the volume of guidebooks expanded enormously with the archetypal work being Thomas Nugent's multi-volume, *The Grand Tour* (1749) which ran into several editions. This book provided exhaustive lists of places to visit, what to see, where to stay as well as information on travel and transport conditions. Significant later works were Mariana Starke's *Letters from Italy* (1800) and *Travels on the Continent* (1820). One of Starke's claims to fame is that she anticipated the star-ratings of modern Michelin guidebooks by using exclamation marks to rank sights in order of interest. Altogether, the comprehensive volumes compiled for the needs of the Grand Tourists influenced the nineteenth-century works of Murray and Baedeker (Hinrichsen 1989) and were thus the antecedents of today's vast guidebook industry.

If these were the main forms of Grand Tour literature, what of their nature? At one level, they are a rich and unique source of material about tourism in an age where official statistics and other forms of evidence scarcely existed (Towner and Wall 1991). There is much invaluable detail on the basic aspects of the Tour: how long it lasted, where the visitors went, where they stayed and what routes they followed. The published accounts, in particular, have been quarried to provide the basis for many studies of the Grand Tour (Bates 1911; Hibbert 1969; Mead 1914; Trease 1967), although Black (1992) has looked more to the unpublished material. However, the more intimate connections between the tourists and the process of creating their literature deserve closer scrutiny. How authentic is this literature, not so much in terms of the basic outline provided, but in giving us an insight into the tourist experience itself? The authenticity of 'travellers' tales' is an issue that runs through the centuries (Adams 1962) and the Grand Tour is no exception. We can be concerned with matters of detail: who wrote the account of the tour? Is this what the tourist was really doing? Is the account plagiarized? Is it a fake? And we can question how far this literature enables us to penetrate the *mentalité* of the tourists. Is this what they were really thinking?

Manuscript diaries and journals seem to convey the immediacy of experience and attitude; the closest we will get to the tourist on a journey. But even this form of literature was subject to later revision and editing. John Evelyn kept a diary of his Grand Tour of 1643–7, which does not seem to have been intended for publication. However, it is clear that he incorporated material from many sources into his work. In the Netherlands, France and Italy he used J. H. von Pflaumern's *Mercurius Italicus* (1628) and John Raymond's *An Itinerary Contuyning a Voyage* (1649). Sections of material passed from one account to another, such that Raymond's work as used by Evelyn was, in turn, based on an earlier work by François Schott: *Itinerarió Italiae* (1600) (De Beer 1955). To make it an even more tangled web, Raymond seems to have copied from the manuscript journal of his uncle and tutor on his Grand Tour, John Bargrave (Sturdy and Henig no date). This wholesale lifting of material from both published and unpublished accounts can distort our view of the Grand Tour. An initial impression can be conveyed of diligent sightseers spending weeks and months touring everything and recording everything in great detail. The reality, if large sections of information were simply copied from elsewhere, may not have been quite like that.

Some Grand Tour diaries, however, were unedited and do seem to bring us closer to the tourist. Boswell's private papers remind us that this form of travel literature can show us a very different side to the institution (Pottle 1952–5). For instance, in Utrecht, Boswell outlines a serious course of study for the law, involving long hours of work. But rapidly this scheme is abandoned in favour of parties and receptions. 'After all', he notes in his journal, 'I am come abroad to see foreign manners as well as to study' (Pottle 1952, 1: 80). In Berlin, the court and art galleries were not the only way of occupying his time:

> About eight, in came a woman with a basket of chocolates to sell. I toyed with her and found she was with child. Oho! A safe piece, into my closet. 'Habs er ein Man?' 'Ja, in den Gards bei Potsdam'. To bed directly. In a minute-over, I rose cool and astonished, half-angry, half-laughing, I sent her off. Bless me, have I now committed adultery? Stay, a soldier's wife is not a wife. (Pottle 1953, quoted in Buzard 1993, 1: 31)

A judicious editing of travel literature was common if it was for wider circulation. Sometimes this editing merely confuses the chronology of a tour. Thus, Addison's *Remarks* has him leaving for Italy one year before he actually departed and then departing that country in 1703, when he had already reached Vienna (Batten 1978: 129). Smollett's *Travels Through France and Italy* (1766) on the other hand, appears to be a series of letters written during his Grand Tour, but some of it was compiled after his return to London (Smollett 1766: xviii).

Far more revealing, however, are the differences between the 'public' face of published Tour literature and the 'private' face of unpublished correspondence. Often these differences were the result of the strained relations between the tourist and the tutor. Tutors frequently wrote the published accounts of tours; their experience as university dons suited them for this harmless drudge, and they generally conveyed the impression of an educational visit with an intelligent and dutiful pupil. An age of patronage left them with little alternative. Edward Wright, for instance, published his *Some Observations made in Travelling through France, Italy, etc.* (1730) after a tour with Lord George Parker, son of the Lord Chancellor, Lord Macclesfield. Wright's worthy work of literature, however, makes no reference to the trouble created by Parker. The agitated correspondence of the British Envoy in Turin and Macclesfield is worth quoting at length as an example of the private travel literature of the Grand Tour:

Letter of the Hon. John Molesworth (Envoy at Turin), February or March 1722:

> [Lord Parker] has been at Trevi nearly two months with a woman of Venice, not very beautiful, but much beloved by him. He lavished so much upon her that he scandalised his servants, some of whom wished to leave him. Lord Parker is a small man. He meant to pass by here after having been to Genoa, but, on the evening of the 22nd last, he had come to a new decision, and the woman was to go back to Venice. However, on the morning of the 23rd, he ordered post horses for Verona, and went off with her, to the amazement of his people. The major-domo wrote to his father, who communicated with the English envoy, in order to have him stopped, in the event of his passing from Novi to Turin, and reply was made that he would be detained for two days. However, he did not come that way.

Letter from Lord Macclesfield to the Hon. John Molesworth, 29 March 1722:

> At present I see only one thing of use, and that to be absolutely necessary, that is to secure her till he be returned hither, either in a monastery, or where he may not know how to find her, and in so close and strict a manner that all commerce by message or letters, much more all interview, may be entirely prevented. To banish her would, in my opinion, be only to send him after her, or with her in some place where there might be less hold of him. To send him on board a ship would be attended with difficulty and noise, and, I doubt, of little advantage in the event; she might come to him, he might be landed wherever he should desire and, however, would be under no control at whatever port the ship should touch ... If he should come alone, there are such strong reasons for him not to bring her to Turin, though he shall not have finally parted with her, that I should hope that you would take rise from that you had heard to give him proper advice. And take care of securing her, wherever he is. (Historical Manuscripts Commission, 1913: 334–5)

Dr John Moore had similar problems with his pupil, the Duke of Hamilton. Moore's published account of the Tour, *A View of Society and Manners* (1781), was highly acclaimed and presented the usual picture of a diligent round of culture, society, etc. in the capitals of Europe. But Moore's private letters home to the Duke's mother is the better literature for studying the reality of this trip. In Geneva for instance, Moore's 'public' account outlines the nature of government and society and the city's 'charmingly variegated scenery'. A letter of 4 July 1772 to the mother, on the other hand, details Hamilton's passion for driving a cabriolet and falling in love, 'so much as to bring him into the habit of Rising in the morning' (Campbell 1910, 2: 340). In Berlin, Moore's book tells of meetings with Frederick the Great, military reviews and court society. The private correspondence reveals that:

> Our scheme was to move to Dresden and thence to Vienna about the beginning of July, but I suspect we shall not go so soon, for I understand that Madame la L is to be here about that time ... Some female planet always influences our Motions; at Present she is Queen of the Ascendant. (Campbell 1910, 2: 393)

The tourist/tutor relationship, could, therefore, generate forms of literature that go beyond the external representation of the Grand Tour. Another relationship which, it might be hoped, would throw further light on the reality of the institution is that between the tourist and his servants. It is disappointing, if not surprising, that few accounts of travels by Grand Tour servants have come down to us. Probably few were written in the first place and the survival rate for records by the less wealthy is rarely good. One or two accounts were published but they show all the discretion and deference we might expect. *Memoirs of an Eighteenth-Century Footman* (1927), outlines the life of John MacDonald who travelled on the Continent many times in that century. But it is a bland account of places seen and places stayed at with none of the revelations we would hope for. Similarly, Matthew Todd's (1968) account of his journeys with a Captain Barlow of Yorkshire from 1814 provides no real extra dimension to our understanding of the reality of travel. In fact, his journal largely imitates the views and expressions of any other conventional travel account.

As the itinerary of the Grand Tour was fairly standardized and as the views expressed in print at any one time rarely differed, so the publication of entirely fictitious accounts was fairly easy. Adams (1962: 11) has termed the eighteenth century 'an age of plagiarism', and it is clear that literacy hacks could boost their income from this trade. John Northall's *Travels through Italy* (1766) has been considered to be one of these (Batten 1978). On the other hand, the great demand for travel books had the effect of encouraging some talented writers, who had to earn their living, to undertake the Grand Tour and publish accounts of greater note. This trend became more pronounced from the second half of the eighteenth century and on into the nineteenth century. Thus we have writers such as Smollett (1766), Sterne (1768) and later Hazlitt (1826), gathering material for publication. Hazlitt's tour of the 1820s was recorded in letters to the *Morning Chronicle*. Travel literature was, therefore, increasingly becoming the domain of the professional writer and this feature continued after the Grand Tour had largely disappeared. Dickens' tour of Italy appeared in 1846 and Henry James was later to publish *A Little Tour of France* (1884). But travel accounts away from the well-worn paths of the Grand Tour were also in demand from the public and Robert Louis Stevenson's (1879) journey to the Cévennes, where he hired a donkey, reflected this trend. There was another critical difference, of course: in the Grand Tour era travel was the motive and literature stemmed from this. At a later period, literature was the motive and travel stemmed from this.

THE CLASSICS AND THE ROMANTICS

So far, we have considered the literature created *by* the Grand Tour but the tourists were also strongly influenced by other forms of writing. These helped shape their choice of destinations as well as the sentiments expressed when viewing people and places. Without doubt, the main literary influence on the tourists were the ancient classics of Rome. From the sixteenth century onwards, the classics were central to élite education and culture throughout Europe. Britain was geographically peripheral to the heart of this classical world and its revival in the Renaissance. Thus, travel to the lands from which their culture derived was essential for the wealthy to reaffirm their identity. Not only were classical sites visited but numerous references to classical literature suffused the travel accounts. Richard Lassels (1686) endorsed the widespread view that 'no man understand Livy and Caesar ... like him who hath made exactly the Grand Tour'. Addison had a copy of Horace with him on his journey and recalled that 'The greatest pleasure I took in my journey from Rome to Naples was in seeing the fields, towns and rivers that have been described by so many Classic Authors,' (Addison 1705: 115).

Indeed, the whole tenor of the Grand Tour until the second half of the eighteenth century, both in terms of its spatial patterns and the sentiments expressed, was essentially 'classical' (Towner 1985). And although this influence declined to some degree, it never disappeared. In the early nineteenth century, Eustace wrote a widely read *Classical Tour Through Italy* (1815). Although the style of writing had changed from the age of Lassels and Addison, he still advised that Virgil, Horace, Cicero and Livy should be the 'inseparable companions of all travellers' (Eustace 1815, 1: 4).

As the eighteenth century progressed, there was a notable increase in the number of travel accounts produced by women. This may partly reflect an increase in the number of women travellers to the Continent (Mains 1966; Meyer 1978). As to whether women produced different travel literature to men, this is unclear. Mains (1966: 11) asserts that 'women tended to see [nature] with the eye of reality, to look at objects for their own sake', in contrast to men, whose perceptions were clouded with literary and historical associations. But an extensive reading of travel literature hardly supports this view. Nevertheless, there may exist subtle differences which further textual analysis may help to reveal.

During the later eighteenth century other literary influences came to bear on the Grand Tourists as the Romantic era gathered momentum. A new interest was found in medieval history and this led eventually to new destinations being sought out and a re-evaluation of monuments that had previously been despised as 'gothic', (Towner 1985). Literary associations were also important and references to writers such as Dante and Petrarch began to creep into the travel accounts. Richard Duppa (1829) included Ravenna in his tour of Italy because of its links with Dante and he visited Vaucluse in France because of Petrarch. Furthermore, the Romantic era also created its own literary heroes and heroines and they rapidly became assimilated into the tourist's world. Pre-eminent among the literary heroes was Byron. His *Childe Harolde's Pilgrimage* (1812) or *The Prisoner of Chillon* (1816) could be found clutched in the hands of a new generation of visitors just as Horace and Livy had been a hundred years before. Places visited by Byron on his continental travels were marked by references in his poem and they rapidly became literary shrines (Buzard 1993; Dangerfield 1978). Other major literary influences included Rousseau's *La Nouvelle Heloïse* (1759), carried around by Byron and Shelly in Switzerland and Goethe's *Italienische Reise* (1786–8). These romantic works began to join the earlier classic texts and established, according to Churchill (1980: 4) 'a thick new layer of literary associations'. Across Europe Buzard (1993) views them as injecting new life into the Grand Tour; it certainly became fashionable for travel writers to drop in references to Byron or Rousseau in their works.

The previous sentence raises an important issue in the interpretation of travel literature. To what extent is it possible to deduce real sentiments from those which appear on the written page? How much is that written page a mask behind which we cannot see? To those who are confident that a relationship does exist between the written and the real emotion, the travel accounts do enable one to trace what tourists thought at any one time, and also to trace how sentiments changed from age to age. Thus, writers such as Brand (1957), Parks (1964) and Golden (1977) have used travel literature as reflections of changing tastes. Batten (1978), on the other hand, has stressed how the conventions of travel writing outshone any real expression of individual opinion.

The truth probably lies somewhere in between. A complex relationship existed between the writer and the reading public. Whilst much of the writing was conventional and simply reflected what was currently fashionable, it is unlikely that an author, at any one time, would record views and opinions which would not resonate with the audience. Thus, public perceptions were influenced by travel writers and they, in turn, influenced what those writers would choose to put in the books they wished to sell. But careful analysis of language is required. Parks (1964) points out that the second half of the eighteenth century developed a 'language of enthusiasm' which colours our understanding of how tourists reacted to scenery. The Romantic era was expressed through the vocabulary of the sublime and picturesque. When Addison was at Geneva at the beginning of the eighteenth century, he wrote of its 'wonderful variety of beautiful prospects' and he reflected on his tour of the lake: 'The greatest Entertainment we found in coasting it were the several prospects of woods, vineyards, meadows, and corn fields which lie on the borders of it' (Addison 1705: 258–60). Was his measured prose masking real joy and enthusiasm? Or, when Marianne Baillie saw paths in the mountains of Savoy in 1818 and longed 'to spring from the confinement of the carriage, and to explore their cold and exquisitely romantic terminations' (Baillie 1819: 106), was she merely replicating fashionable responses? Did she really want to leave the carriage?

Changing attitudes reflected in travel accounts were not just confined to landscapes. Black (1992) and Pine-Coffin (1974) detect a gradual shift in opinion towards a greater toleration of Roman Catholicism abroad by the British during the eighteenth century. People and their cultures were also appraised in new ways. It became popular, by the early nineteenth century, to visit simple 'peasant' societies in addition to the fashionable set. Lady Morgan (1821) wrote of those at Novi and Marianna Starke (1820) of those in Tuscany. Customs and costumes were described in a sentimental way. Mrs Graham (1820) journeyed to the east of Rome to give an account of the 'quiet, simple' people that lived there. But we can never be sure whether these writings reflect a genuine interest or just the fashion of the time. Even the most sophisticated textual analysis will not tease out genuine sensibilities.

THE LITERARY LEGACY OF THE GRAND TOUR

The Grand Tour as an important cultural institution was at its height in the eighteenth century, a period that saw developments in a number of forms of literature. Perhaps the most significant of these was the novel and links have been traced between the evolution of this literary form and travel (Adams 1983; Fussell 1965). Fussell points out that most writers of consequence in the eighteenth century: Defoe, Addison, Fielding, Smollett, Johnson and Sterne among others used travel as a theme in many of their works. Adams shows how certain literary devices, such as the letter form, came from travel literature. Furthermore, the whole structure of many eighteenth-century novels was built around travel. For instance Smollett's *Humphry Clinker* (1771), was itself, in part, a satire on travel literature. However, we have to distinguish between the undoubted influence of travel literature in general on the novel and that of the Grand Tour in particular. In the seventeenth century, some French fiction had heroes going to Italy and the Grand Tour is referred to in English works such as Eliza Haywood's *The Fortunate Foundlings* (1758). Laurence Sterne's *Tristram Shandy* (1759) and Smollett's *Peregrine Pickle* (1751) also have Grand Tour episodes. But in very few notable works does the Grand Tour take centre stage. Most famous of all is Sterne's *A Sentimental Journey* (1768). Yet, although this begins as an account of a tour by coach through France and Italy it quickly moves away into a world of dramatic sketches, philosophical musing and anecdotes.

The departure of *A Sentimental Journey* from a clear focus on the Grand Tour emphasizes an interesting literary paradox. The Grand Tour produced literature in great quantity but very little of any quality, in either fact or in fiction. The only real exceptions are probably Byron and Goethe. Great literary figures went on the Grand Tour in the eighteenth century, yet this experience did not inspire their greatest works. The sights, sounds and experiences of people and places might be expected to stimulate original and exciting works. When the travel theme did inspire good work it was travel at home which was used to greatest effect. Boswell's best travel account was his *Tour to the Hebrides* (1785) with Johnson. Smollett's *Humphry Clinker* is based on a tour of England; he used his material on France and Italy for an entertaining travel account but he did not use it in a more creative work. And, as we have noted above, by the nineteenth century, writers of talent were using travel as a device in the structure of their literature rather than providing accounts of travel *per se*. We can see this in Henry James' *The Portrait of a Lady* (1881). It tells us much about Americans and their friends moving around Europe but it is hardly a novel about a tour of Europe.

Why did the Grand Tour not inspire any great literature? Perhaps it was something to do with its very nature: a largely routine and predictable experience did not provoke imaginative and original thought. Dr Johnson suggests to Boswell that there was little new to say 'of countries so well known' and both found more fertile ground for original views in the Hebrides and Scotland (Boswell 1785; Johnson 1755). This uninspired situation for travel literature on Europe extended right into the nineteenth century. As Pemble (1988: 11) has noted, Tour accounts:

> continued to find publishers and, presumably, readers even when written by authors who revealed little except the poverty of their experience, the triteness of their thought, and the strength of their ability to inflate anecdotes into volumes by means of digression, quotation and tedious drollery.

It was only when writers of talent used travel as a device for exploring characters, relationships and thought that greater literature resulted. If the literary legacy of the Grand Tour has not been to bequeath us works of particular merit or genius, where is its influence still felt? It is in the more mundane field of the guidebook. The sheer volume of affluent travellers abroad created a market for practical guidebooks and a line of descent can be traced from the seventeenth-century works of Lassels and Misson, through Nugent in the eighteenth century, to Starke in the early nineteenth century, to Murray and Baedeker and thence onwards to the Insights, Michelins and Rough Guides today.

That the Grand Tour created little great literature can be illustrated by one final theme. Although the tourist industry in Europe has its modern versions of the Grand Tour in terms of the great cultural treasures of Rome, Venice, Florence, Paris and Vienna (Towner 1996), Grand Tour writers are not celebrated. If the marketing people could, there is no doubt they would make use of them. Robert Louis Stevenson's adventures in the Cévennes formed the basis for a themed trail by the early 1990s (*Independent*, 8th June 1991). Yet, how many visitors to the Leaning Tower of Pisa journey on to Leghorn to see Smollett's grave? How many tourists take Addison's *Remarks* to inspire them in Italy? Some may follow Byron's *Childe Harolde* and visit Lake Geneva with half-remembered lines from *The Prisoner of*

Chillon, but the great mass of Grand Tour literature does not inform tourism today. It is the visitors' Michelin, Insight or Rough Guide, advising them on what to see and how to see it, that focus the main connection between literature, tourism and the Grand Tour.

REFERENCES

Adams, P. G. (1962) *Travellers and Travel Liars*. Berkeley and Los Angeles: University of California Press.

Adams, P. G. (1983) *Travel Literature and the Evolution of the Novel*. Lexington: University of Kentucky Press.

Addison, J. (1705) *Remarks on Several Ports of Italy*. London.

Adler, J. (1989) 'Origins of sightseeing', *Annuals of Tourism Research*, **16**, 7–29.

Baillie, M. (1819) *First Impressions on a Tour of the Continent*. London.

Baker, P. R. (1964) *The Fortunate Pilgrim's Americans in Italy (1800–1860)*. Cambridge, Mass: Harvard University Press.

Bates, E. S. (1911) *Touring in 1600*. London: Constable.

Batten, C. L. (1978) *Pleasurable Instruction. Form and Convention in Eighteenth Century Travel Literature*. Berkeley: University of California Press.

Batts, J. S. (1976) *British Manuscript Diaries of the Nineteenth Century*. London: Centaur.

Black, J. (1992) *The British Abroad: The Grand Tour in the Eighteenth Century*. New York: St Martin's Press.

Boorde, A. (1542) *The Fyrste Boke of the Introduction of Knowledge*. London.

Boswell, J. (1768) *Account of Corsica, with a Journal of a Tour to that Island*. London.

Boswell, J. (1785) *The Journal of a Tour to the Hebrides*. London.

Boswell, J. (1791) *The Life of Samuel Johnson, LLD* (Everyman Edition, 1906, 2 vols. London: Dent).

Brand, C. P. (1957) *Italy and the English Romantics. The Italianate Fashion in Early Nineteenth Century England*. Cambridge: Cambridge University Press.

Broc, N. (1974) *La Geographie des Philosophes: Geographes et Voyageurs français en XVIII siècle*. Paris: Ophrys.

Buzard, J. (1993) *The Beaten Track: European Tourism, Literature and the Ways to Culture, 1800–1918*. Oxford: Clarendon Press.

Campbell, J. D. S. (1910) *Intimate Society Letters of the Eighteenth Century*, 2 vols. London: Stanley Road.

Churchill, K. (1980) *Italy and English Literature, 1764–1930*. London: Macmillan.

Cox, Edward Godfrey (1935–49) *A Reference Guide to the Literature of Travel including Voyages, Geographical Description, Adventures, Shipwrecks and Expeditions*. Seattle.

Curley, T. M. (1976) *Samuel Johnson and the Age of Travel*. Athens, Ga.: University of Georgia Press.

Dangerfield, E. (1978) *Byron and the Romantics in Switzerland, 1816*. London: Ascent.

De Beer, E. S. (1952) 'The development of the guidebook until the early nineteenth century', *Journal of the British Archaeological Society*, 3rd series **4**, 35–46.

De Beer, E. S. (1955) (ed.), *The Diary of John Evelyn*, vol. 2. Oxford: Clarendon Press.

Dent, K. (1974) 'The informal education of the landed classes in the eighteenth century, with particular reference to reading', unpublished doctoral dissertation, University of Birmingham.

Dickens, C. (1846) *Pictures from Italy*. London: Chapman and Hall.

Duppa, R. (1829) *Travels on the Continent*. London.

Eustace, J. C. (1815) *A Classical Tour Through Italy*, 4 vols. London.

Frantz, R. W. (1934) *The English Traveller and the Movement of Ideas, 1660–1732*. New York: Octagon.

Fussell, P. (1962) 'Patrick Brydone: the eighteenth century traveller as representative man', *Bulletin of the New York Public Library*, **66**, 349–63.

Fussell, P. (1965) *The Rhetorical World of Augustan Humanism*. Oxford: Clarendon Press.

Golden, M. (1977) 'Travel writing in the "Monthly Review" and "Critical Review", 1756–1775', *Papers on Language and Literature*, **13**, 213–23.

Harder, H. (1981) *Le Président de Brosses et le Voyage en Italie au dix-huitienne siècle*. Geneva: Slatkine.

Hazlitt, W. (1826) *Notes of Journey through France and Italy*. London.

Hibbert, C. (1969) *The Grand Tour*. London: Putnam.

Hinrichsen, U. (1989) *Baedeker-Katalog*. Holzminden: Verlag Ursula Hinrichsen.

Historical Manuscripts Commission (1913) *Various Collections*, VIII. London: Historical Manuscripts Commission.

Houghton, W. E. (1942) 'The English virtuoso in the seventeenth century', *Journal of the History of Ideas*, **3**, 51–73, 190–219.

Independent, (1991) 'Travel with Dr. Jekyll and Mr. Donkey-beater', 8 June.

James, H. (1881) *The Portrait of a Lady*. Republished Penguin books, Harmondsworth: Penguin.

Johnson, S. (1775) *Journey to the Western Isles of Scotland*. London.

Kaufman, P. (1960) *Borrowings from the Bristol Library 1773–1784*. Charlotsville: University of Virginia Press.

Lassels, R. (1686) *The Voyage of Italy*. London.

MacDonald, John (1927) *John MacDonald: Travels (1745–1779) Memoirs of an Eighteenth-Century Footman*. With an Introduction by John Beresford. London: Routledge.

Mains, J. A. (1966) 'British travellers in Switzerland with special reference to some women travellers between 1750–1850', unpublished doctoral dissertation, University of Edinburgh.

Matthews, W. (1950) *British Diaries: An Annotated Bibliography of British Diaries Written Between 1442–1942*. Cambridge: Cambridge University Press.

Mead, W. E. (1914) *The Grand Tour in the Eighteenth Century*. New York: Houghton Mifflin.

Meyer, P. J. B. (1978) 'No land too remote: women travellers in the Georgian age', unpublished doctoral dissertation, University of Massachusetts.

Misson, M. (1691) *A New Voyage to Italy*. London.

Moore, J. (1781) *A View of Society and Manners in Italy*. 3 vols, London.

Morgan, S. (1821) *Italy*, 3 vols, London.

Nichols, J. (1812–15) *Literary Anecdotes of the Eighteenth Century*, 9 vols, London.

Nichols, J. and Nichols, J. B. (1817–58) *Illustrations of the Literary History of the Eighteenth Century*, 8 vols, London.

Nugent, T. (1749), *The Grand Tour*. London.

Parks, G. B. (1964) 'The turn to the Romantic in the travel literature of the eighteenth century', *Modern Language Quarterly*, **25**, 22–33.

Pemble, J. (ed.) (1988) *The Mediterranean Passion*. Oxford: Oxford University Press.

Pflaumern, J.H. von (1628) *Mercurius Italicus*, Augsburg.

Pine-Coffin, R. S. (1974) *Bibliography of British and American Travel in Italy to 1860*. Florence: Biblioteca di Bibliografica Italiana, 76.

Pottle, F. A. (1952–5) (ed.) *Yale Edition of the Private Papers of James Boswell*, 3 vols. London: Heinemann.

Raymond, J. (1649) *A Itinerary Contayning a Voyage*. London: Printed for Humphrey Moseley.

Schudt, L. (1959) *Italienreisen im 17. und 18. Jahrhundert*. Vienna: Schroll-Verlag.

Smollett, T. (1766) *Travels Through France and Italy*, republished Oxford: Oxford University Press 1981.

Smollett, T. (1771) *Humphry Clinker*, London.

Starke, M. (1800) *Letters from Italy*, London.

Starke, M. (1820) *Travels on the Continent*, London.

Sterne, L. (1768) *A Sentimental Journey*, London.

Stevenson, R. L. (1879) *Travels with a Donkey in the Cévennes*, London.

Sturdy, D. and Henig, M. (nd) *The Gentle Traveller, John Bargrave, Canon of Canterbury*. Abingdon: Abbey Press.

Todd, M. (1968) *Matthew Todd's Journal*, ed. G. Trease. London: Heinemann.

Towner, J. (1984) 'The European Grand Tour (1550–1840): a study of its role in the history of tourism', unpublished doctoral dissertation, University of Birmingham.

Towner, J. (1985) 'The Grand Tour: a key phase in the history of tourism', *Annuals of Tourism Research*, **12**(3), 297–333.

Towner, J. (1996) *An Historical Geography of Recreation and Tourism in the Western World 1540–1940*. Chichester: John Wiley.

Towner, J. and Wall, G. (1991) 'History and tourism', *Annals of Tourism Research*, **18**(1), 71–84.

Trease, G. (1967) *The Grand Tour*. London: Heinemann.

Wright, E. (1730) *Some Observations made in Travelling through France, Italy, etc.*, London.

Chapter 12

La Serenissima: Dreams, Love and Death in Venice

Graham M. S. Dann

INTRODUCTION

If all the world's most famous places were to compete on the simple basis of their ability to attract equally celebrated visitors from abroad, Venice would undoubtedly be among the top ten most desirable destinations. However, were the contest to be limited solely to foreign patrons with a literary flair, *La Serenissima*, as this former Adriatic kingdom, borrowing its title from Roman emperors (Ambros 1993: 15), has been so endearingly called, would probably emerge as outright winner. Even excluding such high-culture notables as Turner and Wagner, or statesmen of the calibre of Napoleon and Disraeli, this north-eastern Italian city has been associated with a whole galaxy of distinguished novelists, poets, letter writers, dramatists and composers of travellers' tales. This list of well-known overseas names reads something like a *Who's Who* and contains such eminent authors as Addison, Browning, Byron, Coleridge, Coryat, de Brosse, Dickens, Emerson, Erasmus, Gibbon, Goethe, James, Maupassant, Montesquieu, Nietzche, Rousseau, Ruskin, Shelley, Stendhal, Voltaire and Wordsworth. The roll call is even more impressive if sons of the soil and domestic literary luminaries are added, for then it is possible to include the likes of Calvino, Dante, d'Annunzio, Goldoni, Gozzi, Machiavelli, Palazzeschi, Pasinetti and Toddi, as well as the notorious Casanova.

This chapter attempts to demonstrate that Venice owes a great deal of its current touristic success to the ways in which it has been textually crafted in the past and continued in the twentieth-century works of writers such as Alfred Andersch, Dorothy Carrington, G. K. Chesterton, Daphne du Maurier, Lawrence Durrell, Hans Habe, L. P. Hartley, Ernest Hemingway, Patricia Highsmith, Erica Jong, D. H. Lawrence, Thomas Mann, Mary McCarthy, Jan (James) Morris, Eric Newby, Marcel Proust, Cecil Roberts, Henri Pierre Roche, Mark Twain, Bernard Vesper, Hugo von Hofmannsthal and Evelyn Waugh. More recent forms of promotional communication, such as travelogues, documentaries, television holiday programmes, tour guides, videos and films, have tended to construct their commentaries and scripts around this substantial literary tradition, so much so that phrase has come to mould gaze, both to anticipate and frame it (cf. Dunn 1998).

Although this veritable mountain of material is difficult to classify due to its complex variety of genres, periodization and sheer abundance, nevertheless three common motifs can be inductively detected – those of dreams, love and death in Venice. Taking each meta-theme (Fjellman 1992: 261) in turn, and after providing examples of their separate treatment, it will be shown how these universals are fundamental to an understanding of tourism itself. In such a manner, the literary account of yesteryear can become the lure piece of today.

DREAMS

I have, many and many a time, thought, since, of this strange Dream upon the water: half-wondering if it lie there yet, and if its name be VENICE.

(Dickens 1989: 127)

In Charles Dickens' *Pictures from Italy*, an account which is actually based on two whirlwind tours commencing from his temporary home in the Palazzo Peschiere in Genoa in November 1844 and from January to April 1845, the chapter on Venice is the only one which does not bear the name of a city in its title. Instead, Venice is referred to as 'An Italian Dream'. Part of the explanation for this lack of designation may be found in Dickens' admission that he had been travelling for so long in his horse-drawn carriage that 'the rapid and unbroken succession of novelties that had passed before me came back like half-formed dreams' (118). In other words, he wished to convey the idea that travel itself is dream-like since it forms a series of impressions that perform 'a jumble in my brain' (119).

However, the main reason why Venice is singled out for such oneiric description, when equally any other Italian city visited by the author could be subject to similar sensory overload, is due more to Venice's unique qualities. For instance, when Dickens arrives by boat, the city appears to him like 'a cluster of tapers' (119). The vessel approaches 'by a dreamy kind of track … gliding up … a phantom street' (119). On being installed in a large canal-side mansion, and having slept the night there, he awakens and experiences 'the glory of the day that broke upon me in this Dream' (120) and 'sparkles of the sun in water', (120) 'great ships lying near at hand in stately indolence; on islands crowned with gorgeous domes and turrets' (121). Cloisters and galleries are described as 'the work of fairy hands' (121), the cathedral as 'gorgeous in the wild luxuriant fancies of the East' (121), the whole scene as 'enchanted' (121).

On entering what is clearly St Mark's, he refers to its 'grand and dreamy structure' (122), of its being 'unreal' and 'fantastic' (122). He thinks he wanders; he dreams that he is led on (122). Water fills this dream of his (123). He speaks of the 'luxurious wonder of so rare a dream' (125) and confesses that:

I stood there in my dream – and looked along the ripple, to the setting sun: before me, in the sky and on the deep, a crimson flush; and behind me the whole city resolving into streaks of red and purple, on the water. (125)

He alludes to 'the errant fancy' of his dream (126), and later that he 'fancied that the great piazza of the Winged Lion was a blaze of cheerful light' (126). Finally, Dickens awakens, though not until his next destination – the old market-place of Verona – and wonders about his strange dream and whether it indeed refers to Venice (127).

Proust is another well-known writer who casts Venice in a dreamlike mould. In his greatest work – *À la Récherche du Temps Perdu* – Proust (1954), through his hero Marcel (by more than mere coincidence, his own forename), depicts Venice as the culmination of a voyage of self-discovery, one that has been fantasized from his early childhood dreams of rural France (see Collier 1989). For Marcel, Venice is the ultimate cultural experience. Its art and architecture provide the subjective structure of meaning, which the text translates into the narrative of a dream. The mind can hence explore its own circular consciousness via a *mise en abyme*, the representation in miniature of images embedded in larger structures.

Venice is phantasm rather than fact. It is a fantasized 'topos' in which images and sensations interface through different layers of time, switching back and forth between today and yesteryear. For instance, Carpaccio's paintings, (particularly the *Sogno di Santa Orsola*), are seen as creations of the self-reflexive dreamer. So, too, are the depicted spires, cupolas and palaces of Venice, which emerge from the hazy sunlight as a realization of dreams, as indeed do the mosaics which represent a kaleidoscope of experiences in which metaphor exchanges place with reality. Thus his imaginary home town of Combray is in Venice and Venice is in Combray. The two are intertwined in Marcel's Arabian nights, where he envisages himself as being led by a genie through the maze of an oriental city. Even St Mark's dissolves into fantasy when Marcel, accompanied by his mother, sails into the baptistery of its ship-like structure. The font, the mosaics, his mother and her shawl, the water, the canals, the candle at the foot of his bed, the church at Combray and St Ursula herself are all merging and flickering elements of his time-transcendent dream. However, in the basilica, the dream can quickly turn to nightmare as beauty becomes tinged with fear, when dragons, serpents and ravenous beasts of prey are encountered alongside graceful birds that drink from running fountains and feed from vases of crystal.

The little dark alleys ('calli'), too, which constitute a mysterious labyrinth wherein Marcel is often terrifyingly lost, break into spatial relief when they open on to the vast, moonlit and magical 'piazza' of St Mark's. That unfolding is also part of the recurring dream-nightmare. However, typically, and in the light of day, when the hero once more returns to the nocturnal scene, he recognizes that he has confused the recollection of his dream with the memory of reality, without appreciating that existence itself may be considered as a subjective projection secreted by the unconscious.

This sense of *déjà vu*, the quintessential blend of strangeness and familiarity is quite evident when Marcel relatedly acknowledges:

One of my dreams was the synthesis of what my imagination had often sought to depict, in my waking hours, of a certain seagirt place and its medieval past. In my sleep I saw a Gothic city rising from a sea whose waves were stilled as in a stained-glass window. This dream in which nature had learned from art, in which the sea had turned Gothic, this dream in which I longed to attain, in which I believed that I was attaining the impossible, was one that I felt I had often dreamed before.

(in Collier 1989: 68)

Interestingly, Proust refers to two authorities in his narrative – Dante and Freud – both of whom set great store by dreams. In the opening canto of his *Inferno* (I, 10–12), for example, Dante writes:

> I cannot tell exactly how I got there,
> I was so full of sleep at that point of my journey
> When, somehow I left the proper way.

(Alighieri 1981: 47)

By way of elaboration, Dante later explains (Inferno XXX, 136–8) that the dreamer, particularly when confronted by harmful (false) situations, wishes that he were only experiencing a dream. He longs for that which is, as if it were not (Alighieri 1981: 176).

Freud is introduced to illustrate the process of waking consciousness, and how it is transformed into reverie by 'dream work'. This situation is evident when Proust transposes light into sound, in writing, for example:

> In later years, in Venice, long after the sun had set, when it seemed to be quite dark, I have seen, thanks to the echo, itself imperceptible, of a last note of light held indefinitely on the surface of the canals as though by the effect of some optical pedal, the reflections of the palaces unfolding as though for ever and ever in a darker velvet on the crepuscular greyness of the water.

(in Collier 1989: 66)

Freud, appropriately enough, also has a dream in Venice. In his *Interpretation of Dreams*, he imagines that he is with his wife looking out across the (blue) lagoon, when he espies a battleship. He confesses to being afraid. She cries out 'Here comes the English warship' and his fear evaporates with the realization that English ships are expected to be given a ceremonial reception (in Bull 1980: 185–6).

Other authors, too, refer to Venice in terms of dreams. William Beckford (1760–1844), for example, a wealthy, if eccentric, artist and romantic writer, speaks of 'a city fading away into a vaporous dream-like existence' (in Carrington 1947: 60). Commentator, Bull (1980: 125), relatedly notes that 'frequently the city floats free of time altogether in the observer's imagination and its vision is recalled as a dream'. In this regard, there is Byron (1989: 407), who, in his preface to the tragedy of *Doje Marino Faliero* writes, 'Everything about Venice is, or was, extraordinary – her aspect is like a dream, and her history is like a romance,' and Samuel Rogers (1842), who, in his *Italy*, relates:

> The path lies o'er the sea
> Invisible; and from the land we went,
> As to a floating city – steering in,
> And gliding up her streets as in a dream.

(in Bull 1980: 125)

and in his journal records, 'St Mark's Place a dream' (in Hibbert 1988: 200).

According to Bull (1980: 126), a dream is a metaphor which helps writers 'convey the unreality of contemporary Venice, conquered and corrupt, compared with the full-blooded substance of the Venetian past'. Thus, Disraeli, in his novel *Contarini Fleming* has the heroine Alceste tell her cousin, 'But the life of a Venetian is like a dream, and you must pass your days like a ghost gliding about a city fading in a vision' (in Bull 1980: 126). Mark Twain (1967: 153, 141), too, refers to Venice as 'old' and 'dreaming', as 'drowsing in a golden mist of sunset'. For him:

> We have been in a half waking sort of dream all the time. I do not know how else to describe the feeling. A part of our being has remained still in the nineteenth century, while another part of it has seemed in some unaccountable way walking among the phantoms of the tenth. (Twain 1967: 156)

Finally, Twain (1967: 160) sums up his visit as follows, 'And so, having satisfied ourselves, we depart tomorrow and leave the venerable Queen of the Republics to summon her vanquished ships, and marshal her shadowy armies, and know again in dreams the pride of her old renown.'

At around the same time, fellow countryman and novelist, William Dean Howells, in his two-volume *Venetian Life*, refers to Venice as 'a city almost in a trance', 'a city full of ghosts or marionettes' (in Bull 1980: 152), while Henry James, in a letter to Katherine de Kay Bronson, states that his stay has taken on the 'semblance of a beautiful dream' (in Bull 1980: 154). A similar sentiment is echoed by Rawdon Lubbock Brown, friend of Effie Ruskin and editor of the *Despatches of the Venetian Ambassador to London*, who, after a sixteen-year sojourn in the city, admits:

> I never wake in the morning but I thank God that he has let me spend my days in Venice ... Sometimes of an evening, when I go to the piazzetta, I am afraid to shut my eyes lest when I open them I should find that it had all been a dream. (in Hibbert 1988: 269)

Sometimes it is a particular experience of Venice that evokes the dream metaphor. Thus, for example, J. W. Cross (husband of George Eliot), when reflecting on his honeymoon and spending lazy days in a gondola, speaks of their constituting 'a delicious dreamy existence' (in Hibbert 1988: 292). James Morris, too, in his well-known description of the reburial of former Patriarch, Pope Pius X, states, 'Then came the dream like barges of the Venetian tradition, their crews in medieval liveries, silver or blue castles at their prows and sterns, heavy draperies trailing in the water behind' (in Hibbert 1988: 322).

However, it is Thomas Mann (1912 (1968)) who, perhaps more than any other writer, captures the oneiric imagery of Venice. Although his novella, *Death in Venice*, clearly refers to the last of the three inductive themes treated here, there is also a great deal in the work that relates to dreams. Those familiar with the story will recall that it features one Gustave von Aschenbach, a widowed poet and aspiring biographer chronicling the life of Frederick the Great. The account opens with Gustave deliberating in a Munich cemetery as to whether he should take a well-earned holiday or retire instead to his country home to press on with the book. For him, travel is like a dream, and so he decides to journey to Venice via Trieste and the

Adriatic resort island of Pula ('And he thought of the melancholy and susceptible poet who had once seen the towers and turrets of his dreams rise out of the waves' (23)). He eventually arrives in 'this most impossible of cities' (24) and repairs to an hotel on the Lido. Here he comes across a Polish family comprising a governess and a mother with two daughters and a son, Tadzio (the latter soon to become the object of his erotic desires). Even after their first encounter, Gustave 'came at length to the conclusion that what seemed to him fresh and happy thoughts were like the flattering inventions of a dream, which the waking sense proves worthless and insubstantial' (33). Thus, he 'went to bed betimes, and passed the night in deep, unbroken sleep, visited, however, by varied and lively dreams' (33). Dreams and dreaming, however, are not confined to the night. On the beach, Gustave gazes out 'dreamily over the blue of the southern sea' (47–8), while Tadzio is 'day dreaming away into blue space' (50), ('He whose preoccupation is with excellence longs fervently to find rest in perfection; and is not nothingness a form of perfection? As he [Gustave] sat dreaming thus ... ' (36)). As the tale develops, Gustave's philosophizing quickly turns to lust. He dreams of an orgy. He visits a barber in order to make himself look younger, leaving 'as in a dream' (78) ('While the rouged and flabby mouth uttered single words of the sentences shaped in his disordered brain by the fantastic logic that governs our dreams' (80)). Gustave relentlessly pursues the object of his salacious desire through Venetian alleyways, in gondolas and back to the beach, driven ever more demented in the process. Later he succumbs to an outbreak of cholera and dies with his passion still unconsummated, the whole saga being a feverish mixture of fantasy and reality.

Reed (1994: cover), in commenting on *Death in Venice*, claims that both Mann and Proust use that city to work through their own identities. The former's concern with 'art and decadence, symbolism and mythology' allows him to discover 'the possibilities and perils of the imaginative life'. For him, 'the flattering and suspect beauty' of Venice is 'half fairy tale, half tourist trap' (60). Although it becomes a fatal and literal snare for Gustave (61), due to its commercial and erotic self-interest (64), the dream-like mixture of realism and symbolism is always present. Certainly, there is the fact of disease, but there are also at the same time its legendary origins on a primitive Indian island inhabited by tigers (64). Homophilia of the present is additionally linked to a mythic past through Gustave's dreams of the orgiastic cult of Dionysus (64–5) and the 'strange dream logic' that incorporates Platonic dialogue (67).

Finally, strangers play an important role in the story. There is a foreigner in the cemetery at the beginning and another on the ferry. The singer at the hotel show also turns out to be an alien, as indeed are the Polish family and Tadzio outsiders to the scene. Dreams, too, it should be noted, are replete with strangers, ephemeral characters who represent real acquaintances.

LOVE

Venice has always been treated in predominantly feminine terms. Back in 1608, Thomas Coryat, for instance, speaks of her as 'a maiden city ... with her virginity untouched' and the 'fairest lady, yea the richest Paragon and Queen of Christendome' (in Bull 1980: 58). Similarly, James Howell, in 1618, refers to Venice as a beauteous maid: 'some have courted her, some bribed her, some would have forced her, yet she hath still preserved her chastity entire' (in Bull 1980: 64–5), and Robert Gray, Vicar of Farringdon, romantically describes her in 1792 as 'the mother of love, gilded by the rays of an evening sun as arising from the waves' (in Carrington 1947: 46).

However, in 1670, Richard Lassels, tutor to the English travelling nobility, departs from this tradition of female innocence. In his *Voyage of Italy*, he declares that 'mother nature hath indulged her even to wantonness' (in Carrington 1947: 42). Later, he speaks of his compatriots' travelling to Venice and spending a whole month 'only to lie with an impudent woman' (in Carrington 1947: 48). John Ruskin, too, in *The Stones of Venice* (1851–3 (1985)), suggests that the city may be less madonna and more whore when he refers to 'four centuries of voluptuous decay' and to Venice as being 'a scene of indolent pleasure' (in Carrington 1947: 70). Likewise, Henry James, describes Venice as a lover full of favours and of possessing her as being an erotic experience – 'you desire to embrace it, to caress it, to possess it' (in Hibbert 1988: 295). Clearly, also, he is talking about a more mature woman, when he states in his *Italian Hours*: 'Dear old Venice has lost her complexion, her figure, her reputation, her self-respect; and yet, with it all, has so puzzlingly not lost a shred of her distinction' (in Bull 1980: 154). Mark Twain (1967: 141–2) continues this imagery when he refers to Venice as the 'widowed bride of the Adriatic ... fallen prey to poverty, neglect and melancholy decay', and Gabriele d'Annunzio echoes this sentiment in *Il Fuoco* when he describes the city as a voluptuous older woman and a terrible temptress (in Bull 1980: 160).

Of these two versions of Venice – innocent maid and licentious harlot – it is the latter which tends to prevail. The essayist, Joseph Addison (1672–1719), for example, observes that in Venice nothing flourishes except pleasure. There is 'something more intriguing in the amours of Venice than those of other countries'. The custom of masquerading provides the opportunities for such adventure. After all, he notes, even the nuns have lovers (in Carrington 1947: 52). Similarly, Lady Mary Wortley Montagu, in her 1739 letter to Lady Pomfret, highlights Venice as a 'centre of pleasure' (in Bull 1980: 104), and Ruskin as a 'scene of indolent pleasure ... a museum of renaissance achievement and renaissance vice' (in Carrington 1947: 70).

'Lady' Anne Miller (1741–81), in her *Letters from Italy*, is a self-confessed, self-titled socialite looking for fun. She speaks of Venetian paintings as providing such delight. She refers to the wedding of a Doge's son and of the bride whose 'bosom was quite bare'. She talks about the Venetians' spending night after night gambling in their little houses – 'casini' (in Carrington 1947: 55). Indeed, Carrington (1947: 59) sums up the likes of Lady Miller when she writes, 'the pursuit of pleasure could be extended, without fear of mockery, right through old age until the grave'.

Goethe (1970) reaches Venice in the autumn of 1786 and attends a ballet. Although the performance itself is booed, his attention is focused rather on the young ladies watching from the balconies who 'considered it their duty to acquaint the audience with every beautiful part of their bodies' (in Bull 1980: 112).

The courtesans of Venice, (which Coryat in the seventeenth century estimates are about 20,000 in number (Hibbert 1988: 180), are in reality, according to Byron, no different from the rest of the female population. As he relates to his biographer, the Irish poet Thomas Moore, 'A lady with one lover is not reckoned to have over-stepped the modesty of marriage – that being a regular thing. Some have two, three and so on to twenty' (in Hibbert 1988: 201).

Venetian men are considered to be no less amorous than the women. According to Coryat, in relation to the gentlemen in their gowns of black cloth in the style of a toga, 'I believe with many that have "prurientem libidinem", they would minister a great incentive and fomentation of luxurious desires' (in Bull 1980: 63). There are also mountebanks in the 'Piazza San Marco' with their 'soveraigne waters and amorous songs' (in Hibbert 1988: 133). As for the gondoliers, they are described as 'venal', 'dishonest' and 'licentious' by Frederick Rolfe (1934 (1986)) in *The Desire and Pursuit of the Whole* (in Carrington 1947: 72). According to Coryat, they place a black cloth over their gondolas so that it is like a tunnel in which their occupants can make love (Hibbert 1988: 134). As Samuel Rogers notes in his journal, the gondola, 'is a conveyance refined and improved upon by the experience and study of the most sensual and luxurious people for many ages' (in Hibbert 1988: 200). Then there are the monks, whom Voltaire observes openly strolling with their pretty girlfriends across St Mark's Square (Bull 1980: 110). Thus, 'everywhere', as Mark Twain (1967: 143) relates, there is a hush, 'a stealthy sort of stillness ... suggestive of recent enterprises of bravos and lovers'.

Naturally, some of this erotic ambience both attracts and rubs off on some of its literary patrons. Rousseau, for example, refers to the amorous trembling that he experiences when he meets some female choristers from the 'scuole' and hears them singing through a church grille. Venice is not the kind of town, he admits, where men abstain from women (Bull 1980: 109). Similarly, Montesquieu in 1728 notes that liberty has turned to licence where men visit working-class girls even in broad daylight (Bull 1980: 84), as does Proust on his second visit to the city (on this occasion, significantly, unaccompanied by his mother) (Bull 1980: 168). Venice is the place where George Sand has an affair with Alfred de Musset in the Hotel Danieli (Bull 1980: 153), as also with the latter's doctor, Pietro Pagello (Hibbert 1988: 298), and where Gabriele d'Annunzio enjoys a liaison with Eleonara Duse (Bull 1980: 160). Venice, too, is the location for George Eliot's honeymoon and where Browning falls in love with Mrs Bronson and her daughter Edid (Hibbert 1988: 292).

In 1816, Byron escapes to Venice from England, thereby eluding the clutches of his mistress Claire Clairmont, the mother of his illegitimate child Clara Allegra, and the scandal of an alleged relationship with his half-sister, Augusta Leigh (Newby 1986: 146). Once settled in 1817, he seduces Marianna Segati, (the spouse of the draper whose apartments he is renting), Margarita Cogni (the baker's wife), 19 year-old Teresa Guiccoli, and countless other women whom he meets at masques and sub-sequently installs in the 'Palazzo Mocenigo' (Bull 1980: 175; Hibbert 1988: 201–15). No small wonder that Shelley, who brings Claire Clairmont (actually Mary Shelley's step sister) to visit Byron in Venice in 1818, reproaches his friend for allowing Venetian parents to bargain with him for their daughters and for their unspeakable practices (Hibbert 1988: 211). Of course, all these exploits pale into insignificance when compared to those of that son of the soil, the legendary Casanova, who refers to the seductions of masked ladies who appear at the 'Erberia' after a night of debauchery (Bull 1980: 92–6), as well as to nuns who engage in serial affairs (Hibbert 1988: 181). Summing up his own feelings, he candidly admits, 'the chief business of my life has always been to indulge my senses; I never knew anything of greater importance' (in Bull 1980: 92).

Venice as a romantic city is also the setting of many fictional accounts of heterosexual love. Shakespeare's (1989) *The Merchant of Venice*, for instance, not only features Portia's admirers, but there is additionally the attachment of Lorenzo and Jessica ('That in a gondola were seen together Lorenzo and his amorous Jessica').

In Proust's (1954) *À La Récherche du Temps Perdu*, Marcel's mistress, Albertine, is a central figure, even though she is obliged to remain behind in Combray. Marcel's experiences in Venice constantly evoke memories of Albertine. At one point she becomes so idolized that she is compared to Mary Magdalene in a Carpaccio painting and to an angel on the 'campanile' of St Mark's (Collier 1989: 9, 23). Marcel imaginatively drapes her in Fortuny gowns which conjure up the palaces of Venice (Collier 1989: 3). The eagle 'motif' in the church of 'San Giorgio degli Schiavoni' is another reminder of her presence since it is the same design as that of her ring (Collier 1989: 7). When Albertine dies, and her image seemingly evaporates from Marcel's memory, the hero now feels free to chase local girls, many of whom are of roughly the same age as Albertine when she and Marcel first met. One such youngster is a Venetian glass-maker. Marcel wishes to take her back to Paris as if she were a painting by Titian. There she can be a mirror reflecting his desire for Albertine who, in turn, mirrors Titian's *Belle aux Deux Miroirs* in the Louvre (Collier 1989: 31–3).

Finally, Venice is associated with a number of well-known gay relationships. William Beckford, for example, is at the age of twenty dispatched abroad on account of his involvement with young boys at home (Hibbert 1988: 157–8). Then there is Frederick William Rolfe (aka. Baron Corvo) whose major (1934 (1986)) work is replete with libellous stories. As a practising homosexual (Bull 1980: 165), he is frequently found in the company of John Addington Symmonds and Horatio Brown, the former widely acknowledged to be having an open affair with a gondolier named Angelo Fustato (Hibbert 1988: 298–300).

Of course, the literary offering *par excellence* which explores such homophilia to the fullest is *Death in Venice*. Here, the writer, von Aschenbach, passionately pursues Tadzio. In a heady mixture of mythology and fantasy, the young Polish boy is depicted as a latter-day Phaeacian, as relaxed and carefree as a character in Homer's *Odyssey* (Sowerby 1986), as a delicate creature who never grows old (Reed 1994: 46–7). On one occasion, he is transformed into the youth Hyacinthus, the object of the jealous desire of two deities, while on another he is revealed as Narcissus with a beguiling smile (Reed 1994: 57–8). In many ways, the figure of Gustave stands for Thomas Mann himself since he represents the kind of author Mann wishes to become (Reed 1994: 8). More saliently, however, Gustave's experiences relate back to Mann's own attachment to the painter Paul Ehrenberg prior to his marriage in 1905 (Reed 1994: 81). Hence, it comes as no surprise to learn from this author that love between men is somehow more romantic than the heterosexual version. Not only does the former exclude any procreative function, but there is consequently room for a more elevated spiritual begetting. As is evident from Socrates' conversation with Phaedrus, the lover looks beyond the individual to the reality from which beauty is borrowed. 'The true lover loves intensely, but always symbolically' (in Reed 1994: 54).

DEATH

From love to death is but a brief mental transition, and the link between the two states is quite evident in many literary accounts of Venice. In Proust, for example, the connection is metaphorically achieved via the previously mentioned Fortuny gowns which adorn Marcel's beloved Albertine. Each dress has a phoenix or peacock motif, and the movement of the birds triggers an association between sexuality and death. The stiffness of the material, too, suggests a certain phallic 'rigor mortis', the peacock's plumed tail calls to mind the church of childhood at Combray, while the phoenix symbolizes the resurrection of the body as it arises anew from the ashes (Collier 1989: 7, 85, 91).

Just as the author, Proust, uses Venice to work through his own identity, so also does Thomas Mann. To this end, the latter similarly employs the love/death relationship. For Gustave von Aschenbach, (as indeed for his creator), love and death respectively represent passion and control, creativity and morality. Thus, travel to Venice is regarded as a mandatory escape from a literary impasse in which 'destination' becomes one with 'destiny'. In this sense a 'vacation (is) a necessary passage to death at an appointed place' (Reed 1994: 11; cf. 10, 42).

Ernest Hemingway (1950), too, creates an association between love and death in his *Across the River and into the Trees*. The story is of a Colonel Richard Cantwell of the US infantry who returns to Venice after the Second World War. He stays at the 'Gritti' where he knows all the staff (particularly the *maître d'* with whom he reminisces), and returns to his favourite haunts, including 'Harry's'. The tale speaks of his affair with the youthful and titled Renata whom he calls 'daughter'. In one of the Colonel's many intimate conversations with Renata, inevitably the subject of his wife comes up, and the following dialogue ensues:

> ' ... Besides the wench is dead.'
> 'Is she really dead ?'
> 'Deader than Phoebus the Phoenician. But she doesn't know it yet.'
> 'What would you do if we were together in the Piazza and you saw her?'
> 'I'd look straight through her to show how dead she was.' (165).

However, the contrast is more fully established shortly afterwards when Cantwell is embracing Renata and the author relatedly observes, 'he only thought of her and how she felt and how close life comes to death when there is ecstasy' (169).

More often than not though, Venice, together with its inhabitants and their customs, is spoken of in terms which solely refer to death. As a *place*, Venice is often regarded as a dismal spot. William Dean Howells, for instance, refers to it in winter as 'the gloomiest place on earth', a 'constant witness to life and death' (in Bull 1980: 152), while Henry James remarks, 'Venetian Life in the large old sense, has long since come to an end, and the essential present character of the most melancholy of cities resides simply in its being the most beautiful of tombs' (in Bull 1980: 154). Similarly, in 1867, Mark Twain (1967: 151) complains about 'the silence, the mildew, the stagnant waters, the clinging weeds, the deserted houses, and the general lifelessness of the place', and Ralph Waldo Emerson about the bilge-water and desolation (Bull 1980: 146). Ruskin, too, though admittedly returning after the death of the woman with whom he had fallen in love, confides to a friend that 'coming back here makes me unspeakably sad' (in Hibbert 1988: 287), a sentiment echoed by Evelyn Waugh who describes the city as 'sinking, shadowed and sad' (in Bull 1980: 155), and Robert Browning (no date: 603, stanza XII) who refers to the place as 'dust and ashes, dead and done with'. Jan Morris (1988: 99), also, is despondent on her return and at the missing sight of the two familiar horses outside the basilica. As she relates, 'The autumn tourists stared at that anguished façade ... Venice was failing before their eyes, and they were only just in time.'

However, it is perhaps Dickens (1989) who, more than most, conjures up the bleakness of Venice. In his *Pictures from Italy*, and more specifically in his *Dream*, he speaks of advancing into 'this ghostly city ... with dark mysterious doors', of 'figures coming down a gloomy archway ... and everywhere the same extraordinary silence' (120). As he happens upon the Bridge of Sighs 'in the distempered horror of my sleep' (120), he sees the Council room where prisoners were taken for interrogation and the door through which condemned prisoners passed for ever, and, in the seeing, confesses 'my heart appeared to die within me' (120). He descends into the prison with its 'dismal, awful, horrible stone cells', where 'no man remained for more than twenty-four hours; being marked for dead before he entered it' (123). In the armoury he encounters a case 'full of accursed instruments of torture' (124), and he enters apartments where 'the furniture, half awful, half grotesque, was mouldering away' (125). No small wonder that he describes his *Dream* as 'monstrous' (124).

Later, Dickens (1973) locates one of his novels in Venice. In *Little Dorrit* (first published in 1857), William Dorrit's family arrives in Venice and repairs to a palace on the Grand Canal. The following passage is provided as a first impression:

> In this crowning unreality, where all the streets were paved with water, and where the deathlike stillness of the days and nights was broken by no sound but the softened ringing of church bells, the rippling of the current, and the cry of gondoliers turning the corners of the flowing streets, Little Dorrit, quite lost by her task being done, sat down to muse. (519)

Soon the story begins to draw on reflections from *Pictures of Italy*. In its references to the Bridge of Sighs and the state prison, for instance, one reads that:

> It was quite a walk, by mysterious staircases and corridors, from Mrs General's apartment – hoodwinked by a narrow side street with a low gloomy bridge in it, and dungeon-like opposite tenements, their walls besmeared with a thousand downward stains and streaks, as if every crazy aperture in them had been weeping tears of rust into the Adriatic for centuries – to Mr Dorrit's apartment. (525)

However, where *Little Dorrit* differs significantly from the dungeon-death imagery of *Pictures from Italy* is in placing it in its opening scene. Here it is transferred from

Marshalsea, the penitentiary where (Dickens' father and) Mr Dorrit was once a penniless inmate, as indeed Amy subsequently recalls in listening to her own father's advice (530). It is precisely this similarity to a prison that enables Little Dorrit to compare Venetian society with the Marshalsea (even though that notorious gaol was only a sixth of the size of the 'palazzo' in which they are currently residing):

> Numbers of people seemed to come abroad, pretty much as people had come into prison: through debt, through idleness, relationship, curiosity, and general unfitness for getting on at home. They were brought into these foreign towns in the custody of couriers and local followers, just as debtors had been brought into prison. They prowled about the churches and picture-galleries, much in the old, dreary, prison-yard manner. (565)

Since incarceration represents lack of freedom and loss of liberty signifies death of the subject, perhaps that is why there are so many references to the latter in the forty-seven pages allocated to Venice in *Little Dorrit*. Tinkler (the valet), for example, announces Amy 'as if she had come to a funeral' (528). Then there is Mrs Gowan's house which is described as having fallen into decay, with botched walls, overrun with vines and having a Venetian odour of bilge-water (543). As for the Gowan dog, Lion, he is declared quite dead, 'as dead as the Doges' (556).

However, and maybe even more poignantly, Byron (1989: 227) conjures up Venice as 'thanatos' in the oft-quoted first stanza of the 4th canto of *Childe Harold's Pilgrimage*:

> I stood in Venice, on the Bridge of Sighs;
> A palace and a prison on each hand:
> I saw from out the wave her structures rise
> As from the stroke of the enchanter's wand:
> A thousand years their cloudy wings expand
> Around me, and a dying Glory smiles
> O'er the far times, when many a subject land
> Look'd to the winged Lion's marble piles,
> Where Venice sate in state, throned on her hundred isles!

Closely linked with Venice and death is the idea of its being a dangerous city. Coryat, for example, is aware of the crime level since he witnesses several associated tortures and executions. Indeed, he alludes to the heads of traitors displayed outside the Doge's palace (Hibbert 1988: 139). Coryat also mentions the ferry boatmen as being 'the most vicious and licentious varlets about all the city', and he comes across some Greeks with 'very blacke' long hair, 'a fashion unseemly and very ruffian like' (in Bull 1980: 58). Then there is James Earl of Perth who, in his letters to his family (written between 1688 and 1696), speaks of the canals as perilous places since they are the haunts of masked robbers (Carrington 1947: 51). Then again, at roughly the same period, there is the anonymous author of *Observations on a Journey to Naples* who refers to a murderer who has killed as many as three-score persons (Carrington 1947: 51).

In more recent times, Daphne du Maurier (1992) locates her short story *Don't Look Now* in Venice. Throughout the fictional account there are several references to death and danger. Featuring a young couple, John and Laura, who decide to take a holiday in Venice after the death of their daughter Christine, the tale involves two elderly psychic sisters who strangely claim to have seen Christine alive and well. Several of the settings are quite eerie – the sinister side streets, the news of a murderer on the loose, the crying of a child, the young girl being pursued by a man and John following her into a canal side house. It is there in the final scene that the child turns out to be an old woman with an enormous head. She throws a knife at him, and it is only at the moment of death that he realizes why he has seen his wife back in Venice, even though she is meant to be in England, having returned in an emergency to take care of their sick son. Laura, whom John has unbelievably seen at the same time, once more in the company of the two sisters travelling down a canal in Venice, has in fact returned a week later for his funeral. Only the sisters' second sight has permitted this fast-forward knowledge of the future. Two passages in particular sum up this saga of death and intrigue by relating it back to the Venetian environment:

> They were at the corner of another dark, empty street, the same as all the others, when they heard the cry – a dying cry, suddenly stopped. It came from one of the houses with its windows closed, black and dead. (14)

and:

> They're right, he thought, when they say Venice is dying. Soon it will all be under water, an under-sea city, and people will come to visit it in boats, looking down at the buildings and churches below them, under the water, like a lost world. He was sad. (20)

If Venice as a place is death-evoking, the same can also be said of some of its *inhabitants*. Richard Lassels, for example, remarks on the attire of the gentlemen of that city. They wear black suits, black stockings and garters, long black gowns and even black caps with black wool edging (Carrington 1947: 45), almost as if they are ready to attend a funeral. Similarly, Shakespeare (1989), in the *Merchant of Venice*, has two of his characters, Salarino and Solanio, dressed in black robes, and Coryat speaks of as many as 3,000 gentlemen in gowns of black cloth in the style of a toga (Bull 1980: 60).

An aura of darkness is carried over to the most popular form of transportation – the coffin-black gondolas (Reed 1994: 43), which Edmund Flagg portrays as 'long, low, black, funereal, hearse-like barques' (in Hibbert 1988: 258) – an image continued by Shelley (1990: 192) in *Julian and Maddalo* (87–9) when he writes, 'So o'er the lagune we glided; and from that funereal bark I leaned and saw the city.' Thomas Mann (1968: 25) likewise, describes a gondola as:

> That singular conveyance come down unchanged from ballad times, black as nothing else on earth except a coffin – what pictures it calls up of lawless, silent adventures in the plashing night, or even more, what visions of death itself, the bier and solemn rites and last soundless voyage.

Mark Twain (1967: 142), too, refers to the gondola in funereal terms:

> We reached Venice at eight in the evening and entered a hearse belonging to the Grand Hotel d'Europe. At any rate, it was more like a hearse than anything else, though to speak by the card, it was a gondola.

According to him, the reason why gondolas are bedecked in black is because the Senate has decreed, 'It's the color of mourning. Venice mourns' (Twain 1967: 150).

Just as a gondola conjures up images of death, so too on occasion do 'gondolieri'. As Byron (1989: 227) has it in the third stanza of the 4th canto of *Childe Harold's Pilgrimage*:

> In Venice Tasso's echoes are no more,
> And silent rows the songless gondolier
> Her palaces are crumbling to the shore,
> And music meets not always now the ear,

and in stanzas xix and xx of *Beppo*:

> Didst thou ever see a Gondola? For fear
> You should not, I'll describe it to you exactly:
> 'Tis a long covered boat that's common here
> Carved at the prow, built lightly but compactly,
> Row'd by two rowers, each called 'gondolier,'
> It glides along the water looking blackly.
> Just like a coffin clapt in a canoe,
> Where none can make out what you say or do.
>
> And up and down the long canals they go,
> And under the Rialto shoot along,
> By night and day, all paces, swift or slow,
> And round the theatres, a sable throng,
> They wait in their dusk and livery of woe,
> But not to them do woeful things belong,
> For sometimes they contain a deal of fun,
> Like mourning coaches when the funeral's done.
>
> (Byron 1989: 626)

Perhaps even more poignantly, in *Death in Venice*, the first ferryman that Gustave von Aschenbach encounters with his broad-rimmed hat and staff reminds him of Hermes, the 'cicerone' of souls to the realm of the dead. It is this ghostly figure who is to transport Gustave across death's river – Charon – and it is he who menacingly reminds his mortal passenger, 'you will pay' (Reed 1994: 78–9).

From Venice as a destination of death, to its inhabitants, gondolas and oarsmen, it is but a short imaginary step to cemeteries and funerals. In this regard, Coryat finds the Venetian last rites very strange:

> For they carry the corpse to church with the handes and feete all naked, and wearing the same apparell that the person wore lately before it died ... or, many a man that hath been a vitious and licentious liver, is buried in the habits of a Franciscan Frier; the reason forsooth is, because they believe there is such virtue in the Frier's cowle, that it will procure the remission of the third part of their sinnes. (in Hibbert 1988: 131)

Erasmus (1965), on the other hand, is more impressed. In his *Colloquia Familiaria*, he observes, 'The Venetians arrange magnificent funerals. For a minimum of expense, any cobbler would have a splendid burial, with a fine bier provided by his guild; and sometimes six hundred monks, dressed in tunics and cloaks, accompany a single corpse' (in Bull 1980: 41).

Then there is Frederick Rolfe wandering as a homeless social outcast through the back streets and graveyards of the city. The following is an autobiographical description of the nearby island cemetery of 'San Michele':

> He slowly paced along cypress-avenues, between the graves of little children with blue or white standards and the graves of adults marked by more sombre memorials. All around were patricians bringing sheaves of painted candles and gorgeous garlands of orchids and everlastings, or plebeians on their knees grabbing up weeds and tracing pathetic designs with deep chrysanthemums and farthing night-lights. Here were a baker's boy and a telegraph messenger, repainting their father's grave-post with a tin of black and a bottle of gold. (in Carrington 1947: 71–2)

However, it is to the Dominican church of the 'Gesuati' ('Santa Maria del Rosario') on the 'Zattere' that he frequently returns, particularly for memorial celebrations:

> A great white hearse reared its pyramid aloft (crowned with a winged orb) in the middle of the crowded fane, where an army of lance-like tapers sprang fearlessly trustful to the height tipped as with auspicious stars. Great was the company of mourners softly illumined below. The voice of the friar in the pulpit ceased. Gentle sad hopeful music poured from the loft, the insisting patience of the violins, the throb of cellos, the resolute concord of organs, weaving intricate networks of harmony round the faithful voices of men chanting the dirge. Then the silent asperging and censing of the mighty bier, and the last prayer for all the dead: 'Requiem aeternam dona eis, Domine; et lux perpetua luceat eis.'

and, he tellingly adds, 'Venice itself was tired, and refrained from dissipation on the night of the Day of the Dead' (in Carrington 1947: 73).

Jan Morris, too, is at her best when providing an account of the re-interment ceremony of Pius X, a memorial procession along the Grand Canal, which, incidentally, reintroduces the idea of the funeral barque:

> A crew of young sailors rowed it (the funeral barge *Bucintoro*) in a slow funereal rhythm, each stroke of the oar summoned by a single drum beat from a ferocious major domo in the well of the ship   a man who, glaring angrily from oarsman to oarsman, and striking his drum with ritual dedication, looked like an old slave-driver between decks on a galley. (in Hibbert 1988: 322)

Lastly, it should also be noted that Venice, as well as having a notoriously high infant mortality rate (Hibbert 1988: 311), is the final resting place of many visitors. Ezra Pound and Igor Stravinsky are buried in 'San Michele' (Bull 1980: 173). Wagner, who in 1858 composed *Tristan and Isolde* in Venice, died of heart failure in that city some twenty-six years later, and Frederick Rolfe anticipated his own demise with the words, 'Once again he went towards the cemetery ... He bought an armful of white rosebuds with his last coin. Let the forgotten Dead remember him, as he remembered them. Let them' (in Carrington 1947: 72). George Eliot marries J. W. Cross in Venice. Subsequently, her husband becomes insane and hurls himself into the Grand Canal. He recovers, but six months later, his more celebrated spouse dies from delayed shock (Hibbert 1988: 291–2). Then there is the poet Shelley, whose child Clara dies in Venice. As his wife adds in a note to *Julian and Maddalo* (Shelley 1990: 204), 'we had scarcely arrived at Venice before life fled from the little sufferer'. Browning, too, is fatally stricken with pneumonia in the 'Ca'Rezzonico'. His body is

transported by gondola to 'San Michele', a premonition of which is reflected in the
tenth stanza of *A Toccata of Galuppi's* where he writes:

> Then they left you for their pleasure
> Till in due time, one by one,
> Some with lives that came to nothing,
> Some with deeds as well undone,
> Death came tacitly and took them
> Where they never see the sun.
>
> (Browning, nd: 602)

Another poet, August von Platen, known for his *Sonnets from Venice*, although
managing to flee the cholera epidemic of the city, later dies in Italy away from his
homeland (Reed 1994: 75). Gustave von Aschenbach, the principal character of
Death in Venice, who half quotes the similarly homophilic Platen on first seeing the
buildings of the city, is, of course, unable or unwilling to escape the plague. As he
staggers out of his deckchair to follow Tadzio into the sea, he is, in fact, following
the fated directions of his soul summoned to a journey beyond Venice (Reed 1994:
71, 75).

DREAMS, LOVE AND DEATH AS TOURISTIC THEMES

Dreams

In summarizing the written accounts of Venice, the following qualities of dreams are
seen to be associated with that city:

1. Dreams are usually nocturnal events. However, day-dreaming can also occur,
    and this type of reverie is replete with fantasy.
2. Dreams permit behaviour *ad libitum*, and the enactment of otherwise unrealiz-
    able desire.
3. Dreams transcend time and typically move back and forth from a past child-
    hood to the present age of adulthood. Dreams are also projective, to the extent
    that they imaginatively construct the future. Since dreams are tense-less, they are
    eminently suited to the treatment of the perennial.
4. Dreams are heightened by an amalgam of impressions that mark out places as
    different – a unique combination of water, light and colour, for example. On
    other occasions, impressions are created by an idiosyncratic experience. Dreams
    are therefore constituted by a pot-pourri of sensations brought about by the
    sheer novelty of travel. Their kaleidoscopic nature is reflected in their mosaic-
    like structure and is often triggered by the stimuli of art or architecture.
5. Dreams can nevertheless override the boundaries of space and culture, parti-
    cularly when they refer to magical locations where cosmopolitan imagery is in
    evidence.
6. Dreams frequently oscillate between strangeness and familiarity. In confusing
    memory with reality, they can thus supply a sense of *déjà-vu* to a given sight.

7.   Dreams can turn into nightmares whenever there is severe loss of control. Where beauty becomes distorted and normality is transformed into fear or madness, the metaphor of a labyrinth is sometimes employed.

All of these observed characteristics have their touristic counterparts.

First, although Thomas Mann has von Aschenbach tormented by the crazed logic of nocturnal dreams, equally he and Tadzio are portrayed as more tranquil day-dreamers. Likewise, Proust speaks of the process of waking and being converted to reverie, the implication being that the light of day is more conducive to calm introspective musing about forthcoming events than dreams by night which focus in a jumbled and uncontrollable fashion on what has already occurred.

Similarly, tourism promotion sets great store by the pre-trip stage when potential package tourists are thumbing through their holiday brochures and photos, the latter being described by Sontag (1979: 16) as incitement to reverie. As Hanefors and Larsson (1998: 750) observe after interviewing a number of such vacationers, here there is:

> The importance of dreaming and fantasizing long before the actual decision to travel is taken. The dreaming act is always there – whether the tourists intend to go or not – and this armchair travel may indeed take place on the living room sofa.

Armchair travel is also referred to by Taylor (1994: 11), who speaks of the illusion of entering another place and period as if through a magic window.

Recognizing the importance of this 'dreaming-up' phase to its marketing efforts, the travel industry frequently alludes to 'dream destinations', 'places where dreams come true', 'paradise', 'fantasy islands', and so on. The appeal is seemingly made to the individual on a one-to-one basis (although in reality to several thousand persons), who can journey to a faraway land, with maybe a significant other, where all is harmony and joy. There are no disturbing pictorial or textual references to troublesome natives. All nasty surprises have been selectively deleted – as in a dream.

Urry (1995: 132) stresses the importance of such anticipation to the touristic experience and how in turn the gaze is moulded (cf. Burns 1999: 32) by a variety of non-touristic influences (including, presumably, the literary). Parrinello (1993: 241), who also highlights the significance of the anticipatory stage of travel, adds that reverie or daydreaming is a dream of compensation, a kind of break in everyday life, rather like Csikszentmihalyi's (1975) micro-flow.

Second, the fantasy component of reverie, as is quite evident in Dickens' allusions to 'phantom streets', 'enchanted scenes', 'fantastic structures', 'the work of fairy hands', etc. is also reflected in Proust's descriptions of Venice and St Mark's, particularly when accompanied by multiple references to his mother and his beloved Albertine. It is precisely in the realm of the erotic that the parent is introduced and repressed, while full rein is given to the infringement of tactile taboo, as indeed is the case of Byron freed from the moral constraints of his home society – his mother country.

Dann (1976) has argued that the possibility of playing out desires that have been proscribed in the tourist's culture of origin constitutes one of the most fundamental types of motivation for travel. Especially where a holidaymaker is unknown and, due no doubt to the temporary nature of tourism, the opportunities for fantasy enactment form an important part of the basic push factors inclining people to journey elsewhere, to a place where they imagine that normative controls will be minimal.

Although sexual fantasies may predominate, there are many other types of tourist fantasy, ranging from naming fantasies and colour fantasies to those more institutional varieties comprising the realms of education, religion, politics and so on, each conjuring up the notion of role reversal *ad libitum*.

Tourism as the world's largest fantasy industry is fully aware of this situation. Consequently, in its promotions the clientele is often portrayed as participating in activities to excess, apparently aided and abetted by happy and carefree host people free from all inhibitions. Hence the frequent pictorial displays of tourists enjoying themselves with unlimited supplies of food and drink, surrounded by readily available natives catering to their every whim.

Fjellman (1992) has noticed a similar tendency in what must surely be the foremost playground dedicated to fantasy – Walt Disney World. Beyond Cinderella's Castle lies Fantasyland, and further on there are 'dreamers' workshops', 'dreamers and doers themes', 'dream finders' and 'dream flights'. All of this ludic pastiche, under the general organizing principle of 'The American Dream', is carefully controlled by commercial interests whose corporate philosophy is summed up by the slogan of General Electric's Horizons, 'If we can dream it, we can do it' (Fjellman 1992: 268). Burns and Holden (1995: 60–3) supply an interesting footnote to the above scenario when they highlight a category of tourist recently identified in a four-nation Global Travel Survey. This type is referred to as a 'dreamer', that sort of person who mainly travels for enjoyment, relaxation and in order to impress others. The implicit argument is that such an individual cannot have fun or ego-enhancement through hedonism unless there is an accompanying notion of limitlessness.

Third, Venice is portrayed in the literature as a dreamy kind of place that permits an omnipresent sensation of timelessness, a city floating free of time (Bull 1980: 125). Nowhere is this attribute more evident than in Proust's Marcel, whose voyage of self-discovery involves a circularity of consciousness harking back to the dreams and experiences of childhood (Collier 1989: 1, 10). Coterminously, Venice may be regarded as a place of destiny that opens up into the years ahead, as can be seen in the poetic visions of Dante's *Divine Comedy*. No wonder that Mark Twain (1967: 156) finds himself so disoriented, living simultaneously in two centuries.

It is this ability to transcend time, to effect a rapid transition from the present to the past and future, and back again, that allows tourism to go beyond the ordinary time of day-to-day living and into extraordinary time (Graburn 1989; Urry 1995). As far as the past is concerned, the travel dream can materialize in the dreamlands of museums, palaces, art galleries and heritage sites which offer individuals the opportunity to identify with the collective past (Horne 1984; Merriman 1991; Robb 1998), and it is this possibility of journeying nostalgically backwards to days of former glory that is particularly apparent in several accounts of Venice.

The past may also be evoked through attractions that focus on childhood. Trips to Beatrix Potter's Hill Top Farm in the English Lake District (Squire 1994), to the home of Santa Claus in Rovaniemi, Finland (Pretes 1995) or to sites of nursery rhymes, such as Jack and Jill in Kilmersdon, Somerset – the latter interestingly organized by a Connecticut company called 'It's About Time' (Milner 1999) – are all examples of the travel industry's awareness of the importance of early memories. So too, of course, is Walt Disney World's dedication to 'all children young and old who believe that dreams can really come true' (Fjellman 1992: 272). Indeed, 'the tourist as child' (Dann 1989: 1996) is a familiar promotional trope that is often applied, not only to Venice as 'somewhere between a freak and a fairytale' (Jan Morris in Jepson 1996), but to a variety of destinations all over the globe.

Orientation to the future is just as frequently encountered, especially where 'the language of tourism' mirrors 'the language of advertising' in its promotional discourse. Through such visual clichés as the open window or the ascending staircase, viewers can be led out of the present scene and into a land of promise and delight (Williamson 1983). As Hanefors and Larsson (1998: 751) relatedly observe, the pictures of the brochures become a source of identity for would-be tourists as they 'imagine their own touristic behavior and dream about their future tourism experiences and even fantasize about desirable feelings while away from home'. Here the touristic project is projected into the future and, via the power of introspection, is imaginatively captured in the future perfect tense as if it had already happened (Dann 1996; Schutz 1972).

Fourth, the richness of sensation produced by Venice evokes equally vivid impressions and literary descriptions. Dickens' (1989: 120) 'sparkles of the sun on the water' or Mark Twain's (1967: 141) 'golden mist of sunset', for example, clearly indicate that this city offers a unique blend of colour and light that can be found in no other place. In other words, it is different, and it is in this difference that its touristic attractiveness resides.

Interestingly, travel writers attempt to capture the *genius loci* by imitating the genre of writers who travel. A good example is Lawrence Durrell's (1986: 15) incredible opening description of Venice as seen from the deck of a ship (in an otherwise rather dull book about Cyprus):

> Venice (at dawn) wobbling in a thousand fresh-water reflections, cool as a jelly. It was as if some great master, stricken by dementia, had burst his whole colour-box against the sky to deafen the inner eye of the world. Cloud and water mixed into each other, dripping with colours, merging, overlapping, liquefying, with steeples and balconies and roofs floating in space, like the fragments of some stained-glass window seen through a dozen veils of rice-paper. Fragments of history touched with the colours of wine, tar, ochre, blood, fire-opal and ripening grain. The whole at the same time being rinsed softly back at the edges into a dawn sky as softly as circumspectly blue as a pigeon's egg.

In spite of the hackneyed metaphor of the paint-box, this purple passage is one that many a copywriter would be quite happy to borrow from in seeking to capture the uniqueness of a destination for potential tourists. By employing a series of vibrant images, this vignette conjures up the kaleidoscopic, stained-glass nature of a dream (seen in Proust) and the jumbled-up nature of travel predicated on ever-increasing doses of novelty (as in Dickens).

There are at least three advantages to employing such oneiric imagery. According to Fjellman (1992: 400), it helps the reader understand the decontextualization of the travel experience. By means of 'discovery rhetoric' (Taylor 1994: 45) it keeps the tour on the move. In choosing description in preference to information and schedules, it makes the dream possible (Parrinello 1993: 244; Taylor 1994: 2).

Fifth, difference can sometimes be portrayed, not so much by stressing the physical boundaries of a place but by overstepping them, in virtually the same way as the globalized tourism industry can choose to disregard national borders. One reason why Venice is so different from many other destinations is that it achieves a unique blend of cultures. Such cosmopolitanism is particularly evident in the Orientalist (Said 1991) images that Venice evokes, as for example in Proust (Collier 1989: 70–1). The city is thus at once both western and eastern, like none other.

Sixth, as is clear in Thomas Mann's account and elsewhere, strangers feature prominently in dreams of Venice, indeed even before von Aschenbach actually sets off on his journey. At the same time, figures from the past and present are introduced (Albertine in Proust, for example) in order to provide sufficient familiarity as to prevent total disorientation in the subject. A similar polar dichotomy extends to settings – Dickens' reference to the Marshalsea, for instance – where a comparison is made with the home environment so that alienation in the place of visitation can be reduced. Yet, as a writer, only Jan Morris (1987: 93) seems openly to acknowledge her reactions to the strangeness of Venice when she confesses that it is:

> A city in which I am always a foreigner. I have little in common with the Venetians; few of their instincts are mine; I move through their city as through some marvellous exhibition, bemused by its beauty and intrigued by its inhabitants, but never for a moment feeling indigenous.

By way of elaboration, it is the commentator Cohen (1972, 1974, 1979) who seizes on the fundamental distinction between strangeness and familiarity so as to supply one of the most fundamental bases for devising a typology of tourists, deriving all the while his theoretical insights from the works of Schutz (1944) and Simmel (1950). In such a manner, Cohen (1979) has enhanced the cumulative understanding of tourism by providing a phenomenology of tourist experiences ranging from the recreational and diversionary (familiarity) to the experiential, experimental and existential (strangerhood) varieties, thereby also allowing knowledge to progress beyond the formulations of Boorstin (1964 (1987)) and MacCannell (1973, 1976 (1989)).

Since night dreams generally borrow from the past and daydreams tend to look towards the future, the previously noted quality of time transcendence has an additional input into the respective interplay between memory (familiarity) and projected reality (strangeness). Thus the sense of *déjà-vu* so frequently experienced by tourists. This sensation is easy enough to comprehend with the concomitant realization that most of the sights, travel and accommodation experiences that they are likely to encounter have already been prefigured in the promotional media of tourism. Moreover, this imagery in turn oscillates between the past (the 'I can do it again', because-of motivation of the repeater) and promise of the future (the satisfaction of desire through unique offerings, in-order-to motivation of the first timer) (cf. Schutz 1972). Hence, the accusation that tourism is tautological in nature (Boorstin 1964 (1987)).

Finally, while many dreams selectively draw on pleasant sensations from the past and sometimes permit the experiences to be carried over into waking dreams, equally there are nightmares – terrifying imaginations inhabited by incubi and other monstrous creatures which produce fear and dread in the subject. Here there seems to be complete loss of control as beauty turns to ugliness and reality becomes distorted. In Venice, such nightmares are frequently portrayed through the metaphor of a labyrinth, the dark alleyways wherein travellers are totally lost and frightened, only to experience relief on emergence when coming again upon a familiar sight. However, once arrived, even the columns of St Mark's square are referred to by Beckford as a 'labyrinth of pillars' (in Carrington 1947: 63).

The actual origin of the labyrinth (British Broadcasting Corporation 1999) probably dates back to 1800 BC with the construction of the massive Faiyum temple complex in a southern Egyptian oasis, an edifice comprising some 3,000 rooms, more than half of them underground. In the adjacent pyramid of Hewara, built during the reign of Amenenhat III, as in later pyramids, the idea was to conceal the burial chambers of the pharaohs by means of an elaborate system of passages, false doors and dead ends. It was this maze-like structure that Herodotus discovered on a trip in 450 BC in seeking to explain the Minoan myth of Theseus' pursuit of the Minotaur in the labyrinth of Cretan Knossos. Much later, in the Middle Ages, cathedrals such as Chartres (AD 1202) included pavement labyrinths (known as the Jerusalem mile) for pilgrims to make a journey of pre-paschal self-discovery to the centre by identifying with the Christian baptismal imagery of Jesus descending into hell (death) in order to rise again (life). The pagan counterpart could be found on practically every English village green – the turf maze with women in the centre (symbolizing the womb) and young male pursuants at the periphery taking wagers on who would get there first. This tradition was enhanced by Morris and maypole dancing, particularly during spring fertility rituals.

Lash (1990: 33–4), relying on Mumford (1966: 313–23), maintains that the principal metaphor of the premodern Gothic city is the labyrinth, a complex system of narrow streets containing the living spaces of the mediaeval guilds. On holy-days, masters, journeymen and apprentices would wind their way in procession through these twisting alleyways, always out of sight of the cathedral, when suddenly they would be in the central square confronted by its mysterious magnificence. Only with the emergence of the Renaissance was the proletarian *gemeinschaftlich* labyrinth rationally displaced by the straight line, with huge boulevards leading directly to piazzas (as in St Peter's, Rome or Haussmann's Paris, for example).

Venice appears to be one of the few major European cities to have preserved this labyrinthine quality, and herein lies its dangerous charm. Marcel is terrified in the tiny 'calli' of the night, his fear only alleviated on entering St Mark's Square by day, a sensation repeated in von Aschenbach's pursuit of Tadzio and in Daphne du Maurier's *Don't Look Now*. However, it is undoubtedly in Dante (referred to by Proust) that the terror of the maze is given its fullest rendering. *The Divine Comedy* commences (Inferno I, 2–6) in a dark wood (the labyrinth) on the outskirts of Inferno.

... I found myself obscured in a great forest
Bewildered, and I knew I had lost the way.
It is hard to say just what the forest was like,

How wild and rough it was, how overpowering;
Even to remember it makes me afraid.

(Alighieri 1981: 47)

In the forest, the traveller encounters the leopard (sensuality), lion (pride) and she-wolf (greed), vices which prevent him from realizing his best aspirations (Higgins 1981: 15). Thereafter, he is successively exposed to the damned, demons, furies and the Minotaur, before being transported via Charon's ferry, Phlegyas' ferry and the barque of souls. All the while, these successive experiences are punctuated by Dante's dreams (of Eagle, of Siren, of Leah) and visions (Higgins 1981: 17). Indeed, the whole work can be considered a dream inspired by a supranational vision of history (Higgins 1981: 13).

Cast in such a literary light, Venice can be interpreted as an unmarked traveller's maze leading to a sign-posted tourist gaze. Unlike in *The Divine Comedy*, however, in contemporary tourism the process is reversible. The independent visitor to Venice can voluntarily forego the crowded and familiar landmarks of St Mark's, the Doge's Palace, the Rialto, the Bridge of Sighs and the Accademia, and only has to step back a couple of blocks into the deserted alleyways of the Dorsoduro in order to experience strangerhood.

Love

The literary framing of Venice as a city of love, as with the theme of dreams, possesses a number of induced qualities:

1. Venice is referred to in essentially feminine terms that sometimes evoke purity, youthful innocence and the sanctity of marriage.
2. Equally, however, Venice is described as a sexually experienced woman given over entirely to the satisfaction of unlimited pleasure. Venetian men-folk are portrayed as the counterpart to such desire.
3. Venice also offers the space for illicit heterosexual liaisons, either those religiously proscribed on the grounds of vows of chastity, or those out of wedlock.
4. In temporal terms, Carnival is the supreme period of licentiousness in Venice.
5. Venice additionally acts as a setting for homosexual encounters.

As before, these characteristics have their touristic analogues.

First, from several visitors to Venice there are portrayals of that city as a 'maiden', 'maid', 'virgin', 'queen' and 'mother of love'. Wordsworth's (1909: 271) sonnet *On the Extinction of the Venetian Republic* continues in this romantic tradition:

Venice, the eldest child of liberty.
She was a maiden city, bright and free;
No guile seduced, no force could violate;
And when she took unto herself a Mate,
She must espouse the everlasting sea.

So, too, does James Howell's description of Venice's 'dainty smooth neat streets, whereon you may walk most days in the year in a silk stockin' and satin slippers, without soiling them' (in Bull, 1980: 64) or Shelley's observation that 'I never visited any country where the people seemed equally linked in love' (in Bull 1980: 138).

These images of purity and undefiled love in turn lead to the preservation of that state for the ideal of marital love. In this regard, George Eliot weds in Venice, while Daphne du Maurier's fictional couple, John and Laura, before their lives dissolve into tragedy, are revealed as going to church and, thus sanctified, as consummating their sacred feelings in a hotel. Then, too, Jan Morris (1987: 94), in her most intimate of books, *Conundrum*, refers to the time when as a man, he, his wife and two children lived for a year in a little red palace on the Grand Canal 'in a condition of more or less ecstasy'.

This romantic spirit which Ambros (1993: 15) reckons finds 'a perfect setting in Venice among winding alleyways and edifices of oriental splendor rising from the sea' has its touristic counterpart in the 'romantic gaze' (Urry, 1990). It refers to the era preceding the 'collective gaze' of mass tourism, a time when the accent is on the moral upliftment of the individual in the contemplation of natural beauty (Barthes, 1984). In Venice, where there are no mountains and scarcely a blade of grass is to be seen, the rural is replaced by the elements of sun, moon and water, thereby allowing 'nature' to be reflected in the pre-modern structures of mediaevalism and orientalism.

The tourism industry in its promotional material seeks to capture this natural lost age of innocence, not only in its ecotourism publicity, but also in its nostalgic rendering of many Third World destinations, whose inhabitants are portrayed in a language of abundance as happily enjoying the wonders of nature (Cazes 1976). In emphasizing their childlike and pristine *joie de vivre*, the text and pictures call forth a similar state in their clientele via a 'tourist as child' rhetoric (Dann 1989, 1996). Premodern cities, such as Venice, receive a similar soft-focus misty treatment with a related stress on 'égotisme à deux', young radiant couples hopelessly in love surrounded by visual clichés which reinforce their mutual attraction (sunsets, tropical flowers, singing gondoliers, etc.) (cf. Krippendorf 1987). The accent is almost entirely on white, youthful, bodily perfection. There are few 'disturbing' pictorial references to minorities, the disabled and the elderly, or to others facing similar social exclusion (Urry 1990).

Second, and as the romantic literature also leads to 'a sorrowful meditation on the passing of beauty' (Ambros 1993: 15), so too does Venice come to be viewed in terms of an older, more sexually experienced woman, given over to wantonness. The marriage imagery dissolves ('melior meretrix quam uxor' (Lassels in Carrington 1947: 48)), and in its place appears hedonism, as is quite evident in the continuation of Jan Morris' (1987: 95) account:

> I know of no more marvellous sensation than to be afloat on the Venetian lagoon slightly drunk with friends in the middle of a summer night … The spectacle used to strike me speechless with pleasure, and handing the tiller to somebody else, I would lie in the bows of the boat, trailing my fingers in the muddy water, submitting to what I still think to have been the most truly libidinous of a lifetime's varied indulgences – the lust of Venice.

Here the sober spouse is replaced by inebriated friends, while ecstasy surrenders to pleasure, libido and lust. The once pure water is now muddied.

Such imagery is transferred to the inhabitants of Venice by Samuel Rogers via the gondola. 'It is a conveyance,' he says, 'refined and improved upon by the experience and study of the most sensual and luxurious people for many ages' (in Hibbert 1988: 200). Mark Twain (1967: 142), however, reserves the moral outcome of such description for the city itself when he states, 'Her glory is departed, and with her crumbling grandeur of wharves and palaces about her, she sits among her stagnant lagoons, forlorn and beggared, forgotten of the World,' while Nietzsche (1911) in *The Olympus of Illusion* is even more damning when he claims, 'Once they came to admire a rare beauty. Today they come to be present at a deathbed' (in Sasse 1993: 242).

The tourism industry has to tread a careful ethical path if it wishes to encourage liaisons among its clients, all the while avoiding their transference to destination people via the exploitative practices of sex tourism (male association with prostitutes) or 'romance tourism' (female association with beachboys and gigolos (cf. Pruitt and LaFont 1995)). Otherwise there is a very real danger that places such as Thailand and Jamaica will themselves become respectively branded with irresponsible imagery. For this reason, the once familiar brochure pictures of dusky maidens beckoning to potential tourists through half-open doors now tend to be replaced by the niche marketing of specific target groups. Members of the young 18–30 set, for instance, can be shown as engaging in mock sexual combat among themselves, just as all inclusive properties, with names like 'Hedonism', are depicted as client-centred love resorts which exclude locals from all but menial roles.

Even so, traces of a patriarchal language of male conquest of females remain attached to a place, as Gritti (1967: 55–61) has shown, for instance, in his critical analysis of the *Guide Bleu*. Here, great, majestic, enormous, imposing, vast castles, churches, fortifications and mountains dominate, while charming, delicious, verdant, fertile, laughing valleys, streams and pretty villages are beaten into sexual submission by a text that is vertically arranged according to the dominant and the dominated. A re-visitation of the literary descriptions of Venice (with their oppositional references to palaces and canals) might reveal the extent to which such verbal imagery obtains. An examination of the descriptions of current promotions should quickly demonstrate whether or not it has been carried over into the media of contemporary marketing.

Third, Venice is often portrayed as a haven for illicit relationships. As has been seen, there are several references in the literature to priests, monks and nuns openly displaying their affections towards members of the opposite sex. This sense of brazen naughtiness is heightened with the unstated realization that these persons are forbidden from entering such amorous liaisons on account of their religious vow of chastity. The fact that they are introduced into salacious descriptions of Venice is probably to create the impression that, since a serious taboo has been infringed, Venice is consequently a place where anything goes.

As for the literary crafters of Venice themselves, several are known to be having extramarital affairs or sexual relationships with under-aged persons. George Sand, Lady Mary Wortley Montagu, Gabriele d'Annunzio, and of course Casanova and

Byron, are famed for their philandering, and stories abound of their quite blatant liaisons. Byron, for example, readily acknowledges that Italian women 'kiss better than those of any other nation' (Jepson 1996). One day in 1819, while living with the Contessa Guiccoli, Thomas Moore (Byron's biographer) decides to visit him in the 'palazzo'. He arrives at 2 p.m. just as the aristocrat is getting up for breakfast! They proceed together across the lagoon in a gondola to the setting of the sun – 'an evening such as romance would have chosen for a first sight of Venice, rising with her tiara of bright towers above the wall' (in Carrington 1947: 66). When Moore and Byron disembark at the Lido in order to amuse themselves with some gentle horse-riding, a crowd of tourists is there to capture a glimpse of the great English lord who, as a romantic *par excellence*, relishes 'the vice and decadence of Venice' (in Carrington 1947:67). In spite of his club foot (Newby 1986: 146), Byron's good looks prevail. No small wonder that when news of his death in Missolonghi reaches Stendahl, the latter refers to his 'Apollonic' quality (Nicolson 1997). Meanwhile, Casanova, 'the greatest libertine of them all', repairs to the Rialto first thing in the morning in order 'to share restorative beverages with those who have passed the night in the excesses of Venus or Bacchus' (Jepson 1996).

The reference to tourists' assembling so as to catch sight of the notorious Byron is interesting since it opens up the possibility of converting the infamous into tourism attractions (Dann 1994*b*). Among such persons, now deceased, there are places associated with the likes of Pancho Villa (the Mexican outlaw reputed to have had as many as twenty-five wives (Perry 1991), Errol Flynn (Jamaica), Lucky Luciano and Al Capone (Cuba), Ernest Hemingway (the Bahamas), and even the Chicago hotel where John F. Kennedy bedded a prostitute minutes before his famous debate with Richard Nixon, all of which have a certain romantic decadence about them. Some places are also visited for their connection with living 'romantics', most of them creatures of the media, e.g., Bimini, where US presidential candidate Gary Hart had an affair with Donna Rice, Baja California – the location for Raquel Welch and her many men, and the city motel where Jimmy Swaggart entertained a call girl. There is even a guidebook entitled *Unauthorized America. A Travel Guide to the Places the Chamber of Commerce Won't Tell You About* (Staten 1990) listing some of these alternative tourism sites. Arguably, visitors patronize these destinations not so much because they wish to emulate their associated characters, but probably because they desire to add a little spice to their own dull existence by somehow participating in the more exciting lives of others. Venice, as a city for lovers, can be appealing for its decadent excesses. Interestingly, however, contemporary travel writers, as part of tourism's promotional machine do not generally follow writers of travel in this respect. Indeed, as Cadwalladr (1998) observes, 'writers of erotica rarely concern themselves with travel or place, while travel writers don't go in for romantic encounters – or if they did, they weren't telling.'

Fourth, whereas licentiousness in Venice is a year-round activity, its culmination occurs during the ten-day period of Carnival immediately preceding Lent – something of a let-down from its eighteenth-century festivities which began on 26 December and lasted for two months! Even so, James Earl of Perth is said to have been impressed with Carnival back in 1695 (Carrington 1947: 51) and John Evelyn is quoted as saying, 'All the world doth repair to Venice to see the folly and madnesse of the Carnevall. 'Tis impossible to recount the universal madnesses of this place during this time of licence' (in Jepson 1996). In the literary accounts of Venice, references have already been encountered to masks, masques, masked balls and masquerading. Not surprisingly, Byron meets several of his lovers at masques, and Casanova finds it easy to seduce masked ladies after a night of debauchery. Addison, too, alludes to masking and the opportunities it offers for amorous adventure.

Carnival, even as a movable feast, is naturally used by the tourism industry, not only in Venice where room rates rise accordingly, but also in other places associated with Catholicism, such as Rio de Janeiro, New Orleans and Port-of-Spain. Some non-Catholic destinations, Barbados and the Bahamas for example, have analogous celebrations, although at different times of the year, which amount to similarly ostentatious street parties and opportunities for revelry.

The idea of carnal indulgence, derived from the Latin 'carnem vale', 'farewell to meat', which takes place before a period of austerity, is also quite in keeping with tourism's excesses and enactments of fantasy *ad libitum*. Indeed, it is at this juncture, when there is a mixture of grotesque, exotic anonymity and dreaming, that the fulfilment of sexual fantasy is at its zenith.

Finally, a number of writers about Venice engage in gay relationships. To the names of Frederick Rolfe, John Symmonds and Horatio Brown can be added that of John Cowper Powys. There is also, of course, Thomas Mann's novella about homosexual love and his own similar involvement. References even crop up in otherwise straight authors such as Henry James, who once describes in his *Italian Hours* a Venetian street urchin as 'the most expressively beautiful creature I have ever looked upon ... this little unlettered Eros of the Adriatic strand' (in Bull 1980: 125).

Apart from Symmond's affair with a gondolier, and one cannot assume that it implies a financial transaction, there are no remunerated arrangements with destination people recorded in these literary accounts. There is thus seemingly no 'romance tourism' with gigolos, just as there are apparently no cited instances of female visitors to Venice offering gifts in cash or kind to locals in exchange for sexual favours.

Although there have been some academic analyses of gay tourism, notably by Hughes (1997) and Pritchard *et al.* (1998), the industry itself is only now beginning to appreciate the monetary rewards it can bring. Certainly, there are cities such as Sydney which manage to attract thousands of visitors to their gay festivities, just as there are cruises which cater exclusively to this sexual preference. However, the imagery of tourist promotions is still predominantly targeted at heterosexuals. Rarely are two men depicted in brochures as sharing hotel accommodation; only, it would seem, in sports activities are they shown together. Where women are featured as couples, it is generally understood that they are friends or relatives rather than lesbians.

Venice, then, while open to all the forms of human amatory expression, is still mainly associated with the male/female variety. In this respect, Venice, like:

> *The Divine Comedy* is a poem, above all, of love. If religion and politics, civic life, literature and philosophy are important ... they are constantly developed and measured

against the parameters of love. The 'story' of *The Divine Comedy* is an account of a man in love ... who journeys beyond the grave to meet once more his lady snatched away by death some ten years before. (Higgins 1981: 13–14)

Death

Just as with dreams and love, the literary association of Venice with death has a number of characteristics:

1. Death is connected with its binary opposite – love – via the metaphor of an accompanied journey.
2. Death is, nevertheless, a very individual experience, one anticipated and made possible through personal reflection on loneliness and time.
3. Verbal images of death are monochromatic and focus on the funereal.
4. Death is also portrayed as loss of liberty through references to incarceration.
5. Death is additionally associated with violence, whose constant threat is only alleviated in everlasting rest.

Again, each of these features has a touristic counterpart.

First, and has been seen in various literary accounts of Venice, love and death are linked via a mythical structure of complementary opposites (Levi-Strauss 1958). Marcel has Albertine, Gustave has Tadzio, Cantwell has Renata and John has Laura. In each pairing there is a tension between passion and control, creativity and morality, and it is precisely this dialectical framework of thesis/antithesis which permits the dynamic notion of becoming to override a static concept of being. Such a state of permanent transition is best captured through the metaphor of a journey. *The Divine Comedy* exemplifies the situation via the allegory of travelling through life and death to the reward or punishment of the hereafter. Here Dante as everyman relies successively on Virgil, Beatrice and St Bernard, as he is led through the realms of Hell and Purgatory to the beatific vision of Heaven. All the while, the oppositional structure is maintained between the guide and the guided, good and evil.

Tourism also employs the meta-theme of a sacred journey. Like life itself, it has a beginning and a middle, just as it most decidedly has an end. Perhaps that is why departing travellers, in spite of the otherwise joy of the occasion, often dissolve into tears when bidding farewell to their assembled family and friends, thereby conjuring up the reciprocal sentiment of 'parting as such sweet sorrow' (Graburn 1989: 26–7). Urry (1995: 6, 15), relying on Heidegger, makes the allied philosophical point that:

Being is made visible in its temporal character and in particular the fact of movement towards death. Being necessarily involves movement between birth and death or the mutual reaching out and opening up of the future, past and present ... Only humans live their lives in awareness of their own finitude.

Burns and Holden (1995: 36), referring to tourist motivation and drawing their inspiration from Freud, relatedly argue that human behaviour oscillates between 'eros' and 'thanatos', the instincts of life and death. The latter, they say, 'channels behaviour into a drive towards death and a release from anxiety and striving, a return to the inorganic state'.

However, the metaphor of a journey is not just restricted to the religious concept of the sacred. Tourism can also be extended to encompass the realm of civil religion (Allcock 1988), which can be seen, for example, in the icons of nationhood and progress that are ubiquitously paraded before visitors to Walt Disney World (Fjellman 1992; Moore 1980) as they travel from the glorious past of Main Street, USA and other assembled Americana to the promise of Tomorrow Land.

Second, although Venice is portrayed in terms of an 'égotisme à deux', it also calls forth self-awareness through isolation and introspection. This feature is particularly evident in another extract from Frederick Rolfe featuring *Santa Maria del Rosario*, a passage referred to by Carrington (1947: 71) as 'one of the loveliest descriptions of Venice ever written':

> He went, every evening, to the sermon and benediction at the church of the Gesuati on the Zattere: first, to pay the prodigious debt of the present to the past – the duty of love and piety to the dead; and, second, for the sake of an hour in quiet sheltered obscurity. The grand palladian temple, prepared for the Month of the Dead, draped in silver and black, with its forest of slim soaring tapers crowned with primrose stars in mid-air halfway up the vault, and the huge glittering constellation aloft in the apse where God in his Sacrament was enthroned, replenished his beauty-worshipping soul with peace and bliss. The patter of the preacher passed him unheard. His wordless prayer, for eternal rest in the meanest crevice of purgatory, poured forth unceasingly with the prayers of the dark crowd kneeling with him in the dimness below. (in Carrington 1947: 71)

What is especially poignant about this vignette is that, in spite of the declared intention to listen to the sermon, the 'patter of the preacher' and the murmuring of the surrounding faithful surrender to the prayer of a lone man carrying out his filial obligations to his ancestors in 'quiet sheltered obscurity', in order thereby to achieve his goal of a happy death.

This individual consciousness of mortality is also heightened whenever the tourist is alone. As Theroux (1977: 419) observes, 'There are many satisfactions in solitary travel, but there are just as many fears. The worst is the most constant: it is the fear of death.' It is thus not surprising to find the 'single' tourist more open to introspection, undistracted by the meaningless chatter of fellow travellers. In this vein, Theroux (1980: 420) confesses, 'Usually, throughout this trip, I had looked out of a train window and thought: what a terrible place to die in,' and elsewhere, 'America must have the most geriatric tourists in the world. For them travel is part of growing old' (Theroux 1977: 247).

Lawrence Durrell (1986: 15) also associates the idea of travel with personal reflection when he states:

> Journeys, like artists, are born and not made. A thousand differing circumstances contribute to them, few of them willed or determined by the will – whatever we may think. They flower spontaneously out of the demands of our natures – and the best of them lead us not only outwards in space, but inwards as well. Travel can be one of the most rewarding forms of introspection, before tellingly adding, 'These thoughts belong to Venice at dawn.'

Later on, however, just as Rolfe before him, Durrell (1986: 19) links the present with the past by inserting a temporal dimension to the contemplation of solitude, 'We had become, with the approach of night, once more aware of loneliness and time – those two companions without whom no journey can yield us anything.'

Although a casual appraisal of tourism may conclude that it is a phenomenon free from the constraints of time or, if not completely liberated, at least operating under the non-ordinary time of liminality, it is Cohen (1986) who notes that tourists of the non-sedentary variety are often as much controlled by a timetable as ever they are at home. Sightseeing is, above all, a scheduled activity. Urry (1995: 19) is even more explicit when he claims that 'humans are not just affected by clock time but are themselves clocks'. However, Taylor (1994: 239) introduces an interesting qualification to the foregoing discussion when he refers to that type of tourism which has a definite focus on the past. Heritage, he says, rather than constituting a sign of decline or morbidity, actually allays anxieties about mortality. Since history predominantly displays an attribute of continuity, it therefore suggests and points to an afterlife. Seen in that light, the disintegration of Venice may offer fresh inspiration and hope to those who behold it.

Third, and not withstanding the above observation, verbal images of death are everywhere in the literary accounts of Venice, ranging from the hearse-like gondolas and decaying buildings to the funeral attire of the inhabitants. Colour disappears, only to be replaced by pictures in black and white. Apart from Venetian dowagers sitting in Florian's whispering about death and money, notes Newby (1985: 69), 'much of the city is crumbling as well as sinking. Everywhere leprous walls and rotting brickwork proclaim the fact' (68). Indeed, he says, what with '[t]he melancholy crying of gulls and tolling of a bell ... It was a hell of a place to end up in on such a day. We might just as well have been on the Mersey for all the genius loci I was able to sop up' (Newby 1985: 56).

Monochrome verbal images both frame and have their counterparts in holiday photography, the one pursuit which, more than any other, marks out the tourist from other people. As Susan Sontag (1979: 42) has it, 'The photographer is super tourist, an extension of the anthropologist, visiting natives and bringing back news of their exotic doings and strange gear.' However, and as MacCannell (1992: 45–6) is quick to point out, it is tourists, rather than primitive peoples, who take on the semblance of death, for they are the ones who appear like returning ancestors or spirits of dead cannibals complete with new faces and skin. As Taylor (1994: 265) relatedly observes, although tourists frequently gaze on the ageing and decrepit, the photographs they take are reminders of their own mortality. Looking afterwards at their pictorial accomplishments leads to the realization that time does not stop, and hence to thoughts of mortality (Taylor 1994: 12).

By way of elaboration, Sontag draws several parallels between photography and death. For her, the camera is similar to the gun, a weapon which shoots (14). The outcome is the snapshot, a still life, a slice of time rather than a flow (17). Unlike a film, here time is frozen (81). In this sense, 'All photographs are memento mori. To take a photograph is to participate in another person's (or another thing's) mortality, vulnerability, mutability' (15; cf. Taylor 1994: 135). The last resting place for these pictures is typically the family album, a collection of dead friends and relatives, whose two-dimensional presence exorcizes the beholder's anxiety over their bodily disappearance (Sontag 1979: 16). Thus, 'photography is the inventory of mortality'. One gazes at people and thinks how much younger they looked when the picture was taken (70). Even so, 'After the event has ended, the picture will still exist, conferring on the event a kind of immortality (and importance) it would never otherwise have enjoyed ... the image world that bids to outlast us all' (11).

Fourth, and particularly in Dickens' (1973) comparison of Venice with the Marshalsea, that city begins to assume all the semblance of a prison. However, it is left to Mark Twain to record the full horrors evoked by the Ducal Palace, the black square replacing the portrait of the beheaded Doge Marino Faliero, the lions' mouths into which were thrust anonymous accusations, the ubiquitous surveillance where even spies were spied upon and the terrible Council of Three:

> The members of that dread tribunal met at night in a chamber to themselves, masked and robed from head to foot in scarlet cloaks, and did not even know each other unless by voice. It was their duty to judge heinous political crimes, and from their sentence there was no appeal. A nod to the executioner was sufficient. The doomed man was marched down a hall and out at a doorway into the covered Bridge of Sighs, through it and into the dungeon and unto death. (Twain 1967: 146–7).

There follow lurid descriptions of the infernal den in which such judgements were passed – the council table, the stations of the inquisitors and executioners, 'the pictures of death and dreadful suffering' (147). Across the 'ponderous stone bridge' (147) and below the water level lay the dungeons of the condemned with their 'damp, thick-walled cells' (148). Here many a patrician languished:

> Without light, air, books; naked; unshaven, uncombed, covered with vermin; his useless tongue forgetting its office, with none to speak to; the days and nights of his life no longer marked, but merged into one eternal eventless night; far away from all cheerful sounds, buried in the silence of a tomb. (148)

Nearby was a small corridor where otherwise forgotten prisoners were brought, only to be garrotted or sewn up in a sack before being taken by boat to some remote spot and drowned (148).

At first sight, it is extremely difficult to conceive of a parallel between the horrors of this totalitarian injustice and contemporary tourism, especially as the latter is so often self-portrayed as the very antithesis of imprisonment and death. Yet, increasingly, commentators as ideologically varied as Adams (1984), Adler (1985), Allcock (1994), Britton (1980), Bruner (1994), Buck (1977), Burgelin (1967), Cassou (1967), Cazes (1976), Dann (1996, 1997, 1999), Eco (1996), English (1986), Enzensberger (1962), Fjellman (1992), Graburn (1983), Gritti (1967), Hollinshead (1993), Krippendorf (1987), Lanfant (1980), Laurent (1967), MacCannell (1992), Moeran (1983), Mohamed (1988), Papson (1981), Pearce (1982), Powell (1988), Rivers (1972), Thurot (1989), Urbain (1993) and Urry (1990, 1995) continue to emphasize that tourism is becoming more and more a vast system of social control which extends from small-scale operators to multinational corporations. Fjellman (1992), for instance speaks of a 'friendly fascism' (24) by which visitors are managed, of boundary maintenance and policing as 'unnatural selection', of censorship and 'cultural spin policing' (29), of the suppression and silencing of counter-messages (96), of de-contextualization as a form of control (31), of re-conceptualization as providing new contexts and control (32). Similarly, Eco (1996) notes that 'visitors must agree to behave like robots', while 'officials regulate their every move' (48), and argues that 'animals earn happiness by being humanized, the visitors by being animalized' (52).

Fifth, Venice is portrayed as a violent city. Once a site of execution and torture, it is now the haunt of masked robbers and murderers on the run, their pursuit of victims through dangerous alleyways, with the sombre churches only too ready to receive the bodies and transport them to their final resting place of 'San Michele'. Eric Newby (1985: 61) manages to capture something of the atmosphere when he arrives one evening by boat and observes, 'Darkness had added itself to the fog; creating the sort of conditions that even Jack the Ripper would have found a bit thick for his work down in nineteenth-century Whitechapel.' Then there is Hemingway (1950) who interrupts his story of Colonel Richard Cantwell in order to insert two reflections on interment. The first occasion is similar to Newby's arrival:

> They passed the long line of boats in the slow canal that carried water from the Brenta, and he thought about the long stretch of the Brenta where the great villas were, with their lawns and their gardens and the plane trees and the cypresses. I'd like to be buried out there, he thought. (Hemingway 1950: 29)

The second is part of a conversation with Renata, one that commences with a question from her:

> 'And you don't want Arlington or Père Lachaise or what we have here?'
> 'Your miserable boneyard.'
> 'I know it is the most unworthy thing about the town. The city rather. I learned to call cities towns from you. But I will see that you go where you wish to go and I will go with you if you like.'
> 'I would not like. That is one thing we do alone. Like going to the bathroom.' (Hemingway 1950: 176)

In the end, Cantwell dies without his companion, just as General Thomas Jackson had done after requesting that he be allowed to cross the river and lie under the shade of some trees (Hemingway 1950: 236). In fact, it is in such a manner that this final scene gives the book its title.

Just as with the previous notion of social control, it is hard to see initially how tourism can be interested in violent death and corresponding places of interment. Indeed, Paul Theroux (1977: 68) regards travel, not so much as immersion in terrifying experiences abroad, but rather as a flight from the media of home, their sensational headlines announcing tales of murder, mayhem, self-destruction and natural disaster.

Be that as it may, today, as in the past, there is a whole segment of the tourism industry dedicated to sites of death and burial. This rapidly expanding type of tourism has been variously described as 'dark tourism' (Foley and Lennon 1996a, 1996b, 1999), the 'dark side of tourism' (Dann 1998), 'twilight tourism' (Campbell

1998), 'thanatourism' (Seaton 1996, 1999), 'tragedy tourism', ' "mea culpa" tourism' (Richter 1999), a tourism that focuses on 'black spots' (Rojek 1993) and 'sensation sights' (Rojek 1997), or simply 'milking the macabre' (Dann 1994*a*). Whatever its designation, this all-important variety of tourism comprises dangerous places of the past (e.g. the Californian gold town of Bodie) or present (Algiers, Belfast), sites of murder and assassination (e.g., the scene of the Charles Manson murders or of John F. Kennedy's slaying), infamous prisons (e.g. Alcatraz, Château d'If, Colditz, the KGB headquarters, Robben Island), hotels (e.g., Hitler's hideout), battlefields (e.g., trips to First and Second World War sites by specialist tour operators such as Holts and Midas), re-enactments of battles (e.g., St Brice's Day Massacre), concentration camps (e.g., Auschwitz, Dachau), deathspots of celebrities (e.g., Hollywood's Grave Line Tour), meetings with the living notorious (e.g., train robber Ronnie Biggs in Rio), museums of morbidity (e.g., Madame Tussaud's Chamber of Horrors), visions of hell morality exhibits (e.g., Singapore's Haw Paw Villa) and cemeteries for celebrities (e.g., Père Lachaise in Paris containing the last remains of Maria Callas, Isadora Duncan, Oscar Wilde and Jim Morrison) (cf. Dann 1994*b*).

It is to this last graveyard that Renata refers in her conversation with Cantwell. Venice's 'San Michele', while not as well patronized as Paris' sixth most-visited site, nevertheless has a fair share of interred notables, including several well-known writers. Venice also has its dark tourism elements with its prisons and places of execution. However, it is probably in its *Death in Venice* imagery that its chief attractiveness resides and that representation, of course, is entirely due to literary crafting.

CONCLUSION

As has been seen, 'The unique quality of Venice has been captured in the work of countless poets and writers. Like no other city Venice has become a place of myth and legend, a literary Fata Morgana' (Ambros 1993: 15). At the same time, 'More guidebooks have been written about Venice than any other city in Europe and few places have been so eulogized' (Rough Guide to the World 1998: 35). It is this connection between the literary account and its subsequent appropriation by the texts of 'the language of tourism' (Dann 1996) that requires some final elaboration. By combining the insights of Butler (1985, 1986) and Squire (1994), it can be observed that the evolutionary process of linguistic transformation commences with authors creating an image of a place. This initial stage is often followed by successive generations of writers who, relying on the works of their predecessors, tend to borrow off, feed on and introduce them into their own accounts. Via the act of publication, this corpus of literary discourse becomes part of a wider and multivocal symbolic system which, read by different audiences with varying interpretations, is incorporated into their daily lives and given new meaning. One such living appli-cation relates to the perceived need to travel from the home environment to another cultural setting, the fulfilment of which is considerably facilitated if the latter is already known through its literary framing. Since places often derive their identity from literary images, the tourism industry can evoke the desire to journey to a given destination by simply referring to various relevant works and authors.

However, since the industry is, above all, employing a language of promotion, its referencing becomes highly selective. It is also moulded by media which eschew lengthy descriptions, substituting them with sound bites and clichés that only accentuate the positive. If persuaded by this hyperbole, tourists are consequently drawn to these freshly formatted locations, even to the point where they patronize the original literary shrines that underpin them. In such a manner, Walter Scott's novels became 'prime factors in the decision of many people to visit the Highlands of Scotland' and 'Burns, Wordsworth, Dickens and Tennyson ... added further literary respectability to a visit to the area' (Butler 1985: 376). Similarly, with Stratford being recast as 'Shakespeare Country', Yorkshire as 'Brontë Country' and Tyneside as 'Catherine Cookson Country', 'this canon of writers creates its own geography' (Taylor 1994: 245) and places thus promoted can profit from their literary linkages (Squire 1994: 104). Not only are people attracted to such locales, but their trips may well include visits to the very nerve centres of these associations – Hardy's cottage in Higher Brockhampton, for example (Butler 1986), or Beatrix Potter's Hill Top Farm (Squire 1994). As Goodey (1994: 157) notes in reference to George Orwell and Wigan Pier, 'it has been place themes deriving from the literary rather than the visual arts which have directed visitors and therefore formed the basis for current marketing strategies'. Moreover, it is precisely because such locations are resonant with verbal descriptions of the nostalgic past that 'it is much more common for heritage guardians to draw on poets and novelists than to use artists and photographers' (Taylor 1994: 245).

In relation to Venice, the foregoing scheme operates as follows. In the beginning, there are a number of foundation accounts. These early renderings of reality may be either impressionistic and based on personal experience, as in the seventeenth century with Coryate's (1905) *Crudities* and Lassels' *Voyage of Italy*, or else fictitious and placeless, as in Dante's fourteenth-century *Divine Comedy*. For a while, Newby (1986: 111) observes, Coryate's was the only handbook for travellers to Venice, until, that is, Lassels' became 'a standard work, the necessary equipment of a travelling gentleman' (Carrington 1947: 43). One such wandering male was James Earl of Perth who visited Italy in 1695 and duly brought along a copy of Lassels. This work, in turn, acted as an input for the letters to his own family which were subsequently published (Carrington 1947: 51). As such, the nobleman was typical of travellers of that period who carried with them 'a library of classical authors in order to verify quotations on the spot' (Paroissien 1989: 13).

Later, there is a reference to William Rose, author of *Letters from the North of Italy*, who, *en route* from Padua to Venice, would often be heard muttering lines from Dante (Bull 1980: 135). Likewise, Proust borrows from the *Inferno* in order to highlight the dreams at the heart of his *Récherche*, just as Dante's fantastic visions are central to his own writing (Collier 1989: 10, 66, 140). Proust also draws heavily on Ruskin (Collier 1989: 5). In fact, he brings most of Ruskin's works with him (Hibbert 1988: 285), only delaying the start of his own *magnum opus* until his mentor has been translated. It should be further noted that Proust postpones his visit to Venice until four months after Ruskin has died since he cannot arrive while the city is still so alive with the Englishman's descriptions (Collier 1989: 16). By the time Rose and Proust reached Venice there were additionally several guidebooks to that city. Indeed, Byron was said to rely on them (Bull 1980: 131).

Dickens (1989: 35), however, seems to be the exception to this general trend of literary dependency, since he claims not to have used many books written on Italy ('I make little reference to that stock of information'), preferring instead to rely on his own previously written letters. Indeed, in order to assemble *Pictures of Italy* one finds him first trying to obtain correspondence from Lady Blessington d'Orsay (Paroissien 1989: 13), herself something of an author with her three-volume *The Idler in Italy* (Bull 1980: 143).

With the advent of mass tourism, the classical text yields to contemporary travel writing, the guidebook, the brochure, the video and the advertisement. Even so, these (post) modern media, via a 'representational loop' (Sturma 1999) draw on earlier romantic, imperial and orientalist literature in order to enhance the mystique of a place. In this recent late capitalist copy it is almost mandatory to include a list of celebrated western visitors (particularly if they are authors who can contribute to the romanticized image of a place). Thus, Herman Melville, Robert Louis Stevenson and James Michener can be called forth and quoted so as to heighten the attractiveness of Polynesia (Sturma 1999). Similarly, producers of modern travelogues on Venice, such as O'Neill and Fay (1994), liberally quote from sources as diverse as Gabriele d'Annunzio and Henry James. Another alludes to a much more recent tradition as if it were part of the present era: 'In fact, Venice does not seem to have changed since the 1960s. All the great ruminations on the city, written more than 30 years ago by writers such as Jan Morris, Mary McCarthy and J. G. Links still seem as pertinent as ever' (Tisdall, 1998*a*). Current guidebooks also sense the need to borrow from the literary past. Thus, Tisdall (1998*b*), the travel writer (above), praises the *Everyman Guide to Venice* (1999) precisely because it includes 'chirpy quips from Byron and Henry James; good chunks of sensual prose from the likes of Thomas Mann and Elizabeth David'.

Why, then, are these influences and references so successful? According to Squire (1994: 116), 'Literary tourism is one medium that allows people to live out certain fantasies, not only about their favorite books or authors, but also a range of other culturally constructed attitudes and values' (about a happy childhood or nostalgia for rural life, for example). Moreover, she says, 'One of the functions of tourism . . . is that it enables people to indulge in dreams and idylls that are set aside when they return home to "ordinary" life' (Squire 1994: 110), and, 'Literary influences are a starting point for other kinds of introspection' (Squire 1994: 111). By pointing to 'dreams', Squire is emphasizing one of the perennial features of tourism identified in the present exercise. When she further stresses the importance of 'introspection' she paves the way for another touristic quality – that of reflection, particularly meditation on mortality.

It is argued here that literary tourism, more than other type, by a successful blend of fact and fiction, truth and belief, can unearth the deeper sentiments of humankind which, by transcending space and time, are common to every individual throughout the ages. By reflecting on dreams, love and death, we can thus identify with the characters of novels and the experiences of real persons. We are able to share in or reject the emotions of Marcel, Little Dorrit and Gustave, just as we can be attracted or repelled by the exploits of Casanova or Byron.

In this respect, Venice, like tourism itself cast in the meta-theme of a journey, may or may not constitute something of a solution to the riddle of existence. More importantly, however, and with Thomas Mann, it poses the following fundamental dilemma, 'Is the last wave of Tadzio's hand the gesture of the death god or the invitation into a life that poor Achtenbusch (sic) has missed?' And the response?

In this city embraced by the sea we realize for the first time that the answer to this question of life and death is a kind of decision. The sea contains all possible worlds. All myths end in the sea, blend into one another and rise again, transformed, out of the depths. (Sasse 1993: 246)

REFERENCES

Adams, K. (1984) 'Come to Tana Toraja "land of the heavenly kings". Travel agents as brokers in ethnicity', *Annals of Tourism Research*, **11**, 469–85.

Adler, J. (1985) 'Youth on the road. Reflections on the history of tramping', *Annals of Tourism Research*, **12**, 335–54.

Alighieri, D. (1981) *The Divine Comedy*, trans. C. Sisson. London: Pan Books.

Allcock, J. (1988) 'Tourism as a sacred journey', *Loisir et Société*, **11**(1), 33–48.

Allcock, J. (1994) 'International tourism and the appropriation of history', in J. Jardel (ed.), *Actes du Colloque International 'Le Tourisme International entre Tradition et Modernité'*. Nice: Laboratoire d'Èthnologie de l'Université de Nice, 219–28.

Ambros, F. (1993) 'La Serenissima', in H. Vestner, (ed.), *Insight Guides: Venice*. Hong Kong: APA Publications, 15–18.

Barthes, R. (1984) *Mythologies*. London: Paladin.

Boorstin, D. (1964 (1987)) *The Image. A Guide to Pseudo Events in America*, 25th anniversary edition. New York: Atheneum.

British Broadcasting Corporation (1999) *Ancient Voices*. BBC2 Television, 19 June.

Britton, R. (1980) 'Let us handle everything. The travel industry and the manipulation of the travel experience', *USA Today*, May, 45–7.

Browning, R. (no date) *Poetical Works of Robert Browning*. Edinburgh: Nimmo, Hay and Mitchell.

Bruner, E. (1994) 'Abraham Lincoln as authentic reproduction: a critique of postmodernism', *American Anthropologist*, **96**(2), 397–415.

Buck, R. (1977) 'The ubiquitous tourist brochure. Explorations in its intended and unintended use', *Annals of Tourism Research*, **4**, 195–207.

Bull, G. (1980) *Venice. The Most Triumphant City*. London: The Folio Society.

Burgelin, O. (1967) 'Le tourisme juge', *Communications* **10**, 65–96.

Burns. P. (1999) *An Introduction to Tourism and Anthropology*. London: Routledge.

Burns, P. and Holden, A. (1995) *Tourism. A New Perspective*. Hemel Hempstead: Prentice-Hall.

Butler, R. (1985) 'Evolution of tourism in the Scottish highlands', *Annals of Tourism Research*, **12**, 371–91.

Butler, R. (1986) 'Literature as an influence in shaping the image of tourism destinations. A review and case study', in J. Marsh, (ed.), *Canadian Studies of Parks, Recreation and Tourism in Foreign Lands*, occasional paper no. 11. Peterborough: Department of Geography, Trent University, 111–32.

Byron, Lord G. (1989) *Byron. Poetical Works*, ed. F. Page. Oxford: Oxford University Press.

Cadwalladr, (1998) 'Cool off with a steamy summer read', *Sunday Telegraph*, 14 June.

Campbell, S. (1998) 'It's a hole new world', *Sunday Telegraph*, 15 November.

Carrington, D. (1947) *The Traveller's Eye*. London: Pilot Press.

Cassou, J. (1967) 'Du voyage au tourisme', *Communications*, **10**, 25–34.

Cazes, G. (1976) 'Le tiers-monde vu par les publicites touristques. Une image mystifiante', *Cahiers du Tourisme*, serie C, no. 33.

Cohen, E. (1972) 'Toward a sociology of international tourism', *Social Research*, **39**, 164–82.

Cohen, E. (1974) 'Who is a tourist? A conceptual clarification', *Sociological Review*, **22**(4), 527–55.

Cohen, E. (1979) 'A phenomenology of tourist experiences', *Sociology*, **13**, 179–201.

Cohen, E. (1986) 'Tourism and time', *World Leisure and Recreation*, **28**(3), 13–16.

Collier, P. (1989) *Proust and Venice*. Cambridge: Cambridge University Press.

Coryate, T. (1905) *Coryats Crudities*. London: James MacLehose & Sons.

Csikszentmihalyi, M. (1975) *Beyond Boredom and Anxiety. The Experience of Play in Work and Games*. San Francisco: Jossey-Bass.

Dann, G. (1976) 'The holiday was simply fantastic', *Revue de Tourisme*, **3**, 19–23.

Dann, G. (1989) 'The tourist as child: some reflections', *Cahiers du Tourisme*, serie C, no. 135.

Dann, G. (1994*a*) 'Tourism: the nostalgia industry of the future', in W. Theobald, (ed.), *Global Tourism. The Next Decade*. Oxford: Butterworth-Heinemann, 55–67.

Dann, G. (1994*b*) 'Hyping the destination image through the rich and (in)famous. The boundaries of name dropping', *Cahiers du Tourisme*, serie C, no. 187.

Dann, G. (1996) *The Language of Tourism. A Sociolinguistic Perspective*. Wallingford: CAB International.

Dann, G. (1997) 'Tourist behaviour as controlled freedom', in R. Bushell (ed.), *Tourism Research. Building a Better Industry. Proceedings of the Australian Tourism and Hospitality Research Conference*, Sydney, 6–9 July. Canberra: Bureau of Tourism Research, 244–54.

Dann, G. (1998) 'The dark side of tourism', *Études et Rapports*, série L, vol. 14.

Dann, G. (1999) 'Noticing notices. Tourism to order', Paper presented to the International Academy for the Study of Tourism, Hotel Esplanade, Zagreb, 28 June–1 July.

Dickens, C. (1973) *Little Dorrit*, ed. J. Holloway. Harmondsworth: Penguin.

Dickens, C. (1989) *Pictures from Italy*. London: Robinson Publishing.

Du Maurier, D. (1992) *Don't Look Now*. Harmondsworth: Penguin.

Dunn, D. (1998) *Home Truths from Abroad. Television Representations of the Tourist*

Destination. Ph.D. thesis, Centre for Urban and Regional Studies, University of Birmingham.

Durrell, L. (1986) *Bitter Lemons of Cyprus.* London: Faber & Faber.

Eco, U. (1996) *Faith in Fakes. Travels in Hyperreality.* London: Minerva Books.

English, E. (1986) *The Great Escape. An Examination of North–South Tourism.* Ottawa: North–South Institute.

Enzensberger, H. (1962) *Einzelheiten.* Frankfurt-am-Main: Suhrkamp Verlag.

Erasmus (1965) *The Colloquies of Erasmus,* trans. C. Thompson. Chicago: University of Chicago Press.

Everyman Guide (1999) *Everyman Guide: Venice.* London: David Campbell.

Fjellman, S. (1992) *Vinyl Leaves. Walt Disney World and America.* Boulder: Westview Press.

Foley, M. and Lennon, J. (1996*a*) 'Heart of darkness', *International Journal of Heritage Studies,* **2**(4), 195–7.

Foley, M. and Lennon, J. (1996*b*) 'A fascination with assassination', *International Journal of Heritage Studies,* **2**(4), 198–211.

Foley, M. and Lennon, J. (1999) *Dark Tourism.* London: Cassell.

Goethe, J. (1970) *Italian Journey 1786–1788.* Harmondsworth: Penguin.

Goodey, B. (1994) 'Art-full places: public art to sell public spaces?' in J. Gold and S. Ward (eds), *Place Promotion. The Use of Publicity and Marketing to Sell Towns and Regions.* Chichester: John Wiley, 153–79.

Graburn, N. (1983) 'The anthropology of tourism', *Annals of Tourism Research,* **10**, 9–33.

Graburn, N. (1989) 'Tourism, the sacred journey', in V. Smith (ed.), *Hosts and Guests. The Anthropology of Tourism,* 2nd edn. Philadelphia: University of Pennsylvania Press, 21–36.

Gritti, J. (1967) 'Les contenus culturels du Guide Bleu. Monuments et sites "a voir"', *Communications,* **10**, 51–64.

Hanefors, M. and Larsson, L. (1998) 'Tourism motives and loyalty', *Annals of Tourism Research,* **25**, 749–52.

Hemingway, E. (1950) *Across the River and into the Trees.* Harmondsworth: Penguin.

Hibbert, C. (1988) *Venice. The Biography of a City.* London: Grafton Books.

Higgins, D. (1981) 'Introduction', in D. Alghieri, *The Divine Comedy,* trans. C. Sisson. London: Pan Books, 7–24.

Hollinshead, K. (1993) 'The truth about Texas', unpublished Ph.D. thesis, Texas A and M University.

Horne, D. (1984) *The Great Museum.* London: Pluto Press.

Hughes, H. (1997) 'Holidays and homosexual identity', *Tourism Management,* **18**(1), 3–7.

Jepson, T. (1996) 'Turning a blind eye to Venetian lore', *Weekend Telegraph,* 26 October.

Krippendorf, J. (1987) *The Holiday Makers. Understanding the Impact of Leisure and Travel.* Oxford: Heinemann.

Lanfant, M-F. (1980) 'Tourism in the process of internationalization', *International Social Science Journal,* **32**(1), 14–43.

Lash, S. (1990) *Sociology of Postmodernism*. London: Routledge.

Laurent, A. (1967) 'Le thême du soleil dans la publicité des organismes des vacances', *Communications*, **10**, 35–50.

Levi-Strauss, C. (1958) *Structural Anthropology*. New York: Basic Books.

MacCannell, D. (1973) 'Staged authenticity: arrangements of social space in tourist settings', *American Journal of Sociology*, **79**(3), 589–603.

MacCannell, D. (1976 (1989)) *The Tourist. A New Theory of the Leisure Class*. New York: Schocken Books.

MacCannell, D. (1992) *Empty Meeting Grounds. The Tourist Papers*. London: Routledge.

Mann, T. (1968) *Death in Venice*. Harmondsworth: Penguin.

Merriman, N. (1991) *Beyond the Glass Case: The Past, the Heritage and the Public in Britain*. London: Leicester University Press.

Milner, C. (1999) 'Jack and Jill's trip up the hill fetches a pail of money', *Sunday Telegraph*, 21 March.

Moeran, B. (1983) 'The language of Japanese tourism', *Annals of Tourism Research*, **10**, 93–108.

Mohamed, M. (1988) 'Moroccan tourism image in France', *Annals of Tourism Research* **15**, 558–61.

Moore, A. (1980) 'Walt Disney World: bounded ritual space and the playful pilgrimage center', *Anthropological Quarterly* **53**, 207–18.

Morris, J. (1987) *Conundrum*. Harmondsworth: Penguin.

Morris, J. (1988) 'On revisiting Venice', in P. Marsden-Smedley and J. Klinke (eds), *Views from Abroad: The Spectator Book of Travel Writing*. London: Paladin, 99–101.

Mumford, L. (1966) *The City in History*. Harmondsworth: Penguin.

Newby, E. (1985) *On the Shores of the Mediterranean*. London: Pan Books.

Newby, E. (1986) *A Book of Travellers' Tales*. London: Picador.

Nicolson, N. (1997) 'Immortal fame and passing faces', *Sunday Telegraph*, 20 July.

Nietzsche, F. (1911) *The Olympus of Illusion* (no publisher).

O'Neill, M. and Fay, S. (1994) 'Private views of Venice', *Condé Nast Traveler*, December, 116–25.

Papson, S. (1981) 'Spuriousness and tourism', *Annals of Tourism Research*, **8**, 220–35.

Paroissien, D. (1989) 'Introduction' in C. Dickens, *Pictures from Italy*. London: Robinson Publishing, 9–34.

Parrinello, G. (1993) 'Motivation and anticipation in post-industrial tourism', *Annals of Tourism Research* **20**, 233–49.

Pearce, P. (1982) *The Social Psychology of Tourist Behaviour*. Oxford: Pergamon.

Perry, V. (1991) 'Museum a shrine to Mexican rebel chief', *Toronto Star*, 21 September.

Powell, A, (1988) 'Like a rolling stone: notions of youth travel and tourism in pop music of the sixties, seventies and eighties', in N. Graburn (ed.), *Kroeber Anthropological Society Papers*, nos. 67–8, pp. 28–34.

Pretes, M. (1995) 'Postmodern tourism: the Santa Claus industry', *Annals of Tourism Research*, **22**, 1–15.

Pritchard, A., Morgan, N., Sedgley, D. and Jenkins, A. (1998) 'Reaching out to the gay tourist', *Tourism Management*, **19**(3), 273–82.

Proust, M. (1954) *À la récherche du temps perdu*, P. Clarac and A. Ferré (eds), 3 vols. Paris: Bibliothèque de la Pléiade.

Pruitt, D. and LaFont, S. (1995) 'For love and money. Romance tourism in Jamaica', *Annals of Tourism Research* **22**, 422–40.

Reed, T. (1994) *Death in Venice. Making and Unmaking a Master*. New York: Twayne Publishers.

Richter, L. (1999) 'The politics of heritage tourism development. Emerging issues for the new millennium', in D. Pearce and R. Butler (eds), *Contemporary Issues in Tourism Development*. London: Routledge, 108–26.

Rivers, P. (1972) *The Restless Generation. A Crisis in Mobility*. London: Davis-Poynter.

Robb, J. (1998) 'Tourism and legends. Archaeology of heritage', *Annals of Tourism Research*, **25**, 579–96.

Rogers, S. (1842) *Italy. A Poem*. London: Edward Moxon.

Rojek, C. (1993) *Ways of Escape: Modern Transformations in Leisure and Travel*. London: Macmillan.

Rojek, C. (1997) 'Indexing, dragging and the social construction of tourist sights', in C. Rojek and J. Urry (eds), *Touring Cultures. Transformations of Travel and Theory*. London: Routledge, 52–74.

Rolfe, F. (1934 (1986)) *The Desire and Pursuit of the Whole. A Romance of Modern Venice*. Oxford: Oxford University Press.

Rough Guide to the World (1998) *The Rough Guide to the World*. London: Rough Guides and Penguin.

Ruskin, J. (1851–53) (1985) *The Stones of Venice*. New York: De Capo Press.

Said, E. (1991) *Orientalism. Western Conceptions of the Orient*. Harmondsworth: Penguin.

Sasse, G. (1993) 'In search of beauty', in H. Vestner (ed.), *Insight Guides: Venice*. Hong Kong: APA Publications, 242–6.

Schutz, A. (1944) 'The stranger: an essay in social psychology', *American Journal of Sociology*, **49**(6), 495–507.

Schutz, A. (1972) *The Phenomenology of the Social World*. London: Heinemann.

Seaton, A. (1996) 'Guided by the dark: from thanatopsis to thanatourism', *International Journal of Heritage Studies*, **2**(4), 234–44.

Seaton, A. (1999) 'War and thanatourism: Waterloo 1815–1914', *Annals of Tourism Research*, **26**, 130–58.

Shakespeare, W. (1989) *The Merchant of Venice*, ed. M. Mahood. Cambridge: Cambridge University Press.

Shelley, P. (1990) *Shelley. Poetical Works*, ed. T. Hutchinson. Oxford: Oxford University Press.

Simmel, G. (1950) 'The stranger', in K. Wolff (ed.), *The Sociology of Georg Simmel*. Glencoe: Free Press.

Sontag, S. (1979) *On Photography*. Harmondsworth: Penguin.

Sowerby, R. (1986) *Homer, The Odyssey: Notes*. London: Longman.

Squire, S. (1994) 'The cultural values of literary tourism', *Annals of Tourism*

Research, **21**, 103–20.

Staten, V. (1990) *Unauthorized America. A Travel Guide to the Places the Chamber of Commerce Won't Tell You About*. New York: Harper & Row.

Sturma, M. (1999) 'Packaging Polynesia's image', *Annals of Tourism Research*, **26**, 712–15.

Taylor, J. (1994) *A Dream of England. Landscape Photography and the Tourist's Imagination*. Manchester: Manchester University Press.

Theroux, P. (1977) *The Great Railway Bazaar*. Harmondsworth: Penguin.

Theroux, P. (1980) *The Old Patagonian Express*. Harmondsworth: Penguin.

Thurot, J. (1989) 'Psychologie du loisir touristique', *Cahiers du Tourisme*, serie C, no. 23.

Tisdall, N. (1998a) 'Unlocking the people's Venice', *Sunday Telegraph*, 26 July.

Tisdall, N. (1998b) 'Are you serious or just flirting?' *Sunday Telegraph Review*, 27 September.

Twain, M. (1967) *The Innocents Abroad*. New York: Airmont Publishing.

Urbain, J. (1993) *L'idiot du voyage. Histoires de touristes*. Paris: Éditions Payot et Rivages.

Urry, J. (1990) *The Tourist Gaze. Leisure and Travel in Contemporary Societies*. London: Sage.

Urry, J. (1995) *Consuming Places*. London: Routledge.

Williamson, J. (1983) *Decoding Advertisements. Ideology and Meaning in Advertising*. London: Marion Boyars.

Wordsworth, W. (1909) *The Complete Works of William Wordsworth*. London and Glasgow: Collins.

Chapter 13

African Sublime: The Dark Continent Joins the Grand Tour

Amber Vogel

AFRICAN NIGHT PIECE

Horace Walpole wrote to Horace Mann, 'Africa is indeed coming into fashion' (vol. 24: 21). This was in 1774, the year James Bruce – to whom Walpole was referring in his letter – arrived in London after a long interval of travel, so he said, in Abyssinia. It should be noted, too, that 1774 was the year of Oliver Goldsmith's death, and that the fashion Walpole mentions was one Goldsmith had been helping to shape. The sometimes-Gothic traces of the Dark Continent in his work will surprise readers who believe that Goldsmith generally limited himself to the domestic, the comic and the sentimental. But because he was prodigious in his absorption and production of texts in many of their popular forms, because Africa was a topic he touched on frequently, and because some of what he wrote about Africa in *Animated Nature* became lore for many readers and even for some travellers in Africa – for a century or so afterward, Goldsmith is actually a good touchstone for several of the subtler points of the evolution of Africa in British literature.

An aspect of Goldsmith's art – and perhaps of his character – is its recurrence to themes, to apparent preoccupations. This might have been a matter of efficiency necessary for a hack-writer. But it also seems to have been a result of Goldsmith's abiding passion and thwarted ambition for exotic travel that African themes and images are interjected even into essays that are ostensibly written on domestic scenes or issues. An obvious example, appearing as Letter 114 in *Citizen of the World*, is a set piece on marriage for love – and its improbability in such a mercenary age as Goldsmith's. The letter presents a parade of the world's eligible women, among whom are 'the black beauties of Benin, (...) the women of Wida with well-scarred faces, and the hideous virgins of Caffraria', as well as 'the virgins of Congo' (266). Letter 115, on the hazard of excessive regard for human nature, describes the Portuguese explorers' arrival 'among the wretched inhabitants of the coast of Africa' (266). Letter 116, about changing fashions in beauty, states that 'in the kingdom of

Loango ladies of the very best fashion are sold for a pig; queens, however, sell better, and sometimes amount to a cow' (268). Here Africa, like China, the home of Goldsmith's fictional correspondent, supplies a counterpoint to European custom. It is often in this style, which poses what is known about the continent as factual but curious to the point of improbability, that Africa finds its way into the nooks and crannies of almost every kind of text Goldsmith produced.

Goldsmith's associates included men like Samuel Johnson (whose well-known disdain of Bruce, his rival as an authority on Abyssinia, does not redound to his credit) having a professional interest in African travellers and their tales. Indeed, the small literary club, among whose first members Goldsmith and Johnson were, grew to include, by 1797, Joseph Banks and James Rennell, leading figures in the African Association. Goldsmith had his own professional interest in writers, from Adanson to Voltaire, who represented a wide range of those producing African materials in his time. In addition, the idiosyncratic Goldsmith's own longing after Asian adventure, his mysterious travels on the Grand Tourist's circuit, his expatriation from Ireland to England, and the strains of melancholy and loss in his work, suggest that he would have been particularly responsive to a number of motifs beginning to cluster around Africa – and hence around travellers there.

In 'Zanzibar; and Two Months in East Africa', serialized in *Blackwood*'s in 1858, Richard Burton both describes and reflects the aesthetic of decay, the rhetoric of loss, that had for decades generated and shaped European interest in Africa:

> African travel in the heroic ages of Bruce, Mungo Park, and Clapperton, had a prestige which lived through two generations; and, as is the fate of things sublunary, came to an untimely end. The public, satiated with adventure and invention, suffers in these days of 'damnable licence of printing' from the humours of severe surfeit. It nauseates the monotonous recital of rapine, treachery, and murder; of ugly savages – the *mala gens*, as was said anent Kentish men, of a *bona terra* – of bleared misery by day, and animated filth by night, and of hunting adventures and hairbreadth escapes, lacking the interest of catastrophe. It laments the absence of tradition and monuments of the olden time, the dearth of variety, of beauty, of romance. Yet the theme still continues to fulfil all the conditions of attractiveness set forth by Leigh Hunt. It has remoteness and obscurity of place, difference of custom, marvellousness of hearsay. Events surpassing, yet credible; sometimes barbaric splendour – at least luxuriance of nature; savage contentment, personal danger and suffering, with a moral enthusiasm. ('Zanzibar' 1–2)

The terms in which Burton describes African travel here, and shows himself rhetorically wandering over the ruins of travellers who have gone before him, recall eighteenth-century literary models generally – and Goldsmith's 'A City Night Piece', in particular. Goldsmith published 'A City Night Piece' twice: in the fourth number of *The Bee*, dated 27 October 1759, and as Letter 112 in *The Citizen of the World*, in 1761.

The theme and wording are re-echoed in *The Vicar of Wakefield*, published in 1766, when the hero's fortunes reach their nadir and he laments, 'To see my children all untimely falling about me, while I continue a wretched survivor in the midst of ruin!' (69). In addition, Arthur Friedman points out that a portion lifted from Goldsmith's *Life of Voltaire*, published earlier that year, reappears in 'A City Night

Piece' (1: 431n2). Wherever Goldsmith repeats himself, it is usually rewarding to investigate. Here is the essay's central passage:

> There will come a time when this temporary solitude may be made continual, and the city itself, like its inhabitants, fade away, and leave a desert in its room.
>
> What cities, as great as this, have once triumphed in existence, had their victories as great as ours, joy as just, and as unbounded; and, with short-sighted presumption, promised themselves immortality. Posterity can hardly trace the situation of some: the sorrowful traveller wanders over the awful ruins of others, and as he beholds, he learns wisdom, and feels the transience of every sublunary possession.
>
> 'Here,' he cries, 'stood their citadel, now grown over with weeds; there their senate-house, but now the haunt of every noxious reptile; temples and theatres stood here, now only an undistinguished heap of ruin.' (382)

Though it never mentions the Dark Continent, Goldsmith's 'A City Night Piece' suggests a cultural source for, or a culture's taste for, such darkness. It suggests, too, a ready-made rhetorical framework in which African travel narratives were set in the eighteenth and nineteenth centuries. Here is the combination of elements – solitude and wilderness, travel and ruin, regret and desire, memory and lament – that form rhetorical patterns put to use by African travellers, commentators and literary artists presenting Africa to a growing, evolving audience. Such deserts, such bleak prospects, fitted what might, adapting an eighteenth-century aesthetic paradigm, be called an African Sublime. It was a powerful aesthetic that endured in an unlikely continent.

WORTHY OF THE PENCIL

In an age when epistemologies could be mapped like a world, Africa was, for many readers, at first most vividly a graphic image, a map set out in a periodical or in a textbook or over the surface of a globe. In 1788, the founders of 'an Association for promoting the Discovery of the Interior Parts of the Africa' noted that, 'while we continue ignorant of so large a portion of the globe, that ignorance must be considered as a degree of reproach upon the present age' (*Analytical Review* June 1788: 222, 223). The botanist Adam Afzelius wrote from Sierra Leone in 1794: 'I am almost determined, if I live till next year, to undertake an expedition through the whole of this unknown part of the globe, an enterprize which no man has yet performed' (quoted in Wadström 2: 129). In a discussion of several accounts of expeditions to discover, or rediscover, ancient cities along the northern coast of Africa, a writer in the *Edinburgh Review* for September 1828 lamented, 'Though we certainly know more of the globe than was known to any older people, it is remarkable that considerable portions of it that were familiar to other generations, have been shut, and lost, as it were, to us' (220). The process of exploring Africa, to know that *terra incognita*, found an impetus in the need to complete the continent's graphic representation – to see the side of the globe hidden from the viewer's eye, to recover the lost as well as to find the undiscovered places on the map, and to see the world whole.

In Johnson's definition of *globe*, 'terraqueous ball', it might be a plaything as much as a planet (*Dictionary* 1: no page). An English idea of landscape, and an English vocabulary to describe it, were just beginning to evolve in the eighteenth century. In a *Spelling Dictionary of the English Language, on a New Plan*, published by John Newbery and (given the evidence of at least one library catalogue) perhaps compiled by Goldsmith, 'landskip' is given as the only spelling (no page). This is the spelling used in Johnson's translation – or, more appropriately, his version – of Jeronimo Lobo's *A Voyage to Abyssinia*, published in 1735. Because Johnson based his own work on the version of Lobo's account heavily edited by Joachim Le Grand and published in 1728, one is tempted to treat the following as an eighteenth-century, rather than as an early seventeenth-century, artefact: 'I doubt whether even the Imagination of a Painter has yet conceiv'd a Landskip as Beautiful as I have seen' (109). Simon Schama explains that *landscape* 'entered the English language, along with herring and bleached linen, as a Dutch import at the end of the sixteenth century. And *landschap* (...) in the colloquial English of the time became a *landskip*' (10). Johnson's *Dictionary* offers this: 'Landscape [*landschape*, Dutch] 1. A region; the prospect of a country. 2. A picture, representing an extent of space, with the various objects in it' (2: no page). Embedded in the word, and not yet too deeply to go unseen, were the notions of 'land shape' and 'land shaping', of a nature designed or ordered, that suited an eighteenth-century view of the world.

It is important to set out how commonly and casually a wide variety of African travel-writers, who were otherwise various in their motives and outlooks, applied the same aesthetic framework and vocabulary to the African landscape. The 'picturesque' and the 'sublime', in particular, recur. Regarding a spot on his first journey, Mungo Park writes, 'the face of the country is every where interspersed with a pleasing variety of hills and vallies; and the windings of the Senegal river, which descends from the rocky hills of the interior, make the scenery on its banks very picturesque and beautiful' (63). Richard Lander writes that the country between Boussa, where Park was killed, and another site 'is hilly, woody, and picturesque, rivalling in beauty any portion between Badagry and Soccatoo' (Captain Clapperton's Last Expedition 1: 142). Even John Speke, considered to be one of the travellers least likely to respond to the felicities of the landscape, draws upon these aesthetic conventions. On his way back from Lake Tanganyika, he writes, 'The country still continues of the same rich and picturesque character' (*What Led to the Discovery of the Source of the Nile*: 283). And, also, 'while in sight of the Victoria N'yanza, we ascended the most beautiful hills, covered with verdure of all descriptions. (...) The whole land was a picture of quiescent beauty, with a boundless sea in the background' (*Journal of the Discovery of the Source of the Nile*: 266–7).

It is difficult to find a difference between many passages in African travel narratives and Arthur Young's description of Lake Windermere, published in *A Six Months' Tour through the North of England* in 1770:

Strain your imagination to command the idea of so noble an expanse of water thus gloriously environed; spotted with islands more beautiful than would have issued from the pencil of the happiest painter. Picture the mountains rearing their majestic heads with native sublimity; the vast rocks boldly projecting their terrible craggy points: And, in the path of beauty, the variegated inclosures of the most charming verdure, hanging to the eye in every picturesque form that can grace landscape, with the most exquisite touches of *la belle nature*. (quoted in Parks: 29)

Even West Africa, renowned for a climate deadly to Europeans, could – though with some reservations – be appreciated for similar topographical beauties, as Sarah Lee and Elizabeth Melville write:

> The appearance of this place is highly picturesque: the mountains, with their forest-covered tops, rising loftily behind the town; and the river winding beautifully, and gradually losing itself in the dark masses of foliage which line its banks. (Lee 1830: 96)

> There are certainly few spots that can boast of so much natural grandeur and beauty as Sierra Leone, yet you feel that the want of wood, the absence of cultivation and of animal life, in the grim bare hills, is neither entirely counterbalanced by the sublimity of the frowning peaks and yawning chasms, nor by the distant prospect of the opposite shore, the silvery river and its sleeping islands. (Melville: 249)

In East Africa, a century after Young, Charles New writes of ascending Kilimanjaro: 'It was a truly magnificent sight. Behind the moving clouds, set up against a sky or purest azure, there it shone motionless and sublime. (...) The aspect presented by this prodigious mountain is one of unparalleled grandeur, sublimity, majesty, and glory' (379–81). And in passages of *How I Found Livingstone* that – given its author's reputation for gaucherie and, worse, for brutality – are surprisingly dulcet, Henry Stanley attempts to define the particular quality of the African landscape with reference to standards of picturesqueness and sublimity with which his wide audience would presumably be familiar:

> This beautiful prospect, glorious in its wild nature, fragrant with its numerous flowers and variety of sweetly-smelling shrubs, among which I recognised the wild sage, the indigo plant, &c., terminated at the foot of Kira Peak and sister cones, which mark the boundaries between Udoe and Ukami, yet distant twenty miles. Those distant mountains formed a not unfit background to this magnificent picture of open plain, forest patches, and sloping lawns – there was enough of picturesqueness and sublimity in the blue mountains to render it one complete whole. (110)

> Stand upon any coign of vantage you like, on the height of some of those great Titanic boulders of syenite which crop up above the crest of the hills around Mgongo Temo, or the rocky humps of Ngaraiso, and you will behold a scene the like of which you never saw before. They are no grand mountains, or sublime heights; there is no picturesqueness about it – you would call it prosaic, monotonous, perhaps, for you will have witnessed the same scene a hundred times before you will have arrived in Uyanzi; but in this excessive monotony there is sublimity. The ocean, churned into foam and wild waves, is sublime; the ocean, slumbering under the equatorial sun, reflecting the deep blue of the firmament – extending without a ruffle you know not how far – is sublime; and so is there sublimity in this view of the great, the infinite, apparently endless extent of forests in Unyamwezi. The foliage is of all the colors of the prism; but as the woods roll away into the distance the calm, mysterious haze enwraps them in its soft shroud; paints them first a light blue, then gradually a deeper blue, until, in the distance, there appears but a dim looming; and on gazing at its faded contour we find ourselves falling into a day-dream, as indistinct in its outline as the view which appears on the horizon. I defy any one to gaze

on such a scene long without wishing that his life would fade away as serenely as the outlines of the forests in Unyamwezi. (520–1)

In *Nature into Art: Cultural Transformations in Nineteenth-Century Britain*, Carl Woodring explains: 'By the late seventeenth century in England "picturesque" meant like a picture by Claude Lorrain or Gaspard Poussin (Dughet) – or one of the more relaxed and less populated scenes of the great Nicholas Poussin' (42). And in *Grand Tours and Cook's Tours: A History of Leisure Travel, 1750 to 1915*, Lynne Withy says, 'To describe a scene as "worthy of the pencil of a Claude" became a stock phrase in travelers' accounts' (43). Woodring's study is of British interpretations of domestic scenery; and Withy's is 'a history of leisure travel' on the well-trodden, over-managed routes along which tourists were likely neither to be lost nor diverted from received opinion. In Africa, these routes were mainly confined to the bit of Egypt in which Thomas Cook had organized package tours in the latter part of the nineteenth century. But the statements by Woodring and Withy may also be applied to narratives of travellers in less-hospitable and less-travelled parts of Africa. Thomas Winterbottom, a physician and ethnologist working in Sierra Leone at the end of the eighteenth century, writes in *An Account of the Native Africans in the Neighbourhood of Sierra Leone*: 'In sailing up these rivers, the eye is charmed with a landscape perpetually varying, which would afford full scope to the genius and pencil of a Claude' (1: 3). In *A Residence at Sierra Leone*, Melville describes 'a ruined house, close enough to form a picturesque feature in a place, the soft quiet beauty of which reminded me of the paintings of Poussin and Claude'; and a band of hunters who, gathered around the cooking-fire at dusk 'present quite a picture that reminds you in its wildness of some of Salvator Rosa's' (6–7; 277). On the other hand, rustic elements in English scenes Melville observes during a visit home 'seemed objects worthy of the pencil of Edwin Landseer' (170).

Interestingly, African explorers sometimes revealed their sense of themselves as being the subjects of art, and considered their appropriateness to the scenes in which they figured. When Hugh Clapperton's company stops at a spot, he writes that 'there we performed an African dance, to the great delight of the surrounding multitude. The *tout ensemble* would doubtless have formed an excellent subject for a caricaturist, and we regretted the absence of Captain Pearce [who was recuperating from an illness] to sketch off the old black caboceer' (*Journal of a Second Expedition into the Interior of Africa*: 14). James Hannington's cartoons, in which he depicted himself as a comic adventurer for the benefit of his children back in England, are charming and, given his death at the hands of Mwanga's men, particularly poignant. Hannington, whose experience in Africa, particularly farther inland, was relatively limited, measured the landscape against images of it seen at home: 'We were now on the verge of the vast and almost waterless plain which lies between Taita and Taveta, and we were warned to expect no water for at least two days. (...) This plain exactly fulfils the idea which I had formed of an African plain from pictures and descriptions before I visited the country' (quoted in Dawson: 355–6). In similar fashion, Hannington had to evaluate his own African experience in terms of an image of another explorer: 'I have often thought of poor Dr. Livingstone's trials, and realized what he went through, for my own experience very closely resembled his. If the picture on the cover of "His Last Journals" is correct, my mode of being carried across deep streams is, I think, better than his' (quoted in Dawson: 285–6). Like Livingstone, whose own death scene was evidently rather grim, Clapperton and Hannington perished in Africa. Having set themselves in what would turn out to be a Gothic landscape, they were doomed to act out its rituals, its inevitable tragedy.

NEW PALMYRAS

In the context of an expedition to the Niger, Lander complains that the 'African sky seldom displays the clear, rich ether, or the beautiful and evanescent touches of the Italian' (*Captain Clapperton's Last Expedition* 1: 307–08). Lander, who at one point in his varied career was a servant to wealthy travellers in Europe, was evidently familiar with the aesthetics of the Grand Tour, which would have prominently featured real Italian landscapes. However, drawing from his own experience, Goldsmith notes in *An Inquiry into the Present State of Polite Learning*, 'Countries wear very different appearances to travellers of different circumstances. A man who is whirled through Europe in a post-chaise, and the pilgrim who walks the grand tour on foot, will form very different conclusions' (442). The versions of the Grand Tour taken by relatively poor men such as Lander and Goldsmith suggest the limits placed on their possible ambitions – the limits placed on those who were educated well enough to harbour ambitions and still poor enough to have those ambitions thwarted. The Grand Tour, which might have served as an undemanding finishing school for some young travellers, was not as accessible – at least not on the same terms – or even as attractive to others. The anonymous Englishman who introduces Michel Adanson's narrative in 1759 writes, 'The love of natural history, and an ardent desire of fame, excited this gentleman very early in life, to exchange his native soil for the burning sands of Senegal' (iv). This same appeal to the 'desire of fame' is made in 'Construction of the Map of Africa', an essay contained in the African Association's Proceedings for 1790. Here James Rennell suggests:

> To the lovers of adventure and novelty, Africa displays a most ample field: but the qualification of local manners, and, in some degree, of habits, must in this case, be superadded to that of language: and this, unquestionably, renders the undertaking more arduous than that of an ordinary tour. But the adventurer in quest of fame, will readily appreciate the degrees of glory attendant on each pursuit. (quoted in Hallett, *Records of the African Association*: 246–7)

In fact, these records of the African Association, which serve as a remarkable travel brochure for the would-be explorer, not only posit a new location for the Grand Tour, but formulate a new motive for it. Africa's attraction increasingly became an economic one. In Africa there were profits to be made in an opening market, natural resources to be exploited, bodies to be acquired for or saved from the slave trade, and – if one wants to tally the spiritual account book – souls to be accrued for a Western god. Even the ruins – or the promise of ruins – of civilizations, the requisite feature of the Grand Tour, could be framed in economic terms – the detritus of wealth and array having its own poignant allure, telling its own cautionary tale.

   The strenuousness of the tour it proposed, paired with the Association's interest in its potential economic benefits, produced travellers from the classes we do not usually associate with the conventional, leisurely tour, unless as paid companions. Some resultant tensions in the social fabric as a result of the opportunities that Africa came to afford could be perceived in the early 1830s, when a lieutenant-governor at Sierra Leone publicly called for a rather better sort of missionary and schoolmaster than 'the inferior class which had accepted the posts, and who simply did so, in his opinion, to enable them "to live like gentlemen"'' (Crooks: 157). In any case, for individual travellers from the lower and middle classes, Africa became an avenue to social advancement, the dividends of which might be a modest profit, as well as glory and the greater good:

> To the British *traveler*, a desire of exchanging the usual excursion from Calais to Naples, for a tour more extended and important, and of passing from scenes with which all are acquainted, to researches in which every object is new, and each step is discovery, may recommend the kingdom of Fezzan. If antiquities be his favourite pursuit, the ruins which shadow the cottages of Jermah and of Temissa promise an ample gratification; or if the study of nature be his wish, the expansive scenes and numerous productions of that uninvestigated soil may equally promote his entertainment and his knowledge. But if a spirit of more adventurous research should induce him to travel with the merchants of Fezzan, discoveries of superior value may distinguish and reward his toil. The powerful empires of Bornou and Cashna will be open to his investigation; the luxurious city of Tombuctou [*sic*], whose opulence and severe police attract the merchants of the most distant states of Africa, will unfold to him the causes of her vast prosperity; the mysterious Niger will disclose her unknown original and doubtful termination; and countries unveiled to ancient or modern research will become familiar to his view. Or should he be willing to join the Cairo caravan, the discovery of the ancient site, and of whatever else may remain of the temple of Jupiter Ammon, may perhaps be attempted with success; for the same causes which gave birth to the springs; and, by their means, to the luxuriant vegetation of the ancient domains of the temple, must still continue to distinguish the fortunate soil. (quoted in Hallett, *Records of the African Association*: 100)

In Africa, then, fresh sets of ruins were now available to a new sort of tourist intrepid enough to discover them and, it goes unspoken, hardy enough to survive the trip.
   When he wrote 'A City Night Piece', Goldsmith might have had a number of archaeological sites in mind. His library held a copy of 'Sandys's Travels, 1637' (Prior: 581). So he might have read, in the dedication to *Relation of a Journey*, George Sandys's commentary on the ruins of Troy and of Constantinople and of empires in general. At the ruins of the Egyptian city Memphis, Sandys asks: 'But why spend I time about that that is not? The very ruines now almost ruinated: yet some few impressions are left, and diuers throwne downe, statues of monstrous resemblance: a scarce sufficient testimony to shew vnto the curious seeker, that there it hath bin' (quoted in Davis: 65). In *An Inquiry into the Present State of Polite Learning*, Goldsmith comments on the interest, then reaching giddy heights, in Italian ruins and their related artefacts:

> In Italy, then, we shall nowhere find a stronger passion for the arts of taste, yet no country making more feeble efforts to promote either. (...) The Virtuosi, (...) in statuary, hang over a fragment with the most ardent gaze of admiration; though wanting

the head and the other extremities, if dug from a ruin, the Torso become inestimable. An unintelligible monument of Etruscan barbarity cannot be sufficiently prized; and anything from Herulaneum excites rapture. (425)

Christopher Hibbert notes that 'a visit to Pompeii and Herculaneum became *de rigueur* for the tourist after 1740' (*Grand Tour*: 192). Other sites, in Italy and the East, excited interest and spawned texts: *The Ruins of Baalbek*, by Robert Wood and James Dawkins, in 1757; *The Ruins of the Palace of the Emperor Diocletian at Spolatro*, by Robert Adam, in 1764; and so on. But the most famous – or, rather, the most rhetorically vivid – of these sites at the time Goldsmith was writing 'A City Night Piece' was Palmyra. This site – which, like Baalbeck, was located in what is now Syria – had been discovered by Wood and Dawkins in 1751. These travellers published a folio, *The Ruins of Palmyra*, in 1753, and were the subject of Gavin Hamilton's painting *The Discovery of Palmyra by Wood and Dawkins*, in 1758 (Joseph Burke: no page).

Based on a verse in the Old Testament – 'And he built Tadmor in the wilderness' (*2 Chronicles*: 8.4) – Palmyra was thought to have been founded by Solomon. Its history, or mythology, since then had been similarly filled with incident. All this was well known in Goldsmith's circle. Goldsmith's *Roman History*, first published in 1769, tells of Palmyra's fall. Hesther Piozzi writes of Johnson:

A young fellow asked him abruptly one day, Pray, Sir, what and where is Palmira: I heard somebody talk last night of the ruins of Palmira. ''Tis a hill in Ireland (replies Johnson), with palms growing on the top, and a bog at the bottom, and so they call it *Palm-mira*.' Seeing however that the lad thought him serious, and thanked him for the information, he undeceived him very gently indeed; told him the history, geography, and chronology of Tadmor in the wilderness, with every incident that literature could furnish I think, or eloquence express, from the building of Solomon's palace to the voyage of Dawkins and Wood. (64)

In *The Decline and Fall of the Roman Empire*, Gibbon notes:

Some English travelers from Aleppo *discovered* the ruins of Palmyra, about the end of the last century. Our curiosity has since been gratified in a more splendid manner by Messieurs Wood and Dawkins. For the history of Palmyra, we may consult the masterly dissertation of Dr. Halley in the Philosophical Transactions: Lowthorp's Abridgment, vol. iii. p. 518. (1: 173, n. 69)

Here Gibbon refers to William Halifax, who went to Aleppo in 1691. Gibbon also seems to refer to a book Goldsmith had in his own library: 'Philosophical Transactions, 3 vols. The same abridged, by Lowthorp and Jones, 5 vols.' (Prior: 582).

An important thematic successor to Gibbon's work, Volney's *Ruins: or, Meditations on the Revolutions of Empires*, first published in 1792, takes Palmyra as its starting point; and the pathetic allure of this site continued to infuse a variety of texts well into the nineteenth century. African travel narratives also referred to this archeological conceit. In the *Edinburgh Review* for September 1828, a writer describes the mixed success of exploration in North Africa. Ptolemeta supplied the requisite remains and evocative 'solitude and desolation'; but another site fell far short of being 'a second Palmyra':

They travelled nine days through a difficult and desolate country; continually encouraged by accounts of the numerous population of this city of stone, and only warned against the impious attempt to remove any of those whom the judgment of Heaven had doomed to remain for ever rooted to that fatal spot. Captain Smith, who was exceedingly at his ease on this head, proceeded with increased alacrity, and passed the tenth night in sleepless expectation that his eyes would open on the pomp of a second Palmyra. In the morning, he hurried to the spot; where he saw a few clumsy modern houses, near which were a number of tombs, on which were sculptured, or rather scratched, some objects which did bear a remote analogy to the figures of men, camels, and horses. As Captain Smith viewed with contempt these rude works of some neighbouring Arabs, his Turkish conductor undertook to open his eyes to their beauties, pointing out, in particular, a horse, and appealing to him whether it had not actually four legs. (231)

In the 1870s, Charles New, a traveller in East Africa, writes: 'Some splendid palmyra groves adorn the shore along which we skirted, greatly exciting our admiration. They reminded us of some pictures we have seen of the magnificent ruins of "Tadmor in the wilderness," also called Palmyra' (248–9).

In *A Dissertation on the Course and Probable Termination of the Niger*, published in 1829, Sir Rufane Donkin describes the destiny of an extant civilization that is bound to fall

under the ill-defined denomination of Sahara – advancing, I repeat, to the annihilation of Egypt and all her glories, with the silence, but with the certainty too, of all-devouring time!

There is something quite appalling in the bare contemplation of this inexorable onward march of wholesale death to kingdoms, to mighty rivers, and to nations; the more so, when we reflect that the destruction must, from its nature, be not only complete, but eternal, on the spot on which it falls! (quoted in *Edinburgh Review* 30 Jan. 1830: 502)

These 'sublime and awful contemplations', as the writer in the *Edinburgh Review* derisively labels them, are the offshoot of Donkin's theory that the Niger was hidden because it had been diverted to 'a course beneath the silicious sands of Africa', and that it became marshland toward the Mediterranean (*Edinburgh Review* 30 Jan. 1830: 502). Once, however, this now-secret part of the river flowed, and – Donkin avers – 'it had its cities, its sages, its warriors, its works of art, and its inundations, like the "Classic Nile"' (quoted in *Edinburgh Review* 30 Jan. 1830: 502). The redoubtable geographer James Macqueen pointed out that the 'absurdity' of Donkin's theory 'was made manifest by the modern discoveries of Denham and Clapperton' (*Blackwood's* Feb. 1832: 213). But that the theory was in circulation at all suggests something about how travellers and readers, having assimilated the conventions both of the Grand Tour and of the Gothic aesthetic, had been trained to expect and interpret – and even hunger after – the glamour and terror of lost civilizations and their artefacts. Such secular relics – whether they existed in actuality or only rhetorically – memorialized the poignancy of human effort that had come to nothing, and the similarly poignant efforts of those people who went in rescue of the evidence of a tragic, but therefore more alluring, human past.

An edition of *The Life and Travels of Mungo Park* first published in 1840 gives a portion of Park's life, constructed from the records of his second journey, the running head 'Picturesque Scenery':

[H]e describes the country as beautiful beyond imagination, with all the possible diversities of rock, sometimes towering up like ruined castles, spires, pyramids, &c. 'We passed one place', he says, 'so like a ruined Gothic abbey, that we halted a little before we could satisfy ourselves that the niches, windows, ruined staircase, &c., were all natural rock. A faithful description of this place would certainly be deemed a fiction.' (187)

An entry in Hugh Clapperton's journal reads: 'Left El Wata, the country around which is well cultivated. The ant-hills here are the highest I have ever seen, being from fifteen to twenty feet high, resembling so many Gothic cathedrals in miniature' (117). Samuel Baker describes a 'fine granite mountain (...) picturesquely dotted over with villages' and 'numerous high rocks of granite, which from a distance produced the effect of ruined castles' (2: 18). New writes, 'Night, too, came on, covering everything with its dark pall, when there we were, shut up in that "dark dungeon of innumerous boughs." What a profound solitude! There seemed to be nothing in the world but ourselves' (407). Here, by means of a slightly misquoted line from Milton's *Comus*, New fittingly evokes the 'arboreal Gothic', in which the Gothic reveals its architectural roots in dense groves and archways of trees (Schama: 229). By the time Mary Kingsley arrives, at the end of the nineteenth century, settlers have built a 'big Wesleyan church (...) in the terrible Africa-Gothic style' that she finds on Cape Coast (22).

OPPRESSIVE TO THE HEART

In his report on Réné Caillié's travels to Timbuctoo, Edme-François Jomard inventories the principal travellers who had attempted to penetrate into Africa: 'Twenty-five Englishmen figure in this list', Jomard reports, 'with fourteen Frenchmen, two Americans, and one German: but there are few of them, alas! since Major Houghton, who have not fallen victims to their heroic devotion' (Caillié: 239). Such lists are ritual in African travel narratives and reports of the period. So, too, are references to such lists, or to *the* list that – somewhere, on Earth or elsewhere – registers all who are lost. For instance, in 1824, an obituary in the *Gentleman's Magazine* announced:

> 1822, September 27th. At Wiled Medinet, a day's journey from Sennaar, from whence he was proceeding in an attempt to penetrate up the sources of the Bahr Cotitaid [*sic*], Captain R. J. Gordon R.N. who had often distinguished himself during the late war. He was third son of Capt. Gordon, of Everton, near Bawtry. His death adds another victim to the melancholy list of those who have perished in the cause of African discovery. (quoted in Hallett, *Records of the African Association*: 235)

The astonishingly long roll of those killed while attempting to explore Africa, particularly in the first decades of the nineteenth century, includes men such as this Capt. Gordon, whose claim to fame is that he succeeded in becoming a 'victim ... in the cause of African discovery'.

The 'melancholy list' was drawn up in a language well known to those who took an interest in African exploration. With frequent use, its vocabulary came to comprise a jargon that journalists, historians and other commentators must have found convenient. However, those who seem to have known this language best and for whom its use was most vital, were the explorers themselves – including many of those 'melancholy' and 'lamented' and 'unfortunate' men on it. The list, which formed a crucial record of their perilous endeavour, of their self-sacrifice, was one that African explorers were aware they could – and probably would – join. Indeed, they seemed to prefer to join rather than be forgotten. Before he and his brother set out in 1830, Richard Lander wrote that 'if, by any casualty or unforeseen misfortune, we perish in Africa, and are seen no more, even then our fate will not be more dismal than that of many of our predecessors in the same pursuit, whose gallant enterprising spirits have sunk into darkness, without a voice to record their melancholy end' (*Captain Clapperton's Last Expedition* 1: xxiii). The Landers' project was, in part, to recover the relics of Mungo Park. On an earlier expedition, Richard Lander had already found traces of lost explorers to be African landmarks as important as anything native to the region. He had said of Boussa, that it was 'chiefly remarkable as the place where the enterprising Mr. Park and his companions came by their melancholy death' (*Captain Clapperton's Last Expedition* 1: 141).

Such recognition of, and even some grim pride in, one's peril in Africa persisted among early colonials. Melville refers to Sierra Leone as 'this grave of Europeans' and 'this "Grave of the British"' (198, 244). Without any apparent sense of irony she notes her reading list: 'We brought out, amongst other books, that on this colony entitled "The White Man's Grave," It is remarkably well written' (185). Here Melville seems to refer to F. Harrison Rankin's *The White Man's Grave: A Visit to Sierra Leone, in 1834*, published in 1836. Alta Jablow writes that the 'image of West Africa as the White Man's Graveyard (. . .) remained as one of the most stable in the entire tradition' of an 'essentially epic literature' produced by and about the explorers of this region in the early nineteenth century (298, 297). Perhaps the epic is, indeed, the form with which to match the narratives of and about Park, Clapperton and their kind. But it seems more appropriate to associate them – and narratives of travel in other regions of Africa – with the more depressive aesthetic cults that were the literary fashion of their own time, and particularly with the whole complement of Gothic ornaments. Among the most important of these was solitude, transported from its soothing, pastoral origins to a thrilling, terrible setting and transfigured there.

In the May 1757 number of the *Monthly Review*, Goldsmith's summary of Edmund Burke's *Philosophical Enquiry into the Origin of Our Ideas of the Sublime and Beautiful* highlights this point: 'All general privations are great, because they are terrible, as vacuity, darkness, solitude, silence' (*Collected Works* 1: 32). George Thompson's *Travels and Adventures in Southern Africa*, published in 1827, exhibits the appropriate response to such sublime 'privations':

> The scenery around this spot is certainly picturesque and imposing in a high degree. The lofty, rugged mountains on the left, crested with clouds, and clothed along their skirts with majestic forests, – those woods irregular, dark, hoary with moss, and ancient-looking almost as the rocks which frown above them, or the eternal ocean itself which murmurs at their feet, – form altogether a scene of grandeur which fills the imagination with magnificent and romantic images; accompanied however with ideas of wildness, vastness, and solitary seclusion, almost oppressive to the heart. (4)

In the latter part of the nineteenth century, when these aesthetic values had been well integrated into the rhetoric, New writes similarly of his ascent of Kilimanjaro:

> The sensations too, which came over me at the idea of the profound solitude, of standing on heights to which no human being had ever before ascended were overpowering. The situation was appalling, there was a grandeur and magnificence about the surroundings which were almost too much for me; instead of exhilarating they were oppressive. (429)

As an example of 'the awe-inspiring wonder which raises the beautiful to the sublime', a late-Victorian scholar (if we may say that a scholar whose treatise was first published in 1906 is a late-Victorian) gives as an example the Victoria Falls (Prickard: xix). Livingstone had discovered these falls in 1855, and they were coming more fully into view for a European audience through word and picture and, in rare instances, first-hand observation. Frank Harris, a somewhat unexpected tourist there, writes of his journey, made in 1896:

> Still, I won through to the Zambesi, and one sunlit morning, for the first time, the great Victoria Falls that dwarf Niagara, burst on me, robed in rainbow mists, as if to hide the depths, while the great Zambesi stretched away to the right, a silver pathway to the far-off sea. The solitude, the scenery, the great river, and the falls, the wild animals of all sorts, and above all, the sense of living in the world as it was a hundred thousand years ago, made this experience the chief event in my life, separating the future from the past and giving me a new starting point. (732)

Central to these responses, as well as to the aesthetic that informs them, is the traveller's solitude. It seems that his experience is essentially his alone. Even those who may bear witness to it can neither fully comprehend it nor fully communicate it, and thus each witness also is alone. It is a paradoxical situation in which the crowded pages of travellers' narratives and their readers' published commentaries pour out to the public accounts of isolation – sagas of extreme physical, intellectual, and emotional privacy – undercut, not only by internal details, but by the nature of their publication. When, in 'A City Night Piece', Goldsmith makes a public record of streets crowded with the undone and the sorrowful, including – his biographers suspect – himself when he arrived in London, the reader must wonder: just how alone is a person who not only has so many fellow sufferers, but an audience, too? Either solitude is such an essential part of the aesthetic that the artist must insist it exists despite all evidence to the contrary, or solitude requires human evidence to validate it, to throw it into relief, to highlight its poignancy. It is, then, in either case, part of a strategy both expected and accepted by the eighteenth-century audiences for 'A City Night Piece'; and it became intrinsic in African travel narratives.

Reviewing a new edition of Goldsmith's essays in the 1920s, Marianne Moore wrote, 'A literary period would not be a period but for personality which makes it what it is and unaccountable charm which can be imparted to it by a single mind – as in the instance of Goldsmith' (209). One may, with some justification, assert that Goldsmith's work imparts some useful understanding of the way a culture began to sift, as an archaeologist would, such literary artefacts as travellers were beginning to recover in Africa – and then, as an artist or poet would, reassemble them into troubling, and therefore aesthetically pleasing, forms. Though his knowledge of the continent encompassed much of what was known by Europeans in his time, Goldsmith refers to Africa with varying degrees of what is always, essentially, incredulity. Even in non-fiction, Goldsmith tends to revert to formulas of satire or fable apparently acceptable to his audience, presenting each African as outline, each 'sketch of an African prospect' not as geography but as unreal landscape 'finished up beyond the utmost reach of art' (*Animated Nature* 1: 220). But in his work can be seen the means by which Africa's landscape came to be framed in such a way that it promised, once it was wholly discovered, to satisfy the traveller's imaginative longing after an exciting combination of danger and beauty. Through Goldsmith, we see how Africa's connection with a tradition of tourism in the eighteenth century that was fed by, and fed into, an interest in the Gothic, and related interests in the graveyard and in ruins and ruination, opened the way for an African Sublime. This is what Stanley sensed in Burton's writing:

> Shall I inform you, reader, what [Burton's] 'The Lake Regions of Central Africa', and subsequently the reports of European merchants of Zanzibar, caused me to imagine the interior was like? It was that of an immense swamp, curtained round about with the fever. (...) In this swamp, which extended over two hundred miles into the interior, sported an immense number of hippopotami, crocodiles, alligators, lizards, tortoises, and toads; and the miasma rising from this vast cataclysm of mud, corruption, and putrescence, was as thick and sorely depressing as the gloomy and suicidal fog of London. (...) The wormwood and fever tone of Capt Burton's book I regarded as the result of African disease. But ever since my arrival on the mainland, day by day the pall-like curtain had been clearing away, and the cheerless perspective was brightening. (Stanley: 93)

Though he might seem to discount the value of Burton's African night piece as accurate reportage, Stanley could not avoid conjuring up similar effects for his own purposes. Indeed, his quest after the lost Livingstone, his own narrative, and his subsequent fame sprang from and relied upon the continuing force of the African Sublime on a wide readership's imagination. It is what the audience for his and other African travel narratives resonated to; it is what African travellers themselves resonated to. Thus we find solitude, essential to this aesthetic, an attitude struck because it was both rhetorically fitting and artistically pleasing, growing from the sort of abstraction employed by Goldsmith, among fictional ruins, to its use in reality, by Livingstone in his last days, in a rondavel near Lake Bangweulu. The epitaph on Livingstone's grave in Westminster Abbey reads, in part:

> For 30 years his life was spent in an unwearied effort to evangelize the native races, to explore the undiscovered secrets, to abolish the desolating slave trade, of Central Africa, where with his last words he wrote: 'All I can add in my solitude is may Heaven's rich blessing come down on everyone, American, English, or Turk, who will help to heal this open sore of the world.' (quoted in Moorehead, *The White Nile*: 119)

Livingstone had, he confided to Stanley, established in his own mind an idea that Africa would provide him an ideal graveyard:

> In passing through the forest of Ukamba, we saw the bleached skull of an unfortunate victim to the privations of travel. Referring to it, the Doctor remarked that he could never pass through an African forest, with its solemn stillness and serenity, without wishing to be buried quietly under the dead leaves, where he would be sure to rest

undisturbed. In England there was no elbow-room, the graves were often desecrated; and ever since he had buried his wife in the woods of Shupanga he had sighed for just such a spot, where his weary bones would receive the eternal rest they coveted. (Stanley: 600–01)

In the event, his body was borne to England and buried in the abbey on 18 April 1874. This was almost exactly one hundred years after Goldsmith's burial, in the ground of the Temple Church, on 9 April 1774. By then, the familiar Grand Tourist had been wholly transformed into the exotic African explorer: a contemplative, essentially solitary figure set down in a beautiful but alien landscape cluttered with real and invented artefacts signifying danger, dissolution, darkness. And Livingstone's heart – poignant and iconographic as Shelley's – had been buried in Africa.

REFERENCES

Adanson, Michel (1759) *A Voyage to Senegal, the Isle of Goree and the River Gambia.* With notes by an English gentleman who resided some time in that country. London: J. Norse.

Afzelius, Adam (1967) *Sierra Leone Journal, 1795–1796*, ed. Alexander Peter Kup. Studia Ethnographica Upsaliensia XXVII. Uppsala: Boktryckeri AB.

Analytical Review. London, 1788–96.

Baker, Samuel White (1867) *The Albert N'yanza, Great Basin of the Nile, and Explorations of the Nile Sources.* (f.p. 1866) 2 vols. London: Macmillan.

Blackwood's Edinburgh Review. Edinburgh, 1822–50.

Burke, Joseph (1976) *English Art 1714–1800.* Oxford: Clarendon Press.

Burton, Richard (1969) *'Zanzibar.' Travelers' Tales from 'Blackwood,'* [1858]. Edinburgh: William Blackwood, 1–21.

Caillié, Réné (1968) *Travels through Central Africa to Timbuctoo and Across the Great Desert, to Morocco Performed in the Years 1824–1828*, (f.p. 1830) 2 vols. London: Frank Cass.

Cameron, Verney Lovett (1877) *Across Africa*, 2 vols. London: Daldy, Isbister.

Chambers's Cyclopaedia of English Literature. 4th. edn. 2 vols. 1892.

Clapperton, Hugh (1966) *Journal of a Second Expedition into the Interior of Africa from the Bight of Benin to Soccatoo.* (f.p. 1829) London: Frank Cass.

Crooks, J. J. (1972) *A History of the Colony of Sierra Leone Western Africa.* (f.p. 1903) Northbrook, IL: Metro Books.

Davies, James A. (1983) *John Forster: A Literary Life.* Leicester: Leicester University Press.

Davis, Richard Beale (1955) *George Sandys, Poet-Adventurer: A Study in Anglo-American Culture in the Seventeenth Century.* London: The Bodley Head.

Dawson, E. C. (no date) *James Hannington: A History of His Life and Work, 1847–1885.* Philadelphia: George W. Jacobs & Co.

Edinburgh Review, or Critical Journal. Edinburgh, 1828–30.

Gibbon, Edward (1843) *The History of the Decline and Fall of the Roman Empire.* (f.p. 1776) Vol. 1. New York: Harper & Brothers.

Goldsmith, Oliver (1966) *Collected Works*. (ed. Arthur Friedman) 5 vols. Oxford: Clarendon Press.

Goldsmith, Oliver (1760) *Spelling Dictionary of the English Language, On a New Plan. For the Use of Young Gentlemen, Ladies, and Foreigners. Being an Introductory Part of the Circle of the Sciences*, (7th edn). London: J. Newbery. [Attributed to Goldsmith.]

Hallett, Robin (ed.) (1964) *Records of the African Association, 1788–1831*. London: Thomas Nelson.

Harris, Frank (1991) *My Life and Loves*. (f.p. 1925) (ed. John F. Gallagher) New York: Grove Weidenfeld.

Hibbert, Christopher (1987) *The Grand Tour*. London: Methuen.

Johnson, Samuel (1756) *A Dictionary of the English Language*. (f.p. 1755) 2 vols. London: K. Knapton.

Johnson, Samuel (1735) 'Introduction', *A Voyage to Abyssinia*. London: A. Bettesworth and C. Hitch.

Kingsley, Mary H. (1904) *Travels in West Africa: Congo Français, Corisco and Cameroons*, (abridged) (f.p. 1897). London: Macmillan.

Krapf, Johann Lewis (1860) *Travels, Researches, and Missionary Labours During an Eighteen Years' Residence in Eastern Africa*. Boston: Ticknor and Fields.

Lander, Richard (1967) *Records of Captain Clapperton's Last Expedition to Africa*, (f.p. 1830) (Travels and Narratives 21) 2 vols. London: Frank Cass.

Lee, Sarah [Mrs Lee.] (1830) 'The Voyage Out', *Friendship's Offering 1830*: 85–96.

The Life and Travels of Mungo Park; with the Account of his Death from the Journal of Isaaco, the Substance of the Later Discoveries Relative to His Lamented Fate, and the Termination of the Niger. New York: Harper & Brothers (1841).

Lobo, Jeronymo [Jeronimo] (1735) *A Voyage to Abyssinia*, trans. Samuel Johnson. London: A. Bettesworth and C. Hitch.

Melville, Elizabeth Helen (1968) *A Residence at Sierra Leone. Described from a Journal Kept on the Spot, and from Letters Written to Friends at Home*, (ed. Mrs Norton) (f.p. 1849) (Travels and Narratives 45) London: Frank Cass.

Moore, Marianne (1928) 'Review of New Essays by Oliver Goldsmith', in *The Complete Prose of Marianne Moore*, ed. Patricia C. Willis, (1987) New York: Viking, 450–3.

Moorehead, Alan (1960) *The White Nile*. New York: Harper.

New, Charles (1971) *Life, Wanderings, and Labours in Eastern Africa*. (f.p. 1873) (Missionary Researches and Travels 16) London: Frank Cass.

Park, Mungo (1971) *Travels in the Interior Districts of Africa*. (f.p. 1799) (Physician Travelers) New York: Arno Press.

Parks, George B. (1964) 'The turn to the Romantic in the travel literature of the eighteenth century', *Modern Language Quarterly*, **25**: 22–33.

Piozzi, Hesther Lynch (1971) *Anecdotes of the Late Samuel Johnson, LL.D., During the Last Twenty Years of his Life* (ed. S. C. Roberts) Westport, CT: Greenwood.

Prickard. A. O. (1906) 'Introduction', *Longinus on the Sublime*. Oxford: Clarendon Press, 1954, v–xxi.

Prior, James (1837) *The Life of Oliver Goldsmith, M. B.* 2 vols. London: John Murray.

Rankin, F. H. (1836) *The White Man's Grave: A Visit to Sierra Leone, in 1834.* London: R. Bentley.

Rebmann, Johannes. Included in Krapf, *Travels, Researches, and Missionary Labours.*

Rennell, James. 'Appendix: geographical illustrations of Mr. Park's journey', *Park, Travels in the Interior of Africa* (f.p. 1799), 9–36.

Schama, Simon (1996) *Landscape and Memory* (f.p. 1995) New York: Vintage.

Speke, John Hanning (1864) *Journal of the Discovery of the Source of the Nile* (f.p. 1863) New York: Harper & Brothers.

Speke, John Hanning (1967) *What Led to the Discovery of the Source of the Nile* (f.p. 1864) (Travels and Narratives 18) London: Frank Cass.

Stanley, Henry M. (1887) *How I Found Livingstone: Travels, Adventures, and Discoveries in Central Africa* (f.p. 1872) New York: Charles Scribner's Sons.

Thompson, George (1962) *Travels and Adventures in Southern Africa* (f.p. 1827) Cape Town: Africana Connoisseurs Press.

Wadström, C. B. (1968) *An Essay on Colonization, Particularly Applied to the Western Coast of Africa*, 2 parts (f.p. 1794–5) (Reprints of Economic Classics) New York: Augustus M. Kelley.

Walpole, Horace (1967) *Yale Edition of Horace Walpole's Correspondence: Horace Walpole's Correspondence with Horace Mann*, ed. W. S. Lewis, Warren Hunting Smith and George L. Lam. Vol. 24. New Haven: Yale University Press.

Winterbottom, Thomas (1969) *An Account of the Native Africans in the Neighbourhood of Sierra Leone* (f.p. 1803) 2 vols. (Cass Library of African Studies. Travels and Narratives 52) London: Frank Cass.

Withy, Lynne (1997) *Grand Tours and Cook's Tours: A History of Leisure Travel, 1750 to 1915.* New York: William Morrow.

Woodring, Carl (1989) 'Sublime, Picturesque, Beautiful', *Nature into Art: Cultural Transformations in Nineteenth-Century Britain.* Cambridge: Harvard University Press, 29–56.

Index

CPSIA information can be obtained at www.ICGtesting.com
Printed in the USA
LVOW11s1242100813

347239LV00006B/98/P